EUROPEAN CONSTITUTIONAL COURTS AND TRANSITIONS TO DEMOCRACY

This book brings together research on democratization processes and constitutional justice by examining the role of three generations of European constitutional courts in the transitions to democracy that took place in Europe in the twentieth century. Using a comparative perspective, the author examines how the constitutional courts during that period managed to ensure an initial full implementation of the constitutional provisions, thus contributing – together with other actors and factors – to the positive outcome of the democratization processes. *European Constitutional Courts and Transitions to Democracy* provides a better understanding of the relationship between transitions to democracy and constitutionalism from the perspective of constitutional courts.

FRANCESCO BIAGI is an Adjunct Professor of Comparative Constitutionalism, a Postdoctoral Research Fellow in Comparative Public Law at the University of Bologna School of Law, and a Researcher at the Center for Constitutional Studies and Democratic Development. From October 2015 to January 2017, he was a Senior Research Fellow at the Max Planck Foundation for International Peace and the Rule of Law (Heidelberg), where he now works as a legal consultant. He is the co-editor of *Political and Constitutional Transitions in North Africa: Actors and Factors* (with Justin O. Frosini, 2015).

ASCL STUDIES IN COMPARATIVE LAW

ASCL Studies in Comparative Law is designed to broaden theoretical and practical knowledge of the world's many legal systems. With more than sixty years' experience, the American Society of Comparative Law has been a leader in the study and analysis of comparative law. By promoting the investigation of legal problems in a comparative light, whether theoretical or empirical, as essential to the advancement of legal science, it provides an essential service to legal practitioners and those seeking reform of the law. This book series will extend these aims to the publication of monographs and comparative studies of specific legal problems.

The series has two series editors. David Gerber is Distinguished Professor of Law and Co-Director of the Program in International and Comparative Law at Chicago-Kent College of Law, Illinois Institute of Technology. He is currently President of the American Society of Comparative Law. Mortimer Sellers is Regents Professor of the University System of Maryland and Director of the Baltimore Center for International and Comparative Law. He is an Associate Member of the International Academy of Comparative Law.

European Constitutional Courts and Transitions to Democracy

FRANCESCO BIAGI
University of Bologna

CAMBRIDGE
UNIVERSITY PRESS

CAMBRIDGE
UNIVERSITY PRESS

University Printing House, Cambridge CB2 8BS, United Kingdom

One Liberty Plaza, 20th Floor, New York, NY 10006, USA

477 Williamstown Road, Port Melbourne, VIC 3207, Australia

314–321, 3rd Floor, Plot 3, Splendor Forum, Jasola District Centre, New Delhi – 110025, India

79 Anson Road, #06–04/06, Singapore 079906

Cambridge University Press is part of the University of Cambridge.

It furthers the University's mission by disseminating knowledge in the pursuit of education, learning, and research at the highest international levels of excellence.

www.cambridge.org
Information on this title: www.cambridge.org/9781108489393
DOI: 10.1017/9781108776783

First published 2020

Printed in the United Kingdom by TJ International Ltd, Padstow Cornwall

A catalogue record for this publication is available from the British Library.

Library of Congress Cataloging-in-Publication Data
NAMES: Biagi, Francesco, author.
TITLE: European constitutional courts and transitions to democracy / Francesco Biagi.
DESCRIPTION: New York : Cambridge University Press, 2019. | Series: Ascl studies in comparative law | Includes bibliographical references and index.
IDENTIFIERS: LCCN 2019038263 (print) | LCCN 2019038264 (ebook) | ISBN 9781108489393 (hardback) | ISBN 9781108702393 (paperback) | ISBN 9781108776783 (epub)
SUBJECTS: LCSH: Constitutional courts–Europe. | Constitutional law–Europe. | Democracy–Europe. | Justice, Administration of–Europe.
CLASSIFICATION: LCC KJC5456 .B525 2019 (print) | LCC KJC5456 (ebook) | DDC 347.4/035–dc23
LC record available at https://lccn.loc.gov/2019038263
LC ebook record available at https://lccn.loc.gov/2019038264

ISBN 978-1-108-48939-3 Hardback

Ai miei genitori, Marina e Marco, e a mio fratello Lorenzo

A mia moglie Elena e a mia figlia Arianna

Contents

Foreword

Giuseppe de Vergottini
Professor Emeritus, University of Bologna

The introduction of constitutional review mechanisms represents one of the key stages characterizing a political regime change in the transition from an authoritarian to a democratic form of government. Taking this as his starting point, Francesco Biagi addresses this topic by examining three different experiences of constitutional transformation. The first historical phase consists of the adoption of new constitutions in the aftermath of the political and institutional reconstruction that took place in Europe after World War II. The second phase is represented by the overcoming of the remaining authoritarian regimes present in Europe, namely the regimes of Salazar and Franco. The third phase consists of the abandonment of socialist constitutionalism in its Leninist version with the collapse of the authoritarian regimes that formed part of the Soviet bloc. Each of these historical phases requires an analysis of the specific constitutional developments. In the first phase the focus is on the Constitution of Italy, in the second phase, on the Constitution of Spain, and in the third phase, on the Constitution of Czechoslovakia.

Biagi rightly places his analysis in the framework of the transitions from authoritarian regimes to democratic systems, a topic that has been examined by political scientists and legal scholars for more than two decades. His research seeks to ascertain the impact of constitutional courts on the new constitutions, especially with regard to the effectiveness of the review of the legislation enacted by the political forces in Parliament. Because the study aims to examine the effectiveness of constitutional review, quite understandably it is not limited to the analysis of the formal constitutional provisions, but also examines the concrete constitutional developments. Therefore, the focus is on the dynamics of the legal systems, and this is why it is useful to rely on transitional studies.

The notion of transition has emerged only in recent years in the domain of constitutional law. In this respect, it should be noted that constitutional law studies tend to focus on the role of the constituent power (the radical change of a constitution and hence of the related political regime) and on constitutional amendments of various kinds ("partial" reforms and at times "total" reforms of the constitution as in the case of Switzerland, Spain, and Austria, and in various postsocialist constitutions). It was mainly political scientists who first examined the topic of regime change, including the notion of *transition*, after which constitutional scholars elaborated the concept of *constitutional transition*.

The term "transition" does not have an unequivocal legal meaning, although it is evident that it refers to a change from something that exists to something emerging in its place. This concept does not cover all the developments and adaptations resulting from the implementation of a constitution, deriving from political or administrative practices and courts decisions (implicit changes), or from formal amendments (explicit changes), provided that the political regime and the form of government have remained the same. Moreover, the constitutional transition does not coincide with the concept of *provisional constitution*, which refers to a constitutional instrument adopted in historical phases characterized by precarious or provisional arrangements prior to the adoption of definitive measures. Except in particular cases, constitutional transitions do not give rise to provisional constitutions. In this respect, an example is given by the case of South Africa, where during the transitional phase a provisional constitution was adopted in 1993, prior to the final Constitution of 1996.

The term "transition" is used particularly to describe the evolution from authoritarian regimes characterized by one-party systems to pluralistic and democratic systems. Political scientists have argued that the transition is a situation on the move and depicted it as a "process." In fact, the transition is a concept that conveys the idea of a dynamic process entailing various phases culminating in that of "consolidation." It is only at this point that, starting as a protest movement against a regime and continuing with the progressive adoption of new principles and rules in the place of the previous ones, the change can be said to be consolidated because the previous regime has been replaced by a new one. From a legal perspective, the transitions culminating in the adoption of new constitutions or in major constitutional reforms accompanying the change of political regime and the form of government are particularly important. The evolution (transition) from authoritarian to democratic institutions has traditionally meant a regime change. This was the case after the collapse of the Fascist and Nazi regimes in the mid-1940s, and then of the Salazar and Franco regimes in the 1970s, or with the generalized rejection of the socialist model in favor of liberal democracy, at least in formal terms, after the fall of the Soviet Union at the end of the 1980s.

In this sense, transition means that one normative scheme consisting of certain principles and rules is replaced by another one. The transition may take place over a period, whereas the adoption of a new constitution is *instantaneous*. The formal constitution, once adopted, is fixed at a certain point in time. The constitution immobilizes the change that has taken place, regardless of whether the process leading to its adoption has come about gradually or suddenly, and until such time as it does not undergo further change, it will remain in force. This does not rule out the possibility that the implementation of its principles will be laborious and complex and that it will take time because the process of consolidation may turn out to be complicated. The implementation of the constitution is always characterized by the adaptation of the principles to the reality. It is in this phase that the gap between the intentions of the constitutional framers and that which is permitted by current circumstances becomes evident.

When the decisions made by the *pouvoir constituant* impose a radical change with respect to the past, as in the three case studies examined in this book, where the previous authoritarian constitutions were abandoned, the developments taking place after the adoption of the new constitution are of the utmost importance. Therefore, the transition displays its effects over time. The formal constitutional provisions provide for a market economy, the regulation and protection of rights, political democracy, and the establishment of a new political culture. In particular, they also provide for constitutional justice. However, all this initially exists only on paper. The principles are nearly always merely aspirations, proposals, and policy statements, and as a result everything is projected forward into the implementation phase and the practices that are later put into place. It is evident that these developments are achieved to various extents and across different time frames, depending on the country.

The study shows the different level of difficulty encountered in effectively establishing constitutional courts. In each country examined in this book the positive factors enabling constitutional justice to take root are discussed, along with the factors causing delay or obstacles, that were to be overcome over time. One of the most problematic factors – affecting all the countries that set up (or tried to set up) a constitutional court – consists of the constraints to the political representation in Parliament due to constitutional review of legislation. Hence the inevitable obstacles that have stood in the way of the concrete development of the courts in certain historical periods.

Among the positive factors, Biagi rightly highlights the leading role played by international human rights courts. A strong influence was exerted by the principles laid down in the treaties regulating the European organizations, with particular reference to the Council of Europe and the European Convention on Human Rights, as well as the European Union. Articles 6 and 49 of the Treaty Establishing the European Community, as amended in 1997, laid down as requirements for accession to the European Union respect for the principles of freedom, democracy, human rights and fundamental freedoms, and the rule of law. In its case law the European Court of Human Rights has effectively contributed to strengthening the role of constitutional courts as the guardians of fundamental rights. Because the international jurisdiction on human rights has gradually taken on a pivotal role in the evolution of contemporary constitutional orders, the supporting role of the Strasbourg Court has made a major contribution to reinforcing the overall role of

European constitutional courts. As pointed out by the author, there can be no doubt that the centrality of the role of the person and human rights has significantly shaped in a democratic sense the completion of the transition in the countries examined in this study, and more in general in all the European experiences.

For the countries that have adopted a liberal democratic regime, numerous factors and elements have contributed to facilitating an effective convergence between the formal constitution and the substantive constitution. However, it is also important not to underestimate the factors that may hinder the role and functions granted by the constitutions to the constitutional courts. Biagi rightly points out that it would be mistaken to assume that the mere establishment of a constitutional court would necessarily lead to an effective recognition of constitutionalism. This observation refers, among others, to the countries involved in the "Arab Spring," but it also concerns the post-Communist European countries. The local culture and constitutional traditions of a country may hinder and delay the implementation of the constitutional safeguards. A constitutional court imposed by external forces without the approval of the local population has a limited chance of success, as shown in the case of Bosnia, where an international treaty (the Dayton Agreement of 1995) concluded by the powers intervening in the region at the end of a bloody conflict determined the framework for the Constitution of the Federation of Bosnia and Herzegovina (consisting of the Croat and the Muslim communities) and of the Serbian Republic of Bosnia Herzegovina. The Constitution, inspired by the principles of liberal constitutionalism, envisaged a Constitutional Court composed not only of national judges but also of foreign judges selected at the international level. However, this plan failed to take account of the popular will, in a framework that was substantially one of international protection. It is evident, then, that such an innovation was characterized by a congenital weakness.

On the whole, the countries emerging from the collapse of the Communist regime adopted constitutions containing a number of significant safeguards: in all cases, reference was made to the principles of liberal democracy, human dignity, pluralism, the rule of law, jurisdictional safeguards, the protection of minorities, and the recognition of constitutional justice, with a wealth of declamatory statements. This vast apparatus of constitutional safeguards could not be accompanied in the short term by the dissemination of a culture of rights, the formation of a democratic political tradition, and a pluralistic information system. In practice, in most of these countries the preexisting cultural climate survived for a long time, favored by the persistence of the nomenclature of the old regime, at times with a devastating resurgence of conflicts between ethnic groups in a climate of bitter and exasperated chauvinism.

In conclusion, the study confirms the pivotal role played by the constitutional courts in affirming the classic values of constitutionalism, with special reference to the protection of individual rights, taking for granted the consolidation of the principle of the separation and balance of powers. The *leitmotiv* is that of the substantive elements of the constitutional safeguards that need to be provided to ensure the effectiveness of the action of the constitutional judges. The analysis of the case law of the constitutional courts in the period following the entry into force of the recent constitutions demonstrates the effective role of the constitutional judges in operating in such a way as to enhance the credibility of the principles contained in these constitutions. In fact, the constitutionalism outlined in the written provisions of the new constitutions was shown to be applied in practice. This enables the author to conclude that thanks to this tenacious and constructive case law, aimed above all at ensuring the effective implementation of fundamental rights, constitutional courts have achieved full legitimation.

Acknowledgments

I wish to thank all those who, at various times and in various ways, gave me precious advice during the research and the drafting of this volume: Giuseppe de Vergottini, Susanna Mancini, Justin O. Frosini, Sana Alsarghali, Rainer Arnold, Giorgio Bongiovanni, Marco Dani, Josu de Miguel, Angela Di Gregorio, Gustavo Gozzi, Giorgio Grasso, Tania Groppi, Andrea Guazzarotti, Ivana Janů, Siraj Khan, David Kosař, Andrea Lollini, Soňa Matochová, Jason Mazzone, Sara Pennicino, Valeria Piergigli, Čarna Pištan, Roberto Romboli, Kathrin Maria Scherr, and Javier Tajadura.

In addition, I wish to extend my sincere thanks to David Gerber and Mortimer Sellers, editors of the book series "ASCL Studies in Comparative Law," for their support for this study.

Finally, I wish to thank Bob Abernethy for having believed in this research project from the very beginning.

Notes on the Text

English translation: Francesco Biagi and William Bromwich.

Originally published as *Corti costituzionali e transizioni democratiche. Tre generazioni a confronto* (il Mulino, Bologna, 2016).

The translation of this work has been funded by the George Lawrence Abernethy Endowment for Research and Publications of the Center for Constitutional Studies and Democratic Development (a partnership between the Johns Hopkins University SAIS Europe and the University of Bologna), and by the Max Planck Foundation for International Peace and the Rule of Law (Heidelberg).

This book is geared toward an international audience. Therefore, several changes have been made to the original Italian version. These include the addition of English-language sources, new materials of interest to an international readership, and explanation of foreign terms.

Introduction

What is the relationship between transitions to democracy and constitutionalism? What role have constitutional courts played in the past in democratization processes? What "lessons" can be drawn from these experiences by countries – such as those involved in the "Arab Spring" – that are currently undergoing a transition from an authoritarian rule? These are some of the key questions this book addresses. Transitions to democracy, on the one hand, and constitutional justice, on the other, are topics that, each in its specific domain, have been the subject of numerous in-depth studies. Transition processes, especially in the early phases, have been analyzed mainly by historians, political scientists, sociologists, philosophers, and economists, and only at a later stage did legal scholars (particularly constitutional law scholars) start to examine these processes. In fact, jurists

> have not been inspired by the topic of "transition," that by its very nature is ambiguous, risky and objectively hard to grasp.... [They] have focused on the "established" order or, at most, on the sensitive phase of the "constituent" power, but it is beyond doubt that – at least in general – they have neglected an analysis of the ... "intermediate" phases, i.e. of the phases of "transition."[1]

In turn, constitutional justice – particularly following the setting up and consolidation of constitutional courts – has become one of the main areas of research for constitutional scholars, especially in light of its central role in liberal-democratic countries. Indeed, it is received opinion that one of the essential requirements of a truly democratic state is the existence of an effective system of constitutional review.

On the contrary, the studies that have sought to bring together these two fields of research are much less common. It is true, however, that in recent years scholars have taken steps to fill this gap: consider, for example, the work of Wojciech

[1] Antonino Spadaro, "La transizione costituzionale. Ambiguità e polivalenza di un'importante nozione di teoria generale" in Antonino Spadaro (ed.), *Le "trasformazioni" costituzionali nell'età della transizione* (Giappichelli 2000), 47.

Sadurski,[2] Herman Schwartz,[3] and Radoslav Procházka[4] on the role of constitutional courts in Central and Eastern Europe following the collapse of Communism, or the studies by Tom Ginsburg on constitutional courts in Asia and their role in the democratization processes,[5] or the research on constitutional courts in individual countries.[6] Moreover, international conferences have recently been held on this topic.[7]

This book is intended to contribute to this strand of research by examining the role of constitutional justice – and more specifically of constitutional courts – in the processes of democratic transition that took place in Europe in the twentieth century. In particular, the volume focuses on three countries: Italy, Spain, and the Czech Republic. These countries provide extremely interesting case studies because their constitutional courts – to use an expression of László Sólyom – belong to the "three generations of European Constitutional Courts,"[8] whose creation is inextricably linked to the three waves of democratic transition that took place in Europe in the twentieth century. The first generation consists of the German and Italian constitutional courts, set up in the 1950s following the defeat of the Nazi and Fascist regimes; the second generation, consisting of the Spanish and Portuguese courts, came into existence after the fall of the authoritarian regimes of Franco and Salazar in the 1970s; finally, the third generation consists of the constitutional courts of the Central and Eastern European countries, that were established after the collapse of the Communist regime. Therefore, unlike other comparative studies that have

2 Wojciech Sadurski, *Rights before Courts: A Study of Constitutional Courts in Postcommunist States of Central and Eastern Europe* (Springer 2014); Wojciech Sadurski (ed.), *Constitutional Justice, East and West: Democratic Legitimacy and Constitutional Courts in Post-Communist Europe in a Comparative Perspective* (Kluwer Law International 2002).

3 Herman Schwartz, *The Struggle for Constitutional Justice in Post-Communist Europe* (University of Chicago Press 2000).

4 Radoslav Procházka, *Mission Accomplished: On Founding Constitutional Adjudication in Central Europe* (Central European University Press 2002).

5 Tom Ginsburg, *Judicial Review in New Democracies: Constitutional Courts in Asian Cases* (Cambridge University Press 2003).

6 E.g., László Sólyom, "The Role of Constitutional Courts in the Transition to Democracy: With Special Reference to Hungary" (2003) 18 *International Sociology*, 133 ff.; Heinz Klug, "South Africa's Constitutional Court: Enabling Democracy and Promoting Law in the Transition from Apartheid" (2008) 3 *Journal of Comparative Law* 2, 174 ff.; Alexei Trochev, *Judging Russia: The Role of the Constitutional Court in Russian Politics 1990–2006* (Cambridge University Press 2008).

7 See, by way of example, the Conference *Advocates or Notaries of Democracy? A Comparative Socio-legal Analysis of the Role of Constitutional Courts in Political Transformation Processes*, Berlin, September 22–24, 2011.

8 Sólyom 2003, note 6, at 135. Due to the fact that it is strictly linked to democratic transition processes, the "numbering" of the generations of constitutional courts begins from the end of World War II even though, as is well known, the first instances of constitutional courts date back to the period between the two world wars. It is for this reason that some legal scholars, when speaking of the first generation, refer to the Czechoslovak and Austrian courts set up in 1920 and the Spanish Court of Constitutional Guarantees established in 1931. See, e.g., Michel Fromont, *La justice constitutionnelle dans le monde* (Dalloz 1996), 17 ff.

focused on just one generation of constitutional courts (such as the one (mentioned above) consisting of the courts of Central and Eastern Europe), this study carries out a *diachronic* comparison, providing an analysis of the role of these courts in three distinct historical phases: the period after World War II, the late 1970s–early 1980s, and the period after the fall of the Berlin Wall.

The main aim of this study is to examine whether and how the constitutional courts of these three generations managed to ensure through their judgments an initial full implementation of the constitutional provisions, thus contributing – together with other actors and factors – to the positive outcome of the democratization processes. In other words, the intention is to better understand, from the perspective of the constitutional courts, the relationship between transitions to democracy and constitutionalism.

The decision to analyze the transitions that took place in Italy, Spain, and the Czech Republic is due to the fact that these countries present certain similar characteristics that make them particularly suitable for a comparative study. In the first place, they all experienced a successful transition to democracy; second, in each case the break with the previous autocratic regime occurred mainly through the adoption of a new democratic constitution, thus giving rise to *constitutional* transitions; third, each of these three countries adopted a parliamentary form of government and granted the power to exercise constitutional review of legislation to an ad hoc body, the constitutional court.

At the same time, it is important to bear in mind the differences between the three cases, including, in particular, the different nature of the previous illiberal regime. Indeed, whereas Fascist Italy and Francoist Spain are usually considered by scholars as *authoritarian* countries, Czechoslovakia was one of the satellite states of the Soviet Union, which were characterized by a *Socialist* regime. This difference is particularly significant because the nature of the previous regime influenced the trajectory of the transition, and, as a result, also the action of the constitutional courts. Suffice it to consider the fact that, unlike what happened in Western Europe, the transitions in Central and Eastern Europe were not just political and constitutional but also economic, aimed at setting up a market economy.

The book consists of five chapters. Chapter 1 sets the stage for the subsequent chapters by defining and discussing some key terms and situating the thesis of the book within the existing academic literature. It begins by putting forward a critique of one of the most established notions (especially among constitutional law scholars) of democratic transition, a notion mainly based on formal elements (the approval of the constitution), while arguing in favor of the concept of *substantive* transition, which encompasses elements of "law in action." Indeed, the analysis of transitions in Europe has highlighted the fact that the entry into force of a new democratic constitution, while representing the most significant element of change and discontinuity between the old and the new legal order, is not in itself sufficient to determine the effective transformation from an authoritarian to a democratic system.

Thus, rather than a *formal* transition, it seems necessary to opt for a *substantive* interpretation of transition, which refers to the period in which the fundamental principles characterizing the new system are enforced. According to this interpretation, the conclusion of the constituent process strictly speaking does not mark the end of the transition and the beginning of the consolidation, but, on the contrary, marks the beginning of the *second phase of the transition*, in which the principles laid down in the constitution are effectively implemented. The outcome of the transition largely depends on this second phase, also in light of the role played by the constitutional courts.

The second part of the first chapter provides a brief overview of the origins of constitutional justice in Europe, from the *Staatsgerichtsbarkeit* to the setting up of the first constitutional courts in Czechoslovakia, Austria, and Spain. The analysis then turns to the reasons leading the European constitutional framers – in the period after World War II – to set up constitutional courts, highlighting the fact that the establishment of these bodies is closely linked to the processes of transition to democracy.

The second, third, and fourth chapters focus, respectively, on the role of the Italian, Spanish, and Czech constitutional courts. Each case study examines the constitution-making process, casting light not only on the specific reasons why the constitutional framers decided to set up a constitutional court but also on the forms of resistance in each country to the establishment of these bodies. Previous experiences of constitutional justice are also analyzed. These chapters then examine the role of the courts within the institutional framework of each country, the issues on which they focused their activity, as well as the factors that either favored or hindered their action, identifying similarities and differences from one country to another.

The Italian Constitutional Court, the focus of the second chapter, belongs to the first generation of constitutional courts, and as a result its configuration and role at the time when it was established were largely experimental, if not a leap in the dark. The constitutional judges, especially during the initial phase (from 1956 until the end of the 1960s) focused on the elimination of the Fascist legislation that continued to severely constrain civil, political, religious, and social liberties. In this way the Court made a break with the past, as it contributed to putting an end to the continuity between Fascism and post-Fascism, at least from a legislative point of view. Indeed, with the striking down of Fascist legislation and the upholding of constitutional rights and freedoms the country experienced a transition from an "uncertain" democracy (that was the case in Italy in 1956) to a "mature" democracy. The role of the *Corte costituzionale* also needs to be assessed in light of the fact that in most cases it was required to take decisions in conflict with the prevailing conservative stance of the government, the parliamentary majority, and the superior courts. The difficult context in which it was operating helps to explain its excessively cautious orientation in certain rulings (e.g., in the field of public order).

Chapter 3 deals with the Spanish Constitutional Court. In this second generation of courts there are fewer unknown factors and more instances of courts in other countries to draw inspiration from, including the Italian Constitutional Court. All this contributed to the establishment and consolidation of constitutional justice. In the period from 1980 to the early 1990s, the Spanish Court dealt with four main issues, concerning the normative value of the constitutional provisions, the preconstitutional legislation, fundamental rights, and the territorial organization of the state. From the very beginning, the *Tribunal constitucional* upheld the normative value of all the provisions of the Constitution, and played an important role in determining whether the preconstitutional laws were in conflict with the provisions of the Constitution laying down fundamental rights and freedoms. Moreover, it succeeded in setting up an effective system of protection of fundamental rights, as well as ensuring a rational functioning of the State of Autonomies. The territorial question represented one of the most complex issues to be addressed, as the outcome of the transition to democracy was largely dependent on this matter. The Spanish case thus highlights how the transition from an authoritarian regime to a democratic form of government may also require a new territorial distribution of powers: in fact, from a highly centralized state under Francisco Franco, Spain became a strongly decentralized country, a *State of Autonomies*.

The fourth chapter examines the role of the Constitutional Court of the Czech Republic, which in the first decade of its operation (from 1993 to the beginning of the new millennium) dealt mainly with the protection of fundamental rights, as well as with cases concerning transitional justice. With reference to this matter, the Court was called on to rule on particularly divisive issues concerning the country's past, such as the law on the illegitimacy of the Communist regime, the laws on the restitution of property, as well as the "lustration laws," which were aimed at preventing individuals involved with the Communist regime, or considered to be in favor of a return to Communism, from occupying higher positions in the state apparatus for a certain period. Compared to the previous generations, a distinguishing feature of this third generation of constitutional courts is the interplay between the democratic transition, constitutional justice, and accession to the Council of Europe and the European Union.

Finally, the concluding chapter brings things together with an analysis of the key lessons drawn from the discussion in the preceding chapters. In particular, it makes a comparison among the three generations of courts *by topic*, rather than country by country. The decision to make a comparison of this kind only in the last part of the book is due to the fact that it appeared necessary (in each of the preceding chapters) to show how the historical, political, institutional, and social context differed profoundly from country to country, above all considering that the transitions under examination are embedded in three markedly different historical periods. This last chapter carries out an analysis of the various types of intervention of the constitutional judges, the reasons for the success of the centralized system of constitutional review, as well as the various factors influencing the activity of the courts. The analysis of the three generations has shown that thanks to the actions carried out during the transition processes, the constitutional courts have managed to achieve full legitimation in their respective constitutional systems and within the dynamics of their respective forms of government. Although their action was not immune to criticism, the constitutional courts emerged as key players of the substantive transitions, reducing the high degree of uncertainty that characterizes the outcome of every transition process.

Although the study focuses on Italy, Spain, and the Czech Republic, numerous references are also made to other European constitutional courts that were set up following the collapse of autocratic regimes (such as the German Constitutional Court, and the other post-Communist constitutional courts), highlighting analogies and differences between individual courts and generations of courts. Moreover, the book makes frequent references to the contributions of historians, political scientists, sociologists, and philosophers, in an attempt to emphasize the complexity and the multiplicity of perspectives associated with this topic. Indeed, in examining the role of constitutional courts in transition processes, an exclusively legal analysis would have been too limited, thus confirming the observation made by Giovanni Bognetti, who argued that

> The comparative constitutional scholar, more than other comparative scholars, ... can and should take account of the historical data provided by other disciplines such as political thought, political science, sociology of law, political history, and so on. All these data, provided by various disciplines, are necessary for the comparative constitutional scholar, who will find them extremely useful and indispensable.[9]

For the purposes of this study, no specific time limit was laid down with regard to the judgments to be examined. On the contrary, the book focuses on all the rulings of the constitutional courts that have had a decisive impact on the democratic transition process, regardless of when they were handed down. Although predictably most of the decisions concern the early years of activity of the courts, reference is also made to rulings delivered even many years after these bodies started to operate. Judgment 290/1974 of the Italian Constitutional Court concerning political strikes is emblematic from this point of view: although handed down 18 years after the Court started its activity (and 26 years after the entry into force of the Constitution), this ruling turned out to be extremely important in the process of democratic transition and consolidation.

It should also be noted that although the book focuses on transitions taking place in the past, it is not intended to be merely an historical inquiry. In fact, the European experience can provide useful insights for constitutional courts in

[9] Giovanni Bognetti, *Introduzione al diritto costituzionale comparato* (Giappichelli 1994), 178–179. See also Ran Hirschl, "From Comparative Constitutional Law to Comparative Constitutional Studies" (2013) 11 *International Journal of Constitutional Law* 1, 1–12.

countries that are currently experiencing (or likely to experience in the future) a transition from authoritarian rule, especially in light of the fact that transitional countries increasingly tend to set up constitutional courts or take measures aimed at strengthening the existing ones. The study is therefore aimed at contributing to a better understanding of the dynamics of what Samuel Issacharoff has called "the era of Constitutional Courts."[10]

[10] Samuel Issacharoff, *Fragile Democracies: Contested Power in the Era of Constitutional Courts* (Cambridge University Press 2015).

1

Democratic Transitions and Constitutional Courts

Le développement de la justice constitutionnelle
est certainement l'événement le plus marquant du droit constitutionnel européen
de la seconde moitié du XXe siècle.

Louis Favoreu[1]

1 DEMOCRATIC TRANSITIONS

"The interval between one political regime and another": this is the definition of transition provided by Guillermo O'Donnell and Philippe C. Schmitter in their seminal book *Transitions from Authoritarian Rule*.[2] This is clearly a wide-ranging notion, encompassing all changes in political regimes. Indeed, although with the "third wave of democratization"[3] transitions have almost by definition become transitions *to democracy*, in actual fact a transition can also be from a democratic form of government to an authoritarian regime (*authoritarian* transitions),[4] or from

[1] Louis Favoreu, *Les Cours Constitutionnelles* (Presses Universitaires de France 1986), 3 ("The development of constitutional justice is undoubtedly the most memorable event of European constitutional law in the second half of the twentieth century").

[2] Guillermo O'Donnell and Philippe C. Schmitter, "Tentative Conclusions about Uncertain Democracies" in Guillermo O'Donnell, Philippe C. Schmitter, and Laurence Whitehead (eds.), *Transitions from Authoritarian Rule* (The Johns Hopkins University Press 1986), 6.

[3] Samuel P. Huntington, *The Third Wave: Democratization in the Late Twentieth Century* (University of Oklahoma Press 1991).

[4] Suffice it to consider the "first and second reverse wave" identified by Huntington 1991, note 3, at 17–21. Although it would be inaccurate to speak of an authoritarian transition, a country that is at present characterized by a serious democratic deficit is Hungary. Indeed, the new 2012 Constitution, with subsequent amendments, has attracted strong criticism from numerous scholars, who have interpreted a number of constitutional provisions as evidence of an antidemocratic tendency that has characterized the country since the electoral victory of the Fidesz Party in 2010. See Gábor Attila Tóth (ed.), *Constitution for a Disunited Nation: On Hungary's 2011 Fundamental Law* (Central European University Press 2012); Michel Rosenfeld,

an illiberal regime to another illiberal regime (of the same or different kind).[5] The transition may also lead to a "political gray zone"[6] where *hybrid* regimes are to be found.[7] These regimes are characterized by the fact that democratic procedures (such as free and fair elections) coexist alongside elements of authoritarian rule (such as violations of fundamental rights and freedoms, and a weak separation of powers).

The study of democratic transition processes developed particularly after the fall of the Berlin Wall in November 1989, when a number of countries in Central and Eastern Europe, after breaking free from the previous Socialist regime, began a transition toward democracy. In this period the analysis of these processes was so highly developed as to justify claims about the emergence of a new discipline called *transitology*.[8]

A variety of factors can lead to a process of democratization: it can be the result of historical events (as in the case of the fall of the Berlin Wall), or the outcome of a gradual evolution of the political system (as was the case in the United States and in some European countries during the "first wave of democratization" [1828–1926]).[9] In other cases it may follow on from the military defeat of an authoritarian regime (as happened after World War II in Germany, Italy, Austria, and Japan), or it may be the consequence of the death of a dictator (as in the case of Spain after Franco's death).

"Editorial. Constitutionalism, Moderation and Compromise: Confronting Threats within and beyond the Constitution" (2011) 9 *International Journal of Constitutional Law* 3–4, 552. It is significant that in the view of Kim Lane Scheppele the 2012 Hungarian Constitution is an "unconstitutional Constitution" (Kim Lane Scheppele, "The Unconstitutional Constitution" [January 2, 2012] *The New York Times*, https://krugman.blogs.nytimes.com/2012/01/02/the-unconstitutional-constitution/ [accessed August 2, 2019]). Another country characterized by serious democratic backsliding in recent years is Poland. See Wojciech Sadurski, "How Democracy Dies (in Poland): A Case Study of Anti-constitutional Populist Backsliding" (2018) *Sydney Law School Research Paper* 18/01; Wojciech Sadurski, *Poland's Constitutional Breakdown* (Oxford University Press 2019).

5 As in the case, for example, of some Asian and African countries. See Thomas Carothers, "The End of the Transition Paradigm" (2002) 13 *Journal of Democracy* 1, 9.

6 Carothers 2002, note 5, at 9.

7 Leonardo Morlino, "The Two 'Rules of Law' between Transition to and Quality of Democracy" in Leonardo Morlino and Gianluigi Palombella (eds.), *Rule of Law and Democracy: Inquiries into Internal and External Issues* (Brill 2010), 41 ff.; Valerie Bunce and Sharon L. Wolchik, "Mixed Regimes in Postcommunist Eurasia: Tipping Democratic and Tipping Authoritarian" (2008) *Società per lo studio della diffusione della democrazia Working Paper* 1/2008, 4. An analysis from a legal point of view of this type of regimes is put forward by Mark Tushnet, "Authoritarian Constitutionalism" (2015) 100 *Cornell Law Review* 2, 391 ff.

8 See Philippe C. Schmitter, "Transitology: The Science or Art of Democratization?" in Joseph S. Tulchin and Bernice Romero (eds.), *The Consolidation of Democracy in Latin America* (Lynne Rienner 1995), 11–41; Valerie Bunce, "Should Transitologists Be Grounded?" (1995) 54 *Slavic Review* 1, 111–125.

9 See Huntington 1991, note 3, at 16–17.

The processes of democratic transition and democratic consolidation are neither straightforward nor rational. Rather, they are extremely complex, and characterized by numerous variables, consisting of *actors* and *factors*.[10]

The actors can be classified into two groups. The first group includes the *institutional* actors, such as the military, the government, Parliament, the judicial authorities, the Head of State, the electoral bodies, the constitutional courts (the focus of the present study), Truth Commissions, and supranational and international bodies. The second group, by contrast, consists of *noninstitutional* actors, such as the civil society, interest groups, and elites. In a hybrid position we find the political parties, which serve as liaison between the institutions and the civil society.

In the same way as the actors, also the factors contributing to the success or failure of the transitions are many and varied. The first group includes *endogenous* factors, such as unexpected events, the nature of the previous nondemocratic regime, the electoral systems, the party systems, religious and philosophical beliefs, the existence of a democratic tradition and culture, the level of economic and social development, the constitutional structure, and the "stateness."[11] The second group, by contrast, consists of *exogenous* factors, such as the international context and influences, as well as the *Zeitgeist*.[12]

Due to the previously mentioned variables, the outcome of every transition process is characterized by a high level of *uncertainty*. The case of the recent transitions in the Arab world is emblematic in this respect. It is well known that since December 2010 a series of revolts and protests against the existing autocratic or

[10] For an analysis of the actors and factors influencing the processes of democratic transition and consolidation in Africa, Latin America, Central and Eastern Europe, and Asia see Juan J. Linz and Alfred Stepan, *Problems of Democratic Transition and Consolidation: Southern Europe, South America, and Post-Communist Europe* (The Johns Hopkins University Press 1996); Luca Mezzetti, *Le democrazie incerte. Transizioni costituzionali e consolidamento della democrazia in Europa orientale, Africa, America Latina, Asia* (Giappichelli 2000); Luca Mezzetti, *Teoria e prassi delle transizioni costituzionali e del consolidamento democratico* (Cedam 2003); Justin O. Frosini and Francesco Biagi (eds.), *Political and Constitutional Transitions in North Africa: Actors and Factors* (Routledge 2015).

[11] "In many countries the crisis of the non-democratic regime is also intermixed with profound differences about what should actually constitute the polity (or political community) and which *demos* or *demoi* (population or populations) should be members of that political community. When there are profound differences about the territorial boundaries of the political community's state and profound differences as to who has the right of citizenship in that state, there is what we call a 'stateness' problem" (Linz and Stepan 1996, note 10, at 16). Serious "stateness" problems arose both in Spain and the Czech Republic (to be discussed, respectively, in Chapters 3 and 4). It should be noted that a "stateness" problem arose also in Italy, with specific reference to Sicilian separatism. However, this issue was resolved by means of the adoption of the Statute of Sicily on May 16, 1946.

[12] The *Zeitgeist*, or spirit of the times, derives from the history of ideas in the German tradition. According to Linz and Stepan 1996, note 10, at 74, "When a country is part of an international ideological community where democracy is only one of many contested ideologies, the chances of transiting to and consolidating democracy are substantially less than if the spirit of the time is one where democratic ideologies have no powerful contenders."

semi-autocratic regimes have been taking place in several North African and Middle Eastern countries, in some cases resulting in the fall of the respective dictators. The widespread nature of these movements gave rise to expressions such as "Arab Spring" or "fourth wave of democratization," reflecting the assumption that these transitions would be successful. On the contrary, in a number of countries, such as Egypt and Libya, the processes of democratization ran into enormous difficulties, making their outcome extremely uncertain.

Another important characteristic of transitions is given by their *provisional nature*. Indeed, the transition is placed in a kind of limbo between one regime and the next. It is a period that is not destined to last forever, but that will lead (or rather, *should* lead) to a new political regime, different from the one that existed before. As a result, a transition may be either long or short depending on the circumstances, but it always has a beginning and an end.

It should be noted that democratic transitions are increasingly linked to the adoption of new constitutions, thus giving rise to *constitutional transitions*.[13] It is evident, however, that not all constitutions mark a real break with the authoritarian past. In the first place, one should consider the *procedure* adopted for drafting the constitution because the nature of a constitution is strictly linked to the way it is drafted. Thus, "[I]t would appear to be unimaginable, for example, for a despot to 'impose' a liberal-democratic Constitution: for it to be genuinely liberal and democratic, it would need to be *decided* (not simply 'accepted', and this is the reason for the weakness of all forms of plebiscite) by the people and/or their representatives."[14] In this connection, the process that led to the adoption of the 2014 Constitution of Tunisia, where a Constituent Assembly was directly elected by popular vote, was far more democratic than the constitution-making process that took place in Morocco, where the 2011 Constitution was drafted by a committee of experts all appointed by the king. The impression, therefore, is that the new Moroccan Constitution represents a modern example of an *octroyée* Constitution.[15]

Secondly, it is evident that also the *content* of the constitution matters. Illiberal regimes often rely on socialist and authoritarian constitutions, or constitutions based on religious fundamentalism. In order to make a clean break with the illiberal past, the new constitution needs to be based on values and principles of liberal-democratic constitutionalism, such as the principle of separation of powers (both horizontal and vertical), the separation between state and religion, the civilian

[13] Giuseppe de Vergottini, *Le transizioni costituzionali* (Il Mulino 1998).

[14] Antonino Spadaro, "La transizione costituzionale. Ambiguità e polivalenza di un'importante nozione di teoria generale" in Antonino Spadaro (ed.), *Le "trasformazioni" costituzionali nell'età della transizione* (Giappichelli 2000), 64.

[15] Francesco Biagi, "The Pilot of *Limited* Change: Mohammed VI and the Transition in Morocco" in Frosini and Biagi 2015 (eds.), note 10, at 56 ff.; Francesco Biagi, "The 2011 Constitution-Making Process in Morocco: A Limited and Controlled Public Participation" in Tania Abbiate, Markus Böckenförde, and Veronica Federico (eds.), *Public Participation in African Constitutionalism* (Routledge 2018), 55 ff.

control of the military, the principle of equality, the safeguarding of fundamental rights, the protection of minorities, the independence of the judiciary, and an effective system of constitutional justice.[16]

However, it is not always the case that a democratic transition requires the adoption of a new constitution. Indeed, as pointed out by Giuseppe de Vergottini, it is also possible for transitions to take place by means of a *reform* of the existing constitution, or even *without amending the constitution at all*.[17] Mexico is an example of a democratic transition that took place by means of constitutional reforms. Indeed, from 1977 onward, a series of constitutional amendments introduced major electoral reforms, which played a prominent role in the democratization process of the country. These reforms made a multiparty system possible, leading in the year 2000 to the alternation of power in a country that for 71 years had been dominated by a hegemonic force, the Institutional Revolutionary Party (*Partido Revolucionario Institucional*).[18]

Another case of particular interest is Portugal, where the constitutional reforms of 1982 and 1989 were crucial to guarantee an effective transition to democracy. Indeed, the Constitution of 1976 made numerous references to a transition toward a society and economy of a Socialist type, but with the amendments of 1982 and 1989, the Council of the Revolution was abolished, a Constitutional Court was established, the powers of the president were reduced in certain respects, and for the most part the ideological references to Socialist-economic principles were eliminated. The amendments to the Portuguese Constitution were so radical as to "give the impression that the body drafting the amendments was in actual fact endowed with constituent powers."[19]

Examples of transitions that, at least initially, took place without any formal constitutional amendments are to be found in the Western Balkans, most notably Serbia and Montenegro, where, until the adoption of the new constitutions (respectively, in 2006 and 2007), the transition was based on the constitutions adopted in the 1990s, and was largely directed by the existing elites.[20]

[16] See de Vergottini 1998, note 13, at 51; Larry Diamond, *Developing Democracy: Towards Consolidation* (The Johns Hopkins University Press 1999), 11 ff.

[17] Giuseppe de Vergottini, *Diritto costituzionale comparato* (Cedam 2013), 269.

[18] On the role of the electoral reforms in the process of democratization in Mexico, see Ricardo Becerra, Pedro Salazar, and José Woldenberg, *La mecánica del cambio político en México. Elecciones, partidos y reformas* (Cal y Arena 2000); Lorenzo Córdova Vianello, "La reforma electoral y el cambio político en México" in Daniel Zovatto and J. Jesús Orozco Henríquez (eds.), *Reforma política y electoral en América Latina 1978–2007* (Editorial UNAM 2008), 653 ff.

[19] de Vergottini 1998, note 13, at 161. See also Giuseppe de Vergottini, "Principio di legalità e revisione della Costituzione portoghese del 1982" in Alessandro Pizzorusso and Vincenzo Varano (eds.), *L'influenza dei valori costituzionali sui sistemi giuridici contemporanei* (Giuffrè 1985), 1154.

[20] See Jens Woelk, *La transizione costituzionale della Bosnia ed Erzegovina* (Cedam 2008), 25.

2 FORMAL TRANSITION AND SUBSTANTIVE TRANSITION

Identifying the "temporal coordinates" of democratic transitions is extremely complicated. Whereas political scientists pay considerable attention to identifying the end of the transition and the beginning of the period of consolidation, as well as to the characteristics distinguishing these two processes,[21] legal scholars often tend to identify the entry into force of the new democratic constitution as the watershed between transition and consolidation. In their view, the adoption of a new constitution represents "the legal expression of a successful transition."[22] However, this formulation seems to be slightly simplistic because it fails to take account of the complexity and the dynamism of these processes. An analysis of the transitions that took place in Europe in the twentieth century shows that the entry into force of a new democratic constitution, while representing the most significant element of change and discontinuity between the old and the new legal system,[23] is not in itself sufficient to give rise to an *effective* transition from autocratic to democratic rule.[24] The constitution serves to formalize the change, but is not in itself sufficient to ensure the effective transformation of the state.

In a more traditional perspective, what distinguishes the transition from the consolidation (from a more specifically legal perspective) is the fact that the transition consists of a period in which the fundamental values and principles underlying the new order are formally laid down in the constitution, whereas the consolidation is the period in which these principles and values become firmly rooted. The question arises, however, as to whether this distinction is more theoretical than substantive: How is it possible to consolidate something that in many respects exists only on paper, and that has not yet been implemented? In this connection reference may be made to the recognition and protection of fundamental rights, that clearly constitute an essential feature of any democracy: at the time they are laid down in the constitution, fundamental rights still have to be implemented, and as a result it makes little sense to claim that they need to be "consolidated." They could be consolidated only if they had already been applied in practice, at least partially. One need only consider the case of Italy, particularly the period following the adoption of

[21] On these debates see Richard Gunther, Hans-Jürgen Puhle and P. Nikiforos Diamandouros, "Introduction" in Richard Gunther, P. Nikiforos Diamandouros, and Hans-Jürgen Puhle (eds.), *The Politics of Democratic Consolidation: Southern Europe in Comparative Perspective* (The Johns Hopkins University Press 1995), 3 ff.

[22] See Ruth Rubio-Marín, "Women and the Cost of Transition to Democratic Constitutionalism in Spain" (2003) 18 *International Sociology*, 253. The author, however, rejects this position.

[23] The fundamental importance of the adoption of a new democratic constitution to mark the break between the old and the new regime is underlined by Bruce Ackerman, *The Future of Liberal Revolution* (Yale University Press 1992), 46 ff., 60 ff., and 69. See also de Vergottini 1998, note 13, at 169.

[24] See Giuseppe de Vergottini, "Costituzionalismo europeo e transizioni democratiche" in Marina Calamo Specchia, Maddalena Carli, Giampiero Di Plinio, and Roberto Toniatti (eds.), *I Balcani occidentali. Le Costituzioni della transizione* (Giappichelli 2008), 4.

the 1948 Constitution: for a long time, and above all until the Constitutional Court started its activity in 1956, many constitutional provisions on fundamental rights were not effectively enforced, while a number of laws dating back to the Fascist regime continued to be applied, although they were clearly inconsistent with the new Constitution.[25]

Therefore, a transition, in the sense of replacement of an authoritarian regime with a completely different one based on new principles and values, cannot be deemed to be complete with the mere entry into force of a new constitution. The risk is to deal with a "façade democracy,"[26] characterized by the paradoxical situation that the new democratic constitution operates within a legal order that in many respects is still de facto authoritarian.[27] In these cases it is possible to speak of *constitutions without constitutionalism*.[28]

It is evident, then, that the traditional (*formal*) meaning of transition does not appear to be capable of encapsulating the process in its entirety. For this reason, it seems necessary to opt for a *substantive* interpretation of transition, which refers to the period in which the fundamental principles characterizing the new system are enforced. On the basis of this interpretation, the conclusion of the constituent process strictly speaking does not mark the end of the transition and the beginning of the consolidation, but, on the contrary, marks the beginning of the *second phase of the transition*, in which the principles laid down in the constitution are effectively implemented. The substantive transition thus goes hand in hand with the enforcement of the constitution, and as a result, to paraphrase a well-known distinction,[29] it

25 As discussed in Chapter 2, Sections 3 and 4.

26 de Vergottini 1998, note 13, at 26; Giovanni Sartori, *Elementi di teoria politica* (Il Mulino 1995), 24 ff.

27 As in the case of Italy in the period 1948–1956 (see Chapter 2, Section 3). A sharp contrast between the provisions of the new constitution and the real conditions of the country could also be seen in various Balkan countries (de Vergottini 2008, note 24, at 7), in Latin America (Atilio A. Borón, "Latin America: Constitutionalism and the Political Traditions of Liberalism and Socialism" in Douglas Greenberg, Stanley N. Katz, Melanie Beth Oliviero, and Steven C. Wheatley [eds.], *Constitutionalism and Democracy: Transitions in the Contemporary World* [Oxford University Press 1993], 339 ff.) and Africa (H. W. O. Okoth-Ogendo, "Constitutions without Constitutionalism: Reflections on an African Political Paradox" in Greenberg, Katz, Oliviero, and Wheatley [eds.] 1993, in this note, at 65 ff.).

28 On the distinction between constitutions and constitutionalism see Stephen Holmes, "Constitutions and Constitutionalism" in Michel Rosenfeld and András Sajó (eds.), *The Oxford Handbook of Comparative Constitutional Law* (Oxford University Press 2012), 189 ff.; Augusto Barbera, "Le basi filosofiche del costituzionalismo" in Augusto Barbera (ed.), *Le basi filosofiche del costituzionalismo* (Laterza 2005), 3 ff.

29 With regard to the distinction between "law in the books" and "law in action" see Harold C. Gutteridge, *Comparative Law: An Introduction to the Comparative Method of Legal Study and Research* (Cambridge University Press 1946); Tullio Ascarelli, "Interpretazione del diritto e studio del diritto comparato" in *Saggi di diritto commerciale* (Giuffrè 1955), 508; Karl H. Neumayer, "Law in the Books, Law in Action et les méthodes du droit comparé" in Mario Rotondi (ed.), *Buts et méthodes du droit comparé* (Cedam 1973), 505 ff.

seems possible to distinguish between a *transition in the constitution* and a *transition in action.*[30]

This second phase tends to be much longer than the first one. Moreover, whereas the formal transition comes to an end at a particular point in time (i.e., the entry into force of the new constitution) the same cannot be said for the substantive transition. Indeed, if the transition process is successful, over time the substantive transition will *fade* into consolidation, without a clear demarcation between these two phases. For this reason, though the transition and the consolidation are conceptually distinct, they may even temporally overlap. Thus, the traditional bipartition between transition and consolidation is insufficient to explain the complexity and the dynamism of the process. The latter, on the contrary, consists of three parts: *formal* transition, *substantive* transition, and *consolidation.* The final outcome is given by the *consolidated democracy.*

In other cases, however, when the substantive transition encounters resistance, the process moves into a "political gray zone" (mentioned previously), where *hybrid* regimes are to be found. Finally, it may be the case that the difficulties prevail, with the consequence that the transition fails and a new autocratic regime takes over.

Every transition, then, is characterized by *uncertainty,* not only because the "rules of the game" are unclear and because it is extremely difficult to predict how long this process will last but also because (as noted) its *final outcome* is uncertain. In particular, *the outcome largely depends on the second phase of the transition, that is the substantive transition.* Indeed, during this phase it becomes clear whether the principles and values laid down in the new constitution are effectively implemented in practice (thus paving the way for consolidation), or whether they remain a dead letter (meaning that the country drifts into a "grey area," with the risk of a restoration of an authoritarian regime). In this second phase, as shown in this book, the role played by the constitutional courts is of the utmost importance.

Before arguing that the establishment of these courts, particularly in the period after World War II, is closely linked to the processes of democratic transition, it seems necessary to provide a brief overview of the origins of constitutional justice.

3 FROM THE *STAATSGERICHTSBARKEIT* TO THE *VERFASSUNGSGERICHTSBARKEIT*

The first experiences of constitutional justice were closely linked to decentralized states. Indeed, in these countries there was a need to create a body to safeguard and preserve the "federative contract," and to bring harmony to the institutional

30 On the distinction between "formal" transition and "substantive" transition see also Francesco Biagi, "Three Generations of European Constitutional Courts in Transition to Democracy" (2014) 2 *Diritto pubblico comparato ed europeo,* 986–988.

pluralism underlying the original *pactum foederis*.[31] In the United States, it is the Supreme Court that is the body that has acted since 1787 as the arbiter between the federal government and the member states, whereas in Europe the origins of constitutional justice, in terms of regulation of competences between the member states by a confederal body, can be traced back to the 1815 German Confederation. Afterward, reference may be made to the Austrian Constitution of 1867, where the *Reichsgericht* was vested with the task of resolving the conflicts between the *Reich* and the *Länder*, and the Swiss Constitution of 1874, in which the Federal Court was granted the power to strike down cantonal laws in conflict with federal law.[32] Moreover, the 1919 Weimar Constitution set up a Constitutional Tribunal (*Staatsgerichtshof*) to resolve not only the conflicts between constitutional bodies within the *Reich* and the *Länder* but also the disputes between the *Reich* and the *Länder*, and between the *Länder*. In the same vein the Austrian Constitution of 1920 provided that the Constitutional Court should rule on conflicts of powers between the *Bund* and the *Länder*.

As a result, nineteenth-century Europe saw the emergence of a particular "type" of constitutional justice, known as *Staatsgerichtsbarkeit*, that was intended to preserve the coexistence between the various levels of political power within the state. On the contrary, what could not be established in Europe until the beginning of the twentieth century (with only a few exceptions) was the type of constitutional justice aimed at safeguarding the fundamental rights laid down in the constitution, namely the *Verfassungsgerichtsbarkeit*.[33] Indeed, in nineteenth-century Europe, a key element for the emergence of this type of constitutional justice was lacking, that is social and political pluralism. It should be noted that the distinction between these two types of constitutional justice was established only after World War II, whereas in the period between the two world wars the *Verfassungsgerichtsbarkeit* was considered to be the continuation and completion of the *Staatsgerichtsbarkeit*.[34]

It is well known that the "European" model of constitutional review, inspired by the theories of Hans Kelsen, was born between the two world wars. This model is characterized by the fact that constitutional review can only be carried out by an *ad hoc* body, the constitutional court (centralized model), thus clearly departing from the "US" system, where all the courts are empowered to exercise a constitutional control of legislation (decentralized model). The first experiences of the European system were given by the Constitutional Courts of Czechoslovakia, Austria, and

[31] See Elena D'Orlando, *La funzione arbitrale della Corte costituzionale tra Stato centrale e governi periferici* (Libreria Bonomo Editrice 2005), 40.

[32] On constitutional justice in nineteenth-century Europe, see Jörg Luther, *Idee e storie di giustizia costituzionale nell'Ottocento* (Giappichelli 1990).

[33] On the distinction between *Staatsgerichtsbarkeit* and *Verfassungsgerichtsbarkeit*, see Alessandro Pizzorusso, "Garanzie costituzionali. Art. 134" in Giuseppe Branca (ed.), *Commentario della Costituzione* (Zanichelli-Il Foro italiano 1981), 21 ff.

[34] See Gustavo Zagrebelsky, *La giustizia costituzionale* (Il Mulino 1988), 22.

Spain. The first was provided by the Constitution of Czechoslovakia of February 29, 1920, followed a few months later by the Austrian Constitutional Court, envisaged by the Constitution of October 1, 1920 (the *Oktoberverfassung*). Then the Spanish Constitution of December 9, 1931 made provision for the Court of Constitutional Guarantees (*Tribunal de garantías constitucionales*).

According to Kelsen, the constitutional court was not a court strictly speaking because it was not responsible for adjudicating on specific situations or events, but exercised an "abstract" control of legislation, striking down laws that were deemed to be incompatible with the constitution, with *ex nunc* effects, or in certain cases, with *pro futuro* effects. In Kelsen's scheme, a court that is entrusted with the power of ascertaining whether a law is compatible with the constitution is not a judicial but a legislative body. In particular, the constitutional court is considered a *negative legislator*: whereas the positive legislator enacts new laws, the negative legislator is responsible for striking down laws that are in contrast with the constitution.[35] This interpretation was intended to head off the risk of a "government of judges" because in that historical period Europe was witnessing the rise of the Free Law Movement (*Freirechtsbewegung*)[36] and the People's Community (*Volksgemeinschaft*)[37] that aimed to free judges from what they considered to be the strict application of the law.[38]

The model outlined by Kelsen was intended precisely to avoid the risk of a government of judges, by requiring them to be subject to the laws and granting the constitutional court the exclusive right to strike down laws in contrast with the constitution. The willingness to prevent a system of constitutional review based on

[35] Hans Kelsen, "Wesen und Entwicklung der Staatsgerichtsbarkeit" (1929) 5 *Veröffentlichtung der Vereinigung der Deutschen Staatrechtslehrer* 2/"La garantie jurisdictionnelle de la Constitution – La justice constitutionnelle" (1929) 5 *Revue de Droit Public et de la Science Politique en France et à l'étranger*. The English translation can be found in "Kelsen on the Nature and Development of Constitutional Adjudication" in Lars Vinx (ed.), *The Guardian of the Constitution: Hans Kelsen and Carl Schmitt on the Limits of Constitutional Law* (Cambridge University Press 2015), 22 ff.

[36] In contrast with legal positivism, the members of the Free Law Movement argued that judges should fill in the gaps and uncertainties in the law, as well as promoting creative jurisprudence. Moreover, jurists were expected to work toward an extension of positive sources, promoting normative sources other than the law. Hence the recourse to custom, administrative and judicial practice, case law, the adoption of comparative method and the findings of other social sciences, in particular sociology, and so on. See Giuseppe Volpe, *L'ingiustizia delle leggi. Studi sui modelli di giustizia costituzionale* (Giuffrè 1977), 29 ff.

[37] In the *Volksgemeinschaft* perspective, when considering a specific case, the judge "is not required to evaluate it on the basis of positive norms, that might not be capable of foreseeing it, but to draw on the more widely established law of the people's community, not only in cases in which a positive norm is lacking, but also where it is deemed that in the specific case the provisions of the applicable positive law are in contrast with the values and goals of the community" (Volpe 1977, note 36, at 98).

[38] See Eduardo García de Enterría, "La posición juridica del Tribunal constitucional en el sistema español: posibilidades y perspectivas" (1981) 1 *Revista española de derecho constitucional* 1, 44.

the US model clearly emerged from Article 89 of the 1920 Austrian Constitution, which explicitly prohibited ordinary judges from exercising a constitutional review of legislation.

Whereas Kelsen's model may be seen as symptomatic of a lack of trust in the judiciary, the origins of the US system of constitutional review reflect the aim of establishing the judiciary above the other branches of government, in particular the legislature. More specifically, the historical and ideological motivations for this approach are rooted in the intention of wealthy American bourgeois families to obtain protection from the courts for their constitutional and, above all, property rights against the risk of abuses and expropriation by the legislative assemblies.[39] From this point of view, nineteenth-century European liberal ideology was markedly different from US liberalism. In Europe, the guiding principle was the reorganization and stabilization of legal systems, for example through the introduction of codes, to reduce the margin of discretion of the judges, and to limit as much as possible the activities of the courts (and in fact, as noted in the preceding text, constitutional review of legislation was entrusted to an *ad hoc* body, a *negative legislator*).[40] In the United States, on the contrary, while carrying out judicial review of legislation, the courts were required to interpret constitutional provisions that were often extremely vague and elastic, with the consequence that they had to incorporate into their reasoning elements of evaluation that were by their very nature discretional and (in the most noble sense of the word) "political."[41] As a result, the trust placed in the judiciary was much greater than in Europe.[42]

4 THE DIFFICULTIES OF THE FIRST EUROPEAN CONSTITUTIONAL COURTS

The first experiences of the European model of constitutional review, especially if one considers the cases of the Czechoslovak and Spanish Constitutional Courts, encountered major difficulties. The reasons for the limited success of these bodies are many and various.

39 See Volpe 1977, note 36, at 157.

40 See Giovanni Bognetti, *Lo spirito del costituzionalismo americano. Breve profilo del diritto costituzionale degli Stati Uniti. La Costituzione liberale* (Giappichelli 1998), 67.

41 Ibid.

42 It should be noted, however, that the judiciary in the United States was not initially a strong branch of government. The Constitution made provision solely for the Supreme Court as the necessary judicial body, delegating to Congress the question of whether and to what extent the lower federal courts should be established. In addition, the Constitution did not specify the number of justices to be appointed to the Supreme Court, with the result that Congress had to determine this number by means of legislation, thus potentially interfering in the composition of the Court and indirectly in its judicial decisions (in this connection, mention should be made of the court-packing plan of Franklin D. Roosevelt).

With regard to the Czechoslovak Constitutional Court, on many occasions the political parties expressed their skepticism, if not their outright hostility, in relation to an institution that was authorized to overrule their decisions, as this constituted a threat to the principle of parliamentary supremacy. In addition, there was a certain tension between the apex courts and the Constitutional Court because the former saw the latter as a potential rival. The "stranglehold" on access is another reason that explains the difficulties encountered by the Constitutional Court. In fact, the bodies entitled to challenge the constitutionality of a law before the Court were only the two Houses of Parliament, the Supreme Court, the Supreme Administrative Court, and the Election Court, and each of them had to act *en banc*. This means that the parliamentary opposition was not granted standing to apply to the Court. Even the ordinary courts were denied the power to suspend a case and refer a question of constitutionality to the Court, as they could only challenge the constitutionality of a law *in abstracto* in the *en banc* session.[43] Furthermore, the constitutional challenge could be raised only within three years of the date when the contested law was enacted. Also the lack of a "federal rationale" appears to have weakened the role of the Constitutional Court: indeed, as discussed previously, at that time constitutional justice was strictly linked to decentralized countries. Czechoslovakia, on the contrary, was a unitary state, and therefore there was no need to resolve disputes between the central government and the substate entities.[44] In light of this situation, it is hardly surprising that in 1931, when the term of office of the judges appointed in 1921 expired, the president and the apex courts delayed appointing new judges for seven years.[45] In fact, between 1931 and 1938, the Court was "*de facto* abolished, or at the very least, suspended."[46] At that point, however, Czechoslovakia was in its final months before the Nazi invasion, and as a result the Court managed to operate for just a few months, until it was suspended in 1939 by Hitler's regime. For all these

43 See the decision of the Supreme Administrative Court of Czechoslovakia, Boh. Adm. 1097/22, 1757/22.

44 On the factors explaining the difficulties encountered by the Czechoslovak Constitutional Court see Zdeněk Kühn and Jan Kysela, "Nomination of Constitutional Justices in Post-Communist Countries: Trial, Error, Conflict in the Czech Republic" (2006) 2 *European Constitutional Law Review* 2, 189; David Kosař and Ladislav Vyhnánek, "The Constitutional Court of Czechia" in Armin von Bogdandy et al. (eds.), *Constitutional Judicial Review* (Oxford University Press, forthcoming); see also the website of the Czech Constitutional Court: www.usoud.cz/en/constitutional-court-of-the-czechoslovak-republic-and-its-fortunes-in-years-1920-1948/ (accessed July 15, 2019). A similar degree of hostility was also encountered when the Constitutional Court of the Czech Republic started its activity (see Chapter 4, Section 3).

45 The Constitutional Court was composed of seven members: three appointed by the President of the Republic (from a list submitted by Parliament or government), two by the Supreme Court, and two by the Supreme Administrative Court. The appointment made by the president had to be countersigned by the prime minister.

46 Pedro Cruz Villalón, *La formación del sistema europeo de control de constitucionalidad (1918–1939)* (Centro de estudios constitucionales 1987), 290. Also the Constitutional Court of the Czech Republic was forced to suspend its activities for reasons relating to the appointment of the constitutional judges (see Chapter 4, Section 3).

reasons, the Court handed down an extremely limited number of judgments, having little impact on Czechoslovak society.

Also the Spanish Court of Constitutional Guarantees encountered enormous difficulties. During its short-lived existence it never enjoyed a position of prestige. Rather, in the view of a number of legal scholars, the experience of the Court represented "one of the least glorious pages"[47] as far as the constitutional order of the Second Republic was concerned. The first ruling of the Court was handed down on June 8, 1934, but the decree issued on May 4, 1937 abolished this body as it was deemed to be in conflict with the principles on which Franco's regime was based. Among the difficulties encountered by the Court, mention should be made of the lack of a *real* support from the political forces for setting it up. The then-president of the Court, Alvaro de Albornoz, claimed in a speech before Parliament that nobody had wanted to establish the Court, no significant political force had supported it and that, on the contrary, it had encountered hostility from the right and the left in equal measure. In 1935 the right-wing forces had tabled a motion for constitutional reform envisaging the abolition of the Court. The following year, the left-wing parties had tabled a motion advocating the removal from office of the constitutional judges in the case of manifest hostility to the Republican institutions, to be determined by a simple majority of the Court.[48] Furthermore, some constitutional framers were supporters of the US system of constitutional review, whereas others, as advocates of the principle of parliamentary sovereignty, were against granting the courts the power to verify the constitutionality of legislative acts, and more in favor of review mechanisms of a political nature.[49] In light of the manifest hostility toward the Court, it is not entirely clear why this body was established. The attempt to provide an arbiter to settle conflicts between the state and the regions, and the influence the prestigious Austrian Constitutional Court exerted over the Spanish constitutional drafters, are two of the reasons put forward by legal scholars to justify the establishment of the Court.[50]

Another aspect that explains the difficulties encountered by the Court of Constitutional Guarantees is that its members were too overtly politicized.[51] The president was not elected by the judges, but by Parliament, and its members included, among the others, a representative of each region of the country, both "autonomous" and "nonautonomous." Even the "technical" members (such as those nominated by the

[47] Eduardo García de Enterría and Tomás-Ramón Fernandez, *Curso de derecho administrativo* (Civitas 1980), 94.

[48] See Cruz Villalón 1987, note 46, at 339.

[49] See Francisco Tomás y Valiente, *Escritos sobre y desde el Tribunal constitucional* (Centro de estudios políticos y constitucionales 1993), 26–27.

[50] See Francisco Rubio Llorente, "Del Tribunal de garantías constitucionales al Tribunal constitucional" (1982–1983) 16 *Revista de derecho político*, 33.

[51] In the view of Pedro J. González-Trevijano Sánchez, *El Tribunal constitucional* (Aranzadi 2000), 49, it was precisely the composition of the Court that was "mainly responsible for its lack of success."

bar association, and the faculties of law) were chosen mainly on the basis of political criteria. As a result, the Court was considered to be equivalent to a "political Chamber."[52]

Moreover, it is important to consider the extremely difficult historical phase in which the Court started its activity. Indeed, the judges had the misfortune to find themselves engulfed in the political conflicts of the time, having to deal with a very complex social and political climate. The result was that the rulings of the Court, influenced by this historical context, "were judged according to parameters of a political nature [and] became the subject of struggle and controversy between the various parties."[53] The case of the law on agrarian contracts approved by the Parliament of Catalonia in 1934 is emblematic. Although the Court declared the law unconstitutional, the Catalan Parliament ignored the ruling and approved another law with the same content. All this took place in a climate of such tension between the central government and the regional government of Catalonia that the president of the Court, Alvaro de Albornoz, was forced to resign.

The tension between the central government and Catalonia, as pointed out in the following text,[54] appears to be a constant in Spanish history: it was to resurface during the process of transition to democracy, with the adoption of a new Statute of Autonomy for Catalonia in 2006, and more recently with the events surrounding the popular consultation for the self-government of Catalonia in November 2014 and with the referendum on secession of October 1, 2017.

As argued by Pedro Cruz Villalón, neither Czechoslovakia nor Spain were sufficiently "*mature*"[55] for the constitutional review of legislation. On the contrary, the political and institutional conditions were much more favorable to the setting up of a Constitutional Court in Austria, and this helps to explain why this Court was far more effective than those in Czechoslovakia and Spain.[56] It should be noted that the Austrian constitution-making process took place with the collaboration of legal scholars of the caliber of Karl Renner, Michael Mayr, and Hans Kelsen, and that the Constitution, that was the outcome of significant compromises between the main political parties, adopted a federal structure based on a balance of powers between the *Länder* and the *Bund*. This "moderate federalism"[57] represented an

[52] Rubio Llorente 1982–1983, note 50, at 31; see also Rosa María Ruiz Lapeña, *El Tribunal de garantías constitucionales en la II República española* (Bosch 1982), xxi ff.

[53] Giancarlo Rolla, *Indirizzo politico e Tribunale costituzionale in Spagna* (Jovene 1986), 77. On the case law of the Court of Constitutional Guarantees see Martín Bassols Coma, *La jurisprudencia del Tribunal de garantías constitucionales de la II República española* (Centro de estudios constitucionales 1981).

[54] See Chapter 3, Sections 1.B and 3.D.

[55] Cruz Villalón 1987, note 46, at 417.

[56] On the Austrian Constitutional Court, see Charles Eisenmann, *La justice constitutionnelle et la Haute Cour constitutionnelle d'Autriche* (Economica-Presses Universitaires d'Aix-Marseille 1986) (reproduction of the 1928 edition).

[57] I.M.ª de Lojendio Irure, "Prólogo" in Cruz Villalón 1987, note 46, at 15.

important feature of the Constitution, in which the Constitutional Court was intended to play a key role. Indeed, constitutional review of legislation served to safeguard the federal structure and the proper demarcation of competences between the *Bund* and the *Länder*. This approach undoubtedly contributes to explaining the effectiveness of the Constitutional Court's action.[58]

It must be stressed, however, that even the Austrian Court encountered serious difficulties. Above all, the constitutional reform of 1929 not only vested the Supreme Court and the Administrative Court with the power to refer questions of constitutionality to the Constitutional Court[59] but also modified the procedure for the appointment of the members of the Court, strengthening the role of the federal government (the Government of the Christian-Social Party, in power at the time), thus upsetting the balance in the composition of the Court. A few years later, by means of a government order of May 23, 1933, the Law on the Constitutional Court was reformed to reduce by half (for an indefinite period) the number of members of the Court, that as a result was unable to perform most of its functions.[60] On April 24, 1934, the adoption of an authoritarian-corporatist Constitution resulted in the demise of democracy in Austria. Indeed, although this new Constitution envisaged a constitutional chamber within the Federal Court to take over the functions of the Constitutional Court, the political conditions prevented any effective constitutional review of legislation.

It should be noted that, in spite of their limited success, the precedents of constitutional justice in Spain and Czechoslovakia played a role that was by no means secondary in the decision to set up a constitutional court after the collapse of the respective authoritarian regimes.[61] In Spain, for example, although references to the Court of Constitutional Guarantees were few and far between, and it was nearly always cited as a negative example, this experience was useful during the constitution-making process to avoid the same mistakes. In the Czech Republic the reference to the 1920 Constitutional Court of Czechoslovakia was important especially from a symbolic point of view: indeed, as recalled in the preceding text, it was the first Constitutional Court in Europe (set up even before the Austrian Court) responsible for constitutional review of legislation. Therefore, for the Czech constitutional framers it would have been hard to justify the interruption of a tradition of constitutional justice of such historical significance.

58 Cruz Villalón 1987, note 46, at 419.

59 On this procedural gateway to the Constitutional Court see Hans Kelsen, "Judicial Review of Legislation: A Comparative Study of the Austrian and the American Constitution" (1942) 4 *The Journal of Politics* 2, 183 ff.

60 Cruz Villalón 1987, note 46, at 266 ff. According to Cruz Villalón, in actual fact the Court could have continued to carry out its functions, but the government order achieved its aim thanks to the complicity, or at least the weakness, of the Court or some of its members (at 273).

61 As discussed, respectively, in Chapter 3, Section 2, and Chapter 4, Section 3.

5 THE CLOSE LINK BETWEEN THE PROCESSES OF DEMOCRATIC TRANSITION AND THE SETTING UP OF CONSTITUTIONAL COURTS AFTER WORLD WAR II

The extraordinary spread of constitutional courts in Europe (and beyond) after World War II should not be taken to mean that it was inevitable that these bodies would be established. *Au contraire*. It is important to bear in mind that the criticisms of the setting up of constitutional courts inspired by Jacobin ideals – based on the principle of the "law as the expression of the general will"[62] and the myth of the representative assembly – continued to be particularly strong. It was precisely these ideas that were cited to undermine the legitimacy of a body entrusted with the power of striking down legislative acts adopted by Parliament, the representative institution *par excellence*. These arguments had a certain resonance within the constituent assemblies in Italy, France, and Spain whenever the issue of constitutional justice was discussed. Whereas in the constituent assemblies of Central and Eastern European countries the setting up of a constitutional court was not seriously contested, the legitimacy of these bodies began to be questioned in Parliament as soon as the courts started their activity. Thus, defeating the dogma of parliamentary supremacy was by no means an easy task.

Interestingly enough, in certain countries the power to review the constitutionality of legislation was granted to bodies *other than* the constitutional court (or the ordinary courts). A particular case is that of Portugal, where a Constitutional Court was established only after the constitutional reform of 1982. Indeed, the 1976 Constitution, adopted after the fall of Salazar regime, had entrusted the power of constitutional review not only to the ordinary courts and the Constitutional Commission but also to the Council of the Revolution, a constitutional body representing the military.[63]

It has to be pointed out that the constituent assemblies do not seem to have been influenced by the limits and difficulties of previous experiences of constitutional justice. In this connection, suffice it to mention the fact that in designing the system of constitutional review, the German constitutional drafters not only refused to be discouraged but even drew inspiration from the *Staatsgerichtshof* of the Weimar Republic,[64] although it was a body that not always performed the role assigned to it

[62] See the seminal book by Raymond Carré de Malberg, *La loi, expression de la volonté générale* (Sirey 1931).

[63] See António Araújo, "A construção da justiça constitucional portuguesa: o nascimento do Tribunal Constitucional" (1995) 30 *Análise Social* 134, 897 ff.; Gonçalo de Almeida Ribeiro, "Judicial Review of Legislation in Portugal: A Brief Genealogy" in Francesco Biagi, Justin O. Frosini, and Jason Mazzone (eds.), *Constitutional History: Comparative Perspectives* (Brill, forthcoming); Giuseppe de Vergottini, *Le origini della seconda Repubblica portoghese* (Giuffrè 1977), 234–235.

[64] See Donald P. Kommers, *The Constitutional Jurisprudence of the Federal Republic of Germany* (Duke University Press 1989), 8–11.

by the Constitution of 1919. In fact, "completely betraying its institutional role and functions,"[65] the Court contributed to the collapse of the constitutional order by means of the well-known ruling of October 25, 1932 on the "coup d'état" in Prussia on July 20 the same year, which de facto paved the way for National Socialism.

What, then, are the reasons leading European constitutional framers to set up a constitutional court in their respective countries? As noted in the following text, there are undoubtedly a number of different reasons, in large part relating to the idea that constitutional courts represented a necessary instrument to mark a clean break with the previous autocratic regime.

A *The "Terrible Lessons" Learned from Autocratic Regimes*

The setting up of the Constitutional Courts in Germany and Italy, as well as the re-establishment of the Austrian Constitutional Court, are undoubtedly based on the "terrible lessons"[66] of the Nazi and Fascist regimes. In a similar way, it was the intention of establishing a true democracy after many years of authoritarian rule that explains the creation of Constitutional Courts in Spain and Portugal,[67] and a decade later in Central and Eastern Europe. As argued by Luis López Guerra,

> the establishment of constitutional jurisdiction is linked with the desire to guarantee democratic constitutional stability in the light of past and present dangers and to prevent constitutional mandates from being eroded and eventually suppressed by a parliamentary majority which disregards the Constitution. The objective of constitutional jurisdiction is to defend the Constitution from possible situations which might threaten its integrity.[68]

In some countries the reaction to the autocratic past gave rise to systems of constitutional review characterized by elements of the American model. Greece, for example, following the fall of the Regime of the Colonels (1967–1974), revived its tradition of constitutional justice by adopting a decentralized system, with a Supreme Court responsible for guaranteeing a uniform interpretation of constitutional provisions.[69] Along similar lines, in Portugal the 1982 constitutional reform envisaged a system characterized by elements of both the centralized model (with the setting up of a Constitutional Court) and the decentralized one (in which the

[65] Volpe 1977, note 36, at 203.
[66] Favoreu 1986, note 1, at 11.
[67] Portugal, as discussed in the following text, is also characterized by elements of the decentralized system of constitutional review.
[68] Luis López Guerra, "The Role and Competences of the Constitutional Court" in European Commission for Democracy through Law, *The Role of the Constitutional Court in the Consolidation of the Rule of Law* (Council of Europe Press 1994), 17.
[69] On the Greek system see Allan R. Brewer-Carías, *Judicial Review in Comparative Law* (Cambridge University Press 1989), 168 ff.

ordinary courts are not allowed to apply laws in conflict with the Constitution).[70] Also in Estonia, in contrast with the choices made in the other Central and Eastern European countries,[71] the framers decided to set up a mixed system, in which constitutional review is exercised by the Constitutional Chamber of the Supreme Court, but at the same time the ordinary courts are required to set aside laws inconsistent with the Constitution.[72]

Similarly, outside Europe, a number of Latin American countries opted for a decentralized system of constitutional review, or decided to create a Constitutional Chamber (*Sala constitucional*) within the Supreme Court.[73] The case of Japan is a particular one: indeed, the adoption of a decentralized model is to be explained largely by the decisive influence of the United States during the constitution-drafting process.[74]

The fact that the setting up of constitutional courts goes hand in hand with the establishment of democratic regimes is confirmed by the *a contrariis* argument that, almost without exception, "no dictatorial and oppressive regime has ever accepted an effective, and not merely nominal, system of constitutional justice."[75] Numerous examples could be mentioned, starting from the collapse of constitutional control of legislation in Hitler's Germany,[76] or in Austria after the *Anschluss* of 1938.[77] Another example is Spain, where, as noted previously, the decree of May 4, 1937 resulted in the abolition of the Court of Constitutional Guarantees. The Socialist regimes are also of interest in this connection, considering that with the exception of Yugoslavia and Poland,[78] constitutional review was never envisaged because it was deemed to

[70] See Araújo 1995, note 63, at 918 ff.; de Almeida Ribeiro forthcoming, note 63.

[71] Where a centralized model of constitutional review was adopted. See Wojciech Sadurski, *Rights before Courts: A Study of Constitutional Courts in Postcommunist States of Central and Eastern Europe* (Springer 2014), 3 ff.; Čarna Pištan, *Tra democrazia e autoritarismo. Esperienze di giustizia costituzionale nell'Europa centro-orientale e nell'area post-sovietica* (Bononia University Press 2015), 162 ff.

[72] See Čarna Pištan, "I sistemi di giustizia costituzionale nei paesi dell'Europa centro-orientale e dell'area post-sovietica" in Luca Mezzetti (ed.), *Sistemi e modelli di giustizia costituzionale* (Cedam 2011, vol. II), 191–192 and 233–234.

[73] See Justin O. Frosini and Lucio Pegoraro, "Constitutional Courts in Latin America: A Testing Ground for New Parameters of Classification?" (2008) 3 *Journal of Comparative Law* 2, 39 ff.

[74] See Norikazu Kawagishi, "The Birth of Judicial Review in Japan" (2007) 5 *International Journal of Constitutional Law* 2, 308 ff.

[75] Mauro Cappelletti, "Dimensioni della giustizia nelle società contemporanee" in *Studi di diritto giudiziario comparato* (Il Mulino 1994), 69.

[76] The last judgment of the Constitutional Court, in which it found that it was not competent to adjudicate the case, was handed down on June 30, 1933.

[77] However, as noted previously, already from 1934 onward, the political conditions prevented any effective constitutional review of legislation.

[78] Constitutional review of legislation was introduced in Yugoslavia in 1963 and in Poland in 1982. In Yugoslavia it was justified by the federal structure of the State, but above all by the system of self-management, whereas in Poland the setting up of the Constitutional Court was intended to be evidence of the democratization process taking place in the country. In Czechoslovakia, as discussed in Chapter 4, Sections 1 and 3, Constitutional Law no. 143 of 1968 envisaged a

be in contrast with the principle of supremacy of the representative assembly. Another example is South Africa during the apartheid era, when the country was characterized by a long struggle between the High Court, that intended to strike down certain racist laws, and the political forces that over the course of many years managed to abolish the courts' power of constitutional review.[79] By way of confirmation of this tendency, one need only consider the case of Hungary, where following the recent democratic deterioration, the powers of the Constitutional Court – which had been considered for a long time one of the most powerful and activist constitutional courts in the world[80] – have been severely curtailed.[81]

The very few constitutional courts that have managed to carry out their functions effectively in spite of the fact that they were operating under authoritarian regimes (as in the case of Egypt under Mubarak[82] and Chile under Pinochet)[83] may be seen as exceptions that confirm the rule.[84]

The "lessons" learned from the experience of authoritarian regimes not only resulted in the setting up and the spread of constitutional courts but also served as an important stimulus for the adoption of other instruments aimed at the protection of fundamental rights and freedoms, such as the European Convention on Human Rights (ECHR), the (old) European Commission of Human Rights, and the

Federal Constitutional Court and a Constitutional Court for each of the two republics that had been established, i.e., the Czech Republic and the Slovak Republic. However, these Courts were never set up.

79 Cappelletti 1994, note 75, at 70.

80 See Alec Stone Sweet, "Constitutional Courts" in Rosenfeld and Sajó (eds.) 2012, note 28, at 826.

81 See Oliver W. Lembcke and Christian Boulanger, "Between Revolution and Constitution: The Roles of the Hungarian Constitutional Court" in Attila Tóth (ed.) 2012, note 4, at 269 ff.; Kriszta Kovács and Gábor Attila Tóth, "Hungary's Constitutional Transformation" (2011) 7 *European Constitutional Law Review* 2, 183 ff.; András Jakab and Pál Sonnevend, "Continuity with Deficiencies: The New Basic Law of Hungary" (2013) 9 *European Constitutional Law Review* 1, 102 ff.

82 In particular, from mid-1980s to the end of the 1990s, a period in which the Supreme Constitutional Court struck down numerous important laws enacted by the regime. See Tamir Moustafa, *The Struggle for Constitutional Power: Law, Politics and Economic Development in Egypt* (Cambridge University Press 2007); Clark B. Lombardi, "Egypt's Supreme Constitutional Court: Managing Constitutional Conflict in an Authoritarian, Aspirationally 'Islamic' State" (2008) 3 *Journal of Comparative Law* 2, 234 ff.

83 See Robert Barros, *Constitutionalism and Dictatorship: Pinochet, the Junta, and the 1980 Constitution* (Cambridge University Press 2002), 255 ff., who shows that, although it was envisaged by the Constitution adopted under Pinochet in 1980, the Constitutional Court played a decisive role in keeping the actions of the regime in check and in promoting the transition to democracy.

84 On the role of judicial bodies in autocratic regimes see Tom Ginsburg and Tamir Moustafa (eds.), *Rule by Law: The Politics of Courts in Authoritarian Regimes* (Cambridge University Press 2008).

European Court of Human Rights. Indeed, it is significant that most member states ratified the ECHR after a period of military conflict and/or authoritarian rule.[85]

B *Distrust toward the Legislature and Fear of the Judiciary*

Another reason that explains the setting up of constitutional courts refers to the distrust toward the legislative branch. The experiences of authoritarian rule in various European countries show that in many cases the legislature represented the greatest threat to people's rights and freedoms,[86] due to its power to commit grave injustices in a systematic manner. Bearing these experiences in mind, constitutional drafters decided to establish constitutional courts so as to provide an effective protection from arbitrary (legislative) power.[87] Indeed, these courts were intended to act as a counterweight to majoritarian institutions, which had often failed to defend people's rights under the previous autocratic regimes.

Furthermore, in a number of cases the decision to adopt a centralized system of constitutional review rather than a decentralized system seems to be linked to a lack of trust in the ordinary courts. However, this was not a lack of trust in judges as such, but a reflection of the fact that they were part of the previous authoritarian regime and/or due to their hesitant stance in the past when called on to rule on constitutional matters.[88]

> How could an American system function – asked Louis Favoreu – in the Federal Republic of Germany, Italy, Spain, or Portugal, with judges from the preceding period of dictatorship named to the courts? Adopting [the US] judicial review in these countries would require "purification" on a massive scale of the corps of magistrates, while one could immediately find a dozen or so constitutional judges

[85] See Tom Allen and Benedict Douglas, "Closing the Door on Restitution: The European Court of Human Rights" in Antoine Buyse and Michael Hamilton (eds.), *Transitional Jurisprudence and the European Convention on Human Rights. Justice, Politics and Rights* (Cambridge University Press 2011), 213.

[86] García de Enterría 1981, note 38, at 45.

[87] With specific reference to Italy see Giovanni Bognetti, *The American Constitution and Italian Constitutionalism: An Essay in Comparative Constitutional History* (CLUEB 2008), 58, who argues that "the main reason why the Italian constituents gave their assent to [the setting up of a system of constitutional review of legislation] probably had to do ... with the experience of Fascism. Most of constituents wished it to be adopted because they believed it could be a useful guarantee against possible future encroachment by the Legislature on civil and political rights of the people."

[88] See Andrew Harding, Peter Leyland, and Tania Groppi, "Constitutional Courts: Forms, Functions and Practice in Comparative Perspective" (2008) 3 *Journal of Comparative Law* 2, 10. For example, with regard to Germany, Ackerman 1992, note 23, at 105, argues that at the beginning the legitimacy of the *Bundesverfassungsgericht* depended largely on the fact that, unlike other courts, none of its judges were associated with the previous authoritarian regime. On the complex task of denazification of the German judiciary after the defeat of Hitler regime, see Ingo Muller, *Hitler's Justice: The Courts of the Third Reich* (Harvard University Press 1991), 201 ff.

> with no prior culpability during those periods, capable of carrying out their duties without mental reservations.[89]

However, the refusal to vest the ordinary courts with the power of constitutional review was not always due to the previously mentioned reasons. In the case of Italy, for example, several members of the Constituent Assembly feared that the judiciary would not make a limited but rather an "extensive – or perhaps ... excessive or uncontrollable"[90] use of constitutional review,[91] and that granting judges such a power would mean allowing them too much discretion and creativity in interpreting the laws: indeed, "if they had wanted to, they could have struck down any law, simply by interpreting the constitutional norm in the sense that they preferred from time to time."[92] In addition to that, many members of the Constituent Assembly had been strongly influenced by the work of the French legal scholar, Eduard Lambert, *Le gouvernement des juges et la lutte contre la législation sociale aux États-Unis*,[93] in which he argued that in the United States the decentralized system of judicial review, along with other factors, had given rise to a judicial supremacy, where the legislature and the executive were subordinate to the judicial branch, thus determining a serious imbalance in institutional power.[94]

In short, either due to a distrust stemming from the authoritarian past, or for the purposes of avoiding a "government of judges," the fact is that entrusting the power of constitutional review to the judiciary was often seen as risky, and this evidently favored the setting up of constitutional courts.

In the constituent assemblies of various European countries the decision to adopt a centralized system of constitutional review rather than a decentralized system was justified also with reference to matters of a technical nature. Indeed, the introduction of the US model in civil law countries (as in the case of continental Europe) would have given rise to inconsistent rulings because the same law might have been set aside by certain judges who deemed it to be unconstitutional but enforced by other judges who found it to comply with the constitutional provisions.[95] Moreover,

89 Louis Favoreu, "American and European Models of Constitutional Justice" in David S. Clark (ed.), *Comparative and Private International Law: Essays in Honor of John Henry Merryman on His Seventieth Birthday* (Duncker & Humblot 1990), 110.

90 Elisabetta Lamarque, *Corte costituzionale e giudici nell'Italia repubblicana* (Laterza 2012), 9.

91 A short time before, e.g., the Court of Cassation had handed down a ruling giving rise to considerable controversy because it had struck down the Legislative Decree of the President of the Council as it was found to be in conflict with the "second provisional Constitution" (as discussed in Chapter 2, Section 1).

92 Lamarque 2012, note 90, at 19.

93 Edouard Lambert, *Le gouvernement des juges et la lutte contre la législation sociale aux États-Unis* (Marcel Giard & Cie 1921).

94 On the influence of this book in Europe, see Alec Stone Sweet, "Why Europe Rejected American Judicial Review: And Why It May Not Matter" (2003) 101 *Michigan Law Review* 8, 2758 ff.

95 On the contrary, it is well known that in common law systems courts' rulings declaring laws unconstitutional, on the basis of the principle of binding precedent often have de facto an *erga*

there was a risk of giving rise to contrasts among courts of different types and levels.[96] In actual fact, these factors, albeit important, were never really decisive in the choice between the two models. Interestingly enough, a number of European and Latin American countries characterized by a decentralized or partially decentralized system of constitutional review have shown that it is possible, by means of suitable measures, to ensure a uniform interpretation of the constitution even in the absence of the principle of binding precedent, which is a distinguishing feature of common law countries.[97] In this sense, there does not appear to be a necessary connection between how constitutional review is exercised (i.e., through a centralized or a decentralized system) and the common law or civil law tradition of a specific country.[98]

C *Constitutional Courts in the Constitution-Making Processes*

Starting from the 1990s, the constitutional drafters of certain countries – probably aware of the role that constitutional courts could play in the processes of democratization – decided to set up these courts even *before* the adoption of the new constitution, thus giving rise to the "paradox of a constituted body co-participating in the constituent process."[99]

omnes effect: indeed, the judgments of the higher courts (and in particular of the Supreme Court) are binding on the lower courts.

96 See Cappelletti 1994, note 75, at 63–64.

97 In some Latin American countries (Bolivia, Colombia, Peru, Guatemala, Mexico) the system of constitutional justice is set up so that the ordinary courts can strike down laws with *inter partes* effects, whereas only the Constitutional Court (or the Supreme Court) can annul a law with *erga omnes* effects. A different solution is adopted in Argentina and Brazil, where Supreme Court rulings formally have *inter partes* effects, but because they are handed down by the judicial body at the highest level, the lower courts are obliged to comply with them, and as a result these rulings de facto have *erga omnes* effects. The situation is different in Venezuela, where Article 321 of the Code of Civil Procedure requires the courts to comply with the case law of the Court of Cassation in analogous cases, to safeguard the integrity of legislation and the uniformity of case law: as a result, in this case the binding effect of the decisions of the Supreme Court has been codified (Frosini and Pegoraro 2008, note 73, at 48–50). In Europe reference may be made to the case of Greece, where the Special Supreme Court is responsible for guaranteeing a uniform interpretation of constitutional provisions. In particular, the Constitution stipulates that the Court has the power to resolve the "controversies on whether the content of a statute enacted by Parliament is contrary to the Constitution" and interpret the "provisions of such statute when conflicting judgments have been pronounced by the Council of State, the Court of Cassation or the Court of Audit.") (Article 100(1)(e)). In Estonia the lack of the principle of binding precedent is dealt with by obliging judges setting aside a law in contrast with the Constitution to refer the matter to the Supreme Court (Article 9 of the Constitutional Review Court Procedure Act of 2002; see Pištan 2011, note 72, at 233–234).

98 As argued by Frosini and Pegoraro 2008, note 73, at 50.

99 Andrea Lollini, *Constitutionalism and Transitional Justice in South Africa* (Berghahn Books 2011), 63.

In Albania, for example, in 1991 a provisional Constitution entered into force,[100] providing for political pluralism, the separation of powers, and the protection of fundamental rights; the following year, for the first time in the country's history, a Constitutional Court was established.[101] In the period from 1992 to 1998 (the year of the adoption of the new Constitution), the Court handed down some important judgments relating to fair trial, and on a number of occasions dealt with transitional justice, ruling in particular on the constitutional legitimacy of the "lustration laws" adopted by the country.[102]

In post-apartheid South Africa, the role played by the Constitutional Court (envisaged by the Provisional Constitution of 1993) was even more decisive. The Court was required to adjudicate on whether the final draft of the Constitution was in contrast with the 34 fundamental constitutional principles that were intended to guide the Constituent Assembly. This control was carried out "scrupulously":[103] indeed, the constitutional judges refused to certify the first draft of the Constitution and obliged the Constituent Assembly to implement numerous changes to ensure compliance of the final version with the 34 principles. Moreover, the Court marked a break with the segregationist past by delivering judgments abolishing the death penalty and prison sentences for debtors, in addition to prohibiting inhuman and degrading treatments, as well as corporal punishments.[104]

Also the Polish Constitutional Court, although set up under the previous Socialist regime,[105] ended up playing a prominent role in the process that led to the adoption of the new Constitution. Indeed, during this long process that lasted eight years (1989–1997), the Court declared some fundamental principles, such as the independence of judicial review, and the separation of powers.[106]

[100] Officially known as "Law on the Major Constitutional Provisions."

[101] The Court was established by Constitutional Act 7561/1992.

[102] Act 7666/1993; Act 8001/1995; Act 8043/1995. With regard to these Acts see Kathleen Imholz, "A Landmark Constitutional Court Decision in Albania" in Neil J. Kritz (ed.), *Transitional Justice: How Emerging Democracies Reckon with Former Regimes. Volume II. Country Studies* (United States Institute of Peace Press 1995), 729 ff.; Kathleen Imholz, "States of Emergency as Pretexts for Gagging the Press: Word Play at Albania's Constitutional Court" (1997) 6 *East European Constitutional Review* 4. A new lustration law entered into force in Albania in 2009 (Act 10034/2008), but it was struck down by the Court in March 2010.

[103] Andrea Lollini and Francesco Palermo, "Comparative Law and the 'Proceduralization' of Constitution-Building Processes" in Julia Raue and Patrick Sutter (eds.), *Facets and Practices of State-Building* (Martinus Nijhoff 2009), 310.

[104] See Lollini 2011, note 99, at 68; Heinz Klug, "South Africa's Constitutional Court: Enabling Democracy and Promoting Law in the Transition from Apartheid" (2008) 3 *Journal of Comparative Law* 2, 174 ff.

[105] The constitutional reform envisaging the Constitutional Court was approved on March 26, 1982, and the Law on the organization and functioning of the Court was adopted on April 29, 1985. The Court finally was established on January 1, 1986.

[106] See Mark Brzezinski, *The Struggle for Constitutionalism in Poland* (Macmillan 2000).

D *The Role of the Council of Europe and the European Union*

Finally, it is necessary to examine the role played by supranational organizations – and more specifically by the Council of Europe and the European Union – in setting up constitutional courts in Central and Eastern European countries following the collapse of the Socialist regime. The Council of Europe, aware of the extremely important functions that these bodies were to carry out in the processes of democratization, strongly recommended their establishment:

> In the admission process [to the Council of Europe], the existence of a constitutional court has been a particularly important point and the Council scrutinized the conditions of the constitutional review. The more the democratic functioning of a given State was uncertain, the more the Council of Europe prescribed measures for strengthening the powers of the constitutional court.[107]

This approach is confirmed by the European Commission for Democracy through Law (better known as the Venice Commission), a consultative body of the Council of Europe on constitutional matters,[108] that repeatedly pointed out that the setting up of a constitutional court was a decisive step in the transition from an authoritarian regime to democracy. One need only consider the opinion of Antonio La Pergola, the founder and then-president of the Venice Commission, who argued that "a good constitutional court is the foundation stone of a sound democracy."[109]

It is decidedly more problematic to ascertain whether the establishment of constitutional courts in Central and Eastern European countries was also linked to the process of European integration. Legal opinion is divided on this point. According to some scholars, the prospect of joining the European Union may have acted as an incentive for the constitutional drafters of these countries to set up constitutional courts. Bruce Ackerman, for example, supports the view that the new political elites in Central and Eastern Europe simply could not ignore the effect their choices would have on the immediate future of their countries, above all with regard to accession to the European Union.[110]

[107] László Sólyom, "The Role of Constitutional Courts in the Transition to Democracy: With Special Reference to Hungary" (2003) 18 *International Sociology*, 153.

[108] Further discussed in Chapter 5, Section 4.E.

[109] See European Commission for Democracy through Law, *Constitution Making as an Instrument of Democratic Transition* (Council of Europe Press 1993), 8; European Commission for Democracy through Law, *Meeting with the Presidents of Constitutional Courts and Other Equivalent Bodies* (Council of Europe Press 1993), 15–16; European Commission for Democracy through Law, *The Role of the Constitutional Court in the Consolidation of the Rule of Law* (Council of Europe Press 1994).

[110] Bruce Ackerman, "The Rise of World Constitutionalism" (1997) 83 *Virginia Law Review* 4, 776–777. See also Radoslav Prochàzka, *Mission Accomplished: On Founding Constitutional Adjudication in Central Europe* (Central European University Press 2002), 17–20; Samuel Issacharoff, "Constitutional Courts and Democratic Hedging" (2010) *Public Law and Legal Theory Research Paper Series*, New York University School of Law, 7.

According to other scholars, this appears to be implausible. Wojciech Sadurski, for example, rightly points out that at the time of the fall of Communism, the prospect of joining the European Union "was still beyond the wildest dreams of the political elites from the region. Most of the constitutional courts were set up at the beginning of the 1990s, that is, well before serious talks about possible membership had begun."[111] In addition to that, Sadurski notes that the official documentation of the European Union, in the sections dealing with the reforms to be adopted in the legal domain, did not include any recommendations about the adoption of Kelsenian-style constitutional review.[112] In any case, this does not detract from the fact that the setting up of constitutional courts in post-Communist Europe was indeed welcomed by the institutions of the European Union because their establishment constituted an important step on the road to democratization.[113]

[111] Wojciech Sadurski, "Judicial Review in Central and Eastern Europe: Rationales or Rationalizations?" (2009) 42 *Israel Law Review* 3, 509.
[112] Ibid.
[113] Daniela Piana, "Bureaucratic and Managerial Cultures in Central Eastern European Courts" in Alberto Febbrajo and Wojciech Sadurski (eds.), *Central and Eastern Europe after Transition: Towards a New Socio-Legal Semantics* (Ashgate 2010), 209.

2

The First Generation

The Case of the Italian Constitutional Court

Il giudizio sulla compatibilità [di una legge con la Costituzione]
deve essere dato una volta per sempre e una volta per tutte dalla Corte costituzionale, garante suprema della certezza della Costituzione.

Piero Calamandrei[1]

1 THE CONSTITUTIONAL COURT IN THE 1948 CONSTITUTION

The Constitutional Court envisaged by the 1948 Italian Constitution is not the first instance of a body reviewing the compliance of laws with the Constitution. Indeed, the draft Constitution of the Neapolitan Republic of 1799, inspired by the ideas of Mario Pagano, provided for an institution, the Council of Ephors (*Corpo degli Efori*), responsible for verifying the constitutionality of all legislative acts.[2] Subsequently, the 1848 Albertine Statute (i.e., the first Italian Constitution) made no provision for the constitutional review of legislation, though the courts partially reviewed the constitutionality of laws on formal grounds. It was only during the "transitional period"[3] (in particular from the promulgation of the "second provisional Constitution"),[4] that the judiciary began to review the constitutionality of

[1] Piero Calamandrei, "La prima sentenza della Corte Costituzionale" (1956) II *Rivista di diritto processuale*, 157 ("Any judgment on the compatibility [of a law with the Constitution] should be handed down once and for all by the Constitutional Court, the supreme custodian of the certainty of the Constitution").

[2] Antonello lo Calzo, "Protosistemi di giustizia costituzionale: il Corpo degli Efori nella Costituzione della Repubblica napoletana del 1799" (2013) 14 *Historia constitucional*, 251 ff.

[3] I.e., in the period 1943 (fall of Mussolini)–1948 (entry into force of the new Constitution). See Carlo Ghisalberti, *Storia costituzionale d'Italia 1848–1994* (Laterza 2002), 389 ff.

[4] Namely, the Lieutenant's Legislative Decree no. 98/1946. The "first provisional Constitution," on the contrary, was given by Lieutenant's Legislative Decree no. 151/1944.

legislation on both formal and substantive grounds.[5] In this connection, mention should be made of Judgment 1212/1947 of the Court of Cassation, that gave rise to heated debate, to the point that it was compared to the landmark ruling of the US Supreme Court, *Marbury* v. *Madison*.[6] In this decision the Court of Cassation struck down, with *inter partes* effects, Article 4 of Legislative Decree no. 44/1946 of the president of the Council, ratifying the provisions of the Ministerial Decrees of July 26, 1944 and June 4, 1945. In the view of the Court, these provisions exceeded the limits of the legislative powers granted to the government on the basis of the "first" and the "second provisional Constitution" because they dealt with "constitutional matters" that were not within the purview of the executive.[7] The Court of Cassation specified that the expression "constitutional matters" was intended to cover "the fundamental principles of the constitutional order" including, *in primis*, the "respect for the separation and coordination of powers." In this particular case, the Court ruled that ordinary judges were responsible for ascertaining the constitutionality of the legislative acts adopted by the government.

In the years after the fall of Fascism the question of constitutional justice was addressed by the main political parties.[8] In general they were in favor of setting up a constitutional court (as in the case of the Republican Party, the Liberal Party, the Christian Democrats, the Action Party, and the Common Man), whereas the position of the Socialist Party was ambivalent. The only political party that came out against the establishment of a constitutional court was the Communist Party. In his speech to the fifth national congress of the Communist Party, Palmiro Togliatti argued that

> if transposed into our system, such an institution (of value in those countries where it has played a historical role, in accordance with the legal and political traditions) would probably have no value .... It is clear that if we wish to have effective safeguards in defence of democracy, we need to seek them elsewhere.

Even among the parties taking a favorable view of the idea of a constitutional court there were various positions, concerning, *inter alia*, the desirability of granting

[5] On the history of the constitutional review of legislation in Italy before the establishment of the Constitutional Court see Mario Battaglini, *Contributi alla storia del controllo di costituzionalità delle leggi* (Giuffrè 1957); Marco Bignami, *Costituzione flessibile, Costituzione rigida e controllo di costituzionalità in Italia (1848–1956)* (Giuffrè 1997).

[6] See Franco Pierandrei, "Ancora sul conflitto fra il Governo-legislatore provvisorio e il potere giudiziario" (1947) I *Giurisprudenza italiana*, 337–338.

[7] In particular, the "second provisional Constitution" laid down that the government would have maintained the legislative power, with the exception of constitutional matters, electoral laws, and the ratification of international treaties.

[8] On the position of the political parties prior to the discussion in the Constituent Assembly see Mario Battaglini and Mattia Mininni, *Codice della Corte costituzionale* (Cedam 1960), 47 ff.

citizens the right to petition the Court directly (a procedure known as *azione popolare*).[9] The nature of the review carried out by the Court represented another sensitive topic of discussion. In particular, the Christian Democrats and the Liberals made plain their opposition to any type of constitutional review that was not exclusively of a judicial nature.

Even before the discussion in the Constituent Assembly, a debate about the need to introduce a system of constitutional review took place in the Committee on the Reorganization of the State, set up by the Minister for the Constituent Assembly, Pietro Nenni, and chaired by Ugo Forti, in the meetings held in January and February 1946 (known as the "Forti Committee"). At the meetings of this committee a series of proposals were put forward, for the most part replicated in the Constituent Assembly. There were those who proposed the setting up of a Court of Constitutional Safeguards (Selvaggi) and those who were in favor of a decentralized system of constitutional review (Gueli), in addition to those who argued that the joint sessions of the Court of Cassation should rule on the constitutionality of legislation (Azzariti).

The committee report made clear that what was considered to be simply a technical matter (the choice between a centralized and a decentralized system) had significant theoretical implications. The report stated that: "If the constitutional review of legislative acts is to be considered as a way of defending the rights of citizens laid down in the Constitution, such constitutional review needs to be entrusted to the judiciary which is responsible for safeguarding the citizens, and is an integral part of that system of protection." On the basis of this model, if a judge considered a statutory act unconstitutional, he/she would deal with the case by applying the provision of the Constitution rather than the statutory act. However, the report continued, if the constitutional review of legislation were to be considered

> a system of review aimed at ensuring that the ordinary legislative process did not invade the sphere of the constituent power, the review process would take on a clearly political character, with the result that it would go beyond the purely judicial sphere, thus going in some respects beyond the aim of protecting the individual rights laid down in the Constitution. A review process of this kind would become occasional and indirect.

In this case the review would need to be carried out by an *ad hoc* body, and any actor would be able to challenge legislative acts, not in the defense of an individual interest but in the "general and abstract [interest] of the integrity of the Constitution."

In short, the report made clear that the need to protect citizens' rights was to be considered *in opposition* to the need to defend the integrity of the Constitution

[9] Although adopting slightly different positions, those in favor of the *azione popolare* were the Christian Democrats, the Socialists, the representatives of the Action Party, and the Republicans.

against any encroachment on the part of the legislative power. Carlo Mezzanotte argued that the first conception was essentially "anthropocentric" because "the safeguarding of fundamental rights ... serves as the pivot around which the entire juridical system rotates," whereas the second conception appeared to be "eminently State-centred" to the extent that "it is based on a vision of constitutional review moving beyond the aim of safeguarding rights, and focusing exclusively on the aim of protecting the Constitution as the paramount interest of the State."[10]

The committee adopted the second view, according to which in order to safeguard the constitutionality of legislative acts there was a need for an *ad hoc* body, a Constitutional Court. The Court could be petitioned by any person, regardless of any detriment to a specific interest, in order to ensure extensive access to the Court on the part of citizens (*azione popolare*). In this sense, the break with the past that it was intended to bring about was evident: in contrast with the previous regime that made no provision for the review of legislative acts on substantive grounds, the idea was to set up a system characterized by wide-ranging review, in an attempt to eliminate every "stranglehold" on access, granting the Court's rulings an *erga omnes* effect. In addition, the intention was to make individual citizens the protagonists of the new democratic regime, "thus ensuring their definitive transition from a condition of subordination to a condition of full citizenship."[11] It should be noted, however, that out of respect for the concept of a centralized system outlined in the preceding text, petitions submitted by citizens were not intended primarily in the defense of individual rights, but rather in the defense of *general and abstract interests*. Indeed, the aim was to eliminate from the legal system the laws in conflict with constitutional principles, *in the interests of all*.[12]

Also the Constituent Assembly expressed from the outset a preference for a centralized model of constitutional review, whereas a decentralized system was not widely supported.[13] A decentralized system was favored among others by Luigi Einaudi, who in the plenary session advocated the introduction of such a model making explicit reference to the system of judicial review in the United States.[14] As mentioned previously,[15] it was above all a fear of a "government of judges" that led

[10] Carlo Mezzanotte, *Il giudizio sulle leggi. Le ideologie del costituente* (Editoriale Scientifica 2014) (first published by Giuffrè in 1979), 26. The author later highlights the limits of this contraposition, underlining the fact that the defense of fundamental rights and constitutional legality are not necessarily divergent aims, but can be conciliated, thus ensuring the supreme objective, which consists of the protection of the principle of the superiority of the Constitution (at 77 ff.).

[11] Bignami 1997, note 5, at 107.

[12] Mezzanotte 2014, note 10, at 20–21.

[13] See Pasquale Pasquino, "The Debates of the Italian Constituent Assembly Concerning the Introduction of a Constitutional Court (1947–1948)" in Pasquale Pasquino and Francesca Billi (eds.), *The Political Origins of Constitutional Courts: Italy, Germany, France, Poland, Canada, United Kingdom* (Fondazione Adriano Olivetti 2009), 104 ff.

[14] *Atti della Assemblea costituente*, February 1, 1947.

[15] Chapter 1, Section 5.B.

the members of the Constituent Assembly to reject this model of constitutional review.

The position advocated by Einaudi was in sharp contrast with the debate that had hitherto taken place. During the meetings of the second subcommittee, set up within the "Committee of the Seventy-Five" (entrusted with the task of preparing the initial draft of the Constitution to be submitted to the plenary session of the Constituent Assembly), the discussion on constitutional adjudication revolved around three proposals: that of Piero Calamandrei of the Action Party, that of Giovanni Leone of the Christian Democrats, and that of Gennaro Patricolo of the mixed group.[16] The latter proposal assigned the "Supreme Constitutional Court" the task of carrying out the constitutional review of legislation and settling "conflicts of attribution" among the powers of the State. There were to be multiple gateways to the Court: a petition or referral could be submitted by a member of Parliament or the government, the judiciary, a regional authority, or at least 500 citizens. The proposal put forward by Leone also envisaged a number of actors who were entitled to refer a case to the "Court of Constitutional Safeguards," including various constitutional bodies, the judicial authorities, and citizens. Constitutional review was provided not just for legislative acts but also for regulations and administrative acts at State or regional level.

Calamandrei put forward a proposal of particular interest, identifying two types of constitutional review of legislation. The first type was similar to the "incidental" method of constitutional review (discussed in the following text), that was the responsibility of the ordinary courts and in the final instance of the "Supreme Constitutional Court." The second type was the "direct" method of constitutional review, which was applicable in more general and abstract terms, to be determined only by the joint sessions of the "Supreme Constitutional Court." Cases could be referred to the Court by a State prosecutor serving as a judicial commissioner, at least 50 members of one of the houses of Parliament, or in the form of a petition by any citizen. However, the decision of the Court only had an advisory role. Its effect was to require the government to propose the complete or partial repeal of the legislative act; in cases in which such a proposal was not adopted, it was to be the duty of Parliament to suspend the validity of the legislation by passing a resolution that would have the same value as a proposal to amend the Constitution.

This model clearly adapted various features of the US system of judicial review, while introducing a series of corrective measures aimed at remedying the problems that this kind of constitutional review would have caused in a civil law country such as Italy, in which the doctrine of binding precedent is not valid. The proposal put forward by Calamandrei was intended both to avoid a monopoly over constitutional

[16] *Atti della Assemblea costituente*, II sottocommissione, II sez., December 6, 1946, as well as January 14–15, 1947. See also Alessandro Pizzorusso, "Garanzie costituzionali. Art. 134" in Giuseppe Branca (ed.), *Commentario alla Costituzione* (Zanichelli-Il Foro italiano 1981), 64 ff.

review being granted to a single body (by assigning this power to the judiciary as a whole, not just to the Constitutional Court), and to ensure the greatest possible uniformity in the interpretation of constitutional provisions.

Furthermore, the fact that the rulings of the joint sessions of the Constitutional Court had an advisory status (intended to put pressure on Parliament to suspend the legislation in question) gave the impression that the Court was a body with a quasi-legislative function. This clearly shows that the ideological climate of the Constituent Assembly was still strongly influenced by the ideas prevalent after the French Revolution, such as the primacy of legislation and the sovereign power of the legislature.[17]

The proposal finally put forward to the plenary session of the Constituent Assembly envisaged the referral of cases to the Court both directly (at the initiative of the government, 50 members of Parliament, a regional council, at least 10,000 voters, or a body or institution authorized by the Law on the Constitutional Court), and by means of the "incidental" method of constitutional review. In the latter case, ordinary courts were granted the power to challenge the constitutionality of laws before the Constitutional Court.

The debate in the Constituent Assembly concentrated mainly on the political aspects, rather than on more technical matters. The positions adopted by the parties were fairly clear cut. There was a "singular convergence"[18] between the left-wing parties (the Socialists and the Communists), heirs to the Jacobin tradition, and the authoritative members of the old liberal school of thought (such as Vittorio Emanuele Orlando and Francesco Saverio Nitti). In both of these groupings, albeit for different reasons, the opposition to the setting up of a Constitutional Court was evident. On the right, it was feared that constitutional review would give rise to practices incompatible with a State based on the rule of law, providing an excuse for failure to comply with the law. On the left, there was a fear that the Court would play a conservative role, rather than supporting reform policies,[19] on the basis of the idea (firmly rooted at the time) that the law was "an instrument of conservation, rather than of transformation."[20] It was also deemed to be unacceptable that in a democracy an institution of a technical nature, not elected by the people, could strike down laws enacted by Parliament, a sovereign body directly elected by the

[17] Mezzanotte 2014, note 10, at 124–125.

[18] Gaetano Silvestri, "Alle origini del modello italiano di giurisdizione costituzionale" in *Genesi ed evoluzione dei sistemi di giustizia costituzionale in Italia, Francia e Spagna*, Quaderni del dottorato di ricerca in Diritto ed Economia dell'Università Federico II di Napoli, no. 5 (2012), 96, www.federalismi.it (accessed July 15, 2019).

[19] This view was put forward for example by Ravagnan, who argued that "In these conditions, if any citizen, belonging to the opposition, were to be able to set in motion the machinery of the Constitutional Court, ... this legislation enacting reforms would be paralyzed, since one institution would wield power over all the others, without deriving its power from the will of the majority" (*Atti della Assemblea Costituente*, II sottocommissione, II sez., January 13, 1947).

[20] Gustavo Zagrebelsky, *La giustizia costituzionale* (Il Mulino 1988), 486.

people. Rather, if there was an institution that should perform that function, it was Parliament.[21] The fear was that the new Constitutional Court would undermine the supremacy of Parliament and the principle of the popular legitimation of power.[22] It is evident, then, that "an enduring Rousseauan strand persisted in Italian political thought, according to which a popularly elected legislature embodies the supreme expression of the general will."[23]

In addition, for these political leaders, the nature and role of the Court appeared in many ways to be an unknown quantity. Togliatti remarked that the Court was a "bizarre idea,"[24] and in the view of Nitti, it was hard to understand "what the day-to-day business of this Supreme Court was supposed to be, as nobody feels the need for it; such a court does not exist in any country, and nobody can say what it would lead to."[25]

A completely different position was taken by most of the other political parties, which were in favor of setting up a Constitutional Court. In particular, the representatives of the Christian Democrats argued that the existence of a Constitutional Court was indispensable to ensure the supremacy and rigidity of the new Constitution, and that without such a court, the Constitution would be reduced to "a romantic statement of principles about the rights of man, a mere expression of wishful thinking,"[26] and it would appear as "a house without a roof, an edifice without a vaulted ceiling."[27] The Court was intended to serve as a bulwark against possible abuses of legislative power,[28] and moreover – thus responding indirectly to the criticisms from the left – it would most certainly not undermine the prerogatives of Parliament, that would have the option of "re-enacting" the laws declared unconstitutional by amending the Constitution.[29]

The deliberations of the Constituent Assembly were concluded with the adoption of a series of articles (Articles 134–137 of the Constitution) providing a fairly clear definition of the powers and nature of the Court, and the general applicability of its rulings, but a decidedly incomplete definition of the procedural gateways to the Court. As a result, on December 2, 1947 the "Arata amendment" was adopted,

[21] Nenni argued that "The sole body that can verify the constitutionality of legislative acts is the National Assembly, Parliament, as there can be no form of review other than that of the people. The proposed Court may consist of the most eminent men, experts in constitutional law, but due to the fact that they have not been elected by the people, they are not entitled to pass judgment on Acts of Parliament" (*Atti della Assemblea Costituente*, March 10, 1947).

[22] See Antonio Ruggeri and Antonino Spadaro, *Lineamenti di giustizia costituzionale* (Giappichelli 2001), 43.

[23] William J. Nardini, "Passive Activism and the Limits of Judicial Self-Restraint: Lessons for America from the Italian Constitutional Court" (1999) 30 *Seton Hall Law Review*, 11.

[24] *Atti della Assemblea Costituente*, March 11, 1947.

[25] *Atti della Assemblea Costituente*, March 8, 1947.

[26] Paolo Rossi (*Atti della Assemblea Costituente*, November 28, 1947).

[27] La Pira (*Atti della Assemblea Costituente*, November 28, 1947).

[28] Codacci Pisanelli (*Atti della Assemblea Costituente*, November 28, 1947).

[29] Ambrosini (*Atti della Assemblea Costituente*, November 28–29, 1947).

postponing the determination of the measures regulating access to the Court to a subsequent phase. The matter was finally settled shortly thereafter, on February 9, 1948, with the approval by the Constituent Assembly, operating on the basis of a time extension (*prorogatio*), of a Constitutional Law concerning "Measures on constitutional review and the guarantees of independence of the Constitutional Court." This provision eliminated the option for individual citizens to petition the Court directly, thus heading in a direction that was diametrically opposed to the prevailing orientation within the "Forti Committee" and the second subcommittee of the Constituent Assembly. Direct access to the Constitutional Court was granted only to the Central Government and the regions ("direct" method of constitutional review). In particular, the Central Government was vested with the power to bring a direct action before the Court and challenge the constitutionality of a regional law, and a region was granted the power to raise a constitutional challenge before the Court against national legislation or laws of other regions when it deemed its authority invaded by either. Moreover, ample space was envisaged for the "incidental" method of constitutional review, thus leading to a considerable extent (also in this case) to a U-turn compared the past. In fact, in the Constituent Assembly, the main concern leading to the adoption of a centralized system was the fear of a "government of judges," whereas now, by making provision for the main pathway of access to the Court to be the "incidental" method of constitutional review, judges were assigned the role of "gatekeepers" of constitutional review.[30] Indeed, under this system when an ordinary judge concludes (either following a request by one of the parties or *ex officio*) that the law that has to be applied to the specific case violates the Constitution, he/she must suspend the case and refer the question of constitutionality to the Court.[31]

Finally, mention should be made of the approval, without extensive discussion, of the seventh transitional and final provision of the Constitution, establishing that, until the entry into force of the Constitutional Court, decisions on constitutional legitimacy were to be taken "in the forms and within the limits existing prior to the entry into force of the Constitution," thus providing for a decentralized system of constitutional review. As noted in the next section, due to the delays in the promulgation of the constitutional laws and statutory acts, the Court began its

[30] In the words of Piero Calamandrei, "La Corte costituzionale e il processo civile" in *Studi in onore di Enrico Redenti nel XL anno del suo insegnamento* (Giuffrè 1951), 199.

[31] On the "direct" and "incidental" methods of constitutional review (also known as "*principaliter*" and "*incidenter*" proceedings) see Vittoria Barsotti, Paolo G. Carozza, Marta Cartabia, and Andrea Simoncini, *Italian Constitutional Justice in Global Context* (Oxford University Press 2016), 52 ff.; Justin O. Frosini, "Constitutional Justice" in Giuseppe Franco Ferrari (ed.), *Introduction to Italian Public Law* (Giuffrè 2008), 196 ff. Specifically, on the role played by the "incidental" method see John Ferejohn and Pasquale Pasquino, "Constitutional Adjudication, Italian Style" in Tom Ginsburg (ed.), *Comparative Constitutional Design* (Cambridge University Press 2012), 300 ff.

deliberations only in 1956, and as a result for eight years the ordinary courts were responsible for the constitutional review of legislation.

2 THE ESTABLISHMENT OF THE CONSTITUTIONAL COURT: A LONG AND COMPLEX PROCESS

In the first few months after the adoption of the Constitution, the impression was that the Constitutional Court would begin its deliberations within a short period. On February 9, 1948, as noted previously, Constitutional Law no. 1 was approved, and on July 14 the same year, a bill was brought forward in the Senate with the provisions later transposed into Law no. 87/1953 ("Provisions on the Establishment and Functioning of the Constitutional Court"). In the view of the government, Constitutional Law no. 1/1948 had already implemented the first paragraph of Article 137 of the Constitution,[32] and as a result there was a need simply to implement the provisions of the second paragraph of this constitutional provision.[33]

At this point, however, the deliberations ground practically to a halt, partly due to the "obstructionism by the majority,"[34] with the government postponing the approval of the legislation required for the enforcement of the Constitution. With regard to the matter at hand, the aim of the majority was to slow down the discussion of the proposed legislation to prevent it from being approved before the end of the first parliamentary term.[35] For their part, the Socialists and Communists attempted to prevent the suspension of discussion of the legislation. Therefore, it is evident that the positions of the political parties in relation to the Constitutional Court were reversed. Indeed, following the elections in April 1948, with the victory of the Christian Democrats and the resounding defeat of the left-wing parties[36] clarifying the balance of power between the two groupings, the members of the Constituent Assembly who had advocated the introduction of a Constitutional Court (including the Christian Democrats) became its strongest opponents, whereas the left-wing

[32] Article 137(1): "A constitutional law shall establish the conditions, forms, terms for proposing judgments on constitutional legitimacy, and guarantees on the independence of constitutional judges."

[33] Article 137(2): "Ordinary laws shall establish the other provisions necessary for the establishment and the functioning of the Court."

[34] Piero Calamandrei, "L'ostruzionismo di maggioranza" (1953) *Il Ponte*, 129 ff. Further details in Section 3 of this chapter.

[35] See Giovanni Bisogni, "Le leggi istitutive della Corte costituzionale" in Ugo De Siervo, Sandro Guerrieri, and Antonio Varsori (eds.), *La prima legislatura repubblicana. Continuità e discontinuità nell'azione delle istituzioni* (Carocci 2004), 75; see also John Clarke Adams and Paolo Barile, "The Italian Constitutional Court in Its First Two Years of Activity" (1958) 7 *Buffalo Law Review*, 251.

[36] The Christian Democrats obtained 48.5 percent of the vote and an absolute majority of seats in the Chamber of Deputies. The Communist and Socialist parties, in an alliance known as the "Popular Front," only gained 31 percent.

parties, who in the debates in the Constituent Assembly had been hostile to the setting up of such a body, now argued that it was fundamental.[37]

The slowing down of the approval of the law was not merely a matter of party politics. There were profound differences of opinion, also of a technical and constitutional nature, concerning the role of the Court and its relations with the constitutional bodies, and these divergences were evident also within the government majority.[38] First of all it is important to bear in mind that the setting up of a Constitutional Court was a major innovation not just in relation to the Italian tradition but also to most of Europe. Moreover, doubts and uncertainties about the completion of the Constitution in terms of constitutional adjudication were present not just among the political parties but also among legal scholars.[39] In addition, alongside the approval of ordinary legislation (Law no. 87/1953), it was decided to approve a new constitutional law (that was to become Constitutional Law no. 1/1953 on "Additional provisions to the Constitution concerning the Constitutional Court") by adopting the procedure laid down in Article 138 of the Constitution (which regulates the procedure for constitutional amendments).

For the approval of the ordinary law no less than five parliamentary readings were necessary. In the bill brought forward by the government,[40] various points were found to be obscure, in some ways embodying a "rather reductive conception of the new body and the functions it was intended to perform."[41] In the Senate a number of amendments were approved, including the elimination of the division of the Court into sections, the prohibition on judges continuing with their previous professional activities, the introduction of what was to become an assessment of the "relevance" of the question of constitutionality, and the adoption of various rules concerning the appointment of the judges. However, it was only during the lengthy readings in the Chamber of Deputies that the Constitutional Court took on its definitive appearance.[42] It was at this stage that, in an awareness of the inadequacies of Constitutional Law no. 1/1948, it was decided to approve not just the ordinary law (Law no. 87/1953) but also a new constitutional law (that was to become Constitutional Law no. 1/1953). With regard to the ordinary law, the most important issues were settled, such

[37] See Mary L. Volcansek, "Bargaining Constitutional Design in Italy: Judicial Review as Political Insurance" (2010) 33 *West European Politics* 2, 280 ff.

[38] See Livio Paladin, *Per una storia costituzionale dell'Italia repubblicana* (Il Mulino 2004), 98.

[39] See Bisogni 2004, note 35, at 80.

[40] See the introductory report in the Senate, Bill no. 23, "Measures regarding the establishment and functioning of the Constitutional Court."

[41] Ugo De Siervo, "L'istituzione della Corte costituzionale in Italia: dall'Assemblea costituente ai primi anni di attività della Corte" in Paolo Carnevale and Carlo Colapietro (eds.), *La giustizia costituzionale tra memoria e prospettive. A cinquant'anni dalla pubblicazione della prima sentenza della Corte costituzionale* (Giappichelli 2008), 58. In particular, one need only consider that the Constitutional Court judges were authorized to pursue their previous careers as judges or university professors, to take part in commissions and to continue with their professional activities.

[42] De Siervo 2008, note 41, at 62.

as the criteria for the appointment of judges, the question of dissenting opinions, the temporal effects of judgments, as well as the resolution of "conflicts of attribution" among the powers of the State.

The Senate then examined the revised legislation, confirming to a large extent the choices made by the Chamber of Deputies. One of the few significant amendments concerned the appointment of one-third of the Constitutional Court judges by the President of the Republic.[43] This was a particularly sensitive matter, discussed at some length in previous parliamentary readings. During the debate in the Chamber of Deputies, the Hon. Fumagalli tabled an amendment stating that the President of the Republic was not free to appoint one-third of the members of the Court, but was bound by the proposal made by the Minister of Justice. This proposed amendment attracted strong criticism because it would work against the attempt to "depoliticize the Constitutional Court, safeguarding it from the hegemony of the majority political parties."[44] In fact, by means of the parliamentary election of one-third of the judges and government control over the appointment of five more, these majority political parties would de facto have the chance to fill the majority of the 15 seats on the Constitutional Court with nominees of their own choosing. After extensive debate in the Senate, the Fumagalli amendment was rejected, thus setting aside the ministerial proposal, while confirming only the countersignature by the president of the Council.

After the approval of Constitutional Law no. 1/1953 and Law no. 87/1953, the most important step required to enable the Court to become operative was the election of its members. The appointments by the highest courts did not give rise to any particular problems.[45] The difficulties were encountered in relation to the parliamentary appointments. On November 15, 1955, after long and arduous deliberation, the Senate and the Chamber of Deputies elected Gaspare Ambrosini and Mario Bracci, supported by the Christian Democrats and the Socialist Party, respectively. At this point the mechanism ground to a halt.[46] Because it was taken for granted that the Christian Democrats were entitled to appoint another candidate, and that the fourth one would be nominated by the Liberals, the contentious point was the appointment of the fifth judge. The Monarchists and the members of the Italian Social Movement, on the one hand, and the Communists, on the other, all felt

[43] According to Article 135 of the Constitution, the Constitutional Court is composed of 15 judges. One-third are nominated by the president of the Republic, one-third by Parliament in joint sessions, and one-third by the ordinary and administrative supreme courts.

[44] Sergio Bartole, *Interpretazioni e trasformazioni della Costituzione repubblicana* (Il Mulino 2004), 91.

[45] The Court of Cassation appointed Ernesto Battaglini, Emanuele Piga (who passed away and was replaced by Francesco Pantaleo Gabrieli), and Giacomo Russo (who passed away and was replaced by Giuseppe Lampis). The Council of State appointed Antonino Papaldo. The Court of Auditors appointed Augusto Ortona (who passed away and was replaced by Mario Cosatti).

[46] See Nicola Tranfaglia, "Per una storia politica della Corte costituzionale" in *Dallo Stato liberale allo Stato fascista* (Feltrinelli 1973), 210.

entitled to appoint their own candidate. This led to a stalemate, resolved above all thanks to the intervention of the President of the Republic, Giovanni Gronchi, and the President of the Chamber of Deputies, Giovanni Leone, who managed to broker an agreement by which the Christian Democrat, Giuseppe Cappi, and the Liberal Party candidate, Giovanni Cassandro, were elected, along with the Communist Party candidate, Nicola Jaeger. Shortly thereafter, the President of the Republic appointed his own five nominees,[47] thus completing the composition of the Court.[48]

The role played by Gronchi deserves further attention. In particular, it should be noted that the establishment of the Constitutional Court, intended as a counter-majoritarian institution, had been achieved thanks to the decisive intervention of the President of the Republic, whose appointment had also been made "in contrast with the majority": in fact, Gronchi was elected by a broad-based political alliance,[49] with minimal support from the Christian Democrats, and as a result his election was seen as an election "against the majority."[50] Moreover, the election of Gronchi highlighted the divisions among the Christian Democrats, and in fact shortly thereafter the centrist political strategy (*centrismo*) drew to a close.

It must be pointed out that the action taken to facilitate the appointment of the Constitutional Court judges by Parliament is just one example of the measures taken by Gronchi to promote the creation of the new Constitutional Court. In his inaugural address on May 11, 1955, he called for "full compliance with the Constitution," to be achieved by means of "updating legislation and customs," and by setting up constitutional bodies, in particular the Constitutional Court.[51] The fact that Gronchi had great faith in constitutional justice is also clear from the speech he made when the Court was sworn in, arguing that the Constitutional Court was

> part of the complex system of checks and balances, acting as a moderator and in some cases as the driving force for legislative and executive activities. The Court is necessary in light of the rigidity of our Constitution, in which the Constituent Assembly placed its hopes for the long-lasting stability of our Institutions.[52]

[47] Namely Enrico De Nicola, Giuseppe Capograssi, Giuseppe Castelli Avolio, Tomaso Perassi, and Gaetano Azzariti.

[48] On the first composition of the Court see Adams and Barile 1958, note 35, at 255–256.

[49] The alliance consisted of the Socialist and Communist parties, some Christian Democrat senators and deputies, some Monarchists, and a significant number of deputies from the Italian Social Movement.

[50] Antonio Baldassarre and Carlo Mezzanotte, *Gli uomini del Quirinale. Da De Nicola a Pertini* (Laterza 1985), 72.

[51] Inaugural address available in Gianfranco Merli and Emo Sparisci (eds.), *Giovanni Gronchi. Discorsi parlamentari* (Senato della Repubblica 1986).

[52] "In occasione del giuramento dei giudici della Corte costituzionale," in Segretariato della Presidenza della Repubblica. Servizio archivio storico, documentazione e biblioteca, *Discorsi e messaggi del Presidente della Repubblica Giovanni Gronchi* (2005), 135.

Gronchi's power of moral suasion was particularly effective, as the Court did perform a fundamental function of reviewing legislation and promoting reforms. As a result, Gronchi came to be known as the "*viva vox Constitutionis*,"[53] and was considered as "the first promoter of the implementation of the Constitution."[54]

Gronchi, however, was not the first Head of State to take action in favor of the Constitutional Court. His predecessor, Luigi Einaudi, had taken measures that, albeit indirectly, favored the Court and more generally constitutional justice. First, he managed to establish the principle that the appointment of five life senators was a power exclusively vested with the president of the Republic. This laid the ground for an even more important achievement on the part of his successor, that is the exclusive right of the president (*atto formalmente e sostanzialmente presidenziale*) to appoint five members of the Constitutional Court.[55] In addition, Einaudi established the exclusive right of the president to send legislation back to Parliament stating the reasons for his decision (presidential veto). Also this measure was particularly important, above all

> at a time when, due to the failure to bring into operation the [Constitutional Court], and the reluctance of the ordinary courts to carry out an effective constitutional review of legislation, there was a keen awareness of the need to put into practice at least a bland form of constitutional review of the legislative acts of Parliament.[56]

In short, presidents Einaudi and Gronchi were the first key allies of the Constitutional Court.

3 1948–1956: THE BLOCKING OF THE SUBSTANTIVE TRANSITION

The adoption of the 1948 Constitution was undoubtedly an extraordinary achievement. Although the work of the Constituent Assembly was initially characterized by wide divergences of opinion, a noble compromise was eventually reached.[57] This compromise reflected the essential components, the "souls" of the Italian political system at the time, that is the Catholics (represented by the Christian Democrats), the traditional working class (represented by the Communist Party and part of the Socialist Party), as well as the Liberals. It is important to bear in mind the historical and political circumstances in which the Constituent Assembly was operating, that were to some extent unique. Italy had just emerged not only from World War II, but

53 In the words of Calamandrei the day after his election. See Piero Calamandrei, "Viva vox Constitutionis" (1955) *Il Ponte*, 809.

54 Baldassarre and Mezzanotte 1985, note 50, at 91.

55 Ibid., at 49.

56 Ibid., at 49–50.

57 See Augusto Barbera, "I principi della Costituzione repubblicana: dal 'compromesso' al radicamento progressivo" (2009) 2 *Rassegna parlamentare*, 314.

also from two decades of authoritarian rule that had had a profound impact on the entire country. This situation led to the natural consequence that one of the main concerns – if not *the* main concern – of the Constituent Assembly was to prevent the repetition of experiences of this kind, and to protect the democratic character of the institutional system that was under construction. This explains why the 1948 Constitution pays great attention to the rights of minorities, provides for a parliamentary form of government, envisages a President of the Council as *primus inter pares* in relation to the other ministers, and provides for "constitutional guarantees bodies" such as the President of the Republic and the Constitutional Court. This series of safeguards is to be explained not just with reference to the historical developments mentioned previously but also to a political matter in the strict sense. During the deliberations of the Constituent Assembly, none of the political parties was in a position to foresee the outcome of the first parliamentary elections, and this meant that no party was able with any degree of certainty to count on being able to win a majority in Parliament. Rather, each and every party was afraid that they would lose. As a result, the fear of an electoral defeat prevailed over the desire to impose their own position.[58]

The formal transition was followed by a phase that was particularly problematic in terms of the implementation of the constitutional provisions. Indeed, the period from 1948 to 1956 was characterized by a "freezing of the Constitution,"[59] in the sense that in many cases important constitutional provisions were not enforced. The opinion of legal scholars in this regard is clear. In 1953, Giorgio Balladore Pallieri argued that "in response to the question as to what enforcement the Constitution had during the first parliamentary term . . . the temptation is to sum up in just one word the disheartening reply: none."[60] In the same year, John Clarke Adams and Paolo Barile underlined that "in spite of the formally effective new Constitution, Italy is actually being governed under much the same laws, and people, as during Fascism . . . the inertia of Parliament and the prejudices of the bureaucracy have resisted most of the changes envisaged in the new Constitution."[61] In 1955, Piero Calamandrei remarked that his essay, entitled "The Constitution and the Legislation to Implement it," should have been entitled "The Unimplemented Constitution" or rather "How to Undo a Constitution." In his view

[58] See Roberto Bin and Giovanni Pitruzzella, *Diritto costituzionale* (Giappichelli 2014), 135. See also Giovanni Bognetti, *The American Constitution and Italian Constitutionalism: An Essay in Comparative Constitutional History* (CLUEB 2008), 66–67.

[59] Paladin 2004, note 38, at 73, uses this expression in particular for the period 1948–1953 but in our opinion this "freezing" continued until 1956.

[60] Giorgio Balladore Pallieri, "La Costituzione italiana nel decorso quinquennio" (1954) *Il Foro Padano*, 60.

[61] John Clarke Adams and Paolo Barile, "The Implementation of the Italian Constitution" (1953) 47 *The American Political Science Review* 1, 83.

> the Constitution . . . has never actually been implemented in the way it is written. Rather, in recent years what has slowly taken place is a steady restoration of the old order, *a regime that is completely different from the one specified in the Constitution*, from which the government has actually moved further away day after day.[62]

In other words, the *substantive* transition had been blocked. The failure to implement provisions relating to fundamental rights was accompanied by the failure to set up bodies such as the Constitutional Court, the High Council of the Judiciary, and the National Council for the Economy and Labour, as well as the failure to set up the ordinary regions and the lack of any legislation regulating the holding of referenda. At the same time a number of institutions from the Fascist era were still in operation, along with those from the "transitional period" that should have been abolished or coordinated with the constitutional provisions (as in the case of special jurisdictional bodies and the Supreme Military Court). Even the High Court of Justice of Sicily continued to operate.

In addition, legislation enacted during the Fascist period but in clear contrast with the Constitution had remained in force, thus perpetuating the *legal continuity* with the previous regime. Mention should be made of the 1930 Criminal Code (also known as *Codice Rocco*), the Code of Criminal Procedure (also enacted in 1930), and the 1931 Unified Code on Public Security (*Testo unico delle leggi di pubblica sicurezza*), considered to be the "three fundamental texts of Fascist tyranny."[63] The fact that the Fascist legislation was transferred *en bloc* to the new democratic regime was also a reflection of the lack of reforms adopted by the government in the period 1943–1948. It must be acknowledged that the government took urgent measures to suppress the institutions characterizing the previous regime (the Fascist National Party, the Grand Council of Fascism, the Special Tribunal for the Defence of the State, and the Chamber of Fascists and Corporations),[64] and that two important decrees were issued (Royal Decree Law no. 25/1944 and Royal Decree Law no. 26/1944) repealing the racial laws and restoring the civil, political and property rights of the Italian and foreign nationals who were deemed to be members of the Jewish "race."[65] However, most of the rest of the preconstitutional legislation (not all of it

[62] Piero Calamandrei, "La Costituzione e le leggi per attuarla" in *Dieci anni dopo. 1945–1955* (Laterza 1955), 211 and 277.

[63] Ibid., at 253.

[64] See Paolo Barile, "Il caso italiano" in Associazione Italiana dei Costituzionalisti (ed.), *La nascita delle Costituzioni europee del secondo dopoguerra* (Cedam 2000), 181–182.

[65] These decrees laid the basis for the measures dealing with restitution, compensation, and reparations, a process that was to develop over the next half century. See Mario Toscano, "L'abrogazione delle leggi razziali: l'Egeli e le restituzioni" in *Commissione per la ricostruzione delle vicende che hanno caratterizzato in Italia le attività di acquisizione dei beni dei cittadini ebrei da parte di organismi pubblici e privati, Rapporto generale* (Presidenza del Consiglio dei Ministri, Dipartimento per l'informazione e l'editoria 2001), 261 ff.; Giuditta Brunelli, "Lili, ebrea e donna, discriminata due volte" (2007) 2 *Quaderni costituzionali*, 396 ff.

Fascist because certain laws dated back to the Unification of the Kingdom of Italy) survived under the new constitutional order.[66]

To cast light on the reasons for the difficulties encountered in the implementation of the Constitution, one should consider above all the political context. The elections of April 1948, resulting in a clear victory for the Christian Democrats and the defeat of the left-wing parties, constituted a kind of watershed, marking the definitive end of the co-operation – characterizing the two-year period in which the Constituent Assembly was at work – between the centrist forces led by the Christian Democrats and the left-wing parties.[67] The profound ideological differences between these political forces ("a domestic version of the Cold War that dominated the international scene")[68] gave rise to the adoption of a tacit agreement, known as the *conventio ad excludendum*, that permanently excluded the Communist Party from any government function, and until 1963 also the Socialist Party, that was not considered to be sufficiently integrated into the system of values of a pluralist democracy. The *conventio ad excludendum* also applied to the Monarchists and the Italian Social Movement, who advocated extreme policies making them unfit to play a role in the executive.

One of the main consequences of this situation was the emergence of a strategy of "obstructionism by the majority," as mentioned in the preceding text. This approach is to be explained not just with reference to the fact that implementing the constitutional provisions would necessarily reduce the room for maneuver enjoyed by the majority. As argued by Paolo Pombeni, it is also necessary to bear in mind that in the menacing climate of reciprocal delegitimation between the government and the opposition, the majority had no intention of giving the left-wing parties the satisfaction of agreeing with one of their fundamental arguments, namely the need to implement the constitutional provisions. Moreover, the implementation of structural reforms would have required a solid government majority that could bring forward these reforms in a short time frame and that would be able to overcome the inevitable internal resistance. In a coalition government, that would have been impossible.[69]

The obstructionism by the majority began to weaken in 1953. In that year the government approved Law no. 148/1953 (denounced by the opposition as the "fraud law" (*legge truffa*)) that was intended to set aside the purely proportional electoral

[66] In contrast (as will become clear in Chapter 3, Section 3.C, and Chapter 4, Section 5), already during the "formal" transition the Spanish Parliament and the Czechoslovak Federal Assembly made a clean break with the previous regime by means of the approval of numerous laws aimed at safeguarding fundamental freedoms.

[67] See Gianfranco Pasquino, "The Demise of the First Fascist Regime and Italy's Transition to Democracy: 1943–1948" in Guillermo O'Donnell, Philippe C. Schmitter, and Laurence Whitehead (eds.), *Transition from Authoritarian Rule: Southern Europe* (The Johns Hopkins University Press, 1986), 45.

[68] Zagrebelsky 1988, note 20, at 489.

[69] Paolo Pombeni, *La Costituente. Un problema storico-politico* (Il Mulino 1995), 148–149.

system, and replace it with a new system awarding a considerable bonus to the majority, that is allocating 65 percent of seats in Parliament to the grouping that managed to obtain half the total number of votes plus one. In the elections held on June 7, 1953, due to a shortfall of just 55,000 votes, this majority bonus was not awarded, and as a result the following year it was decided to repeal the reform and revert to proportional representation. The outcome of the election seriously undermined the leadership of Alcide De Gasperi (that had previously been beyond doubt), and more in general of the Christian Democrats, with the result that the majority was forced on several occasions to make a pact with a wider range of political forces.[70]

Another factor that made a decisive contribution to the failure to implement constitutional provisions was the remarkable degree of *continuity between Fascism and post-Fascism* not just in terms of legal measures but also in terms of *public officials*.[71] In a significant number of cases, prefects, police chiefs, high-ranking officers in the armed forces, civil servants, and judges[72] continued to serve in the same roles as before, with the purges producing only limited results.[73] Indeed, despite the extensive and far-reaching measures adopted in the period 1944–1946 that reflected a firm stance toward the exponents of the authoritarian regime,[74] the attempts to dismiss Fascist officials from the state apparatus were not particularly effective. Initially the repression of Fascist crimes was the responsibility of the Special Assize Courts (*Corti straordinarie d'assise*), under the supervision of the regular courts, which generally speaking enforced the law without handing down unduly lenient sentences. However, these judgments "were lost in a Babel of appeals and counter-appeals"[75] until a series of annulments, postponements, and other expedients ended up overturning the rulings of the courts of first instance.

It is also important to consider the effects of the "Togliatti Amnesty," which was adopted on June 22, 1946. This measure was intended to grant an amnesty to all those who had committed political crimes prior to the Liberation (April 25, 1945), while excluding serious crimes committed by high-ranking civil and political

70 Zagrebelsky 1988, note 20, at 492.

71 See Claudio Pavone, *Alle origini della Repubblica. Scritti su fascismo, antifascismo e continuità dello Stato* (Bollati Boringhieri 1995); Mario Fiorillo, *La nascita della Repubblica italiana e i problemi giuridici della continuità* (Giuffrè 2000).

72 Carlo Guarnieri, *Magistratura e politica in Italia* (Il Mulino 1992), 88, argues that "it was only in rare cases that judges compromised with the old regime were removed from office."

73 Cesare Pinelli, "Cinquant'anni dopo: Gronchi, Tambroni e la forma di governo" (2010) 4 *Quaderni costituzionali*, 758; Alessandro Pizzorusso, "Le stagioni della Costituzione," preface to the final volume of Branca 1981 (ed.), note 16, at XXXVII; Leopoldo Elia, "De Gasperi e Dossetti" (1974) 521, 2084 *Nuova Antologia*, 109, 465; *contra* see Hans Woller, *I conti con il Fascismo. L'epurazione in Italia 1943–1948* (Il Mulino 1997), who argues that purges were carried out only for a short period but on an extensive scale.

74 Among the measures removing Fascists from public office, mention should be made of the Lieutenant's Decrees no. 134/1944, no. 159/1944, and no. 142/1955.

75 Fiorillo 2000, note 71, at 236.

officers, as well as high-ranking military personnel. In actual fact, however, the amnesty was extended to cover criminal offences properly speaking, and as a result it came to be considered "a sort of amnesty for Fascism."[76]

This degree of continuity between the old and the new regime also gave rise to paradoxical situations, as shown by the case of Gaetano Azzariti.[77] Azzariti played a leading role in the Fascist administration: he was the head of the Legislative Office at the Ministry of Justice for more than 20 years, taking part in the drafting of Fascist legislation, including the racial laws, and was appointed president of the Racial Tribunal (*Tribunale della Razza*) in 1939. In spite of his involvement in the regime, in 1945 he was chosen by Palmiro Togliatti as an advisor to the Ministry of Justice, and was also involved in the deliberations of the "Forti Committee." In 1955 he was appointed by the President of the Republic Gronchi as a Constitutional Court judge, and it was Azzariti (and here the paradox is astonishing) who was the authoring judge who drafted the first judgment of the Court (1/1956), declaring for the first time the unconstitutionality of a Fascist-era piece of legislation.[78] In April 1957 he was elected President of the Court, a position he continued to hold until he passed away in January 1961.

The case of Azzariti was not an isolated one. In fact, most of the legal scholars who had embraced the Fascist ideology were reinstated in the universities and the public administration.[79] Therefore, the question that arises is "no longer how to understand how an individual managed to slip through the net that the new State had put in place in order to select those who were to play a part in it from among those who were part of the previous era, but rather why such a net was never put in place, or if it was, why it turned out to be ineffective in almost every case."[80]

4 DECENTRALIZED CONSTITUTIONAL REVIEW AS A "CHANNEL OF CONTINUITY" OF THE STATE

Not even the constitutional review of legislation carried out by the regular courts in the period 1948–1956 managed to "unblock" the substantive transition. Rather, it was the ineffectiveness of such a review that permitted the ongoing application of the Fascist legislation, thus contributing in many ways to the failure to implement the

76 Ibid., at 237. See also Ugo De Siervo, "Attuazione della Costituzione e legislazione antifascista" (1975) *Giurisprudenza costituzionale*, 3267 ff.

77 See Massimiliano Boni, "Gaetano Azzariti: dal Tribunale della razza alla Corte costituzionale" (2014) 4 *Contemporanea*, 577 ff.

78 This ruling is discussed in greater detail in Section 5.A of this chapter.

79 With regard to the Constitutional Court, in addition to Azzariti, mention should be made of Antonio Manca, Gaspare Ambrosini, Luigi Oggioni, and Angelo De Marco (see Boni 2014, note 77, at 606).

80 Boni 2014, note 77, at 606.

1948 Constitution.[81] As argued by Mauro Cappelletti and William Cohen, this period "was still dominated by the strong resistance of those who could hardly adapt to a new conception of law and justice. The ordinary 'career' judge, particularly the elderly judges of the Supreme Court of Cassation and the other appellate courts, did a very poor job in the implementation of a highly programmatic and progressive Constitution."[82]

As mentioned previously, the seventh transitional and final provision of the Constitution stipulated that until the entry into force of the Constitutional Court, decisions on constitutional legitimacy were to be taken "in the forms and within the limits existing prior to the entry into force of the Constitution." This provision, far from being clear, gave rise to a number of questions. One of these concerned the nature of constitutional review, that is whether courts could review the constitutionality of legislation only on formal grounds (as was largely the case under the Albertine Statute) or on both formal and substantive grounds (as was the case during the "transitional period," i.e. 1943–1948). Apart from a few sporadic cases of uncertainty,[83] the judiciary mostly took the view that the courts were entitled to review the constitutionality of legislation on both formal and substantive grounds.[84]

Furthermore, some legal scholars supported the view that in cases in which a court did not find the question of unconstitutionality to be manifestly unfounded, the court would be required to suspend the case until the (future) Constitutional Court ruled on the matter.[85] This reading was rejected in the case law of the ordinary courts, in light of the principle that justice delayed was justice denied.

A decisive influence on the rulings of the courts in the period 1948–1956 was the judgment handed down by the Court of Cassation on February 7, 1948[86] (just more

[81] A largely negative assessment of the constitutional review in this period is put forward by Achille Battaglia, *I giudici e la politica* (Laterza 1982), 124 ff.; Zagrebelsky 1988, note 20, at 494–495; Ruggeri and Spadaro 2001, note 22, at 46–47; Bartole 2004, note 44, at 36–37. A less critical stance is adopted by Pasquale Costanzo, "VII disposizione transitoria e finale" in Branca 1981 (ed.), note 16, at 145 ff.; Bignami 1997, note 5, at 209. The work of the courts is also defended in Gaetano Azzariti, "La mancata attuazione della Costituzione e l'opera della magistratura" (1956) IV *Foro italiano*, 3–5, and Calamandrei 1955, note 62, at 212 and 224.

[82] Mauro Cappelletti and William Cohen, *Comparative Constitutional Law: Cases and Materials* (Bobbs-Merrill Company Publishers 1979), 14.

[83] In 1950 the Court of Cassation and the Council of State examined the question of whether, in the absence of a Constitutional Court, the ordinary courts were entitled to determine the constitutionality of legislative acts (Corte di Cassazione Sezioni Unite, April 27, 1950, in *Foro padano* [1951], 156 ff.; Consiglio di Stato, Sez. V., November 17, 1950, no. 1133, in *Consiglio di Stato* [1950], 740 ff.).

[84] *Ex multis*, see Corte di Cassazione Sezioni Unite Civili, January 15, 1953, 107, 108 and 109, in I *Foro italiano* (1953), 173 ff.

[85] E. Favara, "Ancora sul controllo giurisdizionale di costituzionalità dei provvedimenti legislativi" (1950) IV *Foro padano*, 201–204.

[86] Corte di Cassazione Sezioni Unite Penali, February 7, 1948, in II *Foro italiano* (1948), 58 ff., with opinion by Gaetano Azzariti, "La retroattività di leggi penali anteriori alla nuova Costituzione." This ruling was followed shortly after by Judgment 303/1948 of the Council of State,

than a month after the entry into force of the Constitution). The matter at issue concerned the retroactive application of criminal justice laws prior to the Constitution. The complainants had appealed to the Court of Cassation, requesting, on the basis of Article 25 of the Constitution, the repeal of Lieutenant's Legislative Decree no. 159/1944, that applied retroactive sanctions to Fascist crimes. In ruling on the case, the Court distinguished between *programmatic constitutional provisions* (*norme costituzionali programmatiche*), on the one hand, and *preceptive constitutional provisions* (*norme costituzionali precettive*), on the other, with the latter divided into provisions with immediate application and those with deferred application.[87] In the view of the Court of Cassation, Article 25(2) of the Constitution (according to which "no punishment may be inflicted except by virtue of a law in force at the time the offence was committed") was to be considered a programmatic provision,

> since it did not make any provision concerning the succession of the most favourable laws, but simply made reference to the first paragraph of Article 2 of the Criminal Code.... [This provision] is binding only on the future ordinary legislator, and does not repeal the pre-existing penal laws, that provide penal sanctions for acts committed prior to their entry into force.[88]

in III *Giurisprudenza italiana* (1948), 81 ff., with opinion by Carlo Esposito, "Leggi vecchie e Costituzione nuova."

87 On one hand, the programmatic constitutional provisions are provisions that "contain neither a cogent precept for individuals nor an invitation for Parliament to enact legislation, but only policy guidance shaping ordinary legislation, if and when the legislature deems it to be necessary." On the other hand, preceptive constitutional provisions having immediate application "enter into force immediately in relation to individuals, preventing the enactment of ordinary laws that are in contrast [with the Constitution], or amending or repealing pre-constitutional laws that are in contrast [with the Constitution]." Finally, preceptive constitutional provisions having a deferred application "prevent the enactment of ordinary laws in contrast [with the Constitution], but do not enter into force immediately in relation to individuals, because their entry into force is dependent on the adoption of the implementing legislation" (Calamandrei 1955, note 62, at 228). It should be noted that the reference to "programmatic provisions" could not be considered to be a novelty because various members of the Constituent Assembly, especially those representing the left-wing parties, had already underlined the programmatic nature of certain parts of the Constitution. Once the Constitution entered into force, it was the left-wing parties that were most critical of the consequences of the programmatic nature of these provisions (Mezzanotte 2014, note 10, at 228 ff.). On the issue of the normativity of the Constitution, see Mario Dogliani, *Interpretazioni della Costituzione* (Franco Angeli 1982), 29 ff.

88 The first three paragraphs of Article 2 of the Criminal Code state: "1) No punishment may be inflicted for an act which, pursuant to the law at the time it was committed, did not constitute an offence. 2) No punishment may be inflicted for an act which, pursuant to subsequent legislation, does not constitute an offence; and in cases in which a judgment has been handed down, the execution and penal effects of such judgment shall cease. 3) If the law at the time at which the offence was committed and the subsequent laws are different, the applicable law shall be that providing the more favourable treatment of the defendant, except in cases in which an irrevocable judgment has been handed down."

This line of reasoning was debatable to say the least. It took as its starting point Article 2 of the Criminal Code, highlighting the fact that this was a complete provision, in contrast with the incomplete nature of the constitutional provision (Article 25(2)), without taking account of the fact that these were measures with different objectives, and that in any case the provision on the application of the most favorable legislation did not represent the necessary development of the constitutional provision, also because it was not for the courts to determine the extent to which the legislature should intervene.[89]

With this ruling, the Court of Cassation managed to safeguard the measures (of limited efficacy) dealing with the repression of Fascist crimes,[90] while at the same time adopting an interpretation intended to remain in force until the entry into force of the Constitutional Court. The distinction between programmatic constitutional provisions and preceptive constitutional provisions gave rise to the principle that only preceptive constitutional provisions having immediate application (known as "complete" constitutional provisions) were capable of repealing preconstitutional laws in conflict with the new Constitution.

It is important to underline that the principle laid down by the Court of Cassation, according to which "in general, it may be said that the provisions upholding and safeguarding civil liberty rights ... are, in principle, not just preceptive constitutional provisions, but can also have immediate application," was soon contradicted not only by the case law of the other courts, but also by the Court of Cassation's own rulings. Indeed, that which appeared to be a "presumption of the preceptive nature of constitutional provisions"[91] turned out in many cases to be a *presumption of the programmatic nature* of constitutional provisions: if in many cases Fascist laws incompatible with the Constitution were not struck down, it was because the Constitution – in the view of the courts (especially the superior courts, as explained in the following text) – failed to provide another immediately applicable provision to replace them. For the Fascist laws to be repealed, it was necessary to wait for the legislator to adopt specific laws inspired by the new constitutional principles, to replace those deemed to be incompatible. This approach by the Court of Cassation turned out to be the opposite to the one adopted after the entry into force of the 1848 Albertine Statute, probably also due to the fact that Article 81 of this Statute provided an explicit repeal clause. In fact, the regional Courts of Cassation upheld

89 Bartole 2004, note 44, at 46, recalling some observations by Crosa and Pierandrei.

90 In the words of Andrea Guazzarotti, *L'autoapplicabilità delle norme. Un percorso costituzionale* (Jovene 2011), 159, "the strategy of the Court of Cassation ... had the effect of not casting immediately into doubt the 'legitimation' of the recently adopted Constitution in terms of its intrinsic consistency. Indeed, it would have been paradoxical if the constitutional law inaugurating a legal order in antithesis with the Fascist era had resulted in the repeal of the norms that had just been adopted precisely to mark the discontinuity with the previous regime."

91 In the words of Paladin 2004, note 38, at 76.

the view that the mere adoption of the Albertine Statute resulted in the immediate repeal, *ipso iure*, of all the provisions in contrast with the Statute.[92]

Legal scholars were divided on the distinction between programmatic constitutional provisions and preceptive constitutional provisions. On the one hand, there were those who while recognizing that various constitutional provisions required an implementing legislation, argued that even the constitutional provisions classified as programmatic could repeal the preconstitutional laws in contrast with them, pending annulment by the Constitutional Court.[93] On the other hand, there were scholars who supported a presumption of the programmatic nature of constitutional provisions. They were particularly concerned to avoid a legislative void, and to safeguard the continuity of the legal order, which "rejects the idea of violent shocks and untimely upheavals" that would have inevitably ensued in cases in which the Constitution was applied "in a sudden manner, resulting in a rupture, and a destructive approach to the preceding order."[94] Some scholars even went so far as to argue that the Constitution was addressed exclusively to "future legislators."[95] In between these positions a number of scholars argued that the courts should establish *on a case-by-case basis* whether a given constitutional provision should be applicable immediately or at a later date.[96]

With regard to the case law of ordinary courts, it should be noted that it was by no means "a monolithic bloc."[97] On the contrary, from an analysis of the rulings in the period 1948–1956, two tendencies are to be seen: one concerning the first 12 articles ("Fundamental principles") and the first part of the Constitution ("Rights and duties of citizens"), and the other concerning the second part ("Organization of the Republic").

The first tendency reflects the fact that *it was above all the superior courts that were inclined to support the programmatic nature or the nonimmediate applicability of the constitutional provisions relating to fundamental principles and individual*

92 Battaglia 1982, note 81, at 128. Paladin 2004, note 38, at 79, is fairly skeptical about the efficacy of explicit repeal clauses: "clauses that are formulated in such a generic manner always leave the courts the task of determining the effects of the repeal." As pointed out in Chapter 3, Section 3.B, the 1978 Spanish Constitution includes an explicit repeal clause.

93 See Vezio Crisafulli, *La Costituzione e le sue disposizioni di principio* (Giuffrè 1952); Balladore Pallieri 1954, note 60, at 49 ff.

94 Ernesto Eula, "Magistratura e Costituzione" (1956) IV *Foro padano*, 44.

95 Pietro Virga, "Origine, contenuto e valore delle dichiarazioni costituzionali" (1948) *Rassegna di diritto pubblico*, 280; Azzariti 1956, note 81, at 2 ff.

96 See Paolo Barile and Alberto Predieri, "Efficacia abrogante delle norme della Costituzione italiana" in Piero Calamandrei and Alessandro Levi (eds.), *Commentario sistematico alla Costituzione italiana* (Barbera 1950), 69 ff.

97 With regard to the rulings discussed in this section, see "Rassegna di giurisprudenza sulla Costituzione e sugli Statuti regionali" (1956) *Giurisprudenza costituzionale*, 272 ff.; Romano Canosa and Pietro Federico, *La magistratura in Italia dal 1945 ad oggi* (Il Mulino 1974), 192 ff.

rights, thus preventing the repeal of the Fascist legislation.[98] On the contrary, most of the judges in the lower courts seemed to be more favorable to the new constitutional values, and indeed they were more inclined to support the preceptive nature of constitutional provisions. By way of example, mention should be made of the various interpretations of Article 13 of the Constitution (personal freedom). According to the Court of Cassation, this provision, though deemed to have a preceptive nature, was not immediately applicable, and as a result it could not repeal measures such as *ammonizione*[99] and *confino*[100] laid down in the Unified Code on Public Security. The opposite view was taken by a number of judges in the lower courts, who ruled that Article 13 was a preceptive constitutional provision having immediate application. Similar divergences of interpretation were to be found in relation to Article 16 (freedom of movement). According to the Court of Cassation, this was a programmatic constitutional provision, whereas the lower courts ruled that it was a preceptive constitutional provision having immediate application. Moreover, in spite of a few sporadic initial judgments in which it was considered a preceptive constitutional provision, in most cases the Court of Cassation, unlike the lower courts, ruled that Article 21 of the Constitution (free speech) was a programmatic constitutional provision, as a result of its "generic and abstract formulation." In connection with ethical, social, and economic relations, it was above all the Court of Cassation and the Council of State that supported the programmatic nature of the following provisions of the Constitution: Articles 31 (facilitating the formation of the family),[101] 32 (right to health), 37 (the rights of women and minors to equality of treatment in the workplace), 39 (trade union rights), and 43 (nationalization).

In some cases the positions were reversed,[102] or the rulings were in conflict among each other,[103] but nevertheless this does not seem to question the previously

[98] According to Crisafulli 1952, note 93, at 100–101, "it is evident that . . . especially on the part of the highest courts, a hunting expedition is underway in search of 'programmatic' provisions in the text of the Constitution."

[99] An *ammonizione* is an order issued by the prefect regarding a person suspected of certain behavior, usually criminal. The individual concerned might be subjected to a curfew, prevented from leaving his place of residence without notifying the local police authority and prohibited from associating with certain named persons or classes of person.

[100] *Confino* is a system by which the police could require anyone to move to an isolated and out-of-the-way place, to remain indefinitely under strict police surveillance, without judicial trial and without the right of appeal to the courts.

[101] Hence the legitimacy of the dismissal of nurses who had married, violating the ban in the regulations.

[102] Consider, e.g., the case of Article 40 of the Constitution (right to strike): the only objection to the view that this was to be considered a preceptive constitutional provision of immediate application was raised by the Court of Cremona, that held that until the implementing legislation was enacted, the exercise of the right to strike could not be allowed.

[103] This is the case, e.g., of Article 36 of the Constitution (fair remuneration). In general, the Court of Cassation and the lower courts ruled that it was a preceptive constitutional provision of immediate application, but there were several decisions contradicting this view, stating that it

mentioned tendency. If one considers this stance of the judiciary, it is not surprising then that the lower courts were to become the closest allies of the Constitutional Court in the "struggle" to implement the Constitution.[104]

The other tendency that is discernible in the analysis of the case law of the ordinary courts in the period 1948–1956 concerns the second part of the Constitution, dealing with the "Organization of the Republic." In this case it should be noted that *the courts based their decisions to a large extent on the need to safeguard the continuity of the State and State bodies, as well as to defend their own jurisdiction.* In this connection mention should be made of Article 102 of the Constitution, prohibiting the appointment of extraordinary or special judges, generally considered to be a preceptive constitutional provision having immediate application. However, in practice, this provision was applied only to a limited extent because according to the Court of Cassation the five-year limit laid down by the sixth transitional and final provision of the Constitution for the review of the existing special jurisdictions was deemed to be a recommended time frame rather than a peremptory time limit.

One interesting question concerns Article 111(2) of the Constitution (appeals to the Court of Cassation for violation of the law), which was deemed to be a preceptive constitutional provision. However, the Court of Cassation ruled that an appeal to the Court of Cassation against the rulings of the Supreme Military Court was inadmissible, thus determining that the provision had a programmatic nature, and deeming it to be irrelevant that the one-year time limit imposed on the legislator for the reorganization of the Court had run out (as provided by the sixth transitional and final provision of the Constitution).[105] The result was that for a long time the preexisting system of military justice remained in place.[106]

The courts also ruled that Articles 103(3) (limits on military jurisdiction) and 113 of the Constitution (jurisdictional safeguards against acts of the public administration) were immediately applicable. In the first case, the courts established the immediate applicability of the provision stating that in peacetime the military courts have jurisdiction only over military offences committed by members of the armed forces, thus repealing Article 264(1)(c) of the Peacetime Military Criminal Code, that granted military courts the power to investigate common offences committed by military personnel associated with an abuse of military status or in the exercise of

was to be considered a programmatic constitutional provision. An emblematic judgment was that of the *Pretore* of Palestrina on March 31, 1955, stating that "Article 36 of the Constitution is both a preceptive provision and a programmatic provision, in that it recognizes the right of the worker to sufficient remuneration, that may be determined by the courts pursuant to Article 2099 of the Civil Code, and in that the criteria of proportionality and adequacy of the remuneration require a specific legislative act."

[104] On this point see Section 5.A of this chapter.

[105] The Court of Cassation later ruled that the provision was in fact a preceptive provision, while stating that it could only be implemented after reorganization of the Supreme Military Court.

[106] See Bartole 2004, note 44, at 87. With regard to the sixth transitory and final provision see Rolando Tarchi, "VI disp. trans. e fin." in Branca 1981 (ed.), note 16, at 134 ff.

military service. Along similar lines in the second case the courts determined the immediate applicability of the prohibition on excluding or limiting jurisdictional safeguards to specific kinds of appeal or for specific categories of acts, thus repealing Article 9(1) of Legislative Decree no. 89/1946, that determined the inadmissibility of appeals against a decree issued by the prefect for the transfer of uncultivated land. In both cases, the result was "a reinforcement of the powers of the ordinary jurisdictional authorities and the administrative courts."[107] In all probability the decision (in contrast with the majority of rulings at the time) to repeal the "old" legislative acts may be explained precisely on the basis of the aim of the courts to safeguard their own functions.

It is undoubtedly the case that the decentralized constitutional review of legislation between 1948 and 1956 made a significant contribution to promoting "a widespread 'practical' awareness of the problems of constitutional justice" in Italy.[108] However, if the Constitution was not implemented in its entirety, with the result that the substantive transition was blocked, this depended also on the effects of one of the instruments that was supposed to ensure the implementation of the Constitution, that is the constitutional review of legislation. In this connection, to borrow an expression from Claudio Pavone, decentralized constitutional review, together with the other factors mentioned previously, served as an important "channel of continuity" between Fascism and post-Fascism.[109]

5 THE CONSTITUTIONAL COURT IN THE SUBSTANTIVE TRANSITION

A real turning point in the process of substantive transition came with the establishment of the Constitutional Court in the spring of 1956.[110] In the first 15 years of its activity (known as the first "phase" or "season" of the Court)[111] the Constitutional

[107] Bartole 2004, note 44, at 54.

[108] Costanzo 1981, note 81, at 145.

[109] Pavone 1995, note 71, at 105, refers to the Italian Social Republic as a "channel of continuity."

[110] The Court came into existence on January 23, 1956 and the first public session was held on April 23, 1956. On the structure, organization, competences, and functions of the Court see the following works in English: David G. Farrelly and Stanley H. Chan, "Italy's Constitutional Court: Procedural Aspects" (1957) 6 *The American Journal of Comparative Law*, 314 ff.; Antonio Baldassarre, "Structure and Organization of the Constitutional Court of Italy" (1996) 40 *Saint Louis University Law Journal*, 649 ff.; Mary L. Volcansek, *Constitutional Politics in Italy: The Constitutional Court* (Macmillan Press 2000); Tania Groppi, "The Italian Constitutional Court: Towards a 'Multilevel System' of Constitutional Review?" (2008) 3 *Journal of Comparative Law* 2, 100 ff.; Barsotti, Carozza, Cartabia, and Simoncini 2016, note 31; Justin O. Frosini, "Constitutional Court of Italy" in Rainer Grote, Frauke Lachenmann, and Rüdiger Wolfrum (eds.), *The Max Planck Encyclopedia of Comparative Constitutional Law* (Oxford University Press 2017), 1 ff.

[111] Enzo Cheli, *Il giudice delle leggi* (Il Mulino 1996), 35; Elena Malfatti, Saulle Panizza and Roberto Romboli, *Giustizia costituzionale* (Giappichelli 2007), 317; Groppi 2008, note 110, at 110–111. In contrast with this view, it is also possible to divide the "eras" of the Constitutional Court on the basis of other criteria. For example, Tranfaglia 1973, note 46, at 212 ff., and

Court judges carried out a systematic dismantling of the authoritarian legislation, managing to break the continuity characterizing the legal order until that time. It is interesting to note that no such intervention had been envisaged by the Constituent Assembly: in fact, the role of the Constitutional Court had been conceived for the review of legislation enacted *after* the adoption of the Constitution.[112] In addition, constitutional review "had been envisaged as a means of conservation rather than as a means of initial implementation of the Constitution."[113]

The elimination of the authoritarian legislation did not proceed in a linear fashion, but took place in various stages. From its very first deliberations, the Constitutional Court introduced different types of rulings, in an awareness that the binary distinction between judgments upholding or striking down acts was insufficient to deal with all the cases before the Court. In the initial phase, the constitutional judges handed down the first "exhortative" judgments,[114] "manipulative" judgments,[115] and "interpretative judgments of dismissal."[116] The latter category, considered by most critical scholars as an attempt on the part of the Court to safeguard Fascist legislation,[117] appeared with the very first rulings delivered by the Court (Judgments 3/1956 and 8/1956).[118]

An interesting trend in the constitutional case law of this period is that while starting from a fairly restrictive interpretation of constitutional provisions, over time the Court tended to adopt a *more wide-ranging definition*. As discussed in the following text, this was the case of the right to strike, the permissible aims of which became progressively more extensive.[119] In other cases the Court opted for a radical change of direction compared to previous rulings. Consider in this regard the

Stefano Rodotà, "La svolta 'politica' della Corte costituzionale" (1970) 1 *Politica del diritto*, 37 ff., identify different eras on the basis of the name of the president of the Court.

112 See Zagrebelsky 1988, note 20, at 495.

113 Alessandro Pizzorusso, "Obiettivo sulle ordinanze di rimessione alla Corte costituzionale" (1970) 1 *Quale giustizia*, 86.

114 Namely the judgments in which, faced with norms that can be considered unconstitutional in the abstract, the Court temporarily rejects the challenge apparently justifying the exemption of those norms from constitutional review, and at the same time inviting Parliament with a "warning" to change the statute.

115 These judgments are called "manipulative" because the Court does not just declare the challenged provision unconstitutional, but it modifies or integrates it in some way.

116 With these judgments the Court quashes the challenge because the provision should be interpreted so as to give rise to norm A, which is in pursuance of the Constitution, and not norm B, contained in the order of referral, which is unconstitutional. On these different types of judgments see Frosini 2008, note 31, 200 ff.; Groppi 2008, note 110, at 106 ff.; Vincenzo Vigoriti, "Italy: The Constitutional Court" (1972) 20 *The American Journal of Comparative Law*, 404 ff.; Andrea Simoncini, "L'avvio della Corte costituzionale e gli strumenti per la definizione del suo ruolo: un problema storico aperto" (2004) *Giurisprudenza costituzionale*, 3095 ff.

117 See Section 5.D of this chapter.

118 Judgment 3/1956 concerned the criminal liability of the editor of a newspaper (Article 57 of the Criminal Code), whereas Judgment 8/1956 is examined in Section 5.D of this chapter.

119 See Section 5.C of this chapter.

question of female adultery. Judgment 64/1961 of the Court upheld the legitimacy of Article 559 of the Criminal Code imposing sanctions on adultery committed by a wife but not by a husband. Seven years later, with Judgment 126/1968, the Court struck down this provision as a violation of the principle of equality. A similar change of direction also took place when the Court was called on to determine the constitutionality of the provisions in the Criminal Code and the Unified Code of Public Security concerning incitement to use contraceptives. Whereas Judgment 9/1965 declared the challenge to these provisions to be unfounded, Judgment 49/1971 struck them down as unconstitutional.[120] These changes in the case law of the Constitutional Court seem to have been profoundly influenced by the political culture in those years: in this regard, one need only consider the student protests in 1968 and the strikes in the autumn of the following year.[121]

In various situations the Court played the role of "promoter of reforms" (thus putting pressure on Parliament to adopt legislation to regulate the question at hand), or as a "substitute" for Parliament (especially when Parliament failed to enact legislation in response to a recommendation by the Constitutional Court). With regard to the first of these functions, in addition to the case concerning the non-Catholic religions and certain public order matters (to be discussed further),[122] it is interesting to consider Judgment 33/1960, by which due to violation of Articles 3 and 51 of the Constitution, the Court struck down Article 7, Law no. 1176/1919, that excluded women from all public offices requiring the exercise of political rights. This judgment resulted in an intervention on the part of the legislator. Indeed, following the ruling, Parliament approved Law no. 66/1963, granting women access "to all public offices, professions and public service, including the judiciary, in the various roles, careers and categories, without limits on their responsibilities and career development, except for the requirements laid down by the law."[123]

With regard to the role of the Court as a "substitute" for Parliament, mention should be made not just of the case of the right to strike (to be examined later)[124] but also of the High Court of Justice for Sicily. The 1946 Statute of the Region of Sicily granted this Court the power to rule on the constitutionality of the legislation passed by the Regional Assembly, the laws and regulations adopted by the State in relation to the Statute and their applicability to Sicily, as well as jurisdiction over offences committed by the president and the cabinet members of the region. Although proposals had been put forward aimed at abolishing the High Court, the Constituent Assembly, under pressure from the Sicilian members of Parliament, decided to preserve it. As a result, in 1956, when the Constitutional Court started its

[120] See Section 5.D of this chapter.
[121] See Augusto Barbera, "Dalla Costituzione di Mortati alla Costituzione della Repubblica" in Costantino Mortati, *Una e indivisibile* (Giuffrè 2007), 24–25.
[122] See Sections 5.B and 5.D of this chapter.
[123] Giuditta Brunelli, *Donne e politica* (Il Mulino 2006), 42.
[124] See Section 5.C of this chapter.

deliberations, Italy had two constitutional review bodies, casting doubt on the principle of unity of constitutional justice. Initially the Constitutional Court did not address the problem directly, hoping that the question would be examined by Parliament. The latter, however, "chose not to choose."[125] Finally, it was the Constitutional Court, with Judgment 38/1957, that addressed the issue, stating that

> in light of the constitutional provisions and the other laws cited [Constitutional Law no. 1/1948, Constitutional Law no. 1/1953, and Law no. 87/1953], the principle of unity of constitutional justice, reflected in the unitary nature of the body established to administer it, is not just an essential element of our legal order, but a necessary consequence of our constitutional system.[126]

Furthermore, it is important to stress that from the very beginning the Court tried *to facilitate access to constitutional justice*. For example, Article 1 of Constitutional Law no. 1/1948, and Article 23 of Law no. 87/1953 provide that the question of constitutionality can be raised in the course of a judicial proceeding by a jurisdictional authority ("incidental" method of constitutional review). The Constitutional Court interpreted the concepts of "judicial proceeding" and "jurisdictional authority" in a broad sense, legitimizing various categories of actors as judges *a quibus*, that is entitled to refer questions of constitutionality to the Constitutional Court.[127] Moreover, always with a view to widening access to the Court, the Constitutional Court judges did not hesitate to adjudicate on the matter even when the referrals from the ordinary courts had not fully respected all the procedural rules.[128]

However, despite a number of positive characteristics, the role played by the Constitutional Court was not immune to criticism, and this is why various scholars harshly criticized the judgments delivered in its first phase. For instance, in the opinion of Arturo Carlo Jemolo, the Constitutional Court provided a "relative guarantee" because it was in the habit of accepting "those interpretations of the Constitution that the majority of the country – as represented by the political

[125] Bartole 2004, note 44, at 143.

[126] On this point see Costantino Mortati, "Corte costituzionale e Alta Corte per la regione siciliana" (1956) *Giurisprudenza costituzionale*, 1246 ff. The High Court of Sicily continued to exist, on a smaller scale, as the Court with criminal jurisdiction over the members of the Sicilian regional government, until Judgment 6/1970 of the Constitutional Court was handed down (see Malfatti, Panizza, and Romboli 2007, note 111, at 40).

[127] See Simoncini 2004, note 116, at 3093. Consider, for example, judges in noncontentious proceedings (*procedimenti di volontaria giuridizione*, in which the judge's powers are close to that of an administrative officer) (Judgment 4/1956), Patent commissions (Judgment 42/1958), the Court of Auditors (Judgment 165/1963), and the disciplinary division of the National Bar Association (Judgment 114/1970).

[128] See Roberto Romboli, "I rapporti tra giudici comuni e Corte costituzionale nel controllo sulle leggi in via incidentale in Italia: l'esperienza di 50 anni di giurisprudenza costituzionale" in Luca Mezzetti and Eduardo Ferrer Mac-Gregor (eds.), *Diritto processuale costituzionale* (Cedam 2010), 424.

parties – supported."[129] Nicola Tranfaglia took the view that "the political criterion adopted by the Court [was] normally that of safeguarding the legislation from the Fascist period."[130] Although these opinions appear to be too harsh,[131] it must be admitted that on certain occasions during its first 15 years in office, the Constitutional Court lacked courage, upholding the Fascist legislation even when it was clearly in contrast with the new Constitution. The excessive degree of caution in relation to public order provisions (as noted in the text that follows)[132] is a clear demonstration of this tendency. Therefore, it is probably the case that in some circumstances the Court could have carried out its functions in a more incisive manner and more rapidly.

There are many reasons for this hesitant approach on the part of the Constitutional Court. In part it appears to have reflected a sort of "reverential fear" of the traditional powers of the State, or a fear of leaving a legislative void (*horror vacui*). Moreover, it is important not to underestimate the difficulties that the Court had in establishing itself within a consolidated institutional order. In fact the Court, which represented an absolute innovation in the Italian legal order, "occupied spaces that had previously been the preserve of other powers, performing functions that had been inconceivable in the past, and modifying the power structure and the existing privileges."[133] In addition, the conservative policy orientation of the parliamentary majority, the executive, and the superior courts acted as a significant impediment to the action of the Constitutional Court.

The Italian Constitutional Court, however, managed to make a clean break with the authoritarian past. Indeed, in spite of various instances of uncertainty and timidity, the Court made a decisive contribution to the consolidation of democracy, enabling the country to emerge from the "political gray area"[134] to which it had been confined in the period 1948–1956. In the following sections, an analysis will be put forward with specific reference to the first judgment of the Constitutional Court, as well as the rulings relating to non-Catholic religions, the right to strike, and public order matters. These cases show the most evident characteristics (mentioned already) of the work of the Court, namely its capability to break the legal continuity, its function of "reforms promoter," and its role as a "substitute" for Parliament, but also its extremely cautious approach in certain circumstances.

[129] Arturo Carlo Jemolo, *Tra diritto e storia (1960–1980)* (Giuffrè 1982), 468. In a similar vein see Alessandro Pizzorusso, "Meriti e limiti del processo costituzionale" (1972) *Politica del diritto*, 424–425.

[130] Tranfaglia 1973, note 46, at 240.

[131] According to Paladin 2004, note 38, at 139, such claims are "without real foundation."

[132] See Section 5.D of this chapter.

[133] Aldo Sandulli, *Rapporti tra giustizia comune e giustizia costituzionale in Italia* (Cedam 1968) 7.

[134] In the words of Thomas Carothers, "The End of the Transition Paradigm" (2002) 13 *Journal of Democracy* 1, 9.

A *Judgment 1/1956: The First Ruling Overturning a Fascist Law*

In the period immediately prior to the entry into force of the Constitutional Court, widely divergent approaches continued to be adopted. On the one hand, certain courts and legal scholars took the view that the contrast between the Constitution and preconstitutional legislation could be dealt with only by means of repeal, and that in any case the Constitutional Court could not strike down preconstitutional laws in contrast with programmatic constitutional provisions.[135] Moreover, as noted previously, the governing majority was not in favor of the establishment of the new Court, and this was pointed out by Enrico De Nicola, the first President of the Court, during his inaugural address.[136]

On the other hand, there were those who expressed their dissatisfaction with the fact that Parliament had not brought the existing legislation into line with the new constitutional values, along with their disappointment with the results of decentralized constitutional review in the period 1948–1956, thus arguing that the Constitutional Court should extend its powers to deal with preconstitutional legislation, so as to ensure an effective implementation of the Constitution. The general public had high hopes and expectations for the role of the Court, and in this connection, in the view of Piero Calamandrei, the first judgment of the Constitutional Court "did not betray the expectations of the Italian people."[137]

Regardless of what the prevalent approach in the country was, the first judgment of the Constitutional Court (Judgment no. 1, June 14, 1956) was undoubtedly a milestone in the history of Italian constitutional justice and marked *a turning point in the substantive transition*. With this decision the Constitutional Court demonstrated a keen awareness of its own constitutional identity,[138] and for the first time marked a clean break with Italy's authoritarian past, by declaring the unconstitutionality of a Fascist law.

In particular, the matter referred to the Court concerned the constitutional legitimacy of Article 113 of the Unified Code of Public Security, pursuant to which the distribution of posters or newspapers or the use of public address systems could only take place with the prior authorization of the proper police authority. It should be noted that the 30 referrals on this matter to the Court came from lower courts,

[135] See, e.g., Corte di Appello di Roma, March 1, 1956, in (1956) *Giurisprudenza costituzionale*, 123 ff.; in the literature, arguments of this kind were put forward by Salvatore Lener, "Leggi vecchie e Costituzione nuova" (1953) III *La civiltà cattolica*, 48–49, cited in Bartole 2004, note 44, at 119.

[136] "I do not need to engage in discussions in order to defend that which has quite rightly been stated or to disprove that which has been erroneously stated – amid reservations, doubts, and incomprehension – in relation to … the Constitutional Court, that offers the supreme advantage of protecting the country at all times against the risk of wrong turnings and mistakes."

[137] Calamandrei 1956, note 1, at 149; see also Giuseppino Treves, "Judicial Review of Legislation in Italy" (1958) 7 *Journal of Public Law*, 360.

[138] See Simoncini 2004, note 116, at 3072.

with not a single referral from the Court of Cassation. For a long time the Court of Cassation was reluctant to refer cases to the Constitutional Court even when the contrast between the preconstitutional statutes and the Constitution was evident, thus slowing down the process of eliminating authoritarian legislation. On the contrary, as argued by Valerio Onida, for many years the referrals to the Constitutional Court represented the instrument used by the lower courts "seeking to form an alliance with the Constitutional Court against the Court of Cassation"[139] to implement the Constitution. Indeed, in spite of its cautious approach in certain situations, in the eyes of the lower court judges the rulings of the Court were to be seen as "a great step forward compared to the decidedly anti-constitutional positions that often prevailed in the Court of Cassation."[140]

From this point of view, the lower court judges demonstrated a high degree of consistency in their approach. Indeed, as mentioned in the preceding text, during the period 1948–1956 it was above all the judges in the superior courts who often declared the programmatic nature of the constitutional provisions, whereas the lower courts tended to consider them as preceptive provisions having immediate application. The favorable stance taken by the lower courts in the implementation of constitutional provisions was such that they may be considered to be the closest allies of the Constitutional Court in upholding the principles and values laid down in the Constitution. The tendency of the lower courts to distance themselves from the more conservative positions of the superior courts is also closely connected to the establishment in 1958 of the High Council of the Judiciary, which greatly reduced the influence that the Court of Cassation and the executive exerted over such courts.[141]

Article 113 of the Unified Code on Public Security, it was argued by the appellants, was in contrast with Article 21 of the Constitution (free speech). The President of the Council of Ministers, represented by the State Attorney (*Avvocatura dello Stato*), argued that the Court was not competent to rule on the constitutionality of preconstitutional laws for two reasons. First, "because the preceptive constitutional provisions abrogate conflicting prior laws, and the determination of the existence of such a conflict is the exclusive jurisdiction of the ordinary courts," and second because "programmatic constitutional provisions do not have any effect whatsoever on the validity of laws enacted prior to the Constitution."

In response to these arguments the Court replied tersely, noting that "it is a matter beyond doubt" that it had exclusive competence for judging cases concerning the constitutional legitimacy of laws and acts having the force of law, as established by Article 134 of the Constitution. The Court also held that the claim that

139 Valerio Onida, "L'attuazione della Costituzione tra magistratura e Corte costituzionale" in *Aspetti e tendenze del Diritto costituzionale. Scritti in onore di Costantino Mortati* (Giuffrè 1977), 547.

140 Ibid., at 549–550.

141 See Paladin 2004, note 38, at 147 ff.; Calamandrei 1955, note 62, at 232 ff.

preconstitutional laws were not subject to constitutional scrutiny was without foundation from a "textual" point of view, considering that both Article 134 of the Constitution and Article 1 of Constitutional Law no. 1/1948 referred to "laws" without making any kind of distinction, as well as from a "logical" point of view, considering that in relations between the various sources of law, the Constitution prevailed over ordinary laws, regardless of whether they were enacted prior to or subsequent to the Constitution. In short, the Court defended the absolute primacy of the 1948 Constitution in the hierarchy of legal sources, ruling out the possibility that laws in conflict with the Constitution could remain in force.

In spite of the clear stance taken by the Court on this matter, for a long time the President of the Council continued to intervene in the proceedings before the Constitutional Court, defending the position put forward in relation to Judgment 1/1956 (i.e., the lack of competence of the Court to rule on preconstitutional legislation), and defending the content of the legislative acts in question. The actions of the President of the Council were often aimed at defending the preconstitutional laws or at least certain interpretations of them, even in cases in which the contrast between the 1948 Constitution and the prior legislation was evident. In light of the fact that the President of the Council is not required to play a role in the case, but is only required to be *informed* of the case before the Court (as the *notificatario*),[142] the decision to intervene to defend such a position reflected a clear political stance. As a result, at least with regard to the purported lack of competence of the Court to rule on preconstitutional legislation, and the attempt to defend the content of the Fascist legislation, the intervention of the President of the Council in the cases based on the "incidental" method of constitutional review may be deemed to be of a *political* nature, as an expression of the policies of the government.[143]

Returning more specifically to Judgment 1/1956, it should be noted that the Court handed down a clear ruling also with regard to the distinction between programmatic constitutional provisions and preceptive constitutional provisions,[144] thanks to which (as noted previously) a substantial amount of Fascist legislation had remained in force. The Constitutional Court cleared the ground of any doubt about this matter by ruling that this distinction "may be essential for determining the repeal or otherwise of a legislative act, but it is not decisive in relation to a ruling on

[142] See Massimo Severo Giannini, "Sull'intervento nel processo dinanzi alla Corte costituzionale (giudizi di legittimità costituzionale)" (1956) *Giurisprudenza costituzionale*, 245.

[143] With regard to the intervention of the president of the Council in cases based on the "incidental" method of constitutional review (in particular with regard to the *interests* he is required to represent) see Silvano Tosi, *Il Governo davanti alla Corte nei giudizi incidentali di legittimità costituzionale* (Giuffrè 1963); Roberto Romboli, *Il giudizio costituzionale incidentale come processo senza parti* (Giuffrè 1985); some references can also be found in Alessandro Pizzorusso, Vincenzo Vigoriti and G. L. Certoma, "The Constitutional Review of Legislation in Italy" (1983) 56 *Temple Law Quarterly*, 517–519.

[144] See Vezio Crisafulli et al., "Dibattito sulla competenza della Corte costituzionale in ordine alle norme anteriori alla Costituzione" (1956) *Giurisprudenza costituzionale*, 261 ff.

constitutional legitimacy, since the unconstitutionality of a legislative act can also be the result of its incompatibility with programmatic constitutional provisions."

One matter on which the Court did not seem to express a clear opinion was the distinction between *repeal* and *constitutional illegitimacy*. According to the Constitutional Court, the repeal and constitutional illegitimacy of legislation

> are not identical measures, but operate on distinct levels, with different effects and competences. The scope of application of repeal is more limited than that of constitutional illegitimacy, and the requirements laid down for repeal . . . are much more limited than the requirements for declaring the constitutional illegitimacy of a legislative act.

According to some scholars, the Court used this finding to establish its exclusive competence to determine the constitutional legitimacy of prior legislation,[145] whereas other scholars argued that this formulation could be interpreted as "a scaling back of the powers of the Court to less drastic positions, as if attempting to 'leave the door ajar' to the power of any judge to declare the repeal of prior legislation due to its contrast with preceptive constitutional provisions."[146] In actual fact, however, this question – that was not clarified even by the subsequent rulings of the Constitutional Court[147] – had a limited impact in practical terms because judges, engaged in their "struggle" to implement the Constitution, rather than declaring the repeal of a norm, preferred to refer the case to the Constitutional Court, so as to enable the Court to declare the unconstitutionality of the law with *erga omnes* effects.

With regard to the case at hand, with Judgment 1/1956 the Court held that Article 113 of the Unified Code on Public Security was in contrast with Article 21 of the Constitution, due to the fact that it required *authorization* by the police authority for the exercise of the right to free speech. In particular, according to the Court, this article gave rise to "an excessive extension of discretionary powers, since no limits were laid down within which police activities and powers [should] be contained."

[145] See Calamandrei 1956, note 1, at 151.

[146] Bartole 2004, note 44, at 126. See also Enrico Tullio Liebman, "Invalidità e abrogazione delle leggi anteriori alla Costituzione" (1956) *Rivista di diritto processuale*, 161–163.

[147] Indeed, in Judgment 40/1958, the Court ruled that "questions relating to the compatibility of a legislative act with a constitutional provision are questions of constitutional legitimacy that are the exclusive competence of this Court, even if they concern legislative acts prior to the entry into force of the constitutional provision with which they are incompatible." This ruling, in which the Constitutional Court appeared to rule out the possibility of ordinary judges declaring the repeal of preconstitutional laws, seemed to be cast into doubt by Judgments 1 and 4/1959. On the one hand, the Court once again upheld its exclusive competence in declaring the constitutional illegitimacy of the preconstitutional laws and determined that even if the ordinary courts had repeatedly repealed a specific legislative act, this did not in any way prevent the Court from declaring its unconstitutionality, in the case in which a lower court referred the question to the Constitutional Court. On the other hand, it should be noted that the Constitutional Court never *expressly* prohibited ordinary judges from setting aside a legislative act that was deemed to have been repealed by the Constitution.

In addition, mention should be made of the fact that in an awareness of the "limited compliance of certain public security provisions with the constitutional provisions" the Constitutional Court stated that such a sensitive matter as public order "should be regulated as soon as possible in a satisfactory manner by means of provisions in line with the Constitution." This recommendation to the legislature by the Constitutional Court may be seen as a sign of the intention on the part of the Court to engage and cooperate with the other State institutions, an intention that stands out from the outset as one of the characteristics of the action of the Constitutional Court.[148] In fact, whereas the Court was well aware of its institutional role, it strongly believed that this identity needed to be accepted and confirmed by the constitutional system as a whole.[149] In practice, the Constitutional Court encountered serious difficulties in establishing itself in the new institutional framework, above all due to the obstructionism of the government majority and the superior courts. One need only consider the intervention of the President of the Council of Ministers in the cases based on the "incidental" method of constitutional review (supporting the view that the Constitutional Court was not empowered to rule on the constitutionality of laws enacted prior to the Constitution) or the reluctance on the part of the superior courts to refer questions of constitutionality to the Court. Also in the case under consideration, the majority was by no means inclined to cooperate: the recommendation by the Constitutional Court to modify the Unified Code on Public Security was not considered, and the motions tabled in Parliament to reform it were lost in the intricacies of parliamentary procedure and not approved.[150]

B *The Court and the Non-Catholic Religions: A Stimulus for Reform*

The advent of Fascism marked the beginning of a particularly difficult period for the non-Catholic religions. Indeed, the provisions implementing Law no. 1159/1929[151] (issued by means of Royal Decree no. 289/1930), the Criminal Code, the Unified Code on Public Security, as well as Royal Decrees no. 884/1932 and no. 1080/1932 laid down considerable restrictions on the freedoms granted to non-Catholic religions. Among the limitations laid down by Royal Decree no. 289, mention should be made of Article 1, requiring an application to set up a place of worship to be submitted by a recognized minister of religion, and authorized by royal decree, supported by evidence that the place of worship "was necessary to effectively meet the religious needs of significant groups of worshippers" and "endowed with

[148] See Barsotti, Carozza, Cartabia, and Simoncini 2016, note 31, at 34 ff. and 234 ff.
[149] See Simoncini 2004, note 116, at 3080.
[150] To be discussed in Section 5.D of this chapter.
[151] "Provisions on worship by religious denominations permitted by the State and on marriages celebrated by ministers of these religious denominations."

sufficient resources to cover the maintenance costs." This provision clearly left a wide margin of discretion as to whether these criteria were met.[152]

The 1930 Criminal Code, reflecting the provisions for the State religion, laid down that offending a non-Catholic religious denomination by means of personal insults or acts, or the disruption of religious services, was deemed to be a criminal offence, *but the sanctions were reduced* (Article 406).

Another striking example of the restrictions on non-Catholic religions is to be found in Article 18 of the Unified Code on Public Security, that for many years was one of the main instruments prohibiting and prosecuting prayer meetings even in private homes.[153] Indeed, this provision deemed to be public "even a meeting that, albeit held in private, considering the place where it is held, the number of people taking part, or the purpose or aims of the meeting, has the characteristics of a meeting not of a private nature." Moreover, with Royal Decrees no. 884/1932 and no. 1080/1932, responsibility for policies concerning non-Catholic religions was transferred from the Ministry of Justice to the Ministry of the Interior. This decision, as noted in the following text, gave rise to a series of harmful consequences for these religious minorities.

Completing this series of unfavorable provisions regulating the non-Catholic religions, mention should be made of Circular 600/158, April 9, 1935, issued to the prefects by the Ministry of the Interior, prohibiting religious services held by Pentecostals, deemed to be a denomination incompatible with the restrictions laid down in Article 1 of Law no. 1159/1929.[154] This was to be followed by other circulars (441/027713, August 22, 1939, and 441/02977, March 13, 1940), aimed at intensifying the inspections of the Pentecostals, as well as attacking the Jehovah's Witnesses and the Students of the Bible.[155]

During the debates in the Constituent Assembly many of the proposals intended to strengthen the safeguards for religious minorities "were determined by the wish to react to the recent past ... rather than providing a clear framework of reference for the future development of religious pluralism in Italy."[156] For this reason references to "principles" were eliminated (because it was not the duty of the police to evaluate the merits of the principles of a religious faith) along with references to "public

[152] See Arturo Carlo Jemolo, "Le libertà garantite dagli artt. 8, 19, 21 della Costituzione" (1952) *Diritto ecclesiastico*, 409.

[153] See Gianni Long, *Le confessioni religiose "diverse dalla cattolica." Ordinamenti interni e rapporti con lo Stato* (Il Mulino 1991), 27–28.

[154] See Giorgio Peyrot, "Provvedimenti ostativi dell'autorità di polizia e garanzie costituzionali per il libero esercizio dei culti ammessi" (1951) *Diritto ecclesiastico*, 204, including the text of the circular.

[155] Once again, the texts of the circulars are to be found in Peyrot 1951, note 154, at 204 ff.

[156] Andrea Guazzarotti, *Giudici e minoranze religiose* (Giuffrè 2001), 15.

order" (because it was considered to be too vague a concept to be used as a pretext for prohibiting religious services).[157]

The entry into force of the Constitution, unequivocally recognizing the equality of all religions before the law (Article 8) and the right to exercise a religion whatever it may be (Article 19), introduced an important innovation in contrast with the previously mentioned forms of religious persecution of non-Catholic religious denominations. However, for many years the break with the past was purely a formal matter because religious minorities continued to find themselves in a particularly difficult position. As a result, the continuity of the State was evident also in this field.

In actual fact, positive signs were evident in certain courts' rulings, including those of the superior courts, which, in contrast with their general orientation, found Articles 8 and 19 to be preceptive constitutional provisions having immediate application. However, the minister of the interior (who was responsible for non-Catholic religions) adopted a policy of obstructionism, aimed at maintaining the regulation of these denominations laid down in 1929–1930, and postponing (if not preventing) the conclusion of agreements (*intese*) with non-Catholic religious denominations, as provided for by Article 8(3) of the Constitution. This provision stipulates that the relations of non-Catholic religions with the state "are regulated by law, based on agreements with their respective representatives." The objection to these *intese* was of a procedural nature. Indeed, the representatives of the non-Catholic religious denominations argued that in order to reach an agreement, bilateral negotiations were required, and for this purpose, starting in 1948, a series of petitions and proposals were submitted to the government. The Ministry of the Interior, however, replied that non-Catholic religions were free to submit "practical proposals to the Ministry of the Interior, that would take them into consideration, and put forward the necessary agreements and the legislative provisions." In any case, the Ministry underlined, it was important not to overlook the existence of "legislative measures (Law no. 1159, June 1929, and Regulation no. 289, 28 February 1930), governing non-Catholic religious denominations."[158] The strategy was therefore to adopt a unilateral position: it was the minister, after receiving the application, who was to decide whether and when to conclude an agreement, with the result that the existing legislation remained in force without any amendment.

To remove the obstacles that seemed destined to remain in place for a long time, in 1956, by way of provocation, a bill was put forward signed by La Malfa and other secular deputies, aimed at adopting "specific measures" relating to the procedures

[157] On the debates in the Constituent Assembly see Gianni Long, *Alle origini del pluralismo confessionale. Il dibattito sulla libertà religiosa nell'età della Costituente* (Il Mulino 1990); Vittorio Falzone, *La Costituzione ed i culti non cattolici* (Giuffrè 1953), 23 ff.

[158] Letter from the Minister of the Interior, Scelba, dated May 31, 1952, in Long 1991, note 153, at 36.

for concluding these *intese*, as well as repealing the existing provisions on religious minorities.[159] However, even this attempt was unsuccessful.

It has been rightly pointed out that "although the religious minorities did not gain 'access' to a political solution, they managed to obtain a 'case law' solution."[160] In fact, the entry into force of the Constitutional Court paved the way for the elimination of the most serious restrictions on religious freedom. First of all, Judgment 1/1956, though not primarily concerned with religious minorities, was found to be particularly important because it laid down the principle that preconstitutional legislation could be struck down by the Constitutional Court.

This ruling was followed by Judgments 45/1957 and 59/1958. In the first of these decisions, the Constitutional Court declared the unconstitutionality of Article 25 of the Unified Code on Public Security, with regard to the section that imposed an obligation to provide advance notice of religious services, ceremonies, and religious practices held in private places, but which were open to the public, because it was in contrast with Article 17 of the Constitution (freedom of assembly). The state attorney – that, as noted, tended to defend the preconstitutional legislation – in order to demonstrate the constitutional legitimacy of Article 25 of the Unified Code on Public Security, made reference to the criterion of "specialty," arguing that this particular provision was not in contrast with Article 17 of the Constitution due to the fact that a measure of a general character (in this case, Article 17 of the Constitution) could not derogate from "special" provisions provided for in the prior legislation. However, the Court rejected this argument, ruling that Article 17 "was inspired by such elevated and fundamental requirements of social life as to assume a scope and efficacy of the most general kind, with the result that special provisions would no longer be possible." Moreover, the state attorney, still attempting to demonstrate the constitutionality of Article 25 of the Unified Code on Public Security, made reference to Article 19 of the Constitution (freedom of religion), claiming that the obligation to provide prior notice should be interpreted with a view to ascertaining whether in individual cases the religious services it was intended to hold in the places assigned for that purpose, including the places open to the public, constituted practices that were incompatible with public morality, in order to allow the police authority to prohibit them. Also in response to such arguments, the Court replied in a trenchant manner that "the rule that it is intended to derive from such an interpretation, that for every limitation to a constitutional freedom there is a corresponding power of prevention and control on the part of the police authority, does not exist in our legal order."

[159] Chamber of Deputies, bill no. 2432, "Sull'esercizio dei diritti di libertà religiosa e sulla regolamentazione dei rapporti correnti tra lo Stato e le confessioni religiose diverse dalla cattolica," July 21, 1956.

[160] Guazzarotti 2001, note 156, at 18.

In light of the fact that Article 25 had been applied on numerous occasions to break up and prohibit religious services even in private homes, and that it was considered to be one of the most stringent restrictions on religious freedom, it is clear that this ruling by the Constitutional Court was symptomatic of the fact that times were changing.

Another particularly significant decision was Judgment 59/1958. With this ruling the Court declared the unconstitutionality, due to failure to comply with Articles 8 and 19 of the Constitution, of Article 1 of Royal Decree no. 289/1930 (requiring government authorization for the opening of places of worship and prayer, not only for civil purposes, but also for the purposes of worship) and Article 2 of the same decree (that made the holding of religious services and ceremonies in places of worship conditional on the service being held or authorized by a minister of religion whose appointment had been approved by the ministry responsible).

In striking down these provisions, the Court rejected the argument put forward by the state attorney, concerning the legislative void that would ensue from a ruling declaring the constitutional illegitimacy of these articles. According to the Court, the free exercise of religion was upheld and delimited by the Constitution, in particular by Article 19, "with provisions containing a clear and well defined regulation," while "the relations between the non-Catholic religious denominations and the State, pending the adoption of other measures to be adopted pursuant to agreements, continue to be regulated by the existing legislation, in the part that remains in force, in that it is not detrimental to the freedom of religion safeguarded by the Constitution." In more general terms, the Court stated that the power to determine the constitutional legitimacy of the laws could not be hindered by the ensuing legislative void, and that it was a matter for the "wisdom of the legislator . . . to deal with it in the most rapid and appropriate manner." These remarks are particularly significant, above all in the light of the fact that one of the most frequent criticisms of the Constitutional Court (as noted) is that it tended to adopt an extremely cautious approach in declaring constitutional illegitimacy for fear of creating a legislative void (*horror vacui*).

The two judgments mentioned previously were insufficient to deal with all the problems of religious minorities, but it is undeniable that they had the merit of striking down the provisions that in the past had allowed "the worst abuses," the repeal of which was "forcefully requested."[161] The rulings of the Constitutional Court had the effect of *reducing the pressure from the religious minorities to conclude agreements (intese)*, as well as *reducing the intensity of the repressive policy of the government*. In fact, the initial results soon materialized. In 1961 the government put forward a bill to Parliament relating to the setting up of an invalidity insurance and pension fund for the Catholic clergy. With regard to the proposal put forward in the parliamentary commission to extend the provision to other denominations, the then

[161] Long 1991, note 153, at 40.

minister of the interior, Scelba, responded (presenting a bill of his own) that such a fund should be limited to religious denominations that were "approved" and that in any case Jewish denominations should be excluded because they were regulated by Royal Decree no. 1731/30, which required their invalidity insurance and pension funds to be at the expense of the Jewish community. At this point the evangelical denominations made an attempt to use the legislative provision to conclude an *intesa*, "and they obtained the tabling of amendments that required the membership of the fund for all ministers of religion, whether approved or not, of the denominations that had concluded an agreement for this purpose."[162] Albeit with some difficulty, the government and the religious minorities managed to agree on a solution, that provided that the extension of the invalidity and pension fund to ministers of religion other than Catholicism was conditional on the conclusion of a specific *intesa*.

Whereas, on the one hand, these invalidity and pension agreements (*piccole intese previdenziali*) did not constitute a direct application of Article 8(3) of the Constitution, on the other hand, it is undeniable that in that particular historical period they constituted an important innovation.[163] The Constitutional Court thus not only struck down certain provisions restricting the religious freedoms of the religious minorities but also urged the legislator to adopt measures in favor of non-Catholic denominations (in the form of these invalidity pension schemes).

C *The Right to Strike: The Court as a "Substitute" for Parliament*

The strongly repressive approach of Fascism to the right to strike is well known. Articles 18–22 of Law no. 563/1926 imposed a ban on strikes and lockouts, enforced with criminal sanctions, and these measures (together with the regulations approved with Royal Decree no. 1130/1926) were incorporated into the Criminal Code.

Article 40 of the Constitution, providing that "the right to strike shall be exercised in compliance with the law," marked a clean break with the past. However, during the debates in the Constituent Assembly, a fear was expressed that turned out to be well founded. "I am really afraid – argued the deputy Foa – that if the clause in which the right to strike is laid down makes a generic reference to compliance with the law without specifying the policy to be adopted and the limits of the legislative provisions, then this right will be deprived … of its constitutional value."[164] What

[162] Ibid., at 41.

[163] A further innovation in relation to religious minorities was introduced with Law no. 817/1973, extending to hospitals run by non-Catholic denominations the conditions laid down in Law no. 132/1968. However, the effective implementation of Article 8(3) of the Constitution took place only in the period 1984–1987 (known as "the period of agreements" [*stagione delle intese*]).

[164] *Atti della Assemblea costituente*, May 12, 1947, cited by Umberto Romagnoli, "Art. 40" in Branca 1981 (ed.), note 16, at 291.

happened, as it turned out, is that as a result of the lack of intervention on the part of the legislator, the courts had considerable freedom in interpreting Article 40. On the one hand, they did not hesitate to consider this article as a preceptive constitutional provision,[165] while, on the other hand (particularly in the case of the Court of Cassation), they opted for a fairly restrictive definition of strike action, fully upholding the legitimacy only of economic and professional strikes.[166] In the view of Umberto Romagnoli, courts' rulings of this type were the outcome of multiple factors:

> Judges do not understand only the language of legislation: there is also that of the Ministry of the Interior and the Ministry of Justice; that of the Ministry of Labour, remarkably closely aligned to the position of a "deputy minister of the police"; in addition there is the language of the public prosecutors of the Republic and of the prefects; there is that of the mass media . . .; finally there is the language of university courses where labour law textbooks state that "the law should evolve, but it should not make a great leap forward."[167]

In short, as in the case of religious freedom, the Constitutional Court began its deliberations in a climate that was not particularly favorable to the exercise of the right to strike. This helps to explain why it took several years for the Court to adopt a case law approach in contrast with the judgments delivered by the ordinary courts until that time. Over a period of almost 15 years (from 1960 to 1974) the Constitutional Court intervened progressively in relation to the right to strike, but in an increasingly incisive manner, playing a fundamental role as a "substitute" for Parliament, which continued to fail to adopt the implementing legislation.

In that historical period the right to strike represented an issue of the utmost importance, especially in light of its suitability to give a crucial contribution to the ongoing process of democratization. The Constitutional Court underlined "the essential connection between strike action and the regime of a State."[168] In Judgment 29/1960, for example, providing an historical overview of the right to strike and the right to lockout, the Constitutional Court made reference to the ministerial report on the 1930 Criminal Code, which stated that the prohibition of the right to lockout and the right to strike was intended "to mark a clear transition between the two regimes, and to clearly override the democratic principle, which, vice versa, envisaged the right to form alliances and to call a strike." Moreover, in Judgment 290/1974, the Court underlined the fact that the right to strike was particularly

[165] The only exceptions were the previously mentioned rulings of the Court of Cremona (see note 102).
[166] See Francesco Santoni, *Lo sciopero* (Jovene 1991), 24.
[167] Romagnoli 1981, note 164, at 294.
[168] Gian Carlo Perone, "La giurisprudenza costituzionale in materia di sciopero e serrata" in Renato Scognamiglio (ed.), *Il lavoro nella giurisprudenza costituzionale* (Franco Angeli 1978), 360.

significant in a democratic system by virtue of its function of democratic participation.

The Constitutional Court, in light of the inertia of the legislature, stood in for Parliament, in particular by providing a definition of strike and identifying its limits and permitted objectives.[169] The starting point of its case law is to be found in Judgment 29/1960.[170] In this decision the Court stated that Article 40 of the Constitution was a preceptive constitutional provision having immediate application, and struck down Article 502 of the Criminal Code (that prohibited strikes and lockouts for contractual purposes), based on the assumption that strike action for contractual purposes was the main object of the protection granted by the constitutional provision.

Subsequently, with Judgment 123/1962, the Court took the opportunity to formulate its position on the limits of the right to strike in a more systematic manner. Strikes were defined, by means of express reference to "the tradition upheld by the Constituent Assembly," as "the total abstention from work on the part of subordinate employees, with the aim of defending their economic interests." In the view of the Court, it can be deduced that the right to strike is legitimate only when it is aimed at achieving economic ends due to the fact that Article 40 comes under Title III of the first part of the Constitution, regulating economic rights and duties. The Constitutional Court, however, specified that "the protection granted to [economic rights] cannot be limited simply to matters of remuneration, but extends to all those matters concerning the interests of the workers that are regulated by the provisions under the same Title." In addition, it should be mentioned that the Court seemed to allow solidarity strikes (sympathy strikes) albeit within certain limits.[171] As a result, the "contractual" conception of strike action appeared to be replaced by a more wide-ranging conception of "economic" or "economic-professional" strike.

Whereas in its 1962 ruling the Court had moved beyond the more restrictive definitions of the right to strike, Judgment 31/1969 may be seen as a "great leap forward." First of all, it is necessary to consider the *definition* of strike action: whereas Judgment 123/1962 made reference to a "total abstention from work on the part of subordinate employees" citing "the tradition upheld by the Constituent Assembly,"

169 This substitution – as argued by Costantino Mortati, "Appunti per uno studio sui rimedi giurisdizionali contro comportamenti omissivi del legislatore" (1970) V *Foro italiano*, 160 – was deemed to be fully legitimate: "The failure to enact legislation can quite justifiably give rise to rulings by the Constitutional Court whenever it is deemed necessary to safeguard the values that the Constitution is supposed to protect from the indiscriminate use of a given right. This was the case of the right to strike recognized in Article 40."

170 Previously the Court had handed down rulings on the right to strike and the right to lockout in Judgments 110/1957, 46/1958, and 47/1958.

171 "[T]he suspension of work carried out in support of the demands of an economic nature relating to a strike already taking place, by workers belonging to the same category as the first group of striking workers, can be justified in cases in which there is an affinity between the demands of the first group and the second group of striking workers, based on the view that without the joint action of all the workers their demands run the risk of not being satisfied."

the 1969 ruling referred to "the suspension of work on the part of subordinate employees," in line with "the origin and function assigned to the term in the present historical context." In the first place, the disappearance of the qualifier "total" would appear to legitimate "partial" forms of strike, such as rotating or staggered (on-off) strikes,[172] which were not considered legitimate by some legal scholars.[173] Moreover, the notion of strike action is not "to be identified by means of . . . the static definition upheld by the Constituent Assembly, but by the dynamic definition in a specific historical period."[174]

However, it was in terms of the *aims* of strike action that the most significant innovations took place. Indeed, Judgment 31/1969 determined that strikes were "instrumental for the pursuit of economic and social goods which the constitutional system associates with the need to safeguard and develop the personality [of the worker]." In comparison with the ruling handed down seven years before, what is missing is any reference to Title III of the Constitution, and the term "economic interests" is replaced with "economic and social goods" relating to the safeguarding and development of the personality of the worker. As a result of the extension of the concept of economic strikes adopted by the Court, it became extremely difficult to distinguish between economic strikes (which were considered legitimate) and noneconomic strikes (which were considered illegitimate).[175] At that point the only element missing from the reasoning of the Court was "the last . . . logical and necessary step, i.e., the recognition that the right to strike . . . pertains to the pursuit of any collective interest, over and above the necessary 'economic' aspect."[176]

This "last step" was taken with Judgment 290/1974, in which the Court struck down Article 503 of the Criminal Code, "with regard to the part imposing sanctions on political strikes not aimed at subverting the constitutional order or at hindering or impeding the free exercise of legitimate powers by which popular sovereignty is expressed." As in the case of Judgment 29/1960, the Court took as its starting point the *strong correlation between strike action and the regime of the State*. In the view of the Court, the prohibition of the right to strike laid down by the Fascist regime was motivated by "the logic of a constitutional order that took a repressive stance to all forms of freedom, as well as by a conception of the employment relationship incompatible with the conception to be found in the various articles of the Constitution." On the contrary, the 1948 Constitution "overturned the fundamental principles of that logic, giving ample space to the freedom of individuals and groups,

172 See Valerio Onida, "Luci e ombre nella giurisprudenza costituzionale in tema di sciopero" (1969) *Giurisprudenza costituzionale*, 921.

173 See Alessandro Pace, "Spunti per una delimitazione 'costituzionale' dello sciopero" (1964) *Giurisprudenza costituzionale*, 1452–1453.

174 Perone 1978, note 168, at 380.

175 The Court declared the unconstitutionality of Article 330(1) and (2) of the Criminal Code only with respect "to economic strikes that do not undermine the essential public functions and services deemed to be of preeminent general interest pursuant to the Constitution."

176 Onida 1969, note 172, at 925.

upholding and protecting it with the sole limits that are strictly necessary to safeguard other interests that characterize the new democratic system." By way of confirmation of this argument, the Constitutional Court referred to the fact that the Zanardelli Criminal Code of 1889, inspired by the principles of freedom, did not impose sanctions on political strikes, and that in democracies strikes with political aims were not subject to criminal sanctions. This led on to the observation that Article 503 of the Criminal Code was "an isolated case in the history of our legislation and in a comparative view of democratic systems." Therefore, the Court ruled that it was "the fundamental principles of freedom characterizing the new legal order" that acted as a barrier against indiscriminate sanctions on strikes solely due to the fact that they were of a political nature.

It should be noted that this line of reasoning constitutes one of the rare exceptions to the general view of the Constitutional Court that provisions enacted during the previous authoritarian regime can remain in force in the new system, provided they are not in contrast with the new constitutional principles. On this point Valerio Onida is quite insistent:

> as a rule the Court did not frame the question in terms of a conflict between the old and the new system: on the contrary, it takes as its starting point, often in explicit terms, the view that norms enacted for purposes incompatible with constitutional values, in a political and ideological climate which the Constitution solemnly opposes, may well continue to operate in the new system, given the independence of the normative content from the ideological purposes giving rise to the norm, and given the possibility to bring this normative content in line with the new principles governing the legal order.[177]

It is evident that, on the one hand, this approach facilitated the survival of many laws enacted during the previous regime, while, on the other, it promoted a process by which certain preconstitutional laws were re-examined to bring them into line with the principles of the Constitution.

Returning more specifically to Judgment 290/1974, another particularly important part of this decision is the one concerning the *relationship between the right to strike and Article 3 of the Constitution* (principle of equality). In the view of the Court, allowing strikes in support of the adoption of political measures did not mean allowing workers to acquire a more privileged position than other citizens. Rather, it simply meant "recognizing that which was already clear from the Constitution, i.e. that strikes were an appropriate means, necessarily evaluated in the framework of all the methods for exerting pressure adopted by various social groups, for favouring the pursuit of the ends laid down in Article 3(2) of the Constitution." As a result, according to the Constitutional Court, the right to strike acquired a particularly important value in a democratic order due to its function as a means of democratic

[177] Onida 1977, note 139, at 518–521.

participation. Indeed, it represents "a means for the personal development of the worker and the promotion of his effective participation on the transformation of the economic, social and political context within which he operates."[178] This constitutes a step forward from the "contractual" perspective that had long been adopted not just by most legal scholars but also in the case law of the Constitutional Court.[179]

As mentioned in the preceding text, this incisive intervention on the part of the Constitutional Court was motivated by the failure of Parliament to enact the implementing legislation required by Article 40 of the Constitution. In actual fact, some bills were brought forward at various times, but none of them was approved.[180] However, due to the rather restrictive policies put forward in these bills, and in light of the increasingly progressive case law of the Constitutional Court, it may be argued that the legislative void in which the Court operated was ultimately an advantage. Indeed, this void probably facilitated the adoption of interpretations that were closer to the original spirit of the constitutional proclamation of the right to strike.[181]

D *The Court and Public Order: A Janus-Faced Case Law*

As in any authoritarian regime, the Fascist leaders often sought to justify repressive policies in the name of public order. As argued by Paolo Barile,

> under Fascism the tasks of the police were greatly extended, on the basis of the protection of a "good" that until that time had made only sporadic appearances in the legislative provisions adopted by the Crispi administration, i.e. "public order," often accompanied by the synonym and intensifier "public security" and by the related "public morality" and "common decency."[182]

In particular it was the Unified Code on Public Security that constituted one of the most effective instruments of the Fascist regime for greatly reducing the sphere of individual freedoms.[183] Immediately after the entry into force of the Constitution, there seemed to be no doubt that the Unified Code on Public Security could no

178 Perone 1978, note 168, at 400.

179 On Judgment 290/1974 see Sergio Panunzio, "Lo sciopero politico fra Costituzione e Corte costituzionale" in *Aspetti e tendenze del Diritto costituzionale. Scritti in onore di Costantino Mortati*, note 139, at 927 ff.

180 The first bill was presented by the government to the Chamber of Deputies on December 4, 1951 (*Atti Camera, I Legislatura*, no. 2380). The other bill, far more liberal than the first, was presented by the National Council for the Economy and Labour in 1960.

181 See Onida 1969, note 172, at 917.

182 Paolo Barile, "La pubblica sicurezza" in Paolo Barile, *Scritti di diritto costituzionale* (Cedam 1967), 635.

183 One need only consider measures such as the *ammonizione* and the *confino* (see notes 99 and 100), the power to search private homes on the part of the public security authorities, the regulation of meetings, associations, and the *foglio di via obbligatorio* (see note 192), as well as all the provisions regulating free speech. In addition, it is necessary to consider the powers granted to the prefects and the minister of the interior.

longer exist alongside the new constitutional provisions. In fact, on October 25, 1948, the Senate approved a motion tabled by Gasparotto and Berlinguer, urging the government to bring forward a bill for a new Unified Code on Public Security. The day after, the minister of the interior, Scelba, confirmed that the government intended to take measures to implement this proposal:

> It appears to be undeniable that the Unified Code on Public Security contains fundamental measures that are in sharp and evident contrast with the rights laid down in the Constitution. I am so convinced of this that even before the Constituent Assembly had completed its work and approved the Constitution, I appointed a Commission to keep track of the work of the Constituent Assembly in a scrupulous manner, and to re-examine the public security legislation with a view to making it fully compliant with the measures adopted by the Constituent Assembly and the laws that were being enacted .... The work of the Commission is now almost finished, and I make a formal undertaking before this Senate that by the end of this year I will bring forward a proposal for a new public security legislation to be approved by Parliament.[184]

In actual fact, however, this "formal undertaking" was never respected. Indeed, each time the bill was close to being approved, a pretext for postponing the decision was found, until the first parliamentary term came to an end. This approach, that clearly constituted a form of "obstructionism by the majority," was repeated during the second parliamentary term, and as a result in 1956, when the Constitutional Court started to operate, "one of the police laws that was most harmful to the rights and freedoms in the entire world"[185] had still not been repealed.[186]

In light of this state of affairs, the Constitutional Court was called on to ascertain the constitutionality of numerous articles of this Code.[187] The result was an "extremely contradictory" case law,[188] that may be described as *Janus-like*. On the one hand, as in the case of Judgment 1/1956, the Constitutional Court showed a firm hand, making a start on striking down various articles of the Unified Code on Public Security in contrast with the Constitution, and at the same time making recommendations to the legislature to amend this Code. On the other hand, in many cases the Court adopted an extremely cautious stance, opting for an interpretative judgment of dismissal[189] in cases in which, in actual fact, it could (and should) have declared the provisions unconstitutional.

[184] The speech by the Minister of the Interior, Scelba, is reproduced in Lelio Basso, *Il principe senza scettro* (Feltrinelli 1958), 222.

[185] Balladore Pallieri 1954, note 60, at 51.

[186] On the proposals to reform the Unified Code on Public Security, see S. De Fina, "Testo unico di pubblica sicurezza e Costituzione" (1959) *Giurisprudenza costituzionale*, 964 ff.

[187] Some of the judgments discussed in this section are also analyzed in Malcolm Evans, "The Italian Constitutional Court" (1968) 17 *International and Comparative Law Quarterly*, 616 ff.

[188] Stefano Merlini, "La Corte costituzionale e le leggi di pubblica sicurezza" (1972) *Quale giustizia*, 320.

[189] On this type of judgments see note 116.

To exemplify the firm hand of the Constitutional Court, reference may be made to Judgment 114/1967, which declared the unconstitutionality of the power of the prefects to dissolve associations.[190] With this ruling the Court struck down Article 215 of the Unified Code on Public Security enacted with Royal Decree no. 1848/1926 (vesting the prefects with the power to issue decrees dissolving associations, bodies and institutions established and operating in the Kingdom of Italy that were engaged in activities contrary to the national order of the State, as well as the power to order the confiscation of the assets of the association) and Article 210 of the Unified Code on Public Security of 1931, which included a provision along the same lines. Both provisions were deemed to be in conflict with Article 18 of the Constitution (freedom of association). In its reasoning, the Court upheld the concept (mentioned previously)[191] according to which "the origin and rationale of a legislative provision should not be considered decisive for the proper interpretation of the norm. Rather, it should be considered in terms of its objective structure and its capacity to find a place in the new constitutional order." According to the Constitutional Court, in the case at hand the structure of the norms made clear that they were not intended to pursue an interest safeguarded by the Constitution. The Court went on to state that the provisions referred to the Court for constitutional review were intended to prevent the existence of associations engaged "in any case" in activities contrary to "the national order" or "the political order constituted by the State," whereas in a "State of freedom" such as the one founded by the Constitution, "associations are allowed to engage in activities aimed at modifying the existing political order, provided that this aim is pursued with democratic methods, by means of free debate and without recourse to violence, either direct or indirect."

Still with regard to the freedom of association, mention should be made of Judgment 69/1962, in which the Constitutional Court held that Article 18 of the Constitution established and safeguarded also the *negative* freedom of association, and that this negative freedom was a distinguishing feature of the new democratic state. The Court noted that this constitutional provision should be interpreted in the historical context in which it was adopted, namely

> after a period in which the legislative policy of a totalitarian regime attempted to regulate associations ... under the control of the State, obliging citizens to join specific associations, thus eliminating the freedom of the individual to form associations with others in support of shared legitimate ends, voluntarily adopted and pursued.

It is also important to recall the rulings in which the Court declared the unconstitutionality of measures such as forced repatriation by means of a *foglio di via*

[190] See Paolo Barile, "La salutare scomparsa del potere prefettizio di scioglimento delle associazioni" (1967) *Giurisprudenza costituzionale*, 1249 ff.

[191] See Section 5.C of this chapter.

obbligatorio (Judgment 2/1956)[192] and the *ammonizione* (Judgment 11/1956),[193] due to the fact that they were enforced by an administrative authority instead of the judicial authorities.[194] These decisions acted as a strong stimulus for the legislature, which shortly thereafter adopted Law no. 1423/1956, implementing the recommendations of the Constitutional Court.

With regard to the right to assembly, in addition to Judgment 45/1957 (discussed in the preceding text),[195] mention should be made of Judgment 27/1958, by means of which the Court determined that prior notice was required only for meetings held in public, and not also for those held in a private place, but which were open to the public.[196]

All the judgments mentioned "[illustrate] clearly the part played by the Constitutional Court in removing from the Italian judicial order the last vestiges of the totalitarian régime which had so substantially enlarged the concept of public safety."[197]

The other face of the case law of the Constitutional Court with regard to public order is characterized, as noted already, by excessive caution, with several examples to be found. A number of particularly restrictive rulings were handed down in relation to Article 21 of the Constitution (free speech). By way of example, Judgment 121/1957 found the challenge to the constitutionality of Article 68 of the Unified Code on Public Security to be without foundation. This article laid down an obligation to obtain a licence issued by the police authorities for theatrical performances and for the showing of films in public venues or places open to the public, as well as for opening social clubs, dance schools, and venues for public performances. The Court ruled that the police authorities were not entitled to engage in "any censorship or control over the contents of theatrical or cinematic performances," though they were required to ascertain "whether in particular times, places and

[192] By means of a *foglio di via obbligatorio* a person domiciled in a certain municipality could be compelled to return to that municipality and prohibited, in the absence of prior authorization, from returning to the municipality from which he had been expelled. In particular, the first three paragraphs of Article 157 of the Unified Code on Public Security were found to be unconstitutional. Subsequently, by means of Judgment 72/1963, the Court declared the partial unconstitutionality of Article 162 of the Unified Code on Public Security for the same reason.

[193] On the system of *ammonizione* see note 99. This judgment struck down Articles 164–176 of the Unified Code on Public Security as amended by Lieutenant's Legislative Decree no. 419/1944.

[194] It should be noted that these were not "substitutive" judgments. In other words, the Court did not re-elaborate the provision, standing in for the administrative authorities. In both judgments the Court ruled that dealing with a legislative void arising from a finding of constitutional illegitimacy was a matter exclusively for Parliament.

[195] As examined in Section 5.B of this chapter.

[196] In this ruling the Court struck down the provisions laid down in Article 18 of the Unified Code on Public Security, with regard to the section on meetings held in places other than in a public venue.

[197] Evans 1968, note 187, at 619.

settings, the public performance of such works could give rise to dangerous situations."

In handing down Judgment 2/1957, the Court did not strike down Article 156 of the Unified Code on Public Security, which prohibited begging and collecting money without the authorization of the public security authorities. In this way, rather than giving priority to "the positive liberty to form associations and to enjoy free speech," the Court emphasized "the negative 'right' of citizens ... to avoid the risk of '*harassment*' and '*annoying coercion*.'"[198]

With regard to press freedom, the Court handed down "a not very convincing ruling"[199] – Judgment 38/1961 – in which the challenge to the constitutional legitimacy of Article 111 of the Unified Code on Public Security was declared without foundation. This article laid down an obligation to obtain a licence from the police authorities to operate a printing press or similar device. Moreover, with Judgment 9/1965, the Constitutional Court found Article 553 of the Criminal Code to be compatible with the Constitution, a measure that imposed sanctions on those publicly encouraging the adoption of contraceptives or distributing propaganda in favor of their use, along with Article 112 of the Unified Code on Public Security with regard to the section prohibiting the circulation of writings or drawings aimed at disseminating the use of contraceptives, inducing abortion or illustrating the use of such devices.[200]

In connection with the freedom of assembly, reference should be made to Judgment 54/1961, upholding the compatibility with the Constitution of the norm that envisaged the breaking up of meetings solely due to the lack of prior notice. In the view of the Court, the risk was of a "serious condition of unrest or public danger." With Judgment 120/1957, the Court even upheld the compatibility with the Constitution of Article 654 of the Criminal Code, which laid down criminal sanctions for seditious demonstrations or slogans in public venues or in places open to the public. In the view of the Court, such demonstrations or slogans "always imply an incitement to subversion of the public institutions and a danger to public order."

The case *par excellence* that was indicative of excessive caution on the part of the Constitutional Court concerned Article 2 of the Unified Code on Public Security, which, in the case of urgency or grave public necessity, vested prefects with the power "to adopt indispensable measures to safeguard public order and security." It should be noted that the opinion regarding prefects (who, as noted already, had mostly managed to escape the purge of Fascist officials)[201] was for the most part

[198] Merlini 1972, note 188, at 322. It was only with Judgment 519/1995 that the Court declared the unconstitutionality of nonintrusive begging.

[199] Barile 1967, note 182, at 641.

[200] As noted in Section 5 of this chapter, the Court declared the unconstitutionality of such norms in Judgment 49/1971.

[201] See Section 3 of this chapter.

decidedly negative. Indeed, they were considered to be the "symbol of . . . excessive bureaucratic power" and a "formidable instrument of antidemocratic repression,"[202] and in addition their ample powers were reputed to be "a cancer . . . [in the] Italian parliamentary regime."[203] As noted, the main target of the criticisms was Article 2 of the Unified Code on Public Security, considered to be capable of "turning any prefect into a mini dictator."[204] The Court handed down a ruling on the constitutionality of this provision initially with Judgment 8/1956, finding the claim that the provision was unconstitutional to be without foundation. The Court stated that it was necessary to make reference not to the meaning given to the provision in the system enacting it, but to the significance acquired on the basis of the interpretation given to it by the case law. In line with this interpretation, the Court ruled that the claim that this provision was unconstitutional was without foundation due to the fact that the measures adopted by the prefects were administrative acts adopted in the exercise of their functions, strictly limited in terms of time, for necessary and urgent matters, and bound by the principles of the legal order. As a result, according to the Court, Article 2 did not "subvert the order of public powers, since such measures remained within the legitimate exercise of powers granted to the administrative authorities at local level." The Court also specified that such measures, though capable "in theory of having an impact on all fields within which citizens exercise their rights safeguarded by the Constitution," were not to be "confused with laws or with decree laws, that had another character and other effects." Moreover, in an awareness that it was adopting an interpretation in contrast with the one normally applied in the case law of ordinary courts, the Constitutional Court recognized the fact that this provision could "give rise to arbitrary applications, when applying interpretations other than that adopted by the Court. However, in such cases, the present decision does not rule out a reconsideration of the constitutional legitimacy of the norm contained in the said article." This decision of the Constitutional Court represented one of the very first interpretative judgments of dismissal.

However, the "new" interpretation of the Constitutional Court was not followed by the Court of Cassation, which confirmed its own interpretative approach with a judgment of 1958,[205] upholding the view that prefects were allowed to intervene in relation to the exercise of freedoms recognized by the Constitution in the same way as ordinary law. Due to the fact that this line of reasoning was supported by numerous prefects and courts, the Constitutional Court felt obliged to change tack, and hence also its rulings. In Judgment 26/1961 the Court struck down part of Article 2, that is "only within the limits within which it grants the power to prefects to issue

[202] Basso 1958, note 184, at 270.

[203] Gaetano Salvemini, "Fu l'Italia prefascista una democrazia?" (1952) *Il Ponte*, 21.

[204] These were the words (reported by Basso 1958, note 184, at 223) of the Christian Democrat Umberto Merlin during the debate on the reform of the Unified Code on Public Security.

[205] Corte di Cassazione Sezioni Unite, June 16, 1958, no. 2068, in (1959) *Giurisprudenza costituzionale*, 550 ff.

orders that fail to comply with the principles of the legal order"; in other words, allowing a derogation from the rule according to which fundamental rights recognized in the Constitution can only be regulated by statutory acts. Also in this case there was no lack of negative criticism of the ruling, which according to some scholars was aimed at "not annulling ordinary norms particularly 'favoured' by the executive branch."[206] As highlighted by Sergio Bartole, the problem was that "once again, although it was declared unconstitutional, the text of the Unified Code on Public Security remained intact, since the declaration of unconstitutionality concerned only one of the norms that could be derived from it, that is to say, one of the meanings that could be attributed to it."[207]

Some scholars expressed concern about the use of the interpretative judgments of dismissal, which having first appeared as an extreme remedy to questions that were difficult to deal with, had become a useful but questionable expedient to avoid examining thorny questions.[208] From a practical point of view it is undeniable that these judgments – reflecting an extremely "conservative" approach on the part of the Constitutional Court – often produced deleterious effects in terms of the implementation of the Constitution and the process of "substantive" transition. Indeed, the fear of creating a legislative void[209] resulted in the upholding of legislation that was often incompatible with the 1948 Constitution. However, it is important not to overlook the more cautious assessments made by other scholars, according to which the interpretative judgments of dismissal may have served as a stimulus to judges

206 Tranfaglia 1973, note 46, at 261–262.

207 Bartole 2004, note 44, at 153. Just a few years later another conflict arose, this time even sharper, between the Constitutional Court and the Court of Cassation in relation to another interpretative judgment of dismissal, Judgment 11/1965. The Constitutional Court was required to ascertain, with reference to Article 24 of the Constitution (right to legal defense), the constitutionality of Article 392 of the Code of Criminal Procedure, concerning the applicability of certain defense guarantees in the case of summary *istruzione* proceedings (which are a form of pretrial proceeding), within the criminal justice system. The Constitutional Court overturned the consolidated interpretation adopted by the Court of Cassation (according to which certain defense guarantees were not applicable to the summary *istruzione* proceedings), establishing that the appeal was without foundation. In particular, the Constitutional Court handed down an interpretative judgment of dismissal, stating that the provision had to be interpreted, in line with Article 24 of the Constitution, so as to apply certain defense guarantees also to the summary *istruzione* proceedings. See again Bartole 2004, note 44, at 153 ff.; Giuseppe Campanelli, *Incontri e scontri tra Corte suprema e Corte costituzionale in Italia e in Spagna* (Giappichelli 2005), 219 ff.; John Henry Merryman and Vincenzo Vigoriti, "When Courts Collide: Constitution and Cassation in Italy" (1967) 15 *The American Journal of Comparative Law*, 665 ff.

208 See Tranfaglia 1973, note 46, at 241.

209 This fear was also expressed by the president of the Constitutional Court, Sandulli, in a speech on December 3, 1968 to mark the first 12 years of activity of the Court.

(especially those displaying scant regard for constitutional values) to implement such values in their day-to-day work when applying preconstitutional legislation.[210]

In any case, it should be noted that starting from its first rulings the Constitutional Court, with the support of a number of legal scholars, adopted an innovative interpretative approach that was consolidated in the legal literature and the case law of the superior courts, both ordinary and administrative, only in the 1960s and 1970s. In particular, the Court underlined the need to seek consistency at the constitutional level and to give priority as far as possible to an interpretation capable of bringing existing legislation into line with the Constitution.[211]

6 THE ITALIAN CONSTITUTIONAL COURT: A NEW BODY BREAKING WITH THE PAST AND GOING AGAINST THE TIDE

Traditionally it is argued that the three most significant dates in the process of transition to democracy are July 25, 1943 (the fall of Mussolini), June 2, 1946 (the referendum on the choice between Monarchy and Republic, and the election of the Constituent Assembly), and January 1, 1948 (the entry into force of the Constitution). In addition to these dates, one should also include in this list June 14, 1956, when the first judgment of the Constitutional Court was handed down. Just like the other three, this date marks a clean break with the past and the passage to a new phase. The initial stage (1948–1956) was characterized by the ongoing application of the Fascist legislation in the name of continuity of the State, whereas the subsequent phase (from 1956 until the end of the 1960s) was characterized by the dismantling of this legislation and an increasing implementation of the new constitutional provisions.

Following the first public session of the Constitutional Court (April 23, 1956), Piero Calamandrei argued that: "The Constitution is on the move."[212] In actual fact, considering the exceptional importance that this ruling had on the process of democratization of Italy, this expression could be paraphrased in the sense that "the Constitution *and the transition* are on the move." Moreover, it was precisely by eliminating the authoritarian legislation that the Court managed to achieve *full legitimation* in the constitutional framework, establishing itself as the first

[210] See Onida 1977, note 139, at 541. Onida, however, also argues that in various cases the Constitutional Court adopted a "radically innovative re-reading of the scope of the provision," with the sole purpose of bringing it into line with the Constitution (at 537).

[211] See Livio Paladin, "Costituzione, preleggi e codice civile" (1993) 1 *Rivista di diritto civile*, 24 ff. In this connection mention should be made of the Congress of the National Association of Magistrates, that took place in Gardone in 1965. The final motion of the Congress established by unanimous vote that it was the duty of judges: (1) to apply the provisions of the Constitution directly, in cases in which this was technically possible in relation to the matter before the court; (2) to refer to the Constitutional Court, also *ex officio* by ordinary judges, any laws that could not be reconciled (by means of interpretation) with the principles of the Constitution; and (3) to interpret all the laws in compliance with the principles laid down in the Constitution, that represent the new fundamental principles of the legal order.

[212] See Donatella Stasio, "Consulta garante della democrazia" (21 April 2006) *Il Sole-24 Ore*, 9.

constitutional body to declare unequivocally the *normativity* and *superiority* of the Constitution.

This role in *achieving a break with the past* should be assessed in light of the historical circumstances in which the Court was set up. The Court was part of the first generation of constitutional courts and as a result its status and role, especially at the beginning, were still of a largely experimental kind, if not a leap in the dark. A number of political forces in the Constituent Assembly were opposed to the setting up of the Court. Moreover, in the years following the promulgation of the Constitution, the doubts and uncertainties surrounding the completion of the constitutional project with regard to constitutional adjudication were among the factors further delaying the entry into force of the Court. In addition, mention should be made of the fact that the Italian Constitutional Court was operating in an international context that was radically different from that of the courts of the subsequent generations. Indeed, these later generations (as discussed in the following chapters) were in a position to benefit "from the turning point resulting from the opening up of national legal systems to the influence of the activity and interpretations of supranational and international bodies safeguarding fundamental rights":[213] suffice it to mention here the role played by the European Court of Human Rights.

It is important to consider the fact that the Constitutional Court encountered a series of difficulties in establishing itself within the institutional system particularly due to the obstructionism by the government majority and the superior courts. For example, starting with Judgment 1/1956 the president of the Council of Ministers – acting through the state attorney – intervened (in the cases based on the "incidental" method of constitutional review) in favor of the view that the Constitutional Court was not entitled to rule on the constitutionality of preconstitutional legislation, and in many cases defended the content of the Fascist laws. Moreover, the government majority often adopted a stance that was decidedly conservative, as in the cases when it failed to repeal the authoritarian legislation that was in contrast with the Constitution (e.g., it did not reform the Unified Code on Public Security), or in the cases when it failed to implement the provisions of the Constitution (as in the case of the obstructionism on the part of the Ministry of the Interior in concluding agreements [*intese*] with religious minorities, or the case of the failure to implement Article 40 of the Constitution [right to strike]).[214]

With regard to judicial power, a distinction needs to be drawn. On the one hand, from the entry into force of the Constitution the lower courts judges were generally quite open to the principles and values laid down in the Constitution. This favorable stance was confirmed by the fact that once the Constitutional Court started to operate, an alliance was formed between the Court and these lower courts judges

[213] Oreste Pollicino, *Allargamento dell'Europa ad Est e rapporto tra Corti costituzionali e Corti europee. Verso una teoria generale dell'impatto interordinamentale del diritto sovranazionale?* (Giuffrè 2010), 209.

[214] On these difficulties encountered by the Court see Adams and Barile 1958, note 35, at 260 ff.

aimed at implementing the provisions of the Constitution. On the other hand, the stance of the judges in the superior courts was diametrically opposed. In the period 1948–1956 they often declared the programmatic nature of the constitutional provisions regarding fundamental rights, stating that these programmatic provisions could not repeal the Fascist legislation. After the Constitutional Court took office, the Court of Cassation was quite reluctant to refer questions of constitutionality to the Constitutional Court, although in actual fact there were several cases that deserved to be reviewed by the Constitutional Court.[215]

As a result, in the first phase of its existence the Constitutional Court often seemed like a ship *sailing into the wind*. Its task was all the more difficult considering that the headwinds were represented by the three "traditional" branches of government, that had been present in the country for a long time, with a strong sense of their own identity and authority.[216] For its part, the Court was set up in the face of numerous difficulties, and represented a real innovation in the Italian legal order (and in part also in Europe), at times appearing to be something of an outsider. It is against the backdrop of these considerable difficulties that it is important to highlight the ability of the Court to break the legislative continuity with the past. Moreover, this would appear to explain (at least in part) its excessively cautious stance in certain rulings.

In the first 15 years of its activity the Court did not deal exclusively with the elimination of the preconstitutional legislation in contrast with the 1948 Constitution. One need only consider the important role played by the Court in the regulation of the regional organization of the state.[217] However, it was above all

[215] See Tranfaglia 1973, note 46, at 265; Romboli 2010, note 128, at 420–421.

[216] On the relations between the Constitutional Court and the three branches of government, the statement by the President of the Senate, Merzagora, on February 25, 1960 (reported in [1960] *Giurisprudenza costituzionale*, 454–455) is emblematic: "The position recently taken by the Constitutional Court, reported in a weekly magazine, should not be seen as a mark of obsequiousness to Parliament, and I mean the position that considers the Court to have a 'moderating' and 'propulsive' effect in relation to the Chamber of Deputies and the Senate, placing the Court not only outside but also above Parliament. According to these authoritative statements these functions, together with the supreme powers of the Head of State, that are deemed to be on the same footing as the Court itself, constitute the two, let me repeat, two, pillars of our Constitution. This leads me to state . . . that if there were two – and this is not the case – pillars in the constitutional order, they would be, in a democratic and parliamentary Republic, Parliament and the Government."

[217] On the first ten years of the Constitutional Court's case law concerning the relationship between the State and the regions see Evans 1968, note 187, at 609 ff. It is significant that Giuseppe Guarino, "Stato e regioni speciali nella giurisprudenza della Corte costituzionale" in Ettore Rotelli (ed.), *Dal regionalismo alla regione* (Il Mulino 1973), 129–130 argued that the regions "are as shaped by the Constitutional Court. And no other institution . . . has been subject to the same extent to the influence of the Constitutional Court's case law. . . . There is not one fundamental aspect of regional government that has not been shaped by the rulings of the Court." It should be noted that Guarino, who published this article in 1973, only referred to the five "special" regions (Sicily, Sardinia, Trentino Alto Adige, Valle D'Aosta, and Friuli Venezia Giulia) because the "ordinary" regions were only established in 1970 (see Chapter 5, Section 2).

with the striking down of Fascist legislation and hence the upholding of constitutional rights and freedoms that the country achieved the transition from an *uncertain* democracy (that was the case in Italy in 1956) to a *mature* democracy. This was the key feature, the heart of the *substantive* transition. The other rulings of the Court undoubtedly contributed to the process of democratization, but they did not represent the *condicio sine qua non* for Italy to become a consolidated democracy.

3

The Second Generation

The Case of the Spanish Constitutional Court

En una parte fundamental, la suerte de nuestra Constitución y la posibilidad del arraigo definitivo de la democracia y de la libertad en nuestro suelo van a estar en [las] manos [del Tribunal constitucional].

Eduardo García de Enterría[1]

1 THE TRANSITION TO DEMOCRACY AND THE POLITICS OF CONSENSUS

In the mid-1970s "democratic winds of change" were blowing across southern Europe:[2] in 1974 the Carnation Revolution took place in Portugal, overthrowing the long-lasting regime of António Salazar, and in the same year the Regime of the Colonels was deposed in Greece.[3] In Spain, it was the death of General Francisco Franco Bahamonde, on November 20, 1975, that marked the beginning of the transition to democracy.

[1] Eduardo García de Enterría, "La posición juridica del Tribunal constitucional en el sistema español: posibilidades y perspectivas" (1981) 1 *Revista española de derecho constitucional* 1, 105 ("In a fundamental part, the fate of our Constitution and the possibility for democracy and freedom to definitively take root in our soil will be in [the] hands [of the Constitutional Court]").

[2] Juan J. Linz, "La transición a la democracia en España en perspectiva comparada" in Ramón Cotarelo (ed.), *Transición politica y consolidación democrática. España (1975–1986)* (Centro de investigaciones sociológicas 1992), 435.

[3] On the international context of that period see Guy Hermet, "Environnement international et dimension historique de la transition politique en Espagne" (1984) 8 *Pouvoirs*, 5 ff.; Geoffrey Pridham, "The International Context of Democratic Consolidation: Southern Europe in Comparative Perspective" in Richard Gunther, P. Nikiforos Diamandouros, and Hans-Jürgen Puhle (eds.), *The Politics of Democratic Consolidation: Southern Europe in Comparative Perspective* (The Johns Hopkins University Press 1995), 166 ff.

One of the main characteristics of the Spanish transition, so successful that it served as a model for a number of countries in Latin America and Central and Eastern Europe that were addressing similar processes,[4] was the fact that it was *negotiated*. Indeed, it represented the outcome of a series of compromises and agreements between the government and the opposition, and, more generally, between the leading political actors taking part in the transition. Depending on the point of view, it was either a *reforma pactada* (negotiated reform), or a *ruptura pactada* (negotiated break with the past). The *reforma pactada*, supported by the establishment and the most conservative sectors of society, was aimed at implementing change on condition that it derived from the political system established by Franco, avoiding a clean break with the past. By contrast, the *ruptura pactada*, advocated by the democratic opposition, required discontinuity between the authoritarian regime and the democratic government that was taking shape.[5] Regardless of whether it was a reform or a break with the past (or a blend of the two, a *ruptiforma*),[6] what matters is that in the end a democratic regime was set up, and that this change was brought about by means of compromises and agreements. It was "the dialectic between *reforma* and *ruptura* . . . the key to understanding this process, which was successful thanks to the conclusion of a wide-ranging agreement, with a broad consensus between two positions that were *initially* ideologically opposed to each other."[7]

The negotiated nature of the transition concerned in the first place the *governance of the deep recession* that Spain had been going through since 1973. By means of the Pacts of Moncloa of October 1977 between the government, the opposition, and the trade unions, an austerity program was adopted, reducing public spending, restricting credit, increasing fiscal pressure, and introducing a wage freeze. In return, the government promised to introduce a progressive tax reform, to make the social security system more efficient, and to reorganize the financial system.[8]

The attempt to reach a compromise was decisive also on the *political front*. As soon as he was appointed president of the government in July 1976, Adolfo Suárez

[4] See Luis López Guerra, "The Application of the Spanish Model in the Constitutional Transitions in Eastern and Central Europe" (1998) 19 *Cardozo Law Review*, 1937 ff.

[5] See José M. Maravall and Julián Santamaria, "Political Change in Spain and the Prospects for Democracy" in Guillermo O'Donnell, Philippe C. Schmitter, and Laurence Whitehead (eds.), *Transitions from Authoritarian Rule: Southern Europe* (The Johns Hopkins University Press 1986), 73; José M. Maravall and Julián Santamaria, "Transición política y consolidación de la democracia en España" in José Félix Tezanos, Ramón Cortarelo, and Andrés de Blas (eds.), *La transición democrática española* (Editorial sistema 1989), 187.

[6] Antonio Torres del Moral, *Principios de Derecho constitucional español* (Atomo ediciones 1984), 5, argues that "the concepts of *ruptura* and *reforma* are asymmetrical, but not in contrast with each other .... The *ruptura* is a result, whereas the *reforma* is a method. The reformist method does not initially appear to lead to a *ruptura*, but it may lead to that outcome by means of a series of transformations."

[7] Raúl Morodo, *La transición política* (Tecnos 1985), 110.

[8] See Maravall and Santamaria 1986, note 5, at 86.

González launched an extremely delicate process of negotiation and bargaining with the various political forces aimed at the adoption of the *Political Reform Law*, laying down the basic principles that were to regulate the transition. In other words, the intention was to enact a *ley puente* (bridging law)[9] enabling the country to distance itself from its corporative past and to lay the foundations for a democratic system. This Law, so important for the transition that it was compared to the "crossing of the Rubicon,"[10] was characterized by its capacity to bring about profound changes to the legal order, though in certain respects it was linked to the Francoist past. Mention should be made, for example, of the final provision of the Law, that granted it the status of a "Fundamental Law," and in fact this Law is considered by some scholars as the eighth Fundamental Law of Francoist Spain.[11] In line with this spirit of continuity, it was decided not to include a preamble in the Law because it would have marked a clean break with the previous regime. In addition, the Law ensured the survival of two other institutions inherited from Franco regime, that is the monarchy (which was vested with some extremely important prerogatives), and the Council of the Kingdom.

However, the Law also contained a series of important provisions marking a clear departure from the past: indeed, it laid down the principle of popular sovereignty and the supremacy of the law, guaranteed universal suffrage, and established that fundamental rights and freedoms were inviolable and binding on all state authorities. It should be noted that, in setting up a bicameral system consisting of the Congress of Deputies and the Senate, the Law did not specify whether, in addition to performing ordinary legislative functions, the new Parliament was to serve also as a Constituent Assembly. This matter was decided in the first session of the new *Cortes*, which determined that they were also responsible for drafting the Constitution.

As a result, on November 18, 1976, with an "historical act of *harakiri*,"[12] the Francoist *Cortes* approved by a large majority the Political Reform Law, following

9 Jorge de Esteban, *Tratado de Derecho constitucional* (Universidad Complutense Madrid 1998), 92.

10 Ángel J. Sánchez Navarro, *La transición española en sus documentos* (Centro de estudios políticos y constitucionales 1998), 49.

11 See Pablo Lucas Verdú, *La octava Ley fundamental: crítica jurídicopolítica de la reforma Suárez* (Tecnos 1976). The seven Fundamental Laws regulating the powers of the state in Spain under Franco regime were as follows: *Fuero del Trabajo, Ley Constitutiva de las Cortes, Fuero de los Españoles, Ley del Referéndum Nacional, Ley de Sucesión en la Jefatura del Estado, Ley de Principios del Movimiento Nacional*, and *Ley Orgánica del Estado*.

12 de Esteban 1998, note 9, at 92. According to Morodo 1985, note 7, at 110 ff., the decision by the Francoist *Cortes* to approve the Political Reform Law can be explained with reference to five factors: the position of the king, who was in favor of a transition to democracy; the pressure of public opinion; an awareness on the part of the Francoist political class that its role had come to an end and that its institutions were no longer adequate; the fact that political change was considered to be desirable, as well as inevitable, for Western international interests; and the political strategy pursued by Adolfo Suárez.

the procedure laid down for the Fundamental Laws. The Political Reform Law was ratified by the Spanish people by means of a referendum held on December 15 the same year, and also on that occasion a broad consensus was reached: the turnout was close to 78 percent, and 94 percent of those casting a vote were in favor of the new Law.

The strategy of compromise continued also in the period after the approval of the Political Reform Law. Indeed, the Suárez government launched a series of negotiations with the left-wing parties that in the meantime had joined forces to create the Democratic Coordination or *Platajunta*, a body resulting from the merger of the Democratic Council of Spain (controlled by the Communist Party) and the Platform of Democratic Convergence (controlled by the Spanish Socialist Workers' Party).[13] A short time later, the Platform of Democratic Organizations was set up, bringing together not only the parties that were in the *Platajunta* but also other political forces, thus including almost the entire democratic opposition.

Between the approval of the Political Reform Law and the elections of June 1977, numerous measures were approved marking a strong discontinuity with the past and paving the way for elections. These measures included the abolition of the Public Order Court, which had been responsible for trying political offences under Franco regime; the legal recognition of political parties (with the exception of the Communist Party); the widening of the political amnesty and the recognition of freedom of expression and trade union rights; the dissolution of the National Movement, the single party of the Franco regime; the adoption of the new electoral law; and the adoption of the decree setting up the *Consell General de Catalunya* and the re-establishment of the *Juntas Generales* of the Basque provinces.[14] Furthermore, on April 9, 1977, the government decided to legalize also the Communist Party: at this point "the transition to democracy no longer seemed to have any chance of being reversed."[15]

However, the highest point of the *politics of consensus* was reached with the adoption of the 1978 Constitution, representing the outcome of an agreement between almost all the political forces elected to Parliament in the elections held on June 15, 1977, the first democratic elections after nearly 40 years of dictatorship.[16] The elections were won by the Union of the Democratic Centre, led by Suárez, with 34.4 percent of the vote, followed by the Spanish Socialist Workers' Party with 29.3 percent, that soon gained the support also of the six members elected for the

[13] On the role of the left-wing parties in the transition see Raúl Morodo, "Socialistes et communistes dans la transition" (1984) 8 *Pouvoirs*, 29 ff.; Gregorio Peces-Barba et al., *La izquierda y la Constitución* (Taula de Canvi 1978).

[14] See Sánchez Navarro 1998, note 10, at 54.

[15] Roberto L. Blanco Valdés and Vicente A. Sanjurjo Rivo, "Per comprendere la transizione politica spagnola (un contributo)" in Silvio Gambino (ed.), *Costituzionalismo europeo e transizioni democratiche* (Giuffrè 2003), 458.

[16] See Jordi Solé Tura and Eliseo Aja, "Une élaboration consensuelle" (1984) 8 *Pouvoirs*, 79 ff.

Popular Socialist Party. The Spanish Communist Party emerged as the third party with 9.3 percent of the vote, whereas the post-Francoist right (People's Alliance) attracted 8.2 percent of the vote. The other political forces included the Catalan nationalists (11 seats for the Democratic Pact for Catalonia, and 1 for the Democratic Left of Catalonia), and the Basque nationalists (eight seats for the Basque Nationalist Party, and one for *Euskadiko Ezkerra*). The Basque nationalists, however, as noted in the following text, decided not to vote in favor of the new Constitution.

The agreement between the various political forces was undoubtedly facilitated by the fact that the Union of the Democratic Centre failed to win an absolute majority of seats, thus requiring its members to negotiate with the other parties. However, this was not the only factor that favored the consensus in favor of the adoption of the new Constitution: there was indeed a deep-seated belief, resulting from historical experience, that it was necessary to adopt a constitution acceptable to all parties, or at least the vast majority of them. A constitution considered to favor one political formation in particular would have been deemed to be a failure as it would have once again marginalized a significant part of the Spanish people.[17]

The broad consensus that was achieved in the two houses of Parliament was reflected in society as a whole: in fact, in the referendum of December 6, 1978, the electorate ratified the new Constitution with 87.87 percent of those voting in favor, thus showing the intention of the Spanish people to mark a clear departure from the autocratic past. The Constitution was promulgated by the king on December 27 the same year and entered into force two days later, thus bringing the *formal* transition to a close.

A *The Role of King Juan Carlos*

A pivotal role in the process of democratic transition was played by the monarch, Juan Carlos de Borbón, who had been crowned King of Spain on November 22, 1975, pursuant to the provisions on the succession laid down in the Fundamental Laws of the Franco era.[18] The monarchy facilitated the transition to democracy in various ways. In the days after the death of Franco, Carlos Arias Navarro, a Francoist politician belonging to the most reactionary wing of the regime, who "never accepted the idea of transforming the inherited regime into a pluralist democracy," was appointed as president of the government.[19] His intention was the "post-mortem preservation of the Francoist State."[20] On July 1, 1976 Arias Navarro resigned, and

[17] See Jorge de Esteban, "El proceso constituyente español, 1977–1978" in Tezanos, Cortarelo and de Blas (eds.) 1989, note 5, at 299–302.

[18] It should be noted that the legitimate heir to the throne was not Juan Carlos, but his father, Juan de Borbón (in exile at the time), who formally renounced his claim to the throne on May 14, 1977.

[19] Maravall and Santamaria 1986, note 5, at 81.

[20] Morodo 1985, note 7, at 96.

the king, who in the meantime had made explicit his desire for Spain to move toward a parliamentary democracy, appointed Adolfo Suárez González to replace him. This move was decisive because, as noted already, Suárez was one of the chief architects of change (*el cambio*).

The king also contributed to the democratic transition by ensuring, in his capacity as commander-in-chief of the armed forces, that the military leaders accepted the main consequences of that process, most notably the creation of a state based on regional autonomy. In fact, the armed forces, which were "extremely zealous in their role as guardians of territorial unity and incapable of distinguishing between 'regional devolution' and 'separatism,'"[21] were suspicious of or even hostile to anything connected with the question of regional autonomy, and it is significant that a number of Basque terrorist attacks were aimed at military personnel.

In addition, it is important to consider the role played by the king in the attempted *coup d'état* that took place on February 23, 1981, when Lieutenant-Colonel Antonio Tejero Molina, together with a number of officers from the *Guardia Civil*, stormed Congress, holding the members of Parliament hostage until the following morning. Meanwhile, in Valencia, the lieutenant-general of the third military district, Jaime Milans del Bosch, gave orders to enter the city with tanks, declared the state of emergency, and sought to persuade other members of the military to support the coup. One of the main objectives was to install General Alfonso Armada as president of the government. It was the intervention of Juan Carlos that for the most part determined the collapse of the *golpe*: first of all the king made sure he had the support of the leaders of the armed forces, and during the night made a televised address to the nation in which he took a firm stand against the coup in defence of the Constitution.[22]

Thanks to his crucial role in the democratic transition, Juan Carlos de Borbón was known as "the pilot of change."[23] However, it should be pointed out that *this outcome could by no means be taken for granted*. On the contrary, several indicators initially suggested that he might have favored the continuity with the Francoist regime. Suffice it to mention Franco's address before the *Cortes* on July 22, 1969 to mark the appointment of Don Juan Carlos as his successor at the *Jefatura del Estado*:

> The decision we shall take today should contribute, in a major way, to everything being secured and well secured for the future [*a que todo quede atado y bien atado para el futuro*] .... It must be clear and well understood by Spaniards of today and of future generations that this Monarchy is the one ... that was instaurated through

[21] Maravall and Santamaria 1986, note 5, at 87.

[22] On this crucial moment in Spanish history see Javier Cercas, *Anatomía de un instante* (Literatura Mondadori 2009).

[23] Charles T. Powell, *El piloto del cambio. El Rey, la monarquía y la transición a la democracia* (Planeta 1991).

> the Law on Succession approved on 7 July 1947.... This is the Monarchy of the National Movement, the perennial continuator of its principles, institutions and of the glorious tradition of Spain. For this reason, and in order to implement the provisions on the succession, when the day shall come, the Crown shall be instaurated through the person we are presenting today as the successor.

Following this address, Juan Carlos knelt down and took an oath of allegiance to Franco, the principles of the National Movement and the Fundamental Laws of the Franco regime.

In light of all this, it was not possible to rule out the possibility that Juan Carlos, in order to guarantee the continuity of Francoism, would be reluctant to support democratic reforms. In fact it is significant that the presence of Juan Carlos helped to reassure many of those who feared a clean break with the previous regime.[24] The "great paradox," on the contrary, was that "the King used the absolute powers that had been granted to him by General Franco to dismantle Francoism and to establish a new democratic and parliamentary regime."[25] Indeed, Juan Carlos immediately realized that

> the Crown would have been far more vulnerable in an autocratic regime without a genuine separation of powers than in a democratic Monarchy .... Although it may appear to be surprising, the more the King gave up his powers, the freer he became, the more he distanced himself from political responsibilities, the more he strengthened his institutional role.[26]

In this way, in just three years (1975–1978), Spain accomplished the transition from a Francoist monarchy to a parliamentary and democratic monarchy.[27]

B *The Territorial Organization of the State*

The territorial organization of the state, which is still an extremely sensitive matter in Spain (as discussed in further detail later in the book),[28] represented one of the major obstacles (if not the main obstacle)[29] in the transition to democracy. This was

[24] Ibid., at 19.

[25] Javier Tajadura Tejada, "La legitimidad de la Monarquía parlamentaria" in Carolina León Bastos and Víctor Alejandro Wong Meraz (eds.), *Homenaje al Doctor Jorge Carpizo en Madrid* (Porrúa 2010), 932.

[26] Powell 1991, note 23, at 18.

[27] In the view of Tajadura Tejada 2010, note 25, at 912, it does not make much sense to speak of "restoration of the monarchy" because in actual fact "there was no restoration at all, but the establishment, for the first time in Spanish history, of a democratic Monarchy."

[28] See Section 3.D of this chapter.

[29] See Victor Ferreres Comella, *The Constitution of Spain: A Contextual Analysis* (Hart 2013), 197.

mainly due to the demands made by Catalonia and above all the Basque Country[30] aimed at regaining the forms of autonomy they had enjoyed under the Second Republic.[31] Indeed, during that period, Catalonia and the Basque Country had managed to approve their own Statutes of Autonomy (respectively, in 1932 and 1936), though Franco eliminated these forms of autonomy immediately after coming to power.[32] As a result, the intention of creating a state based on autonomous regions, an "Autonomous State" (*Estado autonómico*) or "State of Autonomies" (*Estado de las autonomías*), after the death of the *Caudillo*, constituted in many ways a reaction to the absolute centralism of the Francoist regime.

The democratic transition was thus inextricably linked to the territorial organization of the state, especially with regard to Catalan and Basque autonomy.[33] According to Guy Carcassonne,

> [national] unity was one of the founding principles of the dictatorship, since the territorial claims, crossing classes and contexts, were one of the essential elements of the anti-Franco struggles, and the issue had a strong symbolic value. Finding a solution to this issue was therefore essential for the future of the new democracy.[34]

In light of this situation, it is not difficult to understand why, after the death of Franco, there was an awareness of the need to restore the autonomous regimes of Catalonia and the Basque country as soon as possible, even before the entry into force of the new Constitution. Francesc de Carreras points out that one of the most popular slogans during the anti-Franco demonstrations in that period was *Libertad, amnistía y estatuto de autonomía*, that is freedom, amnesty, and statute of autonomy.[35] As a result, parallel to the constitution-drafting process, the "provincial autonomous regimes," or "pre-autonomous regimes," were set up. The most significant stages in this process of decentralization were the issuing of the Royal Decree Law 41/1977, that re-established the government (*Generalitat*) of Catalonia, and the

30 In the view of Andrés De Blas, "El problema nacional-regional español en la transición" in Tezanos, Cortarelo and de Blas (eds.) 1989, note 5, at 601, "the problem was and is – fundamentally – a Basque problem."

31 It should be noted that the Spanish Constitution of 1931 envisaged a regional State (defined, in Article 1(2), as an "integral State," to distinguish it from the unitary state and the federal state).

32 With regard to Catalonia, reference should be made to the laws of the *Jefadura del Estado* of April 5, 1938 and September 8, 1939; with regard to the Basque Country, reference should be made to the decree law of June 23, 1937.

33 See Diego Muro and Alejandro Quiroga, "Building the Spanish Nation: The Centre-Periphery Dialectic" (2004) 4 *Studies in Ethnicity and Nationalism* 2, 28 ff.; Eliseo Aja, "Spain: Nation, Nationalities, and Regions" in John Loughlin (ed.), *Subnational Democracy in the European Union: Challenges and Opportunities* (Oxford University Press 2001), 231–232; Enric Martínez-Herrera and Thomas Jeffrey Miley, "The Constitution and the Politics of National Identity in Spain" (2010) 16 *Nations and Nationalism*, 6 ff.

34 Guy Carcassonne, "Les 'nationalités' dans la Constitution" (1978) 8 *Pouvoirs*, 117.

35 Francesc de Carreras, "Prólogo. El federalismo en España" in Javier Tajadura Tejada and Josu De Miguel Bárcena (eds.), *Federalismos del siglo XXI* (Centro de estudios políticos y constitucionales 2014), 22.

Royal Decree Law 1/1978, that set up the pre-autonomous regime of the Basque country and established the General Council as its governing body. In the rest of Spain, the problem of autonomy was not so urgent as to hold up the completion of the constitution-making process. However, the government decided to give in to pressure from the other regions, that aspired not to the "re-establishment" but to the "establishment" of autonomous regimes, thus granting such regimes to other regions where this pressure was nonexistent. Therefore, this *"provisional 'regionalization' of the State"*[36] represented the initial attempt to respond to the centralism of Franco regime.

The territorial organization of the state was a particularly sensitive matter also in light of Basque terrorism, especially on the part of ETA, which engaged in criminal actions that modified a process that would otherwise have been largely peaceful.[37] Terrorist violence escalated during the years of the transition, with the most acute phase from 1978 to 1980.[38] This does not appear to be a matter of chance: in fact, the growth of terrorism may be explained, among other factors, by "the inadequate governance of political change, which resulted in many expectations not being met … and gave rise to a propensity to aggression in certain sectors of society."[39] The delay in granting an amnesty to numerous Basque detainees imprisoned under Franco regime, the reluctance to recognize the symbolic and political aspirations of Basque nationalism (including the failure to recognize in the Constitution the right to self-determination),[40] and the maintenance of a public order policy similar to the

[36] Pedro Cruz Villalón, *La curiosidad del jurista persa, y otros estudios sobre la Constitución* (Centro de estudios políticos y constitucionales 1999), 412. "Pre-autonomous regimes" were set up in Navarra, Galicia, Aragón, Canarias, Valencia, Andalusia, Islas Baleares, Extremadura, Castilla y León, Asturias, Murcía, and Castilla-La Mancha.

[37] See Michel Rosenfeld, "Constitution Making, Identity Building and Peaceful Transition to Democracy: Theoretical Reflections Inspired by the Spanish Example" (1998) 19 *Cardozo Law Review*, 1891 ff.

[38] Maravall and Santamaria 1986, note 5, at 92, point out that "from 1976 to 1982, ETA wounded 540 people and murdered 345, including among the latter some 30 high-ranking military officers. Terrorism also increased throughout these years. Sixty-eight people were killed in the Basque country in 1977, 70 in 1978, and 130 in 1980. At the same time extreme right-wing violence also increased, particularly after 1978, producing 40 deaths and 128 wounded in the Basque country alone."

[39] Fernando Reinares, "Democratización y terrorismo en el caso español" in Tezanos, Cortarelo and de Blas (eds.) 1989, note 5, at 629.

[40] E.g., Juan María Bandrés of the *Euskadiko Ezkerra* underlined during the constituent debates that the right to self-determination "does not necessarily mean separatism or secessionism: self-determination means the right to choose the political future of a people, and to choose it autonomously, without external interference, and implies the right to remain united or to separate – I wish to underline – peaceably according to the will of the majority of the people in a responsible manner" (*Diario de Sesiones del Senado*, August 19, 1978, 40, 1602). The position of the Catalan nationalists was decidedly more moderate, with some exceptions. One just has to think of Lluís Maria Xirinacs, who argued that the "Spanish nation" did not exist, but only the "Spanish State" (*Diario de Sesiones del Senado*, August 18, 1978, 39, 1554). In particular, Xirinacs proposed the creation of a Confederation, and believed that the Constitution, in Article 2, should have recognized and safeguarded "the right to Self-determination of the

one that characterized the previous regime, along with the deep recession the country was facing at the time, were the factors that heightened the feelings of frustration and resentment in Basque society, thus strengthening the hand of the terrorist groups.[41]

The Basque National Party made no attempt to hide its dissatisfaction with the territorial structure envisaged by the Constitution, and in fact when the Constitution was put to the vote, its members were among the very few who either voted against or abstained.[42] In addition, the party called on its supporters to abstain from the constitutional referendum, and this recommendation was to a large extent followed. Whereas the average turnout was 67.1 percent, in the Basque country it was just 44.7 percent. This was a significant result for the Basque nationalists, who were able to claim that the Basque people had rejected the new Constitution.[43]

In the years following the enactment of the 1978 Constitution, the Basque National Party took an ambivalent stance toward the new constitutional order: on the one hand, in 1979 it adopted the Statute of Autonomy of the Basque Country (urging its supporters to vote in favor), whereas, on the other hand, it boycotted all the sessions of the *Cortes* from January to September 1980. Moreover, in 1983 it refused to fly the Spanish flag in the municipalities "controlled" by the party (hence the expression: "the war of the flags"), and until the end of the 1980s, it failed to condemn the use of violence by ETA.[44]

Among the various factors that help to explain this stance, one refers to the procedure by which the Constitution was drafted. Before it was debated in Parliament, Congress appointed a Commission on constitutional affairs and public freedoms, which then appointed a drafting committee (*Ponencia*) entrusted with the task of writing the first draft of the Constitution. This committee consisted of seven members: three from the Union of the Democratic Centre, one from the Spanish Socialist Workers' Party, one from the People's Alliance, one from the Communist Party, and one from the Catalan minority. There were no representatives of the mixed group, or of the Basque minority. In the view of Raúl Morodo, this composition of the *Ponencia* was discriminatory because not all the parliamentary groups were represented. Moreover, according to Morodo, if the Basque minority

peoples of the Confederation and the right to Autonomy of the regions belonging to it. Each people has the right to its own State. Each State is based on its own National Constitution" (Senado, *Proyecto de Constitución*, Enmienda no. 444).

41 See Reinares 1989, note 39, at 629–630.

42 In the Congress the vote was 94.1 percent in favor, and 1.8 percent against (some deputies belonging to the People's Alliance and *Euskadiko Ezkerra*) with 4.1 percent abstaining (the Basque Nationalist Party, some members of the People's Alliance, the mixed group and the Catalan minority). In the Senate the vote was 94.4 percent in favor, and 2.3 percent against (senators of the Basque group and the mixed group) with 3.3 percent abstaining (once again members of the Basque group and the mixed group).

43 See Reinares 1989, note 39, at 633.

44 See Richard Gunther, Hans-Jürgen Puhle, and P. Nikiforos Diamandouros, "Introduction" in Gunther, Diamandouros, and Puhle (eds.) 1995, note 3, at 14.

had been represented, they might not have abstained from voting on the Constitution.[45]

As argued later in the text,[46] by adopting a structure that was from many points of view ambiguous and incomplete, the 1978 Constitution did not manage to provide a satisfactory solution to the issue of the territorial organization of the state. It is difficult to say whether the structure envisaged in the Constitution, that is the creation of a "State of Autonomies," constituted "the only *possible political solution*."[47] What is certain is that the territorial question could not be considered to be resolved, and as a result it ended up having a considerable impact on the *substantive* transition.

2 THE SETTING UP OF THE CONSTITUTIONAL COURT

A "consensual creation":[48] this is the expression used by Antonio Torres del Moral to describe the establishment of the Constitutional Court. Indeed, during the constituent debates, almost all the political forces were in favor of setting up a constitutional review body.[49] The only reservations (it would be misleading to speak of an opposition in the proper sense of the term) came from the members of the Communist Party, who – like their Italian counterparts 30 years earlier – were afraid that such a body would adopt a conservative stance and that it would in some way hinder Parliament's functions. According to Jordi Solé Tura, for example, there was a risk that the Constitutional Court would be "difficult to keep in check"[50] and that it would become "a kind of third Chamber that [would end up] imposing its will on Congress and the Senate . . ., thus putting a brake on their actions."[51]

There are numerous factors that help to explain such a broad-ranging consensus on the establishment of the Constitutional Court. Above all, there was a strong

45 See Morodo 1985, note 7, at 174.

46 See Section 3.D of this chapter.

47 Morodo 1985, note 7, at 203.

48 Antonio Torres del Moral, "El Tribunal constitucional español en negativo: lagunas y rectificaciones; cuestiones disputadas, inéditas, irresueltas, menores y de lege ferenda" in Víctor Bazán (ed.), *Derecho procesal constitucional americano y europeo* (Abeledo Perrot 2010), vol. I, 699.

49 The Spanish constituent debates can be examined only in part because the proceedings of the *Ponencia*, the committee entrusted with writing the first draft of the Constitution, are not in the public domain. However, it is possible to examine the debates on the drafting of the Constitution in the *Cortes*.

50 *Diario de sesiones del Congreso de los Diputados*, June 19, 1978, 92, 3448.

51 *Diario de sesiones del Congreso de los Diputados*, July 20, 1978, 115, 4528. It should be noted that also among the socialists there was a certain degree of skepticism in relation to constitutional review of legislation. Pedro Jover, e.g., underlined his "limited enthusiasm toward constitutional review of legislation. It is not that we deny its theoretical validity; in practice, however, the objectively conservative function that these institutions have played leads us to take an extremely prudent approach" (Pedro Jover, "Tribunal de Garantias Constitucionales" in Peces-Barba et al. 1978, note 13, at 125).

desire to make a clean break with the previous authoritarian regime, and this required, among other things, an effective system of protection of fundamental rights. In this sense a constitutional court seemed to offer the best guarantees. Moreover, a number of European countries had already established such a court, and in fact the Spanish constitutional drafters made reference, in particular, to the Italian *Corte costituzionale* and the German *Bundesverfassungsgericht*.[52]

Another reason that explains the setting up of the Constitutional Court is the fact that the judiciary had not been purged: indeed, although the ordinary judges had been appointed under the Francoist regime, they were not replaced with the advent of democratic government.[53] Bearing this in mind, the drafters preferred to grant an *ad hoc* body the power to ascertain whether the laws enacted by the new democratic Parliament complied with the Constitution or not.[54]

The setting up of the Constitutional Court can also be explained with reference to the regional structure of the country.[55] Also in this case the drafters referred in particular to the Italian and German constitutional courts, which carry out their functions in decentralized countries, thus confirming the strict connection between the decentralized nature of the state and constitutional justice.[56]

By contrast, there does not appear to be sufficient evidence in support of the claim, put forward by some scholars,[57] that the establishment of the Constitutional Court was favored by the fact that Spain had had an analogous court in the past, that is the Court of Constitutional Guarantees (*Tribunal de garantías constitucionales*), envisaged by the 1931 Constitution.[58] Indeed, the constituent debates demonstrate that the references to this Court were few and far between, and it was mainly cited as a negative example.[59] As a result, it may be said that the drafters made an attempt to learn from an unfortunate experience: instead of taking the Court of Constitutional

52 On the influence of foreign sources, see Miguel Herrero de Miñon, "Les sources étrangères de la Constitution" (1984) 8 *Pouvoirs*, 97 ff.; de Esteban 1998, note 9, at 132 ff.

53 Carlo Guarnieri, *Magistratura e politica in Italia* (Il Mulino 1982), 132. On the judiciary during the Francoist regime, see José J. Toharia, "Judicial Independence in an Authoritarian Regime: The Case of Contemporary Spain" (1975) 9 *Law and Society Review* 3, 475 ff.

54 See Victor Ferreres Comella, "The Spanish Constitutional Court: Time for Reforms" (2008) 3 *Journal of Comparative Law* 2, 23.

55 See Cruz Villalón 1999, note 36, at 436.

56 See Chapter 1, Section 3.

57 See, e.g., Francisco Rubio Llorente and Manuel Aragón Reyes, "La jurisdicción constitucional" in Alberto Predieri and Eduardo García de Enterría (eds.), *La Constitución española de 1978* (Civitas 1980), 798, who stress the "force of precedent" of the Court of Constitutional Guarantees; see also Ferreres Comella 2008, supra note 54, at 23.

58 See Chapter 1, Section 4.

59 Among the few favorable references to the Court of Constitutional Guarantees, mention should be made of Francisco Letamendía Belzunce, who was in favor of including in the new Constitutional Court representatives of the Autonomous Communities, as it was the case in the Court of Constitutional Guarantees (*Diario de sesiones del Congreso de los Diputados*, June 16, 1978, 91, 3433–3434).

Guarantees as a model to emulate, they were careful to avoid repeating the same mistakes.[60]

The analysis of the constitution-making process shows that, with regard to constitutional justice, there were not many differences between the articles in the draft Constitution produced by the committee (*Ponencia*) and the final text of the Constitution. The debates (not considered to be particularly relevant)[61] did not focus on the desirability of setting up a Constitutional Court (as was the case in Italy), but rather on the technical aspects concerning the composition of the Court, its independence, and powers.

Among the most significant changes to Title IX of the Constitution (regulating the Constitutional Court), mention should be made, in the first place, of Article 159. The *Informe* of the *Ponencia* modified the project by increasing the number of members of the Court (from 11 to 12), with the result that the Senate was to propose not just three judges but four, the same number as Congress. In addition, the principle of independence was included along with the provision that the members of the Court could not be removed from office. In relation to Article 161 (but also to Article 53(2)), the *Informe* of the *Ponencia* restricted the *recurso de amparo* (which consists of an individual constitutional complaint to the Constitutional Court for the protection of fundamental rights) to the rights and freedoms laid down in Article 14 (principle of equality) and the first section of the second chapter of Title I, in addition to the right to conscientious objection (Article 30(2)). Furthermore, the government was granted the right to impugn before the Constitutional Court the provisions and decisions adopted by the bodies of the Autonomous Communities (*Comunidades Autónomas*). The text of Article 162 was modified by the Commission of Congress, which eliminated the powers of the presidents of Congress and the Senate to refer legislation to the Constitutional Court for constitutional review, and increased from 25 to 50 the number of senators entitled to make such a referral to the Court. In addition, it should be noted that the *Informe* of the *Ponencia* amended Article 164, so that no further appeal against the rulings of the Constitutional Court was allowed.

With regard to the provisions not included under Title IX, the *Informe* of the *Ponencia* stated that the Constitutional Court was also vested with the power of *ex ante* constitutional review of Treaties. Moreover, some significant changes were made to Article 153(a): in addition to replacing the term "historic Territories" with "Autonomous Communities," the *Informe* placed limits on the review of the acts adopted by the Autonomous Communities on the part of the Constitutional Court, establishing that the Court could only verify the constitutionality (and not the legality) of such acts.

[60] See Francisco Tomás y Valiente, *Escritos sobre y desde el Tribunal constitucional* (Centro de estudios constitucionales 1993), 30–31.

[61] See Pedro J. González-Trevijano Sánchez, *El Tribunal constitucional* (Aranzadi 2000), 62.

In addition to gaining the support of almost all the political parties, the Court found supporters outside political circles strictly speaking; indeed, it was able to rely on the support of most public law scholars, many of whom had spent a period of study and research in Italian or German Universities. The result was that "from the very beginning of the constitution-making process . . ., only a few institutions . . . were treated with such noble and general concern of political and technical nature as the Constitutional Court."[62]

The Organic Law of the Constitutional Court (no. 2, October 3, 1979)[63] was rapidly approved adopting the procedure for urgent matters as laid down in Article 103 of the Regulations of Congress in force at the time. The draft version presented to the *Cortes* by the government was preceded by a kind of preamble outlining the purposes and the content of the Law:

> The Constitutional Court, responsible for ensuring the supremacy of the Constitution and for guaranteeing that our legal system is in line with it, is . . . an essential element in the legal and political organization of the State.. . . Our Constitution follows a dominant current of thought of our times, by which the progressive legal regulation of political relations is pursued, in order to strengthen the principle of authority of law. The configuration of this fundamental institution is assigned by the Constitution to an Organic Law, the essential form of which is already sufficiently defined in the Constitution itself, of which the present Law is no more than a further development.[64]

The draft submitted to the *Cortes* was subject to very few modifications, for the most part technical or editorial changes. Among the substantive modifications worthy of note, mention should be made of the fact that a new paragraph was added to Article 28, concerning the nature of organic laws.[65] Moreover, it was specified that cases could be referred to the Constitutional Court *ex officio* by ordinary judges or upon petition of one of the parties to the case (*cuestión de inconstitucionalidad*).

Unlike what happened in Italy,[66] the procedure for the appointment of the first judges of the Constitutional Court – which represented the outcome of negotiations between the Union of the Democratic Centre and the Spanish Socialist Workers' Party – did not give rise to any particular difficulties. Indeed, once the Organic Law

[62] Tomás y Valiente 1993, note 60, at 34.

[63] On this Organic Law see Juan Luis Requejo Pagés (ed.), *Comentarios a la Ley Orgánica del Tribunal Constitucional* (Tribunal Constitucional, Boletín Oficial del Estado 2001).

[64] The complete draft version is to be found in *Tribunal constitucional. Trabajos parlamentarios* (Cortes Generales 1980), 5–29.

[65] Article 28(2) provides that "In the same way the Court may strike down as unconstitutional due to violation of Article 81 of the Constitution the provisions of a decree law, a legislative decree or a law that has not been enacted with the status of an organic law or a legislative provision of an Autonomous Community, in cases in which these provisions regulate matters reserved for the Organic Law or imply the amendment or repeal of a law approved with that status, regardless of the content."

[66] See Chapter 2, Section 2.

had been approved, in the three months after the date of its entry into force – as envisaged in the first transitory provision – Congress, the Senate, and the government submitted to the king their proposals for the appointment of, respectively, four, four, and two judges, who were appointed by the monarch on February 23, 1980.[67] On July 12 the same year the Constitutional Court formally took office, with the result that, some 19 months after the adoption of the Constitution, the Court started its activity. This was a reasonably short period, especially when compared to the time required for the Italian Constitutional Court to take office (eight years). In all probability the rapid establishment of the Constitutional Court was favored by the difficulties associated with the construction of the State of Autonomies, giving rise to the urgent need to appoint an arbiter capable of dealing with these sensitive territorial matters.

In the view of Pedro Cruz Villalón, the decisions concerning constitutional justice made by the constitutional drafters in 1978 (decisions that were "indicative of wisdom and common sense"), along with the rapid approval of the Organic Law in 1979 (that "faithfully implemented the ... provisions of Title IX of the Constitution"), and the first composition of the Constitutional Court in 1980 (that consisted of the "most prestigious legal scholars of the time")[68] indicate that there is reason to claim that the Spanish Constitutional Court was born under a "lucky star."[69]

3 THE FOUR MAIN AREAS OF INTERVENTION OF THE CONSTITUTIONAL COURT DURING THE SUBSTANTIVE TRANSITION

Before examining the role played by the Constitutional Court during the *substantive* transition, it is important to consider the social and political context of Spain in that period. The early years after the entry into force of the Constitution, like those immediately before, were particularly difficult: the deep recession, the regional question, terrorist violence, and the continuation of Francoist integralism all contributed to the impression of a fragile democracy. The elections on March 1, 1979 confirmed the Union of the Democratic Centre as the leading political party in the country, with 34.95 percent of the votes, followed by the Spanish Socialist Workers' Party with 30.50 percent. The position of the Communist Party improved

67 Because at that stage the General Council of the Judiciary had not yet been established, the other two judges appointed by the king upon proposal of that body took office a few months later, i.e. after their appointment on November 7, 1980.

68 The first 12 Constitutional Court judges were Manuel García-Pelayo (president), Jerónimo Arozamena Sierra (vice-president), Francisco Tomás y Valiente, Gloria Begué Cantón, Manuel Díez de Velasco Vallejo, Luis Díez-Picazo y Ponce de León, Rafael Gómez-Ferrer Morant, Ángel Latorre Segura, Aurelio Menéndez Menéndez, Francisco Rubio Llorente, Ángel Escudero del Corral, and Plácido Fernández Viagas.

69 All the quotations are taken from Pedro Cruz Villalón, "El estado del Tribunal constitucional" (2009) 191 *Claves de razón práctica*, 4 ff.

slightly (10.66 percent), whereas the People's Alliance lost votes, falling below 6 percent. A good result was achieved by the nationalist and regional parties.

In spite of his electoral success, President Suárez soon encountered difficulty in holding his party together and implementing his electoral program. Indeed, once the Constitution had been promulgated, with the end of the phase of "high politics,"[70] during which he had turned out to be an outstanding statesman, Suárez was not capable of dealing effectively with the problems of day-to-day administration arising in the postconstitutional phase. For this and other reasons, on January 29, 1981 he decided to resign, and was replaced by Leopoldo Calvo-Sotelo. It was precisely during the investiture of Calvo-Sotelo as president of the government that the attempted *coup d'état* of February 23, 1981 took place.[71]

A real turning point came with the elections of October 28, 1982, when there was a reversal of the fortunes of the main political parties: indeed, the Spanish Socialist Workers' Party became the largest party in Spain, obtaining the absolute majority of seats in Parliament, whereas the Union of the Democratic Centre came close to collapse, with the number of deputies falling from 168 to just 12. The Communist Party also obtained a poor result, losing more than a million votes. The People's Alliance, by contrast, gained a considerable number of votes, becoming the largest opposition party. In Catalonia and the Basque Country, the nationalist parties obtained a good result, confirming or even increasing their representation in Parliament.[72]

These elections, resulting for the first time in an alternation of power from the Union of the Democratic Centre to the Spanish Socialist Workers' Party, represent a "milestone"[73] in the Spanish democratic transition.[74] The Socialists managed to deal with numerous matters that had been left unresolved: indeed, between 1982 and 1989, the first two administrations led by Felipe González launched a process of reforms characterized by the implementation of constitutional provisions relating to fundamental rights, a policy of industrial conversion, the reform of the

[70] Carlos Barrera, *Historia del proceso democrático en España. Tardofranquismo, transición y democracia* (Fragua 2002), 150.

[71] It should be mentioned that during the attempted *coup d'état* Suárez was the only person among those who were present at the Congress, together with General Manuel Gutiérrez Mellado (vice-president of the government) and Santiago Carrillo (leader of the Communist Party), who did not throw themselves to the ground, in spite of the shots fired by the Civil Guard.

[72] On the 1982 elections see José M. Maravall, *La política de la transición* (Taurus 1985), 84 ff.

[73] Maravall and Santamaria 1986, note 5, at 100.

[74] According to some legal scholars, these elections mark the end of the transition. It has rightly been pointed out, however, that the idea that the alternation between parties in government is symptomatic of a consolidated democratic regime would lead to "some rather absurd applications to the real world: according to this criterion, the democratic regimes of Japan and Italy (both of which have survived and thrived but whose governments were dominated by a single party for over four decades) would not have been regarded as consolidated until the 1990s" (Gunther, Puhle, and Diamandouros 1995, note 44, at 12).

military justice system, the campaign against terrorism, the decriminalization of abortion,[75] the reform of higher education, and the development of the welfare state.[76]

The path toward democracy was favored by a pro-European and Atlanticist policy. In 1977, with the unanimous approval of Congress and the Senate, Spain joined the Council of Europe; in 1979 it ratified the European Convention on Human Rights (ECHR),[77] and in 1981 it recognized the right to submit individual applications as laid down in Article 34 of the ECHR.[78] Moreover, in mid-1982, in spite of opposition on the part of the Spanish Socialist Workers' Party and the Communist Party, Spain became a member of NATO. Membership of NATO was confirmed by a referendum in 1986 that was proposed by the socialists, who in the meantime had changed their stance on the issue.

The process of applying for membership of the European Economic Community (EEC) was initiated de facto in February 1978, when Suárez appointed Calvo-Sotelo as Minister for Relations with the EEC. The requirements laid down by the 1978 European Council in Copenhagen (consisting of respect for the principles of pluralist democracy and human rights) were met (albeit with a certain amount of difficulty), and as a result on January 1, 1986, together with Portugal, Spain joined the European Economic Community. Accession to the EEC was a significant achievement, particularly due to the fact that for a long time the Spanish had considered the European Community to be a "democratic dream."[79] In this regard, accession to the EEC brought with it a sense of accomplishment of the democratic transition and provided an "external convalidation" of the new Spanish democracy.[80]

[75] On the importance of the right to abortion for the purposes of promoting gender equality, see Susanna Mancini, *Un affare di donne. L'aborto tra eguale libertà e controllo sociale* (Cedam 2012).

[76] See Blanco Valdés and Sanjurjo Rivo 2003, note 15, at 464.

[77] At the time, for the purposes of joining the Council of Europe, an undertaking by the state to ratify the European Convention on Human Rights was considered to be a matter of purely political significance.

[78] The *optional* recognition of the right of the individuals to apply directly to the Court was eliminated only with the entry into force of Protocol no. 11 in 1998, when the right of individual petition became mandatory.

[79] Alejandro Lorca Corrons, "The Spanish Experience Following Accession," paper presented at the University Association for Contemporary European Studies (1988), cited by Pridham 1995, note 3, at 177.

[80] Pridham 1995, note 3, at 178. It should be noted that in examining the applications submitted by Spain and Portugal (and the one submitted by Greece) the commission did not carry out a detailed evaluation of the content of the constitutions, nor of their effective degree of implementation, but simply highlighted the fact that joining the EEC would undoubtedly "strengthen the European ideal," contributing to the consolidation of democracy of these three countries that had just emerged from a period of authoritarian rule. It is evident that this approach overlooked "the fact that there was not necessarily a correspondence between the formal recognition of certain principles and actual implementation" (Laura Cappuccio, "Le condizioni costituzionali di adesione all'Unione europea" [2005] *Forum di Quaderni*

In light of the preceding, it becomes evident that the social and political context in which the Constitutional Court started its activity, though by no means easy due to the issues that still had to be resolved (including above all the territorial question), was generally favorable to its role as "supreme interpreter of the Constitution."[81] In particular, during the process of substantive transition, the Constitutional Court had to deal with four main issues. First, the Court had to uphold the *normative value of the entire Constitution*. This was a very important issue, especially considering that previous Spanish Constitutions had been interpreted merely as programmatic texts, and even in relation to the 1978 Constitution the Supreme Court (in some of its rulings) and some legal scholars had argued that certain constitutional provisions were not directly applicable.

Second, the Constitutional Court had to deal with *preconstitutional legislation*. In particular, the Court handed down rulings clarifying who was responsible for resolving the contrasts between preconstitutional laws and the 1978 Constitution, and also played an important role in verifying the compatibility of "old" legislation with the new constitutional provisions.

Third, the success of the substantive transition was conditional on the *safeguarding of fundamental rights*: the Constitutional Court contributed in a decisive manner to ensuring the effective protection of these rights, mainly by means of the resolution of the *recursos de amparo* and the identification of the essential content of such rights.

Fourth, the most complex and delicate issue dealt with by the Constitutional Court concerned the *territorial decentralization of the state*. Also in this case the role of the Constitutional Court turned out to be of the utmost importance. By means of a systematic interpretation of the constitutional provisions and the resolution of conflicts of powers between the Central Government and the Autonomous Communities, as well as among the Autonomous Communities, the Court managed to ensure the rational functioning of the system of autonomous government (*sistema autonómico*). This was an extremely complicated task, both in light of the *political* difficulties arising from the construction of the "State of Autonomies," and in light of the fact that the *provisions of the Constitution* dealing with the territorial organization of the state were rather vague and arguably incomplete.

In the following sections, the four main areas of intervention of the Constitutional Court will be discussed, showing, in particular, how the Court managed in a

costituzionali, www.forumcostituzionale.it [accessed July 15, 2019]). In this connection suffice it to consider what happened in Italy (see Chapter 2, Sections 3 and 4).

[81] As laid down in Article 1 of the Organic Law 2/1979. On the position and status of the Constitutional Court in the Spanish legal system see in particular Manuel García-Pelayo, "El 'status' del Tribunal constitucional" (1981) 1 *Revista española de derecho constitucional* 1, 11 ff.

relatively short period to facilitate the passage from a *transition in the Constitution* to a *transition in action*.[82]

A *The Constitutional Court and the Upholding of the Normative Value of the Constitution*

With the exception of the 1931 Constitution (which was to remain in force for only five years), the history of Spanish constitutionalism is characterized by "the almost non-existent normative value"[83] of the constitutions prior to that of 1978. Indeed, based on the French model, they were considered to be primarily political documents, aimed at regulating the organization of state institutions, in particular that of the *Cortes* and the sovereign. Thus, the nineteenth-century Spanish Constitutions[84] were not legally binding, except in cases in which the constitutional provisions were transposed into law. The idea that the Constitution was not a legally binding text was constantly upheld by the Supreme Court (*Tribunal Supremo*), which was of the opinion that the Constitution consisted exclusively of programmatic provisions and that it was the duty of the legislature to implement them to a greater or lesser extent, or even to disregard them entirely.[85] This case law also applied to the Fundamental Laws of the Franco regime: the *Fuero de los Españoles*, for example, a Bill of Rights approved in 1945 specifying the rights and freedoms of Spanish citizens, was considered to be mere window dressing.[86]

It is not surprising then if shortly after its promulgation the normative value of the 1978 Constitution could not be taken for granted. According to some scholars, *all* the provisions of the Constitution were legally binding.[87] This conclusion could be drawn in particular from Article 9(1) of the Constitution, that establishes that "citizens and public authorities are bound by the Constitution and all other legal provisions."[88] On the contrary, other scholars[89] argued that a number of

82 On this distinction, see Chapter 1, Section 2.

83 de Esteban 1998, note 9, at 46.

84 Namely, the Constitution of Cadiz of 1812, the Royal Statute of 1834, as well as the Constitutions of 1837, 1845, 1869, and 1876.

85 See Eduardo García de Enterría, *La Constitución como norma y el Tribunal constitucional* (Aranzadi 2006), 291–292.

86 Ibid., at 291.

87 Ibid., at 63 ff.; de Esteban 1998, note 9, at 226 ff.; Torres del Moral 1984, note 6, at 61 ff.; Paolo Carrozza, "Alcuni problemi della giustizia costituzionale in Spagna" in Alessandro Pizzorusso and Vincenzo Varano (eds.), *L'influenza dei valori costituzionali sui sistemi giuridici contemporanei* (Giuffrè 1985), vol. II, 1112 ff.

88 In the view of García de Enterría 2006, note 85, at 64, it is possible to derive from this provision not only the binding character of the entire Constitution, but "something more, that is to say … a 'higher, superior obligation', according to the traditional expression of North American constitutionalism."

89 See Fernando Garrido Falla, "Artículo 1" in Fernando Garrido Falla (ed.), *Comentarios a la Constitución* (Civitas 2001), 28; Javier Jiménez Campo, "Comentario al artículo 53. Protección

constitutional provisions did not have full normative force, in particular those laying down the "Principles governing social and economic policy," that is Chapter III of Title I of the Constitution (Articles 39–52).[90] Fernando Garrido Falla, for example, highlighted the fact that these provisions were

> imperfect legal norms: in the best case scenario, they give a mandate to the legislator … that, if not respected, does not give rise to any juridical consequences; in other cases, this is not even the case, since they are simply rhetorical statements typical of the program of a political party.

With reference to Article 43(1) (the right to health), and Article 45(1) (the right to an environment suitable for personal development), Garrido Falla argued that these provisions should be considered to be "good intentions and wishful thinking, in the domain of constitutional rhetoric."[91]

The main reason why some legal scholars put forward an interpretation of this kind has to do with the (certainly unsatisfactory) wording of Article 53 of the Constitution, relating to the protection of fundamental rights. The first clause, after stating that the freedoms recognized in Chapter II are binding on all the state authorities, provides that the exercise of these freedoms can only be regulated by law, and that their essential content must be respected. The second paragraph then adds that, only in the case of violation of fundamental rights laid down in Article 14 (principle of equality) and Section I, Chapter II, Title I (Articles 15–29), and the right to conscientious objection provided in Article 30(2), citizens may obtain special protection by means of a preferential and summary procedure before the ordinary courts and, when appropriate, by means of a *recurso de amparo* before the Constitutional Court.

The problem of interpretation arose in relation to Article 53(3). Indeed, after stating that "the recognition, the respect and protection of the principles laid down in Chapter III [principles governing social and economic policy] shall guide legislation, judicial practice and actions by the public authorities," this provision then stipulates that these principles "may only be invoked before the ordinary courts in

de los derechos fundamentales" in Óscar Alzaga Villaamil (ed.), *Comentarios a la Constitución española de 1978* (Cortes Generales, Editoriales de derecho reunidas 1996), vol. IV, 520 ff.

90 The Constitution devotes the whole of Title I (Articles 10–55) to "Fundamental Rights and Duties." Section I of Chapter II (Articles 15–29) deals with "Fundamental Rights and Public Freedoms," regulating the right to life, religious freedom, freedom of communication, freedom of movement, freedom of assembly, etc. Section II (Articles 30–38), concerning the "Rights and Duties of Citizens," regulates the most characteristic aspects of the relations between citizens and the state, based on the model of the countries drawing inspiration from the principles of the social state (regulation of military obligations and conscientious objection, marriage, property, trade union rights, etc.). Finally, Chapter III (Articles 39–52) is devoted to "Principles governing social and economic policy" laying down a series of obligations on the part of the public authorities concerning various aspects of "economic and social relations," such as the family, employment and so on.

91 Garrido Falla 2001, "Artículo 1," at 28 and "Artículo 53," at 976, note 89.

accordance with the legal provisions implementing them." As a result, some scholars argued that the normative force of these principles depended on the laws implementing them, and that until the enactment of such laws, Articles 39–52 were to be considered merely programmatic provisions.

It is evident, then, that the debate among legal scholars in Spain about the normative value of the Constitution reflected in many ways the debate taking place in Italy 30 years before, when the 1948 Constitution came into force. Indeed, on the one hand, there were scholars such as Vezio Crisafulli, who argued that the constitutional provisions should as a rule be considered as "normative provisions" and that "the Constitution [should] be understood and interpreted, in all its parts, *magis ut valeat*,"[92] while, on the other hand, there were those such as Gaetano Azzariti who pointed out the existence of certain provisions "that are not even legal norms properly speaking."[93]

Even an analysis of the case law of the Supreme Court does not result in an unambiguous interpretation of the normative value of the Constitution, and in fact conflicting rulings were often handed down.[94] In a number of cases, the Supreme Court upheld the direct applicability of the constitutional provisions. Reference can be made, for example, to the two judgments of July 3, 1979 concerning enrolment on the Register of Associations of the Masonic societies *Grande Oriente Español* and *Grande Oriente Español Unido*. According to the Supreme Court, Article 22 of the Constitution (right to association) constituted a fully fledged right, the implementation of which at legislative level was necessary "only to specify in detail the limits laid down in general terms in Article 22." In other cases, the Supreme Court, instead of making reference to specific constitutional provisions, sought to implement the Constitution considered in its entirety, by invoking the "constitutional spirit."[95]

However, a number of rulings adopting an opposed interpretation were handed down, in which the direct binding effect of the constitutional provisions was denied. Indeed, in certain cases the Supreme Court declared the programmatic nature of the principle of the hierarchy of legal sources,[96] the principle of equality (Article

[92] Vezio Crisafulli, *La Costituzione e le sue disposizioni di principio* (Giuffrè 1952), 11.

[93] Gaetano Azzariti, *Problemi attuali di diritto costituzionale* (Giuffrè 1951), 98. With regard to this debate, see Chapter 2, Section 4.

[94] On the case law of the Supreme Court on constitutional questions in 1979 and 1980, see Luis Prieto Sanchís, "Dos años de jurisprudencia del Tribunal Supremo sobre cuestiones constitucionales" (1981) 1 *Revista española de derecho constitucional* 1, 2, 3 (respectively, 207 ff., 215 ff., and 191 ff.).

[95] Prieto Sanchis 1981 (no. 1), note 94, at 226. With the judgment of January 26, 1979, the Supreme Court ruled that the sanctions laid down by the law on public order of the previous regime "are devoid of validity and juridical efficacy, since they responded to certain objectives and a concept of legality completely incompatible with ... the fundamentals of the present-day juridical and political organization of the Spanish State, that is endowed with a Constitution setting it up as a social State based on democratic principles, which are opposed to and in contrast with those that served as a legal justification for such sanctions."

[96] Judgment March 26, 1982.

14 of the Constitution),[97] as well as Article 39(2) of the Constitution, which stipulates that "the public authorities ensure the integral protection of children, who are equal before the law regardless of their parentage, and of mothers regardless of their marital status. The law shall consent to the ascertainment of paternity."[98] Among the most controversial cases was the order (*Auto*) of May 2, 1980, in which the Supreme Court ruled that constitutions "are usually merely [texts] of a programmatic nature or a declaration of principles." Therefore, with this decision the Supreme Court seemed to be claiming that the programmatic character of the Constitution did not represent an exception, but rather the general rule. Moreover, in other cases the Supreme Court referred to the Constitution by way of *residual argument* or to reinforce the provisions of the Civil Code, the law on the public administration, and the law on administrative procedure. As a result, the Constitution "was applied to the extent that it coincided with other legal texts in order to reinforce them, and was interpreted in compliance with them."[99]

The analogies with Italy are evident: the extreme difficulty with which the Spanish Supreme Court upheld the binding character of the Constitution brings to mind the case law of the Italian Court of Cassation in the period 1948–1956, when in most instances the Court ruled that the constitutional provisions were merely programmatic provisions. The limited measures taken to purge the judiciary (especially at the higher levels), the lack of a habit of safeguarding fundamental rights, as well as the consolidated practice of considering constitutions merely as nonbinding documents (especially in the Spanish case) are among the principal reasons that explain why the supreme courts of the two countries often adopted this line of reasoning.

If it is the case that with the adoption of the 1978 Constitution[100] "descriptive constitutional law" gave way to "normative constitutional law" (to borrow an expression from Jorge de Estaban),[101] this depended to a large extent on the action of the Constitutional Court. In response to the contrasting opinions among legal scholars and the divergent rulings of the Supreme Court on this point, the Constitutional Court, on the contrary, did not hesitate, from its very first rulings,[102] to uphold the *binding force of the Constitution*, underlining that it was not just an "ordinary" law, but the *norma normarum*, placed at the top of the hierarchy of legal sources:

> it is necessary to bear in mind – as noted by the Court in Judgment 16/1982 – that the Constitution is not simply a set of principles that are neither immediately binding nor directly applicable until implemented by means of legislation; on the

[97] Judgment April 8, 1982 (to be discussed in more detail in the text that follows).

[98] See, e.g., *Auto*, November 26, 1979.

[99] Torres del Moral 1984, note 6, at 2. See the judgments of June 11, 1979, May 5, 1980, June 17 and 19, 1981.

[100] With the partial exception, as noted, of the 1931 Constitution.

[101] de Esteban 1998, note 9, at 71.

[102] See, e.g., Judgments 3/1981 and 9/1981.

> contrary, it is a norm, the supreme norm of our legal system, and as a result both the citizens and the public authorities . . . are subject to it.

In the view of the Court, the immediate applicability was valid in particular for the constitutional provisions laying down fundamental rights. This applicability should not be undermined by the fact that the constitutional provisions envisaged legislation to implement them, and that such legislation had not yet been enacted, because the Constitution should not be considered to be merely a programmatic text.[103] Indeed, even before the legislation implementing the constitutional provisions was adopted, the *basic content* of fundamental rights should be safeguarded.[104] Emblematic in this respect was Judgment 15/1982, relating to the right to conscientious objection (Article 30(2) of the Constitution). In response to the argument put forward by the State Attorney (*Abogado del Estado*), that this right "is not recognized by the Spanish Constitution, since Article 30(2) . . . consists of an open-ended statement, that refers the matter to the legislator not only with regard to the definition of the right, but also with regard to whether it exists or not," the Constitutional Court ruled that the right to conscientious objection was to be upheld, albeit in its most basic form (which in the case under review consisted of the provisional suspension of the duty to carry out military service), even in the absence of legislation implementing the right.

The Constitutional Court also upheld the direct applicability of Article 14 of the Constitution, which proclaims the principle of equality.[105] The immediate normative value of this constitutional provision had been expressly denied in the judgment of a lower court, the *Audiencia Territorial* of Seville on January 31, 1980, and also on appeal to the *Sala Primera* of the Supreme Court on April 8, 1982, in which the Supreme Court ruled that Article 14 was simply "a statement of principle" and that legislation was required to implement it.

Moreover, the Constitutional Court handed down a ruling on the question concerning the "principles governing social and economic policy," establishing that they could not be considered as "norms without content" and that, on the contrary, they should be "taken into consideration in the interpretation of other constitutional provisions and of the laws."[106] The constitutional judges clarified the fact that these principles, "regardless of their content that may be more or less precise, constitute binding provisions, according to what is unequivocally laid down in Articles 9 and 53 of the Constitution," and must therefore "have a bearing on ordinary legislation and the decisions of the courts."[107] As a result, while recognizing that these principles did not enjoy the same safeguards granted to the fundamental rights laid down

[103] In Judgment 185/1988 the Court makes reference to the "special binding force of fundamental rights, not subordinated to any legal intermediation."
[104] On this point see Torres del Moral 1984, note 6, at 65.
[105] Judgment 80/1982.
[106] Judgment 19/1982.
[107] Judgment 14/1992.

in Title I, Chapter II, the Constitutional Court rejected in a decisive manner the previously mentioned opinions according to which such principles should be considered as equivalent to programmatic provisions, or even as little more than "good intentions and wishful thinking."

Taking as a starting point the normative character of the Constitution and its status as *lex legum*, the Constitutional Court derived the *principle of interpretation of legal provisions in compliance with the Constitution* (*constitutional-conform interpretation*).[108] The application of this principle meant that the Constitution was the necessary "framework" for all normative provisions as and when they were applied and interpreted,[109] and that it served to fill the gaps of legal provisions ("integrative interpretation").[110] The principle of interpretation in compliance with the Constitution also gave rise to the obligation to interpret legal provisions in the manner considered to be most favorable for the effective implementation of fundamental rights.[111]

B *The Constitutional Court and Preconstitutional Legislation: Quality More Than Quantity*

Along with Italy, Spain constitutes an emblematic case of how, in the transition from an authoritarian regime to a democratic government, the questions concerning preconstitutional legislation take on particular importance.[112] However, unlike the Italian Constitution, the 1978 Spanish Constitution includes a repeal clause (*Disposición derogatoria*), providing a break in continuity between the old and the new regime.[113] Indeed, this clause expressly repeals the seven Fundamental Laws of the Franco regime (along with the Political Reform Law) and the laws of October 25, 1839 and July 21, 1876 (relating to the provinces of Alava, Guipúzcoa, and Vizcaya), and the third paragraph provides that "likewise, any provisions contrary to those contained in the Constitution are hereby repealed."[114] Due to the fact that this last paragraph did not specify who was responsible for determining noncompliance of the "old" laws with the Constitution, various interpretative approaches were adopted. According to some scholars, it was the Constitutional Court that was

[108] See, e.g., Judgments 4/1981, 19/1982, and 74/1987. On the constitutional-conform interpretation in Spain and other European countries see Maartje De Visser, *Constitutional Review in Europe: A Comparative Analysis* (Hart 2014), 291 ff.

[109] Judgment 79/1991.

[110] Judgment 265/1988.

[111] Judgments 34/1983, 17/1985, and 57/1985. On the consequences of the application of the principle of interpretation in compliance with the Constitution, see García de Enterría 2006, note 85, at 313–314.

[112] See Giancarlo Rolla, *Indirizzo politico e Tribunale costituzionale in Spagna* (Jovene 1986), 211 ff.

[113] See Antonio Hernández Gil, *El cambio político español y la Constitución* (Planeta 1982), 471.

[114] On the repeal clause see José Luis Peñaranda Ramos, "Disposición derogatoria. Constitución y ordenamiento preconstitucional" in Alzaga Villaamil (ed.) 1996, note 89, at 771 ff.

responsible to verify the constitutionality of preconstitutional legislation.[115] Other authors, on the contrary, argued that it was for the ordinary courts to deal with the conflicts between preconstitutional laws and the Constitution, and that the Constitutional Court was empowered only to strike down postconstitutional laws.[116] A *sui generis* solution was put forward by Eduardo García de Enterría, who argued that it was necessary to distinguish between, on the one hand, preconstitutional laws that appeared "*icto oculi*"[117] to be in contrast with the constitutional provisions (in particular, those regulating fundamental rights and the organization and functioning of the powers of the state), and, on the other hand, preconstitutional laws that did not appear to be in evident contrast with the Constitution (i.e., preconstitutional legislation the content of which "was not directly political").[118] In the first case, all courts would be authorized to determine the repeal of preconstitutional laws, whereas in the second case, ordinary courts would have to make a referral to the Constitutional Court.

The question as to which body was to deal with the conflict between preconstitutional laws and the Constitution was finally resolved by the Constitutional Court in its first Judgments (4/1981 and 11/1981). In the first of these two decisions, the Court was required to rule on a referral made by 56 socialist senators, who had impugned a series of legal provisions concerning local government that entered into force prior to the adoption of the Constitution. First of all, the Constitutional Court clarified the distinction between "supervening" unconstitutionality and repeal, noting that:

> the particularity of preconstitutional laws consists ... in the fact that the Constitution is a superior law – on the basis of the hierarchical criterion [*lex superior derogat inferiori*] – as well as a posterior law – on the basis of the chronological criterion [*lex posterior derogat priori*]. The combination of these two criteria gives rise on the one hand to the supervening unconstitutionality and the consequent invalidity of the laws failing to comply with the Constitution, and on the other hand, to their loss of force after the adoption of the Constitution ..., in other words, their repeal.

The Constitutional Court therefore decided that it was competent to rule on whether preconstitutional laws complied with the Constitution: in the event of a conflict between the "old" laws and the new Constitution, the Court was

[115] See Santiago Varela and Miguel Satrústegui, "Constitución nueva y leyes viejas" (1979) 4 *Revista del departamento de derecho político*, 75.

[116] See Manuel Aragón Reyes, "La sentencia del Tribunal constitucional sobre leyes relativas al regimen local, anteriores a la Constitución" (1981) 1 *Revista española de derecho constitucional*, 185 ff. Gumersindo Trujillo, "Juicio de legitimidad e interpretación constitucional: cuestiones problematicas en el horizonte constitucional español" (1979) 7 *Revista de estudios políticos*, 146 ff., by recalling the Italian experience in the period 1948–1956, argued that the conflict between preconstitutional laws and the new Constitution should be resolved by the ordinary courts in the course of the "transitional phase," i.e. until the Constitutional Court started its activity.

[117] García de Enterría 2006, note 85, at 94.

[118] Ibid.

empowered to declare "their supervening unconstitutionality" and "their repeal pursuant to the repeal clause."[119] However, unlike the constitutional review of postconstitutional laws, the Constitutional Court ruled that it did not have a monopoly on the constitutional review of preconstitutional laws, but that such review should also involve the ordinary courts: indeed, these courts should be required to set aside such laws whenever they found that they had been repealed by the Constitution. In the case of doubt, however, they were to refer the question of constitutionality to the Constitutional Court (*cuestión de incostitucionalidad*). The only difference would be the effects of the judgment: the repeal determined by the ordinary courts would have had an *inter partes* effect, whereas the unconstitutionality determined by the Constitutional Court would have had an *erga omnes* effect.[120]

In this ruling the Constitutional Court made reference to the systems adopted in Italy and Germany, but opted for an intermediate solution. In Italy, with Judgment 1/1956 the Constitutional Court had determined its own competence to resolve the conflicts between preconstitutional legislation and the Constitution (even if it had never *expressly* ruled out the possibility that ordinary courts could also determine the repeal of preconstitutional laws).[121] In Germany, by contrast, on the basis of Article 123(1) of the *Grundgesetz* ("Law in force before the *Bundestag* first convenes shall remain in force insofar as it does not conflict with this Basic Law"), the Constitutional Court had established that this conflict should be resolved by the ordinary courts (thus declaring the repeal of the preconstitutional law, if appropriate), rejecting the view that it was a matter of constitutional review.[122]

It should be underlined that the Spanish State Attorney, as the legal representative of the government, had raised an objection to the referral, claiming that the Constitutional Court was not competent to hear the case. Indeed, according to the State Attorney the chronological criterion should have prevailed over the hierarchical criterion, and as a result it should have been the ordinary courts that resolved the

[119] In Judgment 11/1981 the Constitutional Court specified that the failure of preconstitutional laws to comply with the Constitution "may result in a situation of repeal and annulment at the same time."

[120] This decision was not unanimous: in his dissenting opinion, Francisco Rubio Llorente argued that ordinary courts should be granted exclusive competence to review preconstitutional legislation (declaring the repeal of the law, where appropriate), and that the Constitutional Court, also on an exclusive basis, should be responsible to review postconstitutional laws (declaring them unconstitutional, where appropriate).

[121] See Chapter 2, Section 5.A.

[122] However, the *Bundesverfassungsgericht* declared its exclusive competence in the case of "abstract" review of both preconstitutional and postconstitutional laws (i.e., when the referrals were made by political entities such as the federal government, a land government, or one-quarter of the members of the *Bundestag*). See in particular the rulings of February 24, 1953 and August 5, 1966. On the solution adopted in Germany see Luciano Parejo Alfonso, "La Constitución y las leyes preconstitucionales. El problema de la derogación y la llamada incostitucionalidad sobrevenida" (1981) 94 *Revista de administración pública*, 201 ff.

conflict between preconstitutional laws and the Constitution, where necessary determining the repeal of the "old" laws.[123] The State Attorney also argued that striking down laws on constitutional grounds would result in a legislative void within the system. The analogies with the Italian case are evident. In the same way as the State Attorney in Spain, the State Attorney in Italy was opposed to recognizing the competence of the Constitutional Court to verify the constitutionality of preconstitutional laws, arguing that it was a question of repeal and that it was therefore a matter for the ordinary courts to deal with.[124] Admittedly the content of the laws under review was different: in Italy, in most cases they were Fascist laws in evident contrast with the Constitution (as in the case of the provisions of the Criminal Code, the Code of Criminal Procedure, or the Unified Code on Public Security), whereas in Spain the contrast between preconstitutional laws and the Constitution was not so evident because in a number of cases they were laws enacted after the death of Franco, meaning that, within certain limits, they were adopted within a democratic framework. What is important to bear in mind, however, is that neither in Italy nor in Spain is it mandatory for the government (represented by the State Attorney) to appear before the Constitutional Court,[125] and therefore the decision to intervene to support the positions just outlined appears to be the outcome of a specific government's policy.

The Spanish Constitutional Court did not deal with a high number of preconstitutional laws, and this depended on a number of factors. First of all it should be noted that, in the three-month period laid down in the Organic Law of the Constitutional Court,[126] only two referrals for constitutional review (*recursos de inconstitucionalidad*) were made in relation to preconstitutional laws (and such laws had been enacted after the death of Franco): indeed, the political parties and the government did not wish to repeal the "old" laws *en bloc* but intended to deal with them gradually, in an awareness that it was impossible to eliminate all preconstitutional legislation in a short period. In addition, it should be noted that the *cuestión de inconstitucionalidad* was raised by the ordinary courts only in a limited number of cases. Ordinary courts often preferred to uphold the preconstitutional laws because they considered that certain provisions of the Constitution were not directly applicable. This was the case because in spite of the extensive provisions in the Constitution regulating the organization of the judiciary and the rapid approval of the

123 The state attorney adopted an analogous line of reasoning also in Judgment 11/1981.

124 See Chapter 2, Section 5.A.

125 The fact that also in Spain this is simply a possibility and not an obligation is made clear by Article 34(1) of the Organic Law of the Constitutional Court, which provides that the government and other state bodies "can appear before the Court and formulate the observations they consider to be opportune." Therefore, the government *can but is not obliged* to appear before the Court: in addition, if it decides to do so, it can put forward the observations that it deems to be "opportune," and this seems to imply considerations of a political nature.

126 On the basis of the joint effect of Article 33 and the second transitional provision of the Organic Law.

Organic Law governing the General Council of the Judiciary, the Spanish judiciary, which had been appointed under the Franco regime, had still not embraced the democratic values laid down in the Constitution and as a result displayed scant interest in repealing the preconstitutional legislation in conflict with the new democratic Constitution.[127] In other cases, however, the ordinary judges did not refer the question of constitutionality for the opposite reason, that is because they decided to repeal the preconstitutional laws, thus giving immediate application to the provisions of the Constitution. Finally, it should be borne in mind that the first section of the repeal clause of the Constitution (as mentioned in the preceding text) had provided for the repeal of the Fundamental Laws enacted under Franco regime, and that over the three-year period 1975–1978 (as noted later) various laws were enacted aimed at safeguarding the exercise of fundamental rights. In addition, some articles of the Criminal Code were modified, to ensure their compliance with the new social and political scenario.[128]

Whereas the case law of the Constitutional Court in relation to preconstitutional legislation was not particularly substantial in *quantitative* terms, it was undoubtedly significant from a *qualitative* point of view. In fact, the Constitutional Court dealt with questions of great importance concerning, above all, whether the "old" laws complied with the constitutional provisions laying down fundamental rights.

One of the most interesting rulings concerned the *right to strike*.[129] Under the Franco regime, strikes were not granted any protection: indeed, not only were they recognized neither in the Labour Charter (*Fuero del Trabajo*), nor in the *Fuero de los Españoles*, but they were expressly classified as a criminal offence under the Criminal Code of 1944 (Article 222). In the 1960s and 1970s some small steps forward were made, but it was only during the transition to democracy that Royal Decree Law 17/1977 on Labour Relations was enacted, a decree regulating the right to strike and collective labor disputes. Although it afforded an important degree of protection, this measure, enacted at a time when trade unions had not yet been legalized,

[127] Carrozza 1985, note 87, at 1125–1126. The author also makes reference to opinion 1/1979 of the state attorney general, who stated that "the 'indeterminate' and 'general' character of the repeal clause does not prevent preconstitutional legislation in contrast with the Constitution from remaining in force in cases in which it concerns general principles the application of which requires further legislative intervention. The worrying aspect of these statements – Carrozza goes on – consists in the fact that the examples cited by the attorney general refer not only to 'principles governing social and economic relations', but also to 'principles' and 'rights' laid down in Articles 14–29, which the Constitution recognizes as having immediately binding effects" (at 1119).

[128] See Section 3.C of this chapter.

[129] Article 28(2) of the Constitution expressly recognizes "the workers' right to strike in the defence of their interests," and provides that the law regulating the exercise of this right should establish "precise guarantees to ensure the maintenance of essential services for the community."

laid down a fairly restrictive regulation and it is significant that it has been called an "antistrike" provision.[130]

Following the adoption of the Constitution, two opposing interpretations were put forward in relation to Royal Decree Law 17/1977. According to some authors, this decree had been implicitly repealed due to its incompatibility with the new Constitution, whereas for other scholars and for certain courts it was still in force and therefore applicable.[131] In addition to this problem of the compatibility of the provisions of the decree with the Constitution, the other particularly delicate matter was whether the law regulating the right to strike could be a preconstitutional law, rather than an organic law (as specified by Article 81 of the Constitution).

This matter was resolved by the Constitutional Court by means of Judgment 11/1981. In response to a referral for constitutional review by a group of 52 socialist deputies, the Constitutional Court ruled first of all that there was no reason to believe that Royal Decree Law 17/1977 was unconstitutional for reasons concerning the procedure by which it had been approved because it had been adopted in compliance with the procedures required at the time of its enactment. This line of reasoning, combined with a fear of leaving a void in the legislation, led the Court to state that "the legal regulation of the right to strike in our country is provided in … the Royal Decree Law to the extent that it is not in contrast with the Constitution and until such time as a new regulation is laid down by means of an organic law." This decision represented one of the first rulings in which the principle of conservation of legal acts was proclaimed.

Moreover, the Constitutional Court partially upheld the requests of those filing the complaint, striking down certain provisions of the decree and reinterpreting others in the light of the constitutional provisions, thus carrying out a "purging"[132] of the contents of the decree. More specifically, the Constitutional Court laid down a wide-ranging definition of the right to strike, identified the instances in which the exercise of such a right was deemed to be illegitimate, and rejected the idea of the legitimacy of strikes exclusively for matters related to the employment contract, thus paving the way for the "labour strike" model (*huelga laboral*)[133] (adopting, however, an "ambiguous"[134] approach with respect to the right to strike for sociopolitical

[130] Manuel Carlos Palomeque López, "El derecho constitucional de huelga y su regulación en España" in *Derecho del trabajo y razón crítica* (Varona 2004), 139.

[131] On this divergence of opinion see ibid.

[132] Antonio Pedro Baylos, "Diez años de jurisprudencia constitucional: el derecho de huelga" in Manuel Ramón Alarcón Caracuel (ed.), *Constitución y derecho del trabajo: 1981–1991 (Análisis de diez años de jurisprudencia constitucional)* (Marcial Pons 1992), 294.

[133] The term "labour strike" (*huelga laboral*) applies to "the notion of professional worker and to the defence, in general, of all his interests in relation to any kind of claim" (José Vida Soria and Ángel Gallego Morales, "Art. 28.2" in Alzaga Villaamil [ed.] 1996, vol. III, note 89, at 326–327).

[134] See José Luis Monereo Pérez, *Derecho de huelga y conflictos colectivos* (Editorial Comares 2002), 119. In the view of the author, it was only with Judgment 36/1993 that the Constitutional Court recognized "without leaving room for any ambiguity" the legitimacy of sociopolitical strikes, including general strikes.

reasons). Furthermore, the Court ruled in favor of the right to strike for reasons of solidarity and issued the first interpretative guidelines relating to the matter of essential services.

Among the most significant passages in this judgment, mention should be made of the one in which the Court ruled that the right to strike is "consistent with the idea of the social and democratic State based on the rule of law as laid down in Article 1(1) of the Constitution," consistent with "the right granted to the trade unions under Article 7," and also consistent with "the promotion of conditions necessary for the freedom and equality of individuals and social groups to be real and effective (Article 9(2))." By analogy with Judgment 290/1974 of the Italian Constitutional Court,[135] what clearly emerged was the concept of the right to strike as *an instrument of influence and democratic participation of the workers* not just in decisions closely linked to the employment relationship but also in decisions of a *sociopolitical nature*.

The judgment of the Constitutional Court takes on even more importance when considering the fact that, in spite of various attempts[136] and recommendations by the Constitutional Court,[137] Parliament has still not enacted the Organic Law required by Article 28(2) of the Constitution, aimed at regulating the right to strike. The result is that at present the only subconstitutional source regulating the matter continues to be Royal Decree Law 17/1977, as interpreted by Judgment 11/1981. The Constitutional Court – by analogy with the Italian Constitutional Court in relation to Article 40 of the Constitution[138] – was thus called on to play a role as a "substitute" for Parliament.

Another particularly significant ruling concerned the *right to assembly*. Under the Franco regime, this right was recognized only in formal terms because Article 16 of the *Fuero de los Españoles*, which recognized this right together with the right to association, was never implemented in an effective manner. A step forward was made with Law 17/1976, but with the entry into force of the Constitution various problems arose concerning the compatibility between this Law, that laid down a restrictive interpretation, and the 1978 Constitution. This was a delicate matter, above all in light of the fact that the Organic Law implementing Article 21 of the Constitution (that safeguards the right to assembly) was enacted only in 1983. The relationship between the two provisions was clarified by the Constitutional Court with Judgment 36/1982. In that ruling the Constitutional Court established that, in

[135] See Chapter 2, Section 5.C.

[136] Mention should be made in particular of the proposed organic law of 1992, which represented the outcome of an agreement between the government and the trade unions. The procedure for the approval of this proposed legislation was interrupted by the enactment of Royal Decree 534/1993, resulting in the dissolution of the *Cortes*, when the proposed legislation had already been approved by the Senate, with the definitive vote scheduled to be held a few weeks later in Congress.

[137] See in particular Judgment 123/1990.

[138] See Chapter 2, Section 5.C.

order to hold a meeting in a public place, it was not necessary to apply for *authorization* from the Civil Governor of the Province (as required by Article 5 of Law 17/1976), but only to give *prior notice* to the authorities (as laid down in Article 21 of the Constitution). However, the Court held that various procedural matters required by Law 17/1976 (including a 10-day period of prior notice for a meeting to the authorities),[139] were not in conflict with Article 21 of the Constitution and served as "a functional and legitimizing channel of the acts of the public authorities and the citizens for the exercise of this right."[140]

Another decision worthy of note is Judgment 7/1983, relating to the *principle of equality*, with particular reference to the *condition of women in employment*. During the Francoist regime, women were not granted the right to vote, and also in family relations and employment they were subject to several forms of discrimination. In the 1940s and 1950s, for example, in numerous state-sector companies, regulations were adopted requiring a compulsory period of extended leave (*excedencia forzosa*) for women workers who married. These women would have the right to return to work only in the event that they became "head of the household," meaning that pursuant to the family law in force at the time the husband had either died or become mentally or physically disabled and therefore no longer able to work. The aim was clearly to "keep married women outside the labour market."[141]

In 1978 the Constitution was adopted, laying down the principle of equality and nondiscrimination, and in 1980 the Workers' Statute implemented this principle, prohibiting discrimination in the workplace. In light of these provisions, and as a result of the deep recession the country was going through, in the early 1980s many women decided to take legal action to seek reinstatement in the workplace. In Judgment 7/1983 the Constitutional Court heard one of these cases for the first time. The ruling was rather ambivalent. On the one hand, the constitutional judges determined that the preconstitutional provisions that provided the suspension of the employment contract for women workers in the case of marriage constituted a clear case of discrimination on the grounds of sex, thus violating the principle of equality. On the other hand, the Court ruled that it was possible to take action for reinstatement only within the first three years of the promulgation of the

139 A 10-day prior notice period is also laid down in Article 8 of the Organic Law 9/1983 (except in the presence of "serious and extraordinary" reasons, in which case a 24-hour prior notice period is allowed).

140 On this matter see Piedad García-Escudero Márquez and Benigno Pendás García, "Régimen jurídico del derecho de reunión (análisis de la Ley orgánica 9/1983, de 15 de julio)" (1986) 22 *Revista de derecho político*, 206–207; Juan José Solozábal Echavarría, "La configuración constitucional del derecho de reunión" (2001) 5 *Parlamento y Constitución*, 118–119.

141 Ruth Rubio-Marín, "Women and the Cost of Transition to Democratic Constitutionalism in Spain" (2003) 18 *International Sociology*, 246. It should be noted that in 1961, with the enactment of the law on the political, occupational, and employment rights of women, the extended leave became optional and no longer obligatory.

Constitution (December 29, 1978).[142] In the case under examination, the complaints of the petitioners were upheld, due to the fact that the petition was presented in July 1981.[143] In a significant number of cases, however, establishing a three-year time limit meant perpetuating de facto the discriminatory treatment: indeed, it was evident that women could not have foreseen the time limit for the filing of their petitions, nor the date from which this time limit would be calculated.[144] As argued by Ruth Rubio-Marín, then, it was the women who paid "the cost of transition to democratic constitutionalism."[145]

C *The End of a* Burla: *The Constitutional Court and the Creation of an Effective System of Protection of Fundamental Rights*

In Spain, unlike what happened in Italy, it was not necessary to wait for the adoption of the new Constitution to identify the first signs of discontinuity in relation to the authoritarian model of fundamental rights (a model that has been defined as a *burla*, i.e. a farce).[146] Indeed, even in the course of the *formal* transition numerous measures were adopted that, while not affording a level of protection comparable to that which would be provided by the new Constitution, constituted an important step toward the creation of a real system of safeguards for fundamental rights and freedoms. In addition to Law 17/1976 on the right to assembly and Royal Decree Law 17/1977 on employment relations mentioned previously, reference should be made of Law 21/1976 on the right to political association;[147] Law 23/1976, amending certain provisions of the Criminal Code relating to the right to assembly, association, free speech, and work; Royal Decree 3011/1976 regulating conscientious objection; Royal Decree Law 6/1977 on the (partial) reform of the public order law; Royal Decree Law 24/1977 on freedom of expression, and Royal Decree 2644/1977 (which eliminated the monopoly of information of *Radio Nacional de España*, and safeguarded

142 Indeed, in the view of the Constitutional Court, it was necessary to comply with the provisions of the Employment Contract Law, which provided that lawsuits arising from the employment contract came under the statute of limitations (unless otherwise specified) three years after the conclusion of the employment contract. According to the constitutional judges, the three-year period in which an action could be taken to seek remedy against discrimination was calculated starting from the promulgation of the Constitution, that was considered to be a legally binding text.

143 For other cases in which the Constitutional Court upheld the petition presented by the women, see Judgments 8/1983, 13/1983, 15/1983, and 86/1983.

144 For cases in which the Constitutional Court rejected the petitions, see Judgments 58/1984, 15/1985, 59/1993, and 70/1993.

145 Rubio-Marín 2003, note 141, at 239 ff.

146 García de Enterría 2006, note 85, at 80. Referring, in particular, to the *Fuero de los Españoles*, the author argued that it contained "emphatic proclamations of rights the effectiveness of which was entirely conditional on the laws implementing them . . ., laws that either were never enacted . . ., or that regulated the scope or conditions in an arbitrary manner."

147 Later developed by Royal Decree 2300/1976, Royal Decree Law 12/1977, and Royal Decree 125/1977.

the freedom to broadcast general information programs); Law 19/1977 on the freedom to set up and join trade unions;[148] and various provisions granting an amnesty.[149] Also the Pacts of Moncloa of October 1977 laid down certain policy guidelines relating to fundamental rights, concerning in particular freedom of expression, the right to assembly, the right to political association, the reform of the Criminal Code, and the reform of the public order law.[150]

The 1978 Constitution – appropriately defined as a "Constitution of Rights"[151] – provides for a wide-ranging Bill of Rights, including (probably due to the influence of the Portuguese Constitution of 1976)[152] "third-generation" and "fourth-generation" rights, such as the right to privacy, the right to access to culture, the right to housing, and the right to an environment suitable for the development of the individuals. To ensure the protection of these rights, a series of safeguards were envisaged, such as the *recurso de amparo*,[153] and the office of the *Defensor del Pueblo* (with a clear reference to the ombudsman in the Scandinavian countries).

The protection of fundamental rights constituted from the very beginning one of the most important concerns of the Constitutional Court: "nothing involving the exercise of the rights of citizens that the Constitution grants to them – observed the Constitutional Court in Judgment 26/1981 – can ever be considered beyond the competence of this Court." In addition to the decisions mentioned previously concerning the normative value of the Constitution and the question of preconstitutional legislation, the Constitutional Court, in order to realize an effective system of protection of fundamental rights, played a dual role as *supreme guardian* of these rights while also *identifying their essential content*.[154]

148 Later developed by Royal Decree Law 31/1977.

149 See Royal Decree Law 10/1976, Royal Decree Law 19/1977, Royal Decree 388/1977, Royal Decree 1135/1977, and Law 46/1977. See Alicia Gil Gil, "Spain as an Example of Total Oblivion with Partial Rehabilitation" in Jessica Almqvist and Carlos Espósito (eds.), *The Role of Courts in Transitional Justice: Voices from Latin America and Spain* (Routledge 2012), 103 ff.

150 The texts (or part of them) of the previously mentioned legal measures are to be found in Sánchez Navarro 1998, note 10.

151 Pedro Cruz Villalón and Javier Pardo Falcón, "Los derechos fundamentales en la Constitución española de 1978" (2000) 97 *Boletín mexicano de derecho comparado*, 66.

152 See de Esteban 1998, note 9, at 135.

153 It should be noted that there are two types of *recurso de amparo*: the "ordinary" type, before ordinary courts, to which reference is made in the Constitution with the expression "a preferential and summary procedure in the ordinary courts" (Article 53(2)), as regulated by Law 62/1978, and the "extraordinary" type, before the Constitutional Court, to which reference is made in the Constitution with the expression "*recurso de amparo*" (Article 53(2)), even though the Organic Law of the Constitutional Court uses the expression "*recurso de amparo constitucional*" (see Cruz Villalón 1999, note 36, at 495 ff.). In the present study, the term "*recurso de amparo*" is intended as a reference to the individual constitutional complaint before the Constitutional Court, unless otherwise specified.

154 See Roberto L. Blanco Valdés, "La politica e il diritto: vent'anni di giustizia costituzionale e di democrazia in Spagna (appunti per un bilancio)" in Lucio Pegoraro, Angelo Rinella, and Roberto Scarciglia (eds.), *I vent'anni della Costituzione spagnola nella giurisprudenza del Tribunale costituzionale* (Cedam 2000), 29.

The function of supreme guardian of fundamental rights was carried out by ruling on referrals for constitutional review, but above all in response to individual constitutional complaints (*recursos de amparo*), which can be filed (as mentioned previously) in relation to the violations of the principle of equality (Article 14), the rights laid down in Section I, Chapter II, Title I (Articles 15–29), as well as the right to conscientious objection (Article 30(2)). The origins of the *recurso de amparo* can be traced back to Latin American constitutionalism in the mid-nineteenth century,[155] though a similar right to petition the Court was envisaged in the Constitutions of Baden and Bavaria of 1818. This procedural gateway to the Constitutional Court reappeared in the Austrian Constitution of 1920 and was then enshrined in the 1949 German Basic Law with the term *Verfassungsbeschwerde*.

During the drafting of the 1978 Spanish Constitution, the debates about the theoretical construction of the *recurso de amparo* were quite limited.[156] It should be noted, however, that the constitutional drafters were inspired not so much by the Latin American *amparo*, but rather by the German model and the one laid down in the Spanish Republican Constitution of 1931. Moreover, although there was widespread support for including the *recurso de amparo* in the new Constitution, not all the drafters were of the view that it should be the Constitutional Court that should rule in these cases, but rather that the ordinary courts should hear them.[157] The fear (that turned out to be well founded) was that as a result of having to hear petitions of this type, the caseload of the Constitutional Court would be excessive, and it would prevent the Court from carrying out its functions effectively.[158] In the end, however, the *recurso de amparo* was assigned to the competence of the Constitutional Court, in the belief that its introduction responded to the need to safeguard fundamental rights not only in relation to possible infringements on the part of the legislature and the executive but also (and perhaps above all) on the part of the judiciary. In fact, the introduction of the *recurso de amparo* constituted one of the most evident

155 See José Maria Serna de la Garza, "Amparo" in Rainer Grote, Frauke Lachenmann, and Rüdiger Wolfrum (eds.), *The Max Planck Encyclopedia of Comparative Constitutional Law* (Oxford University Press 2016), 1 ff.

156 Ollero Gómez, e.g., noted the fact that the Constitution made no attempt to "provide a precise definition of the concept of *recurso de amparo*" (*Diario de Sesiones del Senado*, September 14, 1978, 55, 2707). On this point see also José Luis Cascajo Castro and Vicente Gimeno Sendra, *El recurso de amparo* (Tecnos 1988), 54–56.

157 Lorenzo Martín-Retortillo Baquer, e.g., argued that: "It is necessary to safeguard rights, but I believe it is preferable to strengthen the ordinary courts . . . and seek effective forms of judicial protection close to the citizens, without having to go all the way to the capital of the Kingdom, that is always rather discriminatory" (*Diario de Sesiones del Senado*, August 30, 1978, 46, 2114; see also *Diario de Sesiones del Senado*, September 14, 1978, 55, 2735). On this issue see Germán Fernández Farreres, *El recurso de amparo según la jurisprudencia constitucional. Comentarios al Título III de la LOTC* (Marcial Pons 1994), 9 ff.

158 See Martín-Retortillo Baquer, *Diario de Sesiones del Senado*, August 30, 1978, 46, 2114.

manifestations of the "lack of trust" of the drafters in relation to the judiciary, which was considered politically and sociologically "preconstitutional."[159]

From a practical point of view, as pointed out by Lorenzo Martín-Retortillo Baquer, the *recurso de amparo* "did not fail to live up to expectations . . ., rather, it provided an effective response to the most ambitious aspirations."[160] The Constitutional Court handed down rulings from the very beginning on a wide range of questions, even though most of them concerned the violation of the right to due process (Article 24 of the Constitution).[161]

Among the most significant decisions, mention should be made of Judgment 3/1981, in which the Court ordered the Ministry of the Interior to proceed with the immediate inclusion (previously denied) of the Spanish Communist Party (Marxist-Leninist) in the register of political parties. In this ruling the Constitutional Court established that the right to set up political parties constituted "a particular form" of the right to association and as a result it was a matter for the *recurso de amparo*.

Another important decision was Judgment 104/1986, concerning the scope and limits of freedom of expression and information (Article 20 of the Constitution). The Constitutional Court, reflecting the content of previous judgments,[162] established in the first place that the freedoms laid down in that article were not just the fundamental rights of every citizen but also represented the recognition and safeguarding of a fundamental political institution, that is the *freedom of public opinion*, indissolubly linked to political pluralism. The Court also specified that when the right to honor comes into conflict with the right to freedom of expression and information, the judge is required to strike a balance between them, as well as carrying out an assessment of the importance of the information and opinions expressed with a view to forming public opinion.

Luis López Guerra has rightly argued that the importance of the *recurso de amparo* consists in the fact that although it is formally aimed at the protection of the individual, in actual fact the decisions of the Constitutional Court have "a dimension that is more 'systemic' than individual."[163] Indeed, the *recurso de amparo* can be lodged against specific acts of the public authorities that infringe fundamental rights: as a result, to bring an end to such infringements, the Constitutional Court can issue instructions *pro futuro* to all state authorities to align their actions in

[159] Pedro Cruz Villalón, "El recurso de amparo constitucional" in Pedro Cruz Villalón, Luis López Guerra, Javier Jiménez Campo, and Pablo Pérez Tremps (eds.), *Los procesos constitucionales* (Centro de estudios constitucionales 1992), 117.

[160] Lorenzo Martín-Retortillo Baquer, "Eficacia y garantía de los derechos fundamentales" in Sebastián Martín-Retortillo (ed.), *Estudios sobre la Constitución española. Homenaje al Profesor Eduardo García de Enterría* (Civitas 1991), vol. II, 613.

[161] See Enrique Guillén López, "Judicial Review in Spain: The Constitutional Court" (2008) 41 *Loyola of Los Angeles Law Review*, 547 ff.

[162] In particular, Judgment 12/1982.

[163] Luis López Guerra, *Las sentencias básicas del Tribunal constitucional* (Centro de estudios políticos y constitucionales 1998), 27.

Rights (ECHR) and the case law of the Court of Strasbourg.[171] This was possible above all by virtue of Article 10(2) of the Constitution, according to which "Provisions relating to the fundamental rights and liberties recognised by the Constitution shall be construed in conformity with the Universal Declaration of Human Rights and international treaties and agreements thereon ratified by Spain." Although it had established on more than one occasion that such treaties did not constitute an autonomous parameter for the constitutional review of domestic legislation,[172] the Constitutional Court recognized that to a certain extent the ECHR and the case law of the Court of Strasburg integrated the content of the fundamental rights laid down by the Constitution.[173] The first decisions in which the Constitutional Court referred to the ECHR and the case law of the Court of Strasburg concerned, for example, the principle of equality,[174] the right to life,[175] and the right to privacy.[176] The possibility to make reference to such an influential Convention and supranational judicial body greatly favored the action of the Constitutional Court, especially in its early years.

D *The Constitutional Court and the "Jurisprudential Construction" of the State of Autonomies*

As highlighted previously, the territorial organization of the state probably represented the most sensitive issue in the transition to democracy. In addition to the difficulties already mentioned (such as the lack of support on the part of the Basque National Party for the new Constitution, the ETA terrorist campaign, and the problems arising from the creation of the "pre-autonomous regimes"), the complexity of the territorial question was also linked to the formulation of the Constitution. One of the most widely discussed characteristics of the new Constitution was the failure to establish a clearly defined territorial structure of the State. It is true that Article 2 of the Constitution proclaims "the indissoluble unity of the Spanish Nation, . . ., and recognizes and guarantees the right to selfgovernment of the nationalities and regions of which it is composed," but this decentralization was not something that would *necessarily* be implemented. Indeed, although the

[171] See Aida Torres Pérez, "Report on Spain" in Giuseppe Martinico and Oreste Pollicino (eds.), *The National Judicial Treatment of the ECHR and EU Laws. A Comparative Constitutional Perspective* (Europa Law Publishing 2010), 458; Mercedes Candela Soriano, "The Reception Process in Spain and Italy" in Helen Keller and Alec Stone Sweet (eds.), *A Europe of Rights: The Impact of the ECHR on National Legal Systems* (Oxford University Press 2008), 421 ff.; Xabier Arzoz, "Constitutional Court of Spain" in Rainer Grote, Frauke Lachenmann, and Rüdiger Wolfrum (eds.), *The Max Planck Encyclopedia of Comparative Constitutional Law* (Oxford University Press 2018), 9–10.

[172] See Judgments 120/1990 and 214/1991.

[173] See, e.g., Judgment 36/1991.

[174] See Judgments 22/1981 and 34/1981.

[175] See, e.g., Judgment 53/1985.

[176] See, e.g., Judgment 114/1984.

Constitution laid down the "principle of autonomous rule" (*principio autonómico*) as one of the pillars of the state, it subordinated the implementation of this principle to the "*principio dispositivo*," according to which the territories would decide for themselves whether to establish an Autonomous Community. It is for this reason that the territorial structure of the State – to borrow an expression from Pedro Cruz Villalón – appeared to be "deconstitutionalized"[177] because (at least from a theoretical point of view) it could have evolved in various ways, without ruling out the possibility that Spain could continue to be a centralized state.

However, as expected, the nationalities and regions constituting the Spanish State decided to establish the decentralized entities envisaged by the Constitution, namely the Autonomous Communities. The first Statutes of Autonomy approved were those of the Basque Country and Catalonia at the end of 1979, whereas the last ones were adopted on February 25, 1983: as a result, in just over four years,[178] with the approval of 17 statutes, the "first phase of construction of the State of Autonomies" was concluded.[179] De facto, it is as if on February 25, 1983 *the constitution-making process had been completed*: indeed, it was only at the initiative of the interested territories (establishing the Autonomous Communities) that the Spanish form of state took on its definitive appearance that, as already noted, had not been clearly delineated by the 1978 Constitution. In other words, the completion of the constituent phase depended on this initiative. This was the case particularly when considering that decentralization in Spain represented a "one-way street, without the possibility of turning back. In short, the process of autonomous rule [*proceso autonómico*] was irreversible."[180] Indeed, the Constitution granted the nationalities and the regions the right to their own form of autonomy, but did not guarantee the right to give it up once it had been acquired.

As evidence of the difficulty of defining the territorial structure of the State, one need only consider that in the first two years of its activity the Constitutional Court adopted extremely vague expressions, such as "form of territorial organization of the State as envisaged by the Constitution,"[181] "complex institution,"[182] or "composite form of State."[183] Today, together with Italy, Spain is considered to be an example of a *regional* state, even though the characteristics of the state are so specific as to

[177] Cruz Villalón 1999, note 36, at 431. It is significant that de Esteban 1998, note 9, at 121, described the 1978 Constitution as "unfinished."

[178] Taking as the starting point December 29, 1978, the date when the Constitution was promulgated.

[179] Francisco Tomás y Valiente, "La primera fase de construcción del Estado de las Autonomías (1978–1983)" (1993) 36 *Revista vasca de administración pública*, 45.

[180] Cruz Villalón 1999, note 36, at 399.

[181] Judgment 26/1982.

[182] Judgment 38/1982.

[183] Judgment 35/1982. On this issue see Pedro Cruz Villalón, "Dos años de jurisprudencia constitucional española" (1983) 17 *Revista de derecho político*, 37–38.

require the use of the original wording, such as "Autonomous State" or "State of Autonomies."

The territorial organization of the state regulated by Title VIII of the Constitution was from the outset subject to harsh criticism on the part of legal scholars: for example, according to Luis López Guerra, it was an "absurd and contradictory construction" and "chaos without hope."[184] For his part, Pedro de Vega highlighted the "political ambiguities and judicial lacunae"[185] and described this part of the Constitution as "unfortunate and problematic."[186] In the presence of such a confusing normative framework – especially with regard to the distribution of competences between the central government and the Autonomous Communities[187] – the Constitutional Court carried out a fundamental task of *interpreting* the constitutional provisions and *resolving the conflicts of powers* between the central government and the Autonomous Communities, and among the Autonomous Communities.[188] In this attempt to fill the gaps and make up for the shortcomings of the Constitution, the Constitutional Court managed to ensure the *rational functioning* of the *sistema autonomico*, thus making "achievable"[189] Title VIII of the Constitution. As a result, the "territorial Constitution" of the Spanish State was formed not only by the 1978 Constitution and the Statutes of Autonomy (that taken together represent the parameter for constitutional review [*bloque de constitucionalidad*, corresponding to the *bloc de constititionnalité* in France])[190] but also by the case law of the Constitutional Court.[191] It is for this reason that Spanish legal scholars often use the expression "jurisprudential construction of the State of Autonomies."[192]

[184] Luis López Guerra, "La segunda fase de la construcción del Estado de las Autonomías" (1993) *Revista vasca de administración pública*, 36.

[185] Pedro De Vega, "Prólogo" in Santiago A. Roura, *Federalismo y justicia constitucional en la Constitución Española de 1978* (Biblioteca nueva 2003), 17.

[186] Pedro De Vega, "Prólogo" in Javier Ruipérez, *La reforma del Estatuto de Autonomía para Galicia* (Servicio de publicacións da Universidade da Coruña 1995), 10.

[187] On the distribution of competences see Luciano Vandelli, *L'ordinamento regionale spagnolo* (Giuffrè 1980); Tania Groppi, *Il sistema di distribuzione delle competenze tra lo Stato e le Comunità Autonome* (Giappichelli 1992).

[188] See Arzoz 2018, note 171, at 7 and 11–12; Guillén López 2008, note 161, at 550 ff.; Elisenda Casanas Adam, "The Constitutional Court of Spain: From System Balancer to Polarizing Centralist" in Nicholas Aroney and John Kincaid (eds.), *Courts in Federal Countries: Federalists or Unitarists?* (University of Toronto Press 2017), 386 ff.

[189] Eliseo Aja and Pablo Pérez Tremps, "Tribunal constitucional y organización territorial del Estado autonómico" in Eduardo Espín Templado and Francisco Javier Díaz Revorio (eds.), *La justicia constitucional en el Estado democrático* (Tirant lo Blanch 2000), 155.

[190] It should be noted that the *bloque de costitucionalidad* also consists of the organic laws and the ordinary laws regulating the scope of the competences of the State and of the Autonomous Communities. See Francisco Rubio Llorente, "El bloque de costitucionalidad" (1989) 27 *Revista española de derecho constitucional*, 9 ff.

[191] See Cruz Villalón 1999, note 36, at 431–435.

[192] See, e.g., Francesc de Carreras, "The Inevitable Jurisprudential Construction of the Autonomous State" in Alberto López-Basaguren and Leire Escajedo San Epifanio (eds.), *The Ways of*

The Constitutional Court was concerned primarily with specifying the *political nature* of the Autonomous Communities, underlining the fact that they enjoyed a degree of autonomy (a *political* autonomy) that was distinct from that of the local authorities provided by Article 137 of the Constitution (i.e., the municipal and provincial authorities), that enjoyed an autonomy that was purely administrative.[193] The granting of legislative powers under the terms of a Statute in the framework laid down by the Constitution demonstrated that the Autonomous Communities were vested with their own decision-making powers because their laws had the same rank and force as legislation enacted by the State. Moreover, in Judgment 4/1981 the Constitutional Court provided a more detailed definition of the unity/autonomy dichotomy, specifying that "autonomy does not mean sovereignty, . . . and since each organization endowed with autonomy constitutes a part of the whole, the principle of autonomy may not in any case be in conflict with that of unity: it is actually within this concept that it acquires its real meaning." The Court also ruled that envisaging "generic and indeterminate supervision" by the state over the activities of the Autonomous Communities represented an infringement of the principle of autonomy because such supervision implied a "hierarchical dependency" of the Autonomous Communities in relation to the state administration.[194]

Furthermore, in its first decisions the Court laid down a *duty of collaboration* between the various public bodies forming part of the state and, in particular, between the central government and the Autonomous Communities. In Judgment 18/1982, for example, the Court stated that "the duty of collaboration derives from the general duty of mutual aid between the State authorities and the Autonomous Communities," and specified that this duty "is implied in the very essence of the form of territorial organization of the State envisaged by the Constitution."[195] The constitutional judges also ruled that the duty of mutual aid and cooperation was linked to the principle of coordination, and that it "is even susceptible to modifying the normal order of competences, when it is not possible to wait for the intervention of the normally competent authorities in the case of urgency or necessity."[196]

The most significant decision, however, in this initial period was Judgment 76/1983, in which the Constitutional Court ruled on the constitutionality of the proposed Organic Law on the Harmonization of the Process of Autonomous Rule (*Ley Orgánica de Armonización del Proceso Autonómico* [LOAPA]). In fact, during

Federalism in Western Countries and the Horizons of Territorial Autonomy in Spain (Springer 2013), 481 ff.

193 See, in particular, Judgment 84/1982.

194 Judgment 6/1982.

195 These principles were also reaffirmed on later occasions, as, e.g., in Judgments 33/1982 and 64/1982.

196 Judgment 95/1984. On the case law of the Constitutional Court in relation to the duty of collaboration, see Aja and Pérez Tremps 2000, note 189, at 166–167; Pedro Cruz Villalón, "La jurisprudencia del Tribunal constitucional sobre autonomías territoriales" in Martín-Retortillo (ed.) 1991, note 160, at 3365–3367.

the initial phase of the construction of the State of Autonomies, a crucial step was taken on July 31, 1981, when the president of the government, Leopoldo Calvo Sotelo, and the leader of the Spanish Socialist Workers' Party, Felipe González, signed the "Autonomy Agreements," aimed at the harmonization of the process of autonomous rule by means of a controversial Organic Law, the LOAPA.[197] The aim of this Law was to regulate in greater detail a series of questions concerning the autonomous regimes that neither the Constitution nor the Statutes of Autonomy had regulated with sufficient clarity, such as the extent of the powers of the state and the Autonomous Communities, the meaning of "basic norms" of the state, the form of transfer of services, the role of the *diputaciones provinciales*, and so on. In Judgment 76/1983, however, the Constitutional Court, in finding that the proposed legislation could be approved neither as an Organic Law nor as a law promoting harmonization (*ley armonizadora*), struck down numerous articles, including a substantial part of Title I of the proposed law. Indeed, in the view of the Court, these were interpretative norms aimed at determining the meaning of a series of constitutional provisions relating, in particular, to the distribution of competences. The Constitutional Court ruled that

> the State legislator [could] not intervene directly in the delimitation of competences by means of an interpretation of the criteria constituting the basis of such a delimitation. Certainly any process of normative development of the Constitution always implies an interpretation of the corresponding constitutional provisions, carried out by those enacting the norms giving rise to such a normative development. However, the ordinary legislator cannot enact norms that are merely interpretative, the purpose of which is to specify the sole meaning, among those possible, to be attributed to a specific concept or precept of the Constitution; indeed, by reducing the various possibilities or alternatives laid down in the Constitution to just one, the legislator is *de facto* completing the task of the constituent power and is thus placed from a functional point of view on the same footing, thus overstepping the line of demarcation between constituent power and constituted power.

It has been rightly pointed out that one of the most problematic aspects of these norms was not so much that they were merely interpretative, but that "this interpretation [purported] to be binding on the autonomous legislator."[198] The ruling clarified the fact that the task of interpretation was assigned, on the contrary, to the Constitutional Court, and that in its role as supreme interpreter of the Constitution, the Court was called on to "safeguard the permanent distinction between the positive determination of the constituent power and the implementation of the

[197] See Santiago Muñoz Machado, *Derecho público de las Comunidades Autónomas* (Civitas 2007), 177–180.

[198] Cruz Villalón 1999, note 36, at 429; see also Pedro Cruz Villalón, "¿Reserva de Constitución? Comentario al fundamento jurídico cuarto de la sentencia del Tribunal Constitucional 76/1983, de 5 de agosto, sobre la Loapa" (1983) 9 *Revista española de derecho constitucional*, 185 ff.

constituted powers, that must not overstep the limits and competences laid down for them."

On closer examination, this distinction between constituent power, constituted power, and the relative role of the interpreter has never been entirely clear. In the view of Pedro de Vega, for example, the creative function of law as carried out by the case law of the Constitutional Court with regard to the territorial organization of the State was so powerful that in actual fact the Constitutional Court

> [has ceased] to be ... the mere guardian of the wishes of the constituent power, rather becoming, simply and directly, its substitute: in fact, the acts of constitutional interpretation, that are the only ones that it should legitimately have performed, have been converted to all intents and purposes into acts of constitutional legislation, inexorably going beyond its role of interpreter and guardian of the Constitution.[199]

In short, in de Vega's view, the Constitutional Court has evolved into "a sort of permanent constituent power."[200]

A number of important rulings were also handed down concerning *economic matters*. The Constitutional Court, in particular, attempted to reconcile territorial pluralism and economic unity, relying primarily on Article 149(1)(13), that grants exclusive powers to the state with regard to "the fundamental principles and the coordination of the general planning of economic activity." This clause provided a means for the Constitutional Court to justify state intervention in matters that appeared in the various Statutes of Autonomy to be reserved exclusively for the Autonomous Communities.[201]

One particularly delicate matter that the Court examined was the use of *languages* other than Castilian in certain Autonomous Communities.[202] In particular, in 1986 the Court handed down a ruling concerning the "linguistic normalization laws" of the Basque Country, Catalonia, and Galicia. The Court ruled, *inter alia*, that the duty to know a language concerned only Castilian (Article 3(1) of the Constitution) and not the other languages (such as *Euskera*, Catalan, and Galician), and laid down a series of principles relating to the use of these languages in the public administration of the Autonomous Communities concerned.[203]

In certain cases, the Court revisited its own case law to bring it into line with changes in the legal order. One case of particular interest concerns the "basic" legislation of the State. In Judgment 69/1988, in particular, the Court cast light on the fact that, in the early years after the entry into force of the Constitution, the state

[199] De Vega 2003, note 185, at 17.
[200] Ibid.
[201] See, e.g., Judgment 75/1989.
[202] On this issue see Giovanni Poggeschi, *Le nazioni linguistiche della Spagna autonómica* (Cedam 2002).
[203] See Judgments 82/1986, 83/1986, and 84/1986.

was not in a position to engage in legislative activity that was "so intense as to manage to immediately configure all the basic guidelines envisaged by the Constitution and the Statutes." For this reason, "extraordinary importance" was assigned to the "substantive concept of 'basic norm,'" whereas the "formal component" was considered to be of secondary importance.[204] According to the Constitutional Court, now that this difficult situation had been overcome, the formal component had become increasingly significant and constituted a "guarantee of legal certainty in the organization of the competences of the State and the Autonomous Communities."

It is also important to stress that from 1987 onward there was a steady decline in the number of cases relating to the "*conflicts of powers*" between the central government and the Autonomous Communities,[205] a decline that was due, *inter alia*, to the interpretation of the constitutional provisions by the Constitutional Court. Regardless of the number of cases referred to the Court (that in any case remained high in comparison with the number of cases dealt with, for example, by the German *Bundesverfassungsgericht*), it must be stressed that the Spanish Constitutional Court contributed in a decisive manner, as underlined by Roberto L. Blanco Valdés, to the "*peaceful* settlement, by means of an approach accepted *a priori* by the parties"[206] of the disputes between the central government and the regions. In light of the fact that the territorial question constituted one of the most delicate issues in Spain and that certain sectors of the population had chosen violent methods as the way to achieve their objectives, it is highly likely that had it not been possible to appeal to the Constitutional Court, many of the political conflicts relating to territorial autonomy would have degenerated, thus hindering the *substantive transition* to democracy.

As is well known, the territorial question has remained a thorn in the flesh of Spanish democracy, especially due to the Catalan independence movement. The Constitutional Court has continued to play a leading role in the evolution of the State of Autonomies, handing down a number of extremely important decisions. In 2010, for example, it declared the unconstitutionality of various provisions of the

[204] The substantive concept of "basic norm" implied that the definition by the State legislator of what was "basic" did not mean that the norm was *effectively* basic, but that it was a matter for the Constitutional Court to determine whether it was really basic. The reference to the formal component, on the contrary, meant that it was a matter for the law to "expressly state the basic scope of the norm," or that the law should be characterized by "a structure capable of demonstrating, directly or indirectly, but without any particular difficulty, its vocation or claim to be a basic norm."

[205] Blanco Valdés 2000, note 154, at 28, provides a breakdown of the number of referrals made every year by the state against the Autonomous Communities, and vice versa: 2 (1980), 13 (1981), 48 (1982), 31 (1983), 65 (1984), 82 (1985), 94 (1986), 65 (1987), 64 (1988), 31 (1989), 27 (1990), 7 (1991), 7 (1992).

[206] Ibid.

2006 Statute of Autonomy of Catalonia (Judgment 31/2010);[207] subsequently, it struck down parts of the 2013 Declaration on the Sovereignty and Right to Decide of the People of Catalonia (Judgment 42/2014),[208] and it delivered many other rulings concerning the various legal measures adopted during the separatist process, up until the referendum on secession of October 1, 2017.[209] The Court's arguments ranged from a position of openness (Judgment 42/2014), where the intention was to create a constitutional framework for the development of the "right to decide" of the Catalans, to less conciliatory positions, as a result of the unilateral nature of the separatist process.[210]

4 REASONS FOR SUCCESS

The Constitutional Court was one of the main actors contributing to the success of the process of democratization, ensuring an effective (and fairly rapid) discontinuity with the Francoist past, if not a clean break properly speaking. As discussed in the previous sections, the Court upheld the normative value of all the provisions of the Constitution, dealt with the issue of preconstitutional legislation, established an effective system of protection of fundamental rights, and by means of its interpretation of the constitutional provisions and the resolution of the conflicts of powers between the central government and the regions, it managed to achieve a rational functioning of the State of Autonomies.

A number of factors can be mentioned to explain why the action of the Constitutional Court was so successful. In the first place it is necessary to bear in mind that the Court belongs to the second generation of constitutional courts, and as a result there were fewer unknown factors and more instances of courts in other countries to

[207] See Manuel Pulido Quecedo, *El Estatuto de Autonomía de Cataluña. Anotado con la jurisprudencia sistematizada de la STC 31/2010, de 28 de junio* (Aranzadi 2010); "Forum. Statuto catalano e giurisprudenza costituzionale" (2011) *Diritto pubblico comparato ed europeo*, 3 ff., with an introduction by Luca Mezzetti and papers by Roberto L. Blanco Valdés, Manuel J. Terol Becerra, Miryam Iacometti, Giovanni Poggeschi, Anna Mastromarino, and Renato Ibrido; Francesco Biagi, "*Estatut de Catalunya* e la crisi di legittimazione del *Tribunal constitucional*" (2011) 1 *Quaderni costituzionali*, 63 ff.

[208] This ruling makes numerous references to another important Judgment of the Constitutional Court, 135/2004, concerning the Proposal for a Political Statute for the Euskadi Community (also known as "Plan Ibarretxe"). On Judgment 42/2014 see Victor Ferreres Comella, "The Spanish Constitutional Court Confronts Catalonia's 'Right to Decide' (Comment on the Judgment 42/2014)" (2014) 10 *European Constitutional Law Review* 3, 571 ff. On secession and self-determination in a comparative perspective, see Susanna Mancini, "Secession and Self-Determination" in Michel Rosenfeld and András Sajó (eds.), *The Oxford Handbook of Comparative Constitutional Law* (Oxford University Press 2012), 481 ff.

[209] See Josu de Miguel Bárcena, "El proceso soberanista ante el Tribunal constitucional" (2018) 113 *Revista española de derecho constitucional*, 133 ff.; Josep M.ª Castellà Andreu, "Tribunal constitucional y proceso secesionista catalán: respuestas jurídico-constitucionales a un conflicto político-constitucional" (2016) 37 *Teoría y realidad constitucional*, 561 ff.

[210] See de Miguel Bárcena 2018, note 209, at 133 ff.

learn from. Moreover, the establishment of a Constitutional Court was never contentious: with the exception of certain objections on the part of the Communist Party, during the constitution-drafting process all the political parties gave their wholehearted support to the setting up of a constitutional review body. The adoption of the Organic Law of the Constitutional Court and the appointment of the first (authoritative) constitutional judges went smoothly, enabling the Court to begin deliberations just a year and a half after the adoption of the new Constitution.

The sociopolitical context in which the Court started its activity, though by no means easy due to a number of unresolved issues (including the territorial question), was on the whole conducive to its role as the supreme interpreter of the Constitution. Indeed, especially in the early phase, the Court benefited from great prestige and authority, and was able to perform its duties in a context in which the main political, social, and institutional actors (*in primis*, the monarchy) were committed to a course of action intended to enable Spain to become a social and democratic state based on the rule of law, as laid down in Article 1 of the 1978 Constitution. In addition, as pointed out by Francisco Rubio Llorente, unlike what happened during the Second Republic, the rulings of the Constitutional Court have always been respected "in a rigorous manner"[211] and, at least until the mid-1980s, there was "a lack of tension"[212] between the Constitutional Court and the ordinary courts. Overall, then, the Constitutional Court was clearly operating in a favorable climate. This is all the more evident when making a comparison with the experience of the Italian Constitutional Court, which, in addition to taking office at the end of a particularly tortuous process, was often hindered in its action by the government majority and the higher courts.[213]

The Spanish Constitutional Court was also able to count on the experience of other European Constitutional Courts (such as the German and the Italian ones) that had had to face analogous problems: consider, for example, the issue of the normative value of the Constitution, the problems arising from preconstitutional legislation, and the political decentralization of the state. Moreover, unlike the first generation of courts, the Spanish Constitutional Court was able to rely on the case law of the European Court of Human Rights, to which it made frequent reference. It was, therefore, with the second generation of constitutional courts that the "solitude" of constitutional courts (to borrow an expression from the former Italian

[211] Francisco Rubio Llorente, *La forma del poder (Estudios sobre la Constitución)* (Centro de estudios constitucionales 1993), 460.

[212] Ibid., at 435 (note 71). As noted already, the tensions between the Constitutional Court and the Supreme Court became increasingly evident from the early 1990s onward (see Section 3.C of this chapter).

[213] See Chapter 2, Section 6.

Constitutional Court judge Sabino Cassese)[214] became less marked, as they increasingly took part in a dialogue with foreign, and especially supranational, courts.

Another factor that, albeit indirectly, was favorable to the action of the Constitutional Court was that, after the death of Francisco Franco, Spain soon joined the European Economic Community: indeed, the need to meet the requirements laid down by the 1978 European Council in Copenhagen accelerated the process of democratization, to the benefit of the work of the Constitutional Court.

However, these observations are not intended to imply that the task of the Constitutional Court was easy: Spain was facing a major recession, was dealing with the sensitive issue of the territorial organization of the state (which had led to terrorist violence), and in 1981 experienced an attempted *coup d'état*. Moreover, some legal scholars and members of the judiciary (especially in the superior courts) adopted a rather conservative stance (e.g., by denying that certain constitutional provisions were legally binding), not to mention the fact that even the government, in certain cases, made attempts to hinder the work of the Court (for example by claiming that the Court was not entitled to rule on preconstitutional legislation).

The impression is that the Spanish transition to democracy – that served as a model (as noted already)[215] for several countries that were addressing similar processes – would have hardly been so successful without the pivotal role played by the Constitutional Court. One of its greatest merits was undoubtedly that of promoting and consolidating a *constitutional culture* in the country: indeed, its case law produced *educational effects*, disseminating not only among legal scholars but also in the civil society as a whole, a series of fundamental constitutional values. These included the normative value of the Constitution (Article 9(1) of the Constitution), the inviolability of human rights (Article 10 of the Constitution), as well as the need to strike a fair balance between "the indissoluble unity of the Spanish nation," on the one hand, and "the right to autonomy of the nationalities and regions of which it is composed," on the other (Article 2 of the Constitution).[216]

214 Sabino Cassese, "La giustizia costituzionale: bilancio di un'esperienza; ovvero il dilemma del porcospino, Prolusione dell'anno accademico 2014–15, Accademia delle Scienze di Torino, 10 novembre 2014" in Sabino Cassese, *Dentro la Corte. Diario di un giudice costituzionale* (Il Mulino 2015), 313.

215 See Section 1 of this chapter.

216 On the educational effects of the case law of the Constitutional Court, see Cascajo Castro and Gimeno Sendra 1988, note 156, at 58–59; Blanco Valdés 2000, note 154, at 23; Manuel Aragón Reyes, "25 años de justicia constitucional en España" in Manuel Carrasco Durán, Francisco Javier Pérez Royo, Joaquín Urías Martínez, and Manuel José Terol Becerra (eds.), *Derecho constitucional para el siglo XXI, Actas del VIII Congreso Iberoamericano de Derecho constitucional* (Thomson-Aranzadi 2006), vol. II, 3655; Pedro Cruz Villalón, "Constitución y cultura constitucional" in Pedro Cruz Villalón, Julio D. González Campos, and Miguel Rodríguez-Piñero y Bravo-Ferrer, *Tres lecciones sobre la Constitución* (Mergablum Edición 1999).

4

The Third Generation

The Case of the Constitutional Court of the Czech Republic

> One of the most striking features of the ongoing transitions to democracy in [Central and Eastern Europe] is the spectacular growth in the role and prominence of constitutional courts and tribunals in shaping the new constitutional order.
>
> Wojciech Sadurski[1]

1 FROM THE VELVET REVOLUTION TO THE BIRTH OF TWO INDEPENDENT STATES

According to Juan J. Linz and Alfred Stepan, "the best descriptive phrase of the transition [in Czechoslovakia] is 'regime collapse.'"[2] Indeed, unlike other Central and Eastern European countries, where the transition process was characterized – as in the case of Spain – by negotiations and compromises (suffice it to mention the "round tables" in Poland and Hungary),[3] in Czechoslovakia the rulers were not able to "negotiate the conditions under which they [would] leave power," nor to "impose rules governing the transition," and as a result they did not manage to "delay the process significantly, or exercise some control of the future."[4] Among the main factors that explain this "collapse," in the view of Linz and Stepan, it is important to

[1] Wojciech Sadurski, "Constitutional Justice, East and West: Introduction" in Wojciech Sadurski (ed.), *Constitutional Justice, East and West: Democratic Legitimacy and Constitutional Courts in Post-Communist Europe in a Comparative Perspective* (Kluwer Law International 2002), 1.

[2] Juan J. Linz and Alfred Stepan, *Problems of Democratic Transition and Consolidation: Southern Europe, South America, and Post-Communist Europe* (The Johns Hopkins University Press 1996), 322.

[3] For a comparison between the transition in Spain and Hungary, see Carmen Gonzáles Enríquez, *Crisis y cambio en Europa del Este: la transición húngara a la democracia* (Centro de investigaciones sociológicas 1993).

[4] Linz and Stepan 1996, note 2, at 322.

note the particularly harsh attitude adopted by the regime, leaving no room for reformist moderates within the party and repressing any form of dissent.[5]

The result was that the regime collapsed rapidly, thus confirming the expectations of Timothy Garton Ash at the beginning of the Velvet Revolution: "Arriving in Prague on Day Seven (23 November), when the pace of change was already breathtaking, I met Václav Havel in the back-room of his favored basement pub. I said: 'In Poland it took ten years, in Hungary ten months, in East Germany ten weeks: perhaps in Czechoslovakia it will take ten days!'"[6] In fact, the Velvet Revolution started on November 17, 1989 (when a student protest aimed at commemorating the first student killed after the Nazi invasion turned into a demonstration against the regime that was brutally repressed),[7] but shortly thereafter, on November 29, the Federal Assembly enacted Constitutional Law no. 135/1989, abolishing the main pillars of the Communist regime. In particular, this Law repealed Article 4 of the 1960 Constitution (that upheld the leading role of the Czechoslovak Communist Party) and amended Article 16(1), eliminating the monopoly of the Marxist-Leninist ideology. Moreover, on December 28, 1989, the Federal Assembly elected as its Chairman Alexander Dubček (the symbol of the Prague Spring),[8] and the day after unanimously elected as president of the country Václav Havel, the celebrated playwright who was one of the most outspoken dissidents opposing the Communist regime.

The most urgent measures to be adopted included the purging of the Federal Assembly and the Czech and Slovak national councils, where the forces of the previous regime predominated. For this purpose, the Assembly passed two Constitutional Laws (no. 183/1989 and no. 14/1990). The first Law provided the co-optation of new deputies to replace those who had resigned, whereas the second Law provided for the recall of the most compromised deputies and the co-optation of new ones to fill the vacant seats. The result was that between December 1989 and January 1990 a number of deputies in the Federal Assembly were replaced and the Communist Party, though still holding a large number of seats, lost the overall majority. As discussed in the following text,[9] this measure was followed in October 1991 by the adoption of a Lustration Law, aimed at preventing former Communist Party leaders, as well as officials and collaborators of the secret police, from occupying high-ranking positions in the state apparatus.

[5] Ibid., at 321.

[6] Timothy Garton Ash, *The Magic Lantern: The Revolution of '89 Witnessed in Warsaw, Budapest, Berlin and Prague* (Random House 1990), 78.

[7] On the Velvet Revolution see Bernard Wheaton and Zdeněk Kavan, *The Velvet Revolution: Czechoslovakia, 1988–1991* (Westview Press 1992); John F. N. Bradley, *Czechoslovakia's Velvet Revolution: A Political Analysis* (Columbia University Press 1992).

[8] Dubček was the leader who attempted to introduce "socialism with a human face." In August 1968, however, the Soviet invasion of Czechoslovakia ushered in the period of "normalization."

[9] See Section 4.A of this chapter.

On June 8–9, 1990 the first free elections after 40 years of Communist rule were held to elect the Federal Assembly, the Czech National Council, and the Slovak National Council. The largest number of votes was cast for the Civic Forum in the Czech Republic, and Public against Violence in the Slovak Republic, namely the two civil movements that had been the leading players in the transition in the respective republics. The Communist Party, though still one of the most important political forces, was no longer the hegemonic party. The coalition of the two leading movements gained an absolute majority in the Federal Assembly, and in July 1990 re-elected Havel as president of the republic. The new federal government consisted of members of the Civic Forum, Public against Violence, and the Christian Democrat Movement.

The outcome of this election was particularly significant in various respects. On the one hand, in expressing a strong preference for the Civic Forum and Public against Violence (movements that were strongly antagonistic to the Communist Party), the electorate made plain their intention to leave behind the old regime and to create a democratic system. On the other hand, the success from the very beginning of the transition of two large national movements in each of the Republics, instead of political parties at the federal level, was undoubtedly a factor that later contributed to the dissolution of the Federation.[10] Indeed, once the common enemy, the Communist Party, had been defeated, the profound differences between the two parties, and more in general between the two republics, began to emerge.[11]

The fact that *the relationship between the Federation and the republics was crucial for the future of the country* was evident also from the choice of name. Initially President Havel proposed to change the name of the country from "Czechoslovak Socialist Republic" to "Czechoslovak Republic." Later a compromise was reached by which the country was to have two official denominations: "Czechoslovak Federal Republic" in Czech, and "Czecho-Slovak Federal Republic" in Slovak. This solution, however, was considered to be unsatisfactory by the Slovaks, and as a result a short time later the name was changed to "Czech and Slovak Federal Republic" (hence the expression: "the Hyphen War").[12]

In the autumn of 1990 the Assembly established a commission to draft a new Constitution, consisting of deputies from the Federal Assembly and the Czech and Slovak national councils. The adoption of this Constitution was considered by many

[10] See Angela Di Gregorio, "Lo scioglimento della Cecoslovacchia: aspetti politico-costituzionali" in Angela Di Gregorio and Alessandro Vitale (eds.), *Il ventennale dello scioglimento pacifico della Federazione ceco-slovacca. Profili storico-politici, costituzionali, internazionali* (Maggioli 2013), 122.

[11] See František Šamalík, "Political Parties and the Split of Czechoslovakia" in Viktor Knapp and Sergio Bartole (eds.), *La dissoluzione della Federazione cecoslovacca* (La Rosa 1994), 85.

[12] Karel Svoboda, "Legal and Political Events between 1989 and 1992" in Knapp and Bartole (eds.) 1994, note 11, at 48.

to be "the acid test of Czechoslovakia's continued existence."[13] In the meantime, the Czech and Slovak national councils were supposed to draft their own constitutions. The main question to deal with was the relationship between the republics and the Federation, but after a year the negotiations between the Czechs and the Slovaks broke down. This breakdown, in addition to highlighting "the danger of the weakening of the Federation, or even of its disintegration,"[14] meant that in the end the Federal Assembly never managed to discuss the draft Constitution. Rather, it was decided to postpone the matter until after the elections, to be held in June 1992.

The weakening of the Federation was also due to the adoption of a series of constitutional laws that resulted in a significant increase in the powers of the two republics. It should be noted that until 1989 the country had been characterized by a strong centralism, even though in 1968 a federal system had been adopted (Constitutional Law no. 143/1968). Indeed, the Czechoslovak Communist Party had acted as a "unifying factor"[15] and therefore, even after the adoption of a federal system, the country had continued, de facto, to be a centralized state.[16] The expansion of the powers of the republics came about mainly with Constitutional Law no. 295/1990 (expanding the powers of the republics in relation to the establishment and control of industrial organizations) and Constitutional Law no. 556/1990 (known as the "Competence Law," transferring a series of powers, especially in the economic sector, from the federal government to the republics). The republics were then granted the right to set up their own police forces, as well as their own television and radio stations, and press agencies.[17] The fact that the "federal issue" was coming to the fore gave rise to the need to transfer certain decisions concerning the assignment of powers between the central government and the republics to an independent (*super partes*) institution, the Constitutional Court.[18] As discussed in the following text,[19] though short-lived, this Court handed down some rulings that were extremely important for the transition process.

On June 5–6, 1992, the second elections for the Federal Assembly after the breakdown of the regime were held, resulting in the triumph of the Civic Democratic Party (ODS) led by Václav Klaus in the Czech Republic, and the Movement

[13] Dušan Hendrych, "Constitutionalism in the Czech Republic" in Jiří Přibáň and James Young (eds.), *The Rule of Law in Central Europe: The Reconstruction of Legality, Constitutionalism and Civil Society in the Post-Communist Countries* (Ashgate 1999), 22.

[14] Svoboda 1994, note 12, at 71.

[15] Viktor Knapp, "The Czechoslovak State from Its Origin to Its Extinction" in Knapp and Bartole (eds.) 1994, note 11, at 38.

[16] It has been rightly pointed out that "a socialist federation could never be a true federation, due to the simple fact that it lacks a pluralistic political system" (Hendrych 1999, note 13, at 22).

[17] See Svoboda 1994, note 12, at 66–68.

[18] See Angela Di Gregorio, "La transizione in Cecoslovacchia. Principali profili di diritto costituzionale" in Silvio Gambino (ed.), *Costituzionalismo europeo e transizioni democratiche* (Giuffrè 2003), 252.

[19] See Sections 3 and 4.A of this chapter.

for a Democratic Slovakia (HZDS) led by Vladimir Mečiar in the Slovak Republic. The Civic Forum and Public against Violence, the winners of the previous 1990 elections, practically disappeared. There were profound differences between the ODS and the HZDS. Whereas the ODS was a liberal party which "favored a Thatcher-like rapid move to the market and a stronger role for the central government," the HZDS was a populist and nationalist force, more inclined to "a slower, more statist Austrian move toward a market and substantially more autonomy for Slovakia."[20] The two parties also adopted a different approach with respect to the abovementioned Lustration Law: indeed, whereas the ODS was its main supporter, most of the HZDS members were against this measure.

The new government of the Federation, consisting of an equal number of members of the Civic Democratic Party and the Movement for a Democratic Slovakia, was particularly weak. It consisted of 10 members compared to 16 in the previous government. In addition, only five ministries were effectively run by ministers, whereas the control of the others (that were expected to be abolished) was assigned to the prime minister and other members of the executive. This weakness was not a matter of chance: rather, it was widely recognized that for the Slovaks the task of the federal government was only to "wind up the Federation,"[21] and for this reason Klaus and Mečiar opted to lead the executives of their respective republics.

The election of the president of the republic provided further evidence of the fact that the Federation was heading for dissolution. Indeed, due to the opposition of a minority of Slovak deputies, Havel received insufficient votes to be re-elected. Because there was no other candidate with any chance of being elected, it was decided (as provided by the constitutional law of the Federation) that the presidential functions were to be assigned to the government, which authorized the prime minister to perform some of these functions, while the other powers of the president were transferred to the Presidium of the Federal Assembly.

Despite a number of attempts, the ODS and HZDS failed to reach an agreement on the issue of the territorial organization of the state, which constituted – along similar lines to the situation in Spain, though for different reasons[22] – the main obstacle to the transition process. According to the ODS, the only possible form of state was the Federation (with a single international law subjectivity), whereas the HZDS insisted on the need to create a confederation, in which both republics would be subjects of international law. However, the ODS made clear that, rather than setting up a confederation, it preferred to create two independent states. At this point the dissolution of the Federation appeared to be inevitable. On July 17, 1992 the Slovak National Council approved a Declaration of Sovereignty, laying

[20] Linz and Stepan 1996, note 2, at 333.
[21] Di Gregorio 2013, note 10, at 132.
[22] See Chapter 3, Section 1.B.

down the right to self-determination, proclaiming the sovereignty of the Slovak Republic,[23] and on September 1, 1992 adopted its own Constitution.[24]

The adoption of the Constitution of the Slovak Republic gave rise to the need to speed up the approval of that of the Czech Republic. Until then the Czech constitutional drafters had focused mainly on the new Federal Constitution, while paying scant attention to the drafting of the Constitution for their own Republic. Indeed, in their view the Czech Constitution was to be subordinate to the federal one. The Constitution of the Czech Republic was approved by the National Council on December 16, 1992, and entered into force on January 1, 1993, the day on which the Czech and the Slovak Republics came into being as autonomous states.

At the federal level, the first measure paving the way for the dissolution of the Federation was Constitutional Law no. 493/1992, which abolished various federal ministries and transferred most of the powers from the federal government to the republics. Subsequently, Constitutional Law no. 541/1992 laid down the principles on the basis of which the property of the Czech and the Slovak Republics was to be divided. The main principles were the territorial principle and the principle of the ratio of the population of the Czech Republic to that of the Slovak Republic (based on a criterion of two-to-one in favor of the Czech Republic). On November 25, 1992 the Federal Assembly approved by a slim majority Constitutional Law no. 542/1992 on the extinction of the Czech and Slovak Federal Republic. In particular, this Law stipulated that the Federation would cease to exist on December 31, 1992, and that the states that were to succeed it were the Czech and Slovak republics. These measures were adopted at a time when the process of dissolution of the Federation – based on a political decision – was already at an advanced stage, thus leaving the legislator only two alternatives: "either to legalize this process, or not to do so, and risk unconstitutional developments."[25]

It should be underlined that the decision to dissolve the Federation was taken *without holding a referendum*, even though Constitutional Law no. 327/1991 required a popular consultation in the event that one of the republics decided to leave the Federation. The decision not to comply with the provisions of this Law was essentially the result of political factors. Indeed, on the one hand, the parties did not intend to characterize the dissolution of the Federation as a secession on the part of

[23] Susanna Mancini, "Il fallimento di un *mariage de raison*: la dissoluzione della Repubblica federativa ceca e slovacca" (1993) 4 *Nomos. Le attualità del diritto*, 103–105, argues that Slovakia did not want to dissolve the federation by means of the Declaration of Sovereignty. Rather, the aim of this document was "to show that the governing Slovak bodies did not intend to reach an agreement with the Czechs on economic policy, to express their lack of trust in President Havel, to warn that Slovakia did not intend to compromise." As a result, *the consequences* of the Declaration were more far-reaching than originally intended.

[24] For a comparative analysis of the Constitutions of the Czech Republic and the Slovak Republic, see Rett R. Ludwikowski, *Constitution-Making in the Region of Former Soviet Dominance* (Duke University Press 1996), 169 ff.

[25] Svoboda 1994, note 12, at 83.

the Slovak Republic, while, on the other hand, it was well known that the majority of the population was opposed to the dissolution, or at the very least would have preferred the decision to be taken by referendum and not imposed "from above."[26] In actual fact, it has been rightly pointed out that, although the procedure for the separation of the two republics cannot

> be considered as a secession strictly speaking . . . it is undeniable that the effect was identical, and it could not have been otherwise, since in cases in which a federation consists of only two Member States, their separation, regardless of the procedure adopted, inevitably leads to the dissolution of the pre-existing nation.[27]

Moreover, the intention of the leaders of the political parties not to take account of public opinion in making such an important decision was hardly justifiable, especially in light of the fact that the country was going through a process of emancipation from the Communist regime.

Numerous factors can explain the dissolution of the Federation. First of all, mention should be made of the *nationalist tendencies* that could be found in Slovakia (but to some extent also in the Czech Republic, although they were less visible). Slovak nationalism – in the sense of opposition to the "Prague-centrism"[28] – characterized the entire history of Czechoslovakia, from its origins as a sovereign state,[29] emerging with greater intensity following certain events such as the Prague Spring and the transition to democracy after the collapse of the Communist regime. One of the main obstacles to maintaining a federal system was the *Socialist Constitution* of 1960–1968, which, though subject to far-reaching reforms in the period 1989–1992,[30] had remained in force. In the context of the new democratic system, the serious shortcomings of this Constitution became more and more evident: suffice it to mention the mechanisms that hindered the decision-making processes.

[26] According to opinion polls held in July 1992, 82 percent of Czechs and 84 percent of Slovaks believed that this decision should be taken by citizens in a referendum. Moreover, in having to choose between a federation, a confederation or a separation, both for the Czechs (46 percent) and the Slovaks (47 percent) the least preferred option was a separation. But this is not all: with regard to the form of the State (either a confederation or a federation), both the Czechs (62 percent) and the Slovaks (38 percent) considered the best option to be a federation (even though for the Slovaks a confederation came a close second, with 35 percent of the votes). The results of the opinion polls are reported in Linz and Stepan 1996, note 2, at 329, quoting Sharon L. Wolchik, "The Politics of Ethnicity in Post-Communist Czechoslovakia" (1994) 8 *East European Politics and Societies* 1, 176 ff.

[27] Mancini 1993, note 23, at 109.

[28] Di Gregorio 2013, note 10, at 118.

[29] Katarina Mathernova, "Czecho?Slovakia: Constitutional Disappointments" in A. E. Dick Howard (ed.), *Constitution-Making in Eastern Europe* (Woodrow Wilson Center Press 1993), 59, recalls the fact that the official ideology of the First Republic, established in 1918, was "the existence of a single 'Czechoslovak nation,' bound by one government and cemented by one language." However, the Slovaks "never accepted this concept, and it remains the aspect of President Masaryk's political views most criticized by Slovaks."

[30] In this three-year period more than 50 constitutional laws were enacted.

Economic factors also played a considerable role: as mentioned previously, the Czech Republic intended to speed up the transition to a market economy, whereas the Slovak Republic was in favor of a more gradual approach.[31] In addition, the new leaders were characterized by a strongly *antipolitical* and *anti-institutional stance* (especially in the case of Havel), and were *reluctant to set up statewide political parties*.[32] Finally, as argued by Sergio Bartole, the dissolution of the Federation can be explained by "the impossibility of finding an alternative to . . . the unifying force, the federalizing role of the Czechoslovak Communist Party."[33]

2 THE CZECH REPUBLIC: CONTINUITY WITH THE PAST, INTERNAL QUESTIONS, AND EUROPEAN INTEGRATION

From a *legal* perspective, the *continuity* between the Czech and Slovak Federal Republic and the Czech Republic was extremely evident. In fact, Article 112 of the Czech Constitution stipulates that "the constitutional order"[34] consists of the Constitution; the Charter of Fundamental Rights and Basic Freedoms;[35] the constitutional laws adopted pursuant to the Constitution; those constitutional laws of the National Assembly of the Czechoslovak Republic, the Federal Assembly of the Czechoslovak Socialist Republic and the Czech National Council defining the state borders of the Czech Republic; the constitutional laws adopted by the Czech National Council after June 6, 1992. This continuity was also confirmed by Constitutional Law no. 4/1993 on the measures concerning the dissolution of the Czech and Slovak Federal Republic. This Law confirmed the validity for the territory of the Czech Republic of the constitutional laws, the laws and the other legislative acts of the Federal Republic in force on the day of its dissolution. However, it was not possible to apply those provisions which were contingent only on the existence of the Federation and on the integration of the Czech Republic in it. The Law also transferred the powers of several bodies of the Federation to the corresponding institutions of the Czech Republic.[36]

In addition to dealing with its recent past, after becoming an independent state the Czech Republic turned its attention to settling accounts with the previous Communist regime, a matter that the Federation had already begun to address.

[31] See Jaromír Vepřek, "The Economic Dimension of the Split of Czechoslovakia" in Knapp and Bartole (eds.) 1994, note 11, at 243 ff.

[32] See Linz and Stepan 1996, note 2, at 331–332.

[33] Sergio Bartole, "Introduzione: The Crisis of the Czechoslovak Federalism and the Prospects for Federalism in Europe" in Knapp and Bartole (eds.) 1994, note 11, at X–XI.

[34] The Czech Republic is characterized by a "poly-textual constitution, that is a constitution consisting of several separate documents, which all possess constitutional force and content" (Maxim Tomoszek, "The Czech Republic" in Dawn Oliver and Carlo Fusaro [eds.], *How Constitutions Change: A Comparative Study* [Hart 2011], 42).

[35] On this Charter see Section 5 of this chapter.

[36] E.g., the powers of the Federal Assembly were transferred to the Czech National Council, those of the federal government to the government of the Czech Republic, and so on.

Indeed, as outlined in the text that follows, a series of transitional justice measures were adopted, such as the lustration laws, the law on the illegitimacy of the Communist regime, and the laws on the restitution of property.

The continuity between Czechoslovakia and the Czech Republic was also evident at a *political and institutional level*.[37] The first parliamentary term (1992–1996) was characterized by the fact that in the first six months the Czech representative body was the National Council within the Federation, elected in June 1992. As from January 1, 1993, with the Czech Republic as an independent state, the parliamentary term continued by means of the Chamber of Deputies, that at that stage was the only House of Parliament that had been set up. Indeed, the Constitution did not specify the date for the first elections of the Senate, and as a result of this uncertainty they were only held in 1996.[38] The Civic Democratic Party (ODS) under the leadership of Klaus, having failed to obtain a majority, formed a center-right coalition government consisting of the Christian Democratic Union and the Civic Democratic Alliance (ODA), a liberal party that was set up after the break-up of the Civic Forum. During the period 1992–1996, the ODS strengthened its political identity and clarified the fundamental points of its electoral program, namely the dismantling of the state apparatus, control of inflation and public spending, monetary stability, implementation of the recommendations of the International Monetary Fund, as well as economic and political integration with Europe.[39]

In the 1996 elections, the ODS remained the leading political party in the country, with 29.6 percent of the vote, while the Social Democratic Party (ČSSD) came a close second with 26.4 percent. These elections also saw a decline in support for the Communists, who only obtained 10 percent of the vote, i.e. four percentage points less than in the 1992 elections. The minority government formed by Klaus was short-lived; indeed, due to a major recession, problems within the executive, and a series of financial scandals concerning the ODS, Klaus was forced to resign in November 1997.

The early elections of June 1998 were particularly significant.[40] For the first time the ČSSD emerged as the leading party (32.3 percent of the vote), followed by the ODS (27.7 percent) and the Communists (11 percent). However, in order to be able to govern, the Social Democrats had to sign an agreement – said to be "infamous" by

37 For a more detailed analysis of the political and institutional developments in these early years, see Angela Di Gregorio, *Repubblica Ceca* (Il Mulino 2008), 83 ff.

38 See Ivo Slosarcik, "Rapports: Czech Republic. The Reform of the Constitutional Systems of Czechoslovakia and the Czech Republic in 1990–2000" (2001) 7 *European Public Law* 4, 542–543; Vojtech Cepl and David Franklin, "Senate, Anyone?" (1993) 2 *East European Constitutional Review* 2, 58–60; Jan Kysela, "Bicameralism in the Czech Republic: Reasons, Functions, Perspectives" in Jörg Luther, Paolo Passaglia, and Rolando Tarchi (eds.), *A World of Second Chambers* (Giuffrè 2006), 1003 ff.

39 See Di Gregorio 2008, note 36, at 90.

40 On these elections see Radim Marada, "The 1998 Czech Elections" (1998) 7 *East European Constitutional Review* 4, 51 ff.

some scholars[41] – with the ODS, that offered "external" support in Parliament (agreement known as the "Opposition Agreement"). Although this could not be considered a grand coalition as the ODS did not form part of the government, this party was granted a key role because it was to be consulted on the adoption of the most important decisions, and it was also given the presidencies of both houses of Parliament and the right to appoint the president of the Supreme Auditing Office (Article 97 of the Constitution). The Constitutional Court held that it lacked jurisdiction to determine the legitimacy of this agreement, but it ruled that it was not in contrast with the provision on free political competition (Article 5 of the Constitution).[42] As discussed in the text that follows,[43] the agreement between these two parties could have jeopardized the process of democratic transition, due to the fact that the ČSSD and the ODS introduced numerous changes to the electoral law, thanks to which they could have obtained an overwhelming majority, whereas the minor parties would have run the risk of not gaining any seats in Parliament at all. However, the Constitutional Court struck down most of this law (Judgment Pl. ÚS 42/2000).[44]

During these first parliamentary terms, major economic reforms were adopted, concerning in particular privatization schemes, along with reforms of the justice system and the public administration.

A crucial step in the process of democratization was taken when the country joined the Council of Europe and the European Union (EU), in addition to joining NATO in 1999. To become a member of the Council of Europe, states were required to meet a series of requirements, including being a "European State" and a "pluralist parliamentary democracy."[45] Moreover, from 1990 onward, the standard practice required countries applying to join the Council of Europe to ratify the European Convention on Human Rights (ECHR),[46] and with the Vienna Declaration on October 9, 1993 respect for the rights of national minorities also became a requirement. Interestingly, one of the key factors taken into account with regard to the ability of the state to comply with the basic principles of the Council of Europe (i.e., the principle of the rule of law and respect for fundamental rights) was the setting up of a system of constitutional justice.[47]

41 Radoslav Procházka, *Mission Accomplished: On Founding Constitutional Adjudication in Central Europe* (Central European University Press 2002), 156.

42 See "Czech Republic" (1998) 7 *East European Constitutional Review* 4, 11.

43 See Section 5.A of this chapter.

44 See Section 5.A of this chapter.

45 This expression implied the existence of free and fair elections and the safeguarding of local autonomy.

46 The obligation to ratify the ECHR was laid down in the Vienna Declaration of October 9, 1993. Prior to this, the undertaking by the state to ratify the Convention was taken into consideration only from a political standpoint (see Chapter 3, Section 3).

47 See in particular the Ekman Report of January 29, 1991 on the application for membership submitted by the Czech and Slovak Federal Republic (doc. no. 6380) (available in Council of Europe, *Documents: Working Papers*, vol. VII, Strasburg 1991). On the conditions for

The Czech and Slovak Federal Republic had joined the Council of Europe on February 21, 1991, and the Czech Republic became a member on June 30, 1993. For the purposes of the application submitted by Czechoslovakia, one extremely important factor was the adoption of the Charter of Fundamental Rights and Basic Freedoms, that produced a sort of "ticket effect"[48] for membership in the Council. Joining this supranational organization constituted an important step in the transition process, especially from a formal point of view, since it represented one of the very first external recognitions of the progress of the Czech Republic toward the creation of a fully democratic legal order. From a substantive standpoint, however, it should be underlined that with regard to the admission of Central and Eastern European countries, the Council of Europe applied the conditions for membership *in a much less stringent manner that in the case of previous enlargements*. Indeed, this enlargement, that was "extensive and hurried," produced "a sort of *ex post* implementation of the conditionality criterion, in the sense that the admission of the state to the Council of Europe was not the consequence of meeting the protection standards required by the Convention, but [represented] in many ways the starting point for the achievement of those standards."[49]

The process of accession to the EU began as soon as the Czech Republic became an independent state. On January 17, 1996 an official application for membership was submitted, whereas the first opinion of the European Commission on the application was issued on July 15, 1997. This opinion is of particular interest as it provides an insight into the state of advancement of the democratization process.[50] The application was assessed on the basis of the criteria laid down by the Copenhagen Council of 1993,[51] as well as the recommendations of the European Council in Madrid of 1995.[52] *These conditions were more stringent* than those laid down by

membership for Central and Eastern European countries see Jean-François Flauss, "Les conditions d'admission des pays d'Europe centrale et orientale au sein du Conseil de l'Europe" (1994) 5 *European Journal of International Law* 1, 401 ff.

48 Karel Klíma, *Constitutional Law of the Czech Republic* (Aleš Čeněk 2008), 116.

49 Oreste Pollicino, "Corti europee e allargamento dell'Europa: evoluzioni giurisprudenziali e riflessi ordinamentali" (2009) 1 *Il Diritto dell'Unione europea*, 5–6.

50 See europa.eu/rapid/press-release_DOC-97-17_en.pdf (accessed July 30, 2019).

51 The economic and political requirements were the following: "Membership requires that the candidate country has achieved stability of institutions guaranteeing democracy, the rule of law, human rights and respect for and protection of minorities, the existence of a functioning market economy as well as the capacity to cope with competitive pressure and market forces within the Union. Membership presupposes the candidate's ability to take on the obligations of membership including adherence to the aims of political, economic and monetary union." See www.europarl.europa.eu/enlargement/ec/cop_en.htm (accessed July 30, 2019).

52 For the purposes of accession, the Council underlined the need "to create the conditions for the gradual, harmonious integration of those States, particularly through the development of the market economy, the adjustment of their administrative structures and the creation of a stable economic and monetary environment." See www.europarl.europa.eu/summits/mad1_en.htm (accessed July 30, 2019).

the European Council in Copenhagen of 1978, in relation to the applications submitted by Spain, Greece, and Portugal. In particular, greater emphasis was placed on the principle of the rule of law and the protection of minorities.

The assessment by the European Commission of the application by the Czech Republic was largely positive. In addition, it was undoubtedly a more reliable assessment compared to the past. Indeed, unlike the cases of Spain, Portugal, and Greece (where the degree of effective application of the Constitution was not scrutinized), in the case of the Central and Eastern European countries the commission examined *more closely* whether the "law in the Constitution" corresponded to the "law in action." In the conclusions of the commission's opinion it was stated that "The Czech Republic presents the characteristics of a democracy, with stable institutions guaranteeing the rule of law, human rights, and respect for and protection of minorities." At the same time, however, it was underlined that "[e]fforts to improve the operation of the judiciary and to intensify the fight against corruption must be sustained." Furthermore, there were "some weaknesses in laws governing freedom of the press" along with "a problem of discrimination affecting the Roma, notably through the operation of the citizenship law."[53] From an economic point of view the country was considered to be an efficient market economy, market mechanisms were deemed to be largely well functioning, and significant results had been achieved in terms of economic stabilization, while the unemployment rate was one of the lowest in Europe. However, it was noted that in the ensuing years further initiatives would be needed to strengthen corporate governance and the financial system.

The commission thus believed that the Czech Republic had met the accession criteria, and for this reason recommended starting negotiations for the country to become a member of the EU, bearing witness to the fact that the process of democratization was well advanced. On May 1, 2004, together with nine other states (including Slovakia),[54] the

[53] On the problems of discrimination affecting the Roma see Jirina Šiklová and Marta Miklusakova, "Law as an Instrument of Discrimination: Denying Citizenship to the Czech Roma" (1998) 7 *East European Constitutional Review* 2, 58 ff. For a comparative perspective on the Central and Eastern European countries see István Pogány, "Minority Rights and the Roma of Central and Eastern Europe" (2006) 6 *Human Rights Law Review* 1, 1 ff.

[54] The process of joining the EU was much more complicated for Slovakia than for the Czech Republic. In 1997 the European Commission expressed a negative opinion with regard to opening negotiations for accession to the EU, in light of the fact that the requirements laid down by the European Council in Copenhagen of 1993 had not been met. Indeed, according to the Commission, the Slovak government "d[id] not sufficiently respect the powers devolved by the constitution to other bodies and . . . too often disregard[ed] the rights of the opposition." In addition, the independence of the judiciary was weak and the protection of the rights of minorities was insufficient. See europa.eu/rapid/press-release_DOC-97-20_en.pdf (accessed July 30, 2019).

Czech Republic (that in 2001 had amended its Constitution to be able to join the EU)[55] became a member of the European Union.[56]

In the case of the Czech Republic (and of Central and Eastern European countries more generally), the process of joining the EU had a major influence on the *substantive* transition to democracy.[57] It was not simply the fact that, as in the case of Spain, the possibility of becoming a member of the EU served as a decisive stimulus for speeding up the process of democratization. In the case of post-Communist European countries, there was also a reason of a *procedural* nature.[58] Indeed, the setting of objectives to be achieved for the purposes of accession, the increasingly stringent conditions to be satisfied, and the periodic monitoring aimed at verifying the effective progress of the reforms had the effect of directing and regulating the democratic transition processes. The path to follow in order to reach the final objective was specified with considerable precision, with detailed instructions and more rigorous monitoring than was the case in the past. For all these reasons it is possible to speak of a *"proceduralization" of the substantive transitions to democracy*.

3 ACCEPTANCE AND REJECTION OF THE CONSTITUTIONAL COURT

Kasia Lach and Wojciech Sadurski have underlined that, following the collapse of the Communist regime, in Central and Eastern Europe constitutional courts were "such an obvious institutional element of the newly designed democratic systems that the need to set [them] up was neither seriously debated nor questioned."[59] These courts – as confirmed by László Sólyom – were seen as "a 'trade mark' or ... proof of the democratic character of the respective country."[60] In the Czech Republic the introduction of a system of constitutional review was debated, but "due partly to its indisputability in general terms, [it] did not make it onto the list of

55 Constitutional Law no. 395/2001 introduced sovereignty limitations and regulated the accession procedure. Indeed, Article 10(a) stipulates that "Certain powers of Czech Republic authorities may be transferred by treaty to an international organization or institution. The ratification of a treaty under paragraph 1 requires the consent of Parliament, unless a constitutional act provides that such ratification requires the approval obtained in a referendum."

56 Pursuant to Constitutional Law no. 515/2002, the Czech Republic's membership of the EU was to be ratified by means of a referendum, that was duly held on June 13–14, 2003, with 77 percent voting in favor of accession.

57 On the accession to the EU of these countries, see Neil Walker, "Central Europe's Second Constitutional Transition: The EU Accession Phase" in Adam Czarnota, Martin Krygier, and Wojciech Sadurski (eds.), *Rethinking the Rule of Law after Communism* (Central European University Press 2005), 341 ff.

58 See Laura Cappuccio, "Le condizioni costituzionali di adesione all'Unione europea" (2005) *Forum di Quaderni costituzionali*, www.forumcostituzionale.it (accessed July 30, 2019).

59 Kasia Lach and Wojciech Sadurski, "Constitutional Courts of Central and Eastern Europe: Between Adolescence and Maturity" (2008) 3 *Journal of Comparative Law* 2, 217.

60 László Sólyom, "The Role of Constitutional Courts in the Transition to Democracy: With Special Reference to Hungary" (2003) 18 *International Sociology*, 134.

the constitution makers' primary concerns."[61] Indeed, there were numerous reasons that made the establishment of a constitutional court almost "inevitable." In the first place, it is necessary to consider the "emulation factor," in the sense that the constitutional drafters were keenly aware of the fundamental role played by the constitutional courts of previous generations in democratic transition processes. In particular, they drew inspiration from one of the most important European constitutional courts, the German *Bundesverfassungsgericht*. Moreover, as mentioned already,[62] the prospect of joining the Council of Europe provided an important stimulus for setting up a constitutional court because the Council strongly recommended the creation of a system of constitutional justice.

However, the reasons that more than anything determined the establishment of the Constitutional Court of the Czech Republic were *the strength of the previous experiences of constitutional justice in the region*, and the *lack of trust in the judiciary*. With regard to the first reason, it must be pointed out that a decision of the constitutional drafters *not* to set up a Constitutional Court would have constituted a break (that would have been difficult to explain) with a long-standing tradition of constitutional justice. Indeed, Czechoslovakia had made provision for a Constitutional Court from its origins as a sovereign state in the Constitution of February 29, 1920. In spite of enormous difficulties, this Court represented an extremely important experience especially from a symbolic standpoint because it constituted the very first instance of a constitutional court based on Kelsen's model of constitutional justice, even prior to the Austrian Court.[63]

The second experience of constitutional justice in the region dates back to Constitutional Law no. 143/1968, pursuant to which Czechoslovakia became a federal state, albeit only in formal terms. In addition to the Federal Constitutional Court, provision was made for a Constitutional Court in each of the two republics. However, this was a purely theoretical precedent considering that none of these courts was ever established. The lack of political will to set up a body of this type is reflected in the Czech legal opinion of the time, according to which the Constitutional Court was simply "the blind glorification of a bourgeois institution set up without a scientific Marxist preparation."[64]

The third experience of constitutional justice is that of the Constitutional Court of the Czech and Slovak Federal Republic, established by means of Constitutional Law no. 91/1991. This Court was granted extensive powers: it was entrusted with verifying the constitutional legitimacy of laws and other legislative acts, interpreting

[61] Procházka 2002, note 40, at 68.

[62] See Chapter 1, Section 5.D.

[63] On the Constitutional Court envisaged by the Constitution of February 29, 1920 see Chapter 1, Section 4.

[64] This is the opinion of Professors Blahoz and Matousek as reported by Jean-Pierre Massias, *Justice constitutionnelle et transition démocratique en Europe de l'Est* (Les Presses Universitaires de la Faculté de Droit de Clermont-Ferrand 1998), 300.

the meaning of the constitutional laws of the Federal Parliament, ascertaining the validity of the dissolution of a political party, as well as resolving conflicts over the assignment of powers between the bodies of the Federation, between the bodies of the Federation and those of the republics, and between the bodies of the republics.[65] As noted previously, the setting up of the Constitutional Court was determined above all by the existence of a "federal question" within the country, and it is significant that the first ruling of the Court concerned the assignment of powers between the Federal Ministry of Telecommunications and the corresponding Slovak Ministry.[66] The Court started to operate in February 1992, but ceased to exist just 11 months later, on December 31, when the Czech and Slovak Federal Republic was dissolved. In this short period the Federal Court handed down certain rulings that were extremely important for the transition to democracy, such as the one dealing with lustration (to be discussed)[67] and the one concerning the provisions of the Criminal Code prohibiting hate speech.[68] In spite of its short life span, the Federal Court exerted a significant influence on the case law of the Constitutional Court of the Czech Republic. Indeed, "many interpretative techniques and constitutional principles developed by the [Federal Constitutional Court] were subsequently adopted by the Czech Constitutional Court and thus the [Federal Constitutional Court]'s case law served as an important building block of Czech constitutionalism."[69]

Another factor that explains the setting up of the Constitutional Court of the Czech Republic is the lack of trust in the judiciary, and in particular in the superior courts, including the Supreme Court. This is hardly surprising, especially considering that for many years in Czechoslovakia the courts were under the almost absolute control of the Communist Party. In fact, there was no self-governing body of the judiciary, the Supreme Court judges were appointed by the National Assembly, and their promotion always depended on the will of the party. The apex courts in the Socialist countries were considered to be "bastions" of the regime and "their task was to keep the ordinary courts 'in line,' i.e., to supervise and control them."[70] The lower-court judges were required to follow the guidelines handed down by the superior courts containing the interpretation to be given to important legal issues. In spite of a fairly rapid turnover of judges (especially in the lower courts) in the

65 See Peter Kresák, "Le riforme costituzionali nella Repubblica federale cecoslovacca" (1992) 3 *Quaderni costituzionali*, 448–450.

66 See Herman Schwartz, "The New East European Constitutional Courts" in Howard (ed.) 1993, note 29, at 193.

67 See Section 4.A of this chapter.

68 Pl. ÚS 5/92.

69 David Kosař and Ladislav Vyhnánek, "The Constitutional Court of Czechia" in Armin von Bogdandy et al. (eds.), *Constitutional Judicial Review* (Oxford University Press, forthcoming).

70 Michal Bobek, "Quantity or Quality? Reassessing the Role of Supreme Jurisdiction in Central Europe" (2009) 57 *The American Journal of Comparative Law* 1, 44.

transition from the Communist regime to the democratic order,[71] for a considerable time the judiciary in the Czech Republic continued to be characterized by an "absence of mental independence,"[72] as well as by the strong persistence of "communist legal thinking."[73] This was also due to the fact that several Communist-era judges in the apex courts maintained their position, thus "retain[ing] their influence within the Czech judiciary."[74]

The process leading to the setting up of the Constitutional Court of the Czech Republic was extremely rapid. Indeed, the law on the Court (Law no. 182/1993) was approved on June 16, 1993, and the appointment by President Havel (confirmed by the Chamber of Deputies)[75] of 13 judges (out of a total of 15) took place at the beginning of July in the same year.[76] As a result, just seven months after the entry into force of the Constitution, the Court was able to begin deliberations.

The Czech Constitutional Court encountered a number of difficulties, above all in the first few years of its activity. Along with many other constitutional courts in post-Communist Europe, the Court had to deal with a particular situation that Pavel Holländer (former vice-president of the Czech Court) referred to as "the paradox of acceptance and rejection" of constitutional courts.[77] Indeed, on the one hand, the Court benefited from widespread support among the population, but, on the other hand, strong hostility toward the Court was shown by the ordinary judges, Parliament, President Klaus, and certain legal scholars.

The reasons for the contrast between the Constitutional Court and the ordinary judiciary concerned the powers of the Court to review the constitutionality of the rulings handed down by the ordinary courts. Article 87(d) of the Constitution

[71] In 2001 around 60 percent of Czech judges had spent fewer than 10 years on the bench. In the case of certain judges, this turnover took place spontaneously, whereas for others it was due to the fact that they were too compromised with the previous regime. See Zdeněk Kühn, "The Democratization and Modernization of Post-Communist Judiciaries" in Alberto Febbrajo and Wojciech Sadurski (eds.), *Central and Eastern Europe after Transition: Towards a New Socio-Legal Semantics* (Ashgate 2010), 181.

[72] Michal Bobek, "The Fortress of Judicial Independence and the Mental Transitions of the Central European Judiciaries" (2008) 14 *European Public Law* 1, 107. In his view, "Czech judges perceive themselves as docile interpreters of the will of the legislator. Critical thinking and critical morality … is non-existent or very rare" (at 107).

[73] Kühn 2010, note 70, at 182.

[74] David Kosař, *Perils of Judicial Self-Government in Transitional Societies* (Cambridge University Press 2016), 170.

[75] Pursuant to Article 84 of the Constitution, judges are appointed by the president with the consent of the Senate. In the case of the initial appointments, however, because the Senate had not yet been established, the task of confirming the choices made by the president was carried out by the lower chamber.

[76] With regard to the remaining two judges, one was appointed in the autumn of 1993, the other in the spring of 1994.

[77] Pavel Holländer, "The Role of the Czech Constitutional Court: Application of the Constitution in Case Decisions of Ordinary Courts" (1997) 4 *Parker School Journal of East European Law*, 445.

provides that the Court has jurisdiction "over constitutional complaints against final decisions or other encroachments by public authorities infringing constitutionally guaranteed fundamental rights and basic freedoms," and Article 89(2) stipulates that the "decisions of the Constitutional Court are binding on all authorities and persons." However, the judges in the ordinary courts, in particular in the apex courts, believed that they were excluded from the category of "public authorities" and as a result they argued that they were not required to comply with the decisions of the Constitutional Court. The problem of the binding nature of the rulings of the constitutional courts in relation to the ordinary courts was quite a common one in Central and Eastern Europe,[78] but it became a matter of particular concern above all in the Czech Republic. The contrast between the Supreme Court and the Constitutional Court (which became extremely evident with Judgment Pl. ÚS 38/1999)[79] was so intense that (as in the case of Italy and Spain) it gave rise to the expression "the war of the Courts." The charge leveled against the Constitutional Court was that in various instances this body did not limit itself to ascertaining the constitutionality of the decisions of the ordinary courts, but it had turned into a de facto "appeal court."[80] The tensions between the Constitutional Court and the ordinary courts diminished considerably (though not entirely)[81] starting from the

78 E.g., on the case of Poland see Lech Garlicki, "Constitutional Courts versus Supreme Courts" (2007) 5 *International Journal of Constitutional Law* 1, 57 ff.; Rafał Mańko, "'War of Courts' as a Clash of Legal Cultures: Rethinking the Conflict between the Polish Constitutional and Supreme Court over 'Interpretive Judgements'" in Antonia Geisler, Michael Hein, and Siri Hummel (eds.), *Law, Politics, and the Constitution: New Perspectives from Legal and Political Theory* (Peter Lang 2014), 79–92. For a comparative overview of the complex interactions between constitutional courts and ordinary courts see also Maartje De Visser, *Constitutional Review in Europe: A Comparative Analysis* (Hart 2014), 377 ff.

79 This case concerned the Jehovah's Witnesses, who refused to carry out military service or the alternative civil service. According to the Constitutional Court this continuous refusal for religious reasons was deemed to be one crime continuing over time, and not a series of different crimes, and as a result the principle of *ne bis in idem* (the principle that the defendant could not be tried for the same offence more than once) was applicable. The Supreme Court, on the contrary, held that each refusal constituted a distinct criminal act, and therefore decided not to accept the ruling of the Constitutional Court. The result was that "the system of justice [was put] into a deadlock" (Jiří Přibáň, "Judicial Power vs. Democratic Representation: The Culture of Constitutionalism and Human Rights in the Czech Legal System" in Sadurski [ed.] 2002, note 1, at 381).

80 Procházka 2002, note 40, at 162.

81 Another more recent example of the tensions between the Constitutional Court and the ordinary judiciary is that of the Slovak Pension Saga, in which the Supreme Administrative Court repeatedly refused to follow the case law of the Constitutional Court. The clash then moved to the European level, involving the Court of Justice of the EU. See Zdeněk Kühn, "Ultra Vires Review and the Demise of Constitutional Pluralism: The Czecho-Slovak Pension Saga, and the Dangers of State Courts' Defiance of EU Law" (2016) 23 *Maastricht Journal of European and Comparative Law*, 185 ff.; Kosař and Vyhnánek, forthcoming, note 68.

new millennium, when the ordinary judges began to recognize the binding force of the Constitutional Court's rulings.[82]

Even certain legal scholars, relying on the principle of parliamentary sovereignty, argued that the decisions of the Constitutional Court were not binding and hence Parliament could enact legislation containing provisions that had been declared unconstitutional by the Court in one of its previous judgments.[83] Words were followed by deeds. In fact, this position was adopted in some cases by Parliament, which manifestly ignored previous rulings handed down by the Court. One of the most interesting cases concerns Law no. 268/1998, on the abolition of part of the supplementary salary payments for certain public officials, including judges. This Law was part of a package of austerity measures aimed at dealing with the economic difficulties that the country was facing in that period. The abolition of one of the two supplementary monthly payments attracted widespread public support, as it was seen as a way of addressing the economic crisis. However, with Judgment Pl. ÚS 13/1999, the Court struck down the part of the Law that included judges among the public officials who were to lose the supplementary monthly payment, based on the argument that a measure of this kind violated the principle of the independence of the judiciary. In spite of this decision, a short time later the Chamber of Deputies approved fresh austerity measures, concerning the same public officials and with almost the same provisions as the law that had just been declared unconstitutional. The Senate sent the proposed legislation back to the Chamber of Deputies, stating that it needed to comply with the ruling of the Court. However, the Chamber of Deputies chose to ignore both the recommendation of the Senate and the judgment of the Constitutional Court, approving the law in its original version.[84] The matter was settled when the question was referred once again to the Court, which found the law in line with the Constitution.[85] However, it should be noted that the Court has ruled on the constitutionality of judicial salaries 15 times so far, in most cases striking down the proposed salary cuts.[86]

82 See Zdeněk Kühn, "Making Constitutionalism Horizontal: Three Different Central European Strategies" in András Sajó and Renáta Uitz (eds.), *The Constitution in Private Relations: Expanding Constitutionalism* (Eleven International Publishing 2005), 224.

83 This position, defended by Vladimír Mikule and Vladimír Sládecek, is mentioned in Přibáň 2002, note 78, at 385.

84 See Přibáň 2002, note 78, at 387–388. Similar cases occurred also in other countries, such as Bulgaria. See Sergio Bartole, "Le nuove democrazie dell'Europa centro-orientale alle loro prime prove" in Sergio Bartole and Pietro Grilli di Cortona (eds.), *Transizione e consolidamento democratico nell'Europa centroorientale. Élites, istituzioni partiti* (Giappichelli 1998), 202.

85 Judgment Pl. ÚS 18/99. See Wojciech Sadurski, "Constitutional Courts and Constitutional Culture in Central and Eastern European Countries" in Febbrajo and Sadurski (eds.) 2010, note 70, at 107.

86 Namely Judgments Pl. ÚS 13/99, Pl. ÚS 18/99, Pl. ÚS 16/2000, Pl. ÚS 11/02, Pl. ÚS 34/04, Pl. ÚS 43/04, Pl. ÚS 9/05, Pl. ÚS 55/05, Pl. ÚS 27/07, Pl. ÚS 13/08, Pl. ÚS 12/10, Pl. ÚS 16/11, Pl. ÚS 33/11, Pl. ÚS 23/09, and Pl. ÚS 28/13.

A series of conflicts took place also between the President of the Republic, Klaus, and the Court. Klaus had been one of the leading critics of the Constitutional Court, having often accused it of excessive activism. The new appointments of constitutional judges in 2003 provided the president with an excellent opportunity to try to create a Court that was as similar as possible to his own idea of what a Constitutional Court should be. However, he encountered strenuous opposition from the Senate (which, as mentioned already, was required to confirm the appointment of the judges), where the majority of members belonged to the rival party, the ČSSD. The reasons for the disagreement concerned whether formerly active politicians could be appointed to the Court, as well as whether certain judges could be appointed for a second term of office.[87] The first time the Senate rejected the presidential nominees was on July 16, 2003, but the high point of the conflict came on August 6, when the Senate rejected three out of four nominees. The situation was so serious that during the summer of 2003 the number of judges serving on the Court fell below 12, the quorum required for handing down rulings. It was only in the autumn of 2004 that the Court managed to reach the threshold of 12 judges.[88] For more than a year, then, the activity of the Czech Constitutional Court remained "frozen." The "nomination saga"[89] concluded in December 2005, when all the vacancies on the bench were finally filled.

Another episode that is emblematic of the strained relations between President Klaus and the Constitutional Court occurred in 2006, when Klaus dismissed the Chief Justice of the Supreme Court, Iva Brozova.[90] However, the Constitutional Court, to which the matter had been referred, struck down the law that allowed the president to dismiss the chief justice, on the grounds that it undermined the principle of the independence of the judiciary.[91] Klaus took the view that the ruling of the Court was "an example of judicial corporatism" and a "threat to democracy."[92]

It is in light of this particular situation of "acceptance and rejection" that the role of the Constitutional Court in the process of substantive transition to democracy must be examined. As discussed in the following sections, the Court focused on two main fields. The first sphere of intervention – that was common to many other constitutional courts in the region – concerned *transitional justice*. In particular, the Court was called on to verify the constitutionality of the laws dealing with the

[87] See Zdeněk Kühn and Jan Kysela, "Nomination of Constitutional Justices in Post-Communist Countries: Trial, Error, Conflict in the Czech Republic" (2006) 2 *European Constitutional Law Review* 2, 196–198.

[88] Ibid., at 198–199.

[89] Lach and Sadurski 2008, note 58, at 227.

[90] See Kühn 2010, note 70, at 188–191.

[91] Judgment Pl. ÚS 18/06. On this decision see Zdeněk Kühn, "Judicial Independence in Central-Eastern Europe: The Experience of the 1990s and 2000s" (2011) 1 *The Lawyer Quarterly*, 34 ff.

[92] As reported by Sadurski 2010, note 84, at 110.

Communist past, such as the lustration laws, the law on the illegitimacy of the Communist regime, and the laws on the restitution of property. The second sphere of intervention concerned the *safeguarding of fundamental rights and freedoms*, that had been systematically violated under the previous regime. Among the numerous judgments delivered in this field, special attention will be devoted to the decisions concerning the status of the European Convention on Human Rights and international treaties, as well as those on the right to vote and the electoral system.

Many constitutional courts of the third generation, such as the Polish, the Hungarian, and the Slovakian Courts, were called on to resolve major political disputes between the branches of government.[93] Although in the Czech Republic the Constitutional Court was less involved in these political conflicts, there were a few significant cases. In Judgment Pl. ÚS 14/01, for example, the Court ruled on the conflict between the president and the government regarding the appointment of the board members of the Czech National Bank. The constitutional judges held that the president could act unilaterally and appoint all board members of the National Bank without the countersignature of the prime minister.[94]

The fact that the Czech Court was less involved in the resolution of political disputes compared to many other post-Communist Courts can be explained (at least in part) by taking account of

> the context in which the transition begins, that from the very beginning is not favorable to a decisive role of the Court in the political sphere .... Since the new democratic elite, with the support of public opinion, immediately initiates far-reaching political and economic reforms, as well as a ... rapid process to implement European standards with a view to future membership of the EU, there is no room for constitutional disputes about the real scope of the powers of Parliament and the Government and their approach to decision-making and legislation.[95]

With regard to access to the Court, one of the most widely utilized procedural gateways was the individual constitutional complaint, by which citizens could petition the Court directly, albeit within certain limits, including the requirement to have exhausted all other judicial remedies. In the early years, for example, the Court received a number of complaints dealing with rehabilitation and the restitution of property. However, if the Court played a prominent role in the process of democratization, it was also because public authorities (in particular the president of the Republic) and parliamentary minorities often challenged the constitutionality of legislative acts, thus enabling the Court to rule on cases concerning transitional justice and the protection of fundamental rights.[96]

93 See Chapter 5, Section 2.

94 See Kosař and Vyhnánek, forthcoming, note 68.

95 Di Gregorio 2003, note 18, at 268.

96 On the procedural gateways to the Constitutional Court see Angela Di Gregorio, "Ricorso incidentale e ruolo dei cittadini nella tutela dei diritti e libertà fondamentali dinanzi alla Corte

4 DEALING WITH THE PAST: THE COURT AND TRANSITIONAL JUSTICE

In the definition adopted by Rudi G. Teitel, transitional justice refers to "the conception of justice associated with periods of political change, characterized by legal responses to confront the wrongdoings of repressive predecessor regimes."[97] Therefore, the ultimate aim of transitional justice may be summed up in the well-known expression "*to deal with the past.*" The idea is that it is not possible to establish a new phase of democracy and liberty without coming to terms with the past, and in particular with those who have committed atrocities of various kinds.[98] The key issues that must be dealt with are essentially two: the first concerns *acknowledgment* (whether to "remember" of "forget" the abuses), and the second refers to *accountability* (whether or not to prosecute or otherwise impose sanctions on the perpetrators).[99]

The picture is further complicated when it comes to choosing the methods for addressing the past. History shows that a number of responses have been given, varying from one country to another, though it is possible to identify four main strategies.[100]

The first strategy consists of prosecuting the perpetrators of crimes committed under the previous regime. This was the official policy adopted vis-à-vis the collaborators of the Nazi regime in most of the Western countries occupied by the Germans during World War II.

The second strategy consists of granting an amnesty. In certain situations, the elites unilaterally grant themselves this act of clemency before the transition gets underway. In other cases, the amnesty is the outcome of negotiations between the outgoing and the incoming leaders. Another possibility is when the democratic forces decide to grant a pardon to those who committed crimes in the past. This was the case of Spain after the death of Francisco Franco.[101] While it is the case that the main beneficiaries of a series of clemency measures adopted in 1976 and 1977 were individuals who had opposed the authoritarian regime, pardons were also granted to

costituzionale ceca" (2014) 1 *Diritto pubblico comparato ed europeo*, 362 ff.; Kosař and Vyhnánek, forthcoming, note 68.

97 Ruti G. Teitel, "Transitional Justice Genealogy" (2003) 16 *Harvard Human Rights Journal*, 69. See also Ruti G. Teitel, *Transitional Justice* (Oxford University Press 2000).

98 See Jon Elster, *Closing the Books: Transitional Justice in Historical Perspective* (Cambridge University Press 2004).

99 See Mary Albon, "Project on Justice in Times of Transition: Report of the Project's Inaugural Meeting" in Neil J. Kritz (ed.), *Transitional Justice: How Emerging Democracies Reckon with Former Regimes. Volume I. General Considerations* (US Institute of Peace Press 1995), 42. On the arguments for and against these positions see Samuel P. Huntington, *The Third Wave: Democratization in the Late Twentieth Century* (University of Oklahoma Press 1991), 211 ff.

100 See Luc Huyse, "Justice after Transition: On the Choices Successor Elites Make in Dealing with the Past" in Kritz (ed.) 1995, note 98, at 337 ff.

101 See Chapter 3, Sections 1 and 3.C.

officials and members of the police force engaging in acts of repression under Franco.

The Italian case is to be found midway between the first and the second strategy. Indeed, initially it was decided to prosecute the members of the Fascist regime (albeit with limited results), whereas subsequently, in June 1946, an amnesty was granted (known as the "Togliatti amnesty"). In Italy, therefore, there was no clear choice between criminal prosecution and granting a pardon.[102]

The third strategy, based on the principle "amnesty, but not amnesia,"[103] consists in setting up a Truth and Reconciliation Commission, as in the case of postapartheid South Africa.[104] The purpose of this body is not to prosecute or punish, but to ascertain the truth, casting light on human rights violations and ensuring that what happened in the past does not fall into oblivion, but remains alive in the memory of the collectivity. The underlying rationale for establishing these commissions is that general knowledge of the truth is not sufficient in itself, but rather there is a need for official recognition of the injustices suffered in the past.[105]

The fourth strategy is the one pursued mainly in post-Communist Europe, where "lustration"[106] measures were adopted with the intention of preventing those closely associated with the previous regime from occupying higher positions in the state apparatus. Both the Constitutional Court of the Czech and Slovak Federal Republic and the Constitutional Court of the Czech Republic – like many other constitutional courts in Central and Eastern Europe – were called on to verify the constitutionality of these lustration laws. The Czech Court also ruled on the legitimacy of other transitional justice measures adopted in the country, namely the Law on the illegitimacy of the Communist regime and the laws on the restitution of property.

A *The Defense of Democracy: The Federal Court, the Czech Court, and the Lustration Laws*

As noted earlier, lustration laws were the measures most frequently adopted in Central and Eastern Europe to deal with the Communist past. It must be emphasized, however, that the number of individuals affected by these laws varied considerably from one country to another,[107] and that the constitutional courts, depending

[102] See Chapter 2, Section 3.

[103] Huyse 1995, note 99, at 338.

[104] See Andrea Lollini, *Constitutionalism and Transitional Justice in South Africa* (Berghahn Books 2011).

[105] For a comparative analysis of Truth Commissions see Priscilla B. Hayner, *Unspeakable Truths: Transitional Justice and the Challenge of Truth Commissions* (Routledge 2011).

[106] This term comes from the Latin *lustratio* meaning purification, expiation.

[107] In general, however, the number of people affected by these measures was quite limited. Suffice it to consider the cases of Czechoslovakia and Germany, that enacted lustration laws that are considered to be the harshest. The number of those subject to lustration who were

on the respective countries, handed down very different rulings.[108] Although it is a long time since the collapse of the Communist regime, some countries in the region have continued to adopt lustration laws even in recent years, providing evidence that the "specter" of Communism has not been entirely eliminated.[109]

Czechoslovakia was one of the first countries in Central and Eastern Europe to adopt a lustration law (Law no. 451/1991, approved on October 4, 1991). This measure was intended to prevent individuals involved with the Communist regime, or considered to be in favor of a return to Communism, from occupying higher positions in the state apparatus.[110] In particular, it prohibited former Communist Party leaders, as well as officials and collaborators of the secret police (StB), from occupying high-level positions in the state administration for a period of five years, i.e. until January 30, 1996.[111] Individuals subject to lustration measures had the right to appear before a commission set up by the Ministry of the Interior and to appeal against the decisions of this commission before the civil courts.[112]

In addition to the Movement for a Democratic Slovakia,[113] also the International Labour Organization harshly criticized the Law, as it was deemed to be in conflict with Convention No. 111 on Discrimination (Employment and Occupation) 1958, and recommended that it be referred to the Constitutional Court.[114] Havel also raised several objections, arguing that the Law had gone "far beyond the original

removed from their position was 7 percent in Czechoslovakia, and 3 percent in the Czech Republic and Germany. See Angela Di Gregorio, *Epurazioni e protezione della democrazia. Esperienze e modelli di 'giustizia post-autoritaria'* (Franco Angeli 2012), 207.

108 See Mark S. Ellis, "Purging the Past: The Current State of Lustration Laws in the Former Communist Bloc" (1996) 59 *Law and Contemporary Problems* 4, 181 ff.; Wojciech Sadurski, *Rights before Courts: A Study of Constitutional Courts in Postcommunist States of Central and Eastern Europe* (Springer 2014), 343 ff.; Di Gregorio 2012, note 106, at 177 ff.

109 E.g., in 2010 and 2011 the Constitutional Courts of Albania, Romania, Poland, and Macedonia struck down entirely or in part the lustration laws adopted in their respective countries.

110 See Marco Clementi, "Un aspetto della transizione in Cecoslovacchia e nella Repubblica Ceca: la legge di lustrazione" in Gambino (ed.) 2003, note 18, at 285 ff.

111 This concerned, specifically, the higher ranks of the armed forces, the intelligence agency, the police, the office of the president, the legislative and executive bodies of the Federation and the two republics, the Constitutional Court and the Supreme Court, the presidium of the Academy of Science, the radio, the television, the press agencies, public limited companies where the state was their majority owner, the railways, the Central Bank, and the universities. The measure also affected judges, state attorneys, attorney office investigators, notaries public, state arbitrators, and candidates for these offices.

112 However, not all officials were granted the power to seek redress because the Czech authorities believed that for certain categories of people there was "little doubt" that they "did indeed work for the secret police" (Jiri Pehe, "Parliament Passes Controversial Law on Vetting Officials" in Neil J. Kritz [ed.], *Transitional Justice: How Emerging Democracies Reckon with Former Regimes. Volume II. Country Studies* [US Institute of Peace Press 1995] 553).

113 On the opposition to the law by the Movement for a Democratic Slovakia, see Section 1 of this chapter.

114 International Labour Organization, Decision on the Lustration Law (GB.252/16/19, February 28, 1992, 252nd Session).

intentions."[115] He proposed a series of amendments to Parliament, but they were not approved. Because the Constitution in force at the time did not grant the head of state the power to send legislation back to Parliament, in the end he was forced to promulgate the Law.[116]

The lustration law was referred to the Constitutional Court of the Czech and Slovak Federal Republic by a group of 99 members of the Federal Assembly. According to the referral, it violated a number of provisions of the Constitution, the Charter of Fundamental Rights and Basic Freedoms, the Constitutional Law on the Czechoslovak Federation of 1992, and a series of international human rights treaties. However, in Judgment Pl. ÚS 1/92, the Court upheld most of the Law, stressing that its adoption was justified by the need to safeguard the security of the state and its members, and by the fact that it was applicable only for a limited period.

The Court took as the starting point of its reasoning the fact that under the previous regime a number of individuals who met the criteria laid down by the Central Committee of the Communist Party had been hired in the public administration, security sector, justice system, economic sector, and armed forces. These criteria consisted of "political maturity, a creative Marxist-Leninist approach to the solution of problems, and the determination to consistently bring the party's policies to life." The result was that until 1989 all the key positions at every level of the state administration were controlled by the Communist Party. In light of this situation, the Court ruled that this "calculated and malicious conduct" represented a "source of destabilization and danger, which could easily threaten the developing constitutional order," and consequently declared the Law in line with the Constitution. According to the constitutional judges,

[115] Sergio Bartole, *Riforme costituzionali nell'Europa centro-orientale. Da satelliti comunisti a democrazie sovrane* (Il Mulino 1993), 41.

[116] The objections raised to this Law concerned the fact that it provided for collective rather than individual responsibility; was based on a presumption of guilt (because the burden of proof was reversed, as it was up to the citizen to demonstrate the lack of any connection to the party and the secret police); did not take into consideration the circumstances of the individual case; violated the principle of equality before the law; was based on the dossiers of the State Security Police, which were inaccurate, incomplete, or falsified; and allowed no exemptions for those who had been forced to collaborate or who had been members of the Party only for a limited period (see David Kosař, "Lustration and Lapse of Time: 'Dealing with the Past' in the Czech Republic" [2008] 4 *European Constitutional Law Review* 3, 470; Jirina Šiklová, "Lustration or the Czech Way of Screening" [1996] 5 *East European Constitutional Review* 1, 57 ff.). By contrast, those who defended this Law made reference, *inter alia*, to the exceptional circumstances in which it was adopted; the fact that the aim of the Law was not to seek revenge but to respond to the needs of those who, unable to forgive or forget, demanded some kind of sanction. Moreover, the lustration law was intended to prevent former members of the Communist regime from hindering the process of democratization, in the belief that it was extremely unlikely that those who had been the driving force of the regime until a short time before could be converted into genuine supporters of the democratic reforms. See Mark Gillis, "Lustration and Decommunisation" in Přibáň and Young (eds.) 1999, note 13, at 66 ff. On the problematic nature of this type of measures see also Vojtech Cepl, "Ritual Sacrifices" (1992) 1 *East European Constitutional Review* 1, 24–26.

> A democratic state has not only the right but also the duty to assert and protect the principles upon which it is founded .... A democratic state is ... entitled to make all efforts to eliminate an unjustified preference enjoyed in the past by a favored group of citizens ... where such preference was accorded exclusively on the basis of membership in a totalitarian political party .... In a democratic society, it is necessary for employees of state and public bodies ... to meet certain criteria [such] as loyalty to the democratic principles upon which the state is built.

In the view of the Court, this provision did not constitute discrimination since the Law applied only to a limited group of people and for a limited period (i.e., until December 31, 1996, when the Court expected the process of democratization to be concluded), and also because those subject to lustration measures had the right to appeal to the courts.

In addition, the Federal Court put forward an argument (later elaborated in greater depth by the Czech Constitutional Court) based on the "theory of values," underlining that the values that characterize the two regimes (Communist and democratic) are completely different: "the concept of the law-based state does not have to do merely with the observance of any sort of values and any sort of rights, even if they are adopted in the procedurally proper manner." Rather, this concept mainly refers to respect for "those norms that are not incompatible with the fundamental values of human society." The Court also pointed out that the construction of a law-based state, which has as its starting point a discontinuity with the previous illiberal regime in relation to values, may not adopt criteria of formal and material legal continuity based on a different system of values, even when this formal legal continuity is permitted by the legal order. In the view of the Court, respect for the continuity of the old system of values would not constitute a guarantee of legal certainty, but rather a betrayal of the new values, and a threat to legal certainty, and it would also undermine the citizens' belief in the credibility of the democratic system. In short, according to the Court the previous regime could not be considered to be "legitimate" although it was "legal."

In 1995 the Parliament of the Czech Republic extended the validity of the Law for a further five-year period (until December 31, 2000). Havel once again raised objections and decided to refer the Law back to Parliament, because, unlike 1991, the new Constitution of the Czech Republic (Article 50) granted this power to the head of state. According to the president, this extension was tantamount to publicly recognizing the incapacity of the country to become a normal democracy, showing that it was not capable of addressing by democratic means the attempts to reinstate the Communist regime.[117] However, after Parliament had reapproved the Law without introducing any amendments, the president was forced to promulgate it.

In 2000 Parliament voted once again to extend the time limit both of Lustration Law no. 451/1991 (known as "Great Lustration Law") and Lustration Law

[117] See Clementi 2003, note 109, at 296.

no. 279/1992 (known as "Small Lustration Law," which specifically applied to certain positions within the Ministry of Interior, the police, and the Penitentiary Service). These laws were intended to remain in force until the entry into force of the law on public servants in administrative authorities.

On March 2, 2001 both lustration laws were referred to the Constitutional Court by 44 deputies. According to the complainants, the country was now in a totally different situation compared to 1992. Indeed, the three traditional branches of government had been set up democratically, and the key positions in the state apparatus and other public bodies were no longer occupied by persons linked to the previous regime. This meant that acts of subversion or a possible return to the Communist regime were no longer a risk for the country, and as a result the reasons justifying the lustration measures no longer existed. The complainants also stressed the fact that the Federal Court had upheld the constitutional legitimacy of the lustration law given its "transitory nature," as it was intended to remain in force for a five-year period.

Judgment Pl. ÚS 9/01 confirmed the decision adopted by the Czechoslovak Court a decade earlier.[118] The Court dealt first of all with the issue of the "transitory nature" of the Law, underlining the fact that the Federal Court had not indissolubly linked the validity of the Law to 1996, but had simply stated that the process of democratization could be expected to be complete by that year. Moreover, according to the Czech Court, the degree of development of a democracy was "a social and political question, not a constitutional law question," and for this reason it was not in a position to ascertain the completion or the noncompletion of the democratization process. In addition, while sharing the opinion expressed by the complainants that the public interest was now less intense and urgent compared to 1992, the Court (coming to the core of its reasoning) stated that the requisites of loyalty to the interests of the State and the democratic principles on which it is based were not the prerogative solely of countries in transition but of all democratic systems. According to the Court, the State had not only the right, but also the duty "to defend itself," making express reference to the concept, frequently cited by the European Court of Human Rights, of "a democracy capable of defending itself."[119]

[118] David Robertson, "A Problem of Their Own, Solutions of Their Own: CEE Jurisdictions and the Problems of Lustration and Retroactivity" in Wojciech Sadurski, Adam Czarnota, and Martin Krygier (eds.), *Spreading Democracy and the Rule of Law? The Impact of EU Enlargement on the Rule of Law, Democracy and Constitutionalism in Post-Communist Legal Orders* (Springer 2006), 89, points out that in the view of the Court the "world was judged not to have changed enough" to be able to overturn the 1992 ruling of the Federal Court.

[119] The Court referred to the cases *Glasenapp* v. *Germany* (1986), *Vogt* v. *Germany* (1995), and *Pellegrin* v. *France* (1999). This position recalls the "doctrine of positive obligations" developed by the European Court of Human Rights in relation to "antisystem" political parties: "the power of the State to intervene *beforehand* against a party (i.e., before its illiberal intentions are put into practice following the seizure of power) is in line with the positive obligations incumbent on states by virtue of Art. 1" (Andrea Guazzarotti, "Art. 11. Libertà di riunione e

After pointing out that the lustration laws adopted in Central and Eastern European countries were still in force, the Court concluded that a democratic state, not just in the period immediately after the collapse of the authoritarian regime, "can tie an individual's entry into state administration and public services . . . to [the fulfillment of] certain prerequisites, in particular . . . the requirement of (political) loyalty."

The judgments on lustration laws delivered by the other postcommunist constitutional courts differ considerably from the decisions of the Czechoslovak and Czech Constitutional Courts. One of the most emblematic cases is that of the Hungarian Constitutional Court, according to which the argument that lustration was intended to defend the process of democratization from those who were compromised with the previous Communist regime could not be upheld because the transition was now complete and should thus be considered as an historical fact (Judgment 60/1994).[120] For this reason, the principles to be applied to ascertain the constitutionality of the law were to be the same as those applied in a normal democratic society founded on the rule of law. This ruling was in line with the approach adopted by the Court from the beginning of its activity, according to which "the revolution in the change of political regime [was to be] achieved within the constitutional framework, according to the constitutional methods of a State based on the rule of law."[121]

The fact that the constitutional courts of Central and Eastern Europe delivered such different judgments on the lustration laws is to be explained not just in relation to the specific characteristics of each country[122] but also in light of the fact that for a considerable period of time they did not receive any "indication" from the European Court of Human Rights. Indeed, although the Strasbourg Court had often dealt with cases concerning transitional justice,[123] the first ruling on lustration was handed down only in 2004,[124] many years after the collapse of the Communist regime. The European Court of Human Rights ruled that, in general, measures of this kind were not in contrast with fundamental rights, as long as certain conditions were met. In particular, the measures were required to be temporary and subject to

di associazione" in Sergio Bartole, Pasquale De Sena, and Vladimiro Zagrebelsky [eds.], *Commentario breve alla Convenzione Europea dei Diritti dell'Uomo* [Cedam 2012], 440).

120 It should be noted that the measure was enacted in 1994, i.e. five years after the beginning of the transition process. In Czechoslovakia, by contrast, the law was adopted in 1991.

121 Antal Adam, "Il sistema di governo parlamentare in Ungheria" in Gambino (ed.) 2003, note 18, at 242.

122 E.g., according to a number of scholars, the reason why the Federal Constitutional Court and then the Czech Court upheld the lustration laws is that the regime maintained a hardline stance until the very end, unlike Poland and Hungary, where the transition was negotiated. See the debate "Peaceful Transitions to Constitutional Democracy: Transcript of the Proceedings" (1998) 19 *Cardozo Law Review*, 1977–1978.

123 See Antoine Buyse and Michael Hamilton (eds.), *Transitional Jurisprudence and the European Convention on Human Rights: Justice, Politics and Rights* (Cambridge University Press 2011).

124 *Sidabras and Dziautas* v. *Lithuania*, July 27, 2004 (Apps. 55480/00 and 59330/00). See Kosař 2008, note 115, at 472–473.

constant monitoring, it was necessary to adopt a certain degree of "individualization," the application of such laws to the private sector was considered to be an aggravating factor, and so on.

As mentioned already, in the Czech Republic the lustration measures were intended to remain in force until the adoption of the law on public servants in administrative authorities. This law, however, approved in 2002 (Law no. 218/2002), did not expressly repeal the lustration measures. In addition, the provisions of the law relating to "political loyalty" were rather limited and not particularly stringent. Subsequently, the lustration measures were no longer referred to the Constitutional Court, nor to the European Court of Human Rights, and Parliament preferred not to repeal them. All this appears to confirm that in the Czech Republic the lustration law is considered to be "part of the *material* Constitution"[125] (emphasis added) as well as an essential symbol of the transition.

B *The Break with the Past: The Court and the Law on the Illegitimacy of the Communist Regime*

Law no. 198/1993 ("Law on the Illegitimacy of the Communist Regime and on Resistance against it") represented another important transitional justice measure. The main reason that explains the adoption of this Law was that until then only a few members of the previous regime had been convicted for crimes committed in the past. This was not only due to the statute of limitations laid down by the previous regime, but also to the fact that the time elapsed made it extremely difficult to investigate offences committed many years before.

The preamble to the Law included a particularly strong moral condemnation of the Czechoslovak Communist Party, that was held responsible for the "systematic destruction of the traditional values of European civilization," "the intentional violation of human rights and freedoms," "moral and economic decay," "the replacement of a functioning market economy by a command economy," "the destruction of traditional principles of ownership," "the abuse of education, science and culture for political and ideological goals," as well as "the destruction of the environment." Because the Communist regime was considered to be "criminal" and "illegitimate," the citizens who had opposed it deserved sympathy and rehabilitation, and their behavior was deemed to be "just, morally justifiable and honorable." In practical terms, the Law lifted the statute of limitations for crimes committed between 1948 and 1989, in cases in which, for political reasons

[125] Di Gregorio 2012, note 106, at 235. On the notion of "material" Constitution see Costantino Mortati, *La Costituzione in senso materiale* (Giuffré 1940), 138. The available commentaries on Mortati's work in English include Massimo La Torre, "The German Impact on Fascist Public Law Doctrine – Costantino Mortati's 'Material Constitution,'" and Giacinto Della Cananea, "Mortati and the Science of Public Law: A Comment on La Torre" in Christian Joerges and Navraj Singh Ghaleigh (eds.), *Darker Legacies of Law in Europe* (Hart 2003), 305 ff. and 321 ff.

incompatible with the fundamental principles of a democratic State, the defendants had been acquitted.

Among the various reasons why this Law encountered strenuous resistance was the fact that it did not take account of the "evolution" of various members of the regime. Indeed, it has been rightly stressed that many of those who were active and committed Communists in the 1940s and 1950s became "reform Communists" in the 1960s and took part in the 1968 Prague Spring. Some of them, having in the meantime become well-known dissidents, were active in the Velvet Revolution.[126] In short, the Law failed to take into consideration the differences between "hardline Stalinists" and the "Dubcekite reformers."[127]

A short time after its entry into force, the Law was referred to the Constitutional Court by a group of 41 deputies. On December 21, 1993, in its first ruling (Pl. ÚS 19/93), the Court upheld the entire Law. Three main issues were examined. In the first place, the Court considered the objection according to which the Law was unconstitutional with regard to the part declaring the illegitimacy of the Communist regime. According to the complainants, the legitimacy of the previous regime was based on the principle of the continuity of the law because the Czech Republic was one of the legitimate successor states to Czechoslovakia and it had inherited a number of laws and international obligations. This continuity of domestic and international legislation was an "indication of the legitimacy of the … political regime" in the period 1948–1989, and was aimed at ensuring legal certainty. The complainants also argued that the Law's condemnation of the Communist regime could be used by the legislator as the basis for sanctions in criminal, employment, and other laws.

The Court first dismissed the latter argument by pointing out that the condemnatory language found in the Law was simply a statement of the "moral-political viewpoint of the Czech Parliament" toward the previous regime, without any legal significance. With respect to the first objection (namely that declaring the Communist regime as illegitimate was inconsistent with legal certainty), the Court argued that it was necessary to rely on the principles on which the constitutional order of the Czech Republic was founded. In particular, the Court made a distinction between the constitutions adopted in the period between the two world wars and those enacted after the collapse of the authoritarian regimes (such as that of the Czech Republic), unequivocally upholding *a material conception of a state based on the rule of law*. Whereas the constitutions adopted in the period between the two world wars were deemed to be "neutral with regard to values" and constituting an institutional and procedural framework that could be filled with a "very diverse political content," the 1993 Constitution of the Czech Republic was "not founded on neutrality with regard to values," was not a "mere demarcation of institutions and

[126] See Herman Schwartz, "The Czech Constitutional Court Decision on the Illegitimacy of the Communist Regime" (1994) 1 *Parker School Journal of Eastern European Law*, 393.

[127] Šiklová 1996, note 115, at 252.

processes," but rather "it incorporate[d] into its text also certain governing ideas, expressing the fundamental, inviolable values of a democratic society." The Court also emphasized that the Czech Constitution had accepted and respected the principle of legality as part of the general conception of a "law-based state." However, according to the Court positive law does not give rise to obligations solely in terms of formal legality, but rather the interpretation and application of the legal provisions is subordinated to their substantive aims, and the law must have due regard for the respect of the fundamental values of a democratic society and the use of these legal provisions needs to be commensurate to these values. The Court concluded it reasoning by stressing that even when there is a "continuity of old laws" there is a discontinuity in relation to the "values [of] the old regime," and as a result "this conception of the constitutional state rejects the formal-rational legitimacy" of "the *formal* law-based state" (emphasis added).

The Court then turned to the issue of the statute of limitations for criminal offences. According to the complainants, the fact that Article 5 of the Law excluded from the statute of limitations the period 1948–1989 because in that lapse of time there had been no "legitimate convictions or acquittals," represented a violation of the principle of legal certainty and the ban on the retroactive application of criminal laws. except for those more favorable to the defendant. However, the Court determined that this provision was not in contrast with the Constitution because "indispensable components" of the statute of limitations consisted of the "intention, efforts and readiness on the part of the state to prosecute a criminal act." These requisites, however, were not in place under the Communist regime, with the result that the statutory limitation period in actual fact did not exist, and therefore the statute of limitation was in itself "fictitious." The Court held that the presumed legal certainty for those responsible for offences not brought to justice for political reasons in actual fact represented "a source of legal uncertainty [for the] citizens." Moreover, in its view allowing the offender's legal certainty to prevail

> would mean conferring upon a totalitarian dictatorship a stamp of approval as a law-based state, a dangerous portent for the future: a sign that crime may become non-criminal, so long as it is organized on a massive scale and carried out over a long period of time under the protection of an organization so empowered by the state.

As in the case of the lustration law, a diametrically opposed approach (that is to say, a *formalistic* approach) was adopted by the Hungarian Constitutional Court (Judgment 11/1992) when it was called on to rule on a similar measure, i.e. the Law of November 4, 1991 concerning serious crimes not prosecuted for political reasons committed between 1944 and 1990. In the view of the Court, only the laws in force at the time when the alleged crime was perpetrated could be applied, including the statute of limitations in force at the time. Once the statutory limitation period had elapsed, the defendant had acquired the right not to be brought to justice. Moreover, according to the Court, it was not possible to take account of arguments that, in order to justify the validity of the Law, relied on the "unique historical circumstances" of the transition.[128]

The final matter addressed by the Czech Constitutional Court concerned Article 6 of Law no. 198/1993, which granted the courts the power to quash or reduce convictions previously handed down for crimes that were not covered by Law no. 119/1990 on judicial rehabilitation. In particular, the courts could exercise this power in cases in which in the course of the proceedings it was demonstrated that the actions of the defendant were aimed at defending fundamental rights, using means that were not disproportionate. Also in this case, this provision was not held to be in contrast with the Constitution. Indeed, the Court argued that criminal offences aimed at the protection of human rights were interpreted at that time as offences against the regime and consequently they were punished very harshly. For this reason, the re-examination of these decisions did not constitute an "infringement," but rather a "restoration of the principle of ... equality," by means of a reasonable reduction or, where appropriate, the overturning of the conviction.

C *Remedy for Injustices: The Court and the Laws on the Restitution of Property*

Unlike what happened in Western Europe, Central and Eastern European countries also experienced *economic* transitions.[129] Indeed, following the collapse of the Communist regime, one of the priorities of these countries was to ensure the transition from a command economy based on state ownership of the means of production to a market economy. At the end of the 1980s, Czechoslovakia was one of the most centralized economies in the Communist world. Compared to countries such as East Germany and Hungary (where small businesses were tolerated) or Poland (where private land ownership was maintained), in Czechoslovakia, with the exception of the black market, the private sector was practically extinct: almost 100 percent of the economy of the country was in the public sector.[130]

As a result, privatization became one of the main objectives of the new government. Immediately after the beginning of the transition, Constitutional Law no. 100/1990 was approved, laying down the equality of the various forms of property, and in particular establishing that the state was to ensure equal protection for all property owners (individual citizens, legal entities, and the state). Law no. 427/1990 (known

[128] See Alajos Dornbach, "Retroactivity Law Overturned in Hungary" (1992) 1 *East European Constitutional Review* 1, 7–8; Krisztina Morvai, "Retroactive Justice Based on International Law: A Recent Decision by the Hungarian Constitutional Court" (1993–1994) *East European Constitutional Review* 2, 4/3, 1, 32–34.

[129] See Mario Ganino, "Democrazia e diritti umani nelle costituzioni dei Paesi dell'Europa orientale" in Mario Ganino and Gabriella Venturini (eds.), *L'Europa di domani: verso l'allargamento dell'Unione* (Giuffrè 2002), 127.

[130] See Michael Kraus, "Settling Accounts: Postcommunist Czechoslovakia" in Kritz (ed.) 1995, note 111, at 569.

as the "Small Privatization Law") promoted privatization in services, commerce, and production (except for agricultural production), whereas Law no. 91/1999 (known as the "Large Privatization Law") was decisive for the privatization of state enterprises, state financial institutions, and other state organizations. In addition, the Civil Code was amended, a Code of Commerce was adopted,[131] and institutions such as the Federal Office for Economic Competition and the Antitrust Authorities in the Republics were set up.

The issues relating to the transition to a market economy and privatization were closely connected to the measures adopted by the Federal Parliament aimed at remedying the injustices committed by the Communist regime between 1948 and 1989. In April 1990, Law no. 119/1990 on judicial rehabilitation was approved, allowing Czechoslovak citizens who had been imprisoned for political reasons to request that the court verdict against them be declared null and void, and to demand financial compensation from the state. Because in many cases the regime had confiscated property, one of the forms of redress envisaged was the restitution of property.

The first law on the restitution of property concerned the clergy. Indeed, the Communists had arrested a number of priests and nuns and had confiscated ecclesiastical property, such as churches, parishes, and monasteries. Thanks to this law, approved in June 1990, several properties were returned.[132] Afterward, Law no. 403/1990 was approved (known as the "Small Restitution Law"), for the benefit of those whose property had been confiscated between 1955 and 1959 during the processes of nationalization. In February 1991, the Law on Extrajudicial Rehabilitation was approved (Law no. 87/1991, known as the "Large Restitution Law"), providing various forms of redress for those who had been dismissed from their jobs, imprisoned without trial, or forced by the courts to sell their property or to "donate" it to the State. This Law ensured the restitution to the previous owners of property nationalized or confiscated by the Communists between 1948 and 1989, or alternatively it offered financial compensation in cases in which restitution in kind was not possible. Moreover, in May and December 1991, "Land Restitution Laws" were approved, giving the original owners the right to regain property that the state had collectivized into cooperative farms in the 1950s.[133]

[131] On these Codes see Gianmaria Ajani, *Diritto dell'Europa orientale* (Utet 1996), 255 ff. and 335.

[132] See Kraus 1995, note 129, at 575–576. Another important "Church Restitution Law" was adopted in 2012 (Law no. 428/2012). The Constitutional Court has ruled on the constitutionality of Church Restitution Laws in several cases: see, e.g., Judgments Pl. ÚS 9/07 and Pl. ÚS 10/13.

[133] See Michael L. Neff, "Eastern Europe's Policy of Restitution of Property in the 1990's" (1992) 10 *Dickinson Journal of International Law* 2, 368–370; Richard W. Crowder, "Restitution in the Czech Republic: Problems and Prague-nosis" (1994) 5 *Indiana International and Comparative Law Review*, 237 ff.

The adoption of these measures gave rise to a very intense debate.[134] The thorniest question concerned the *time span to which restitution would apply* because it was not clear whether it should start from the Communist *coup d'état* (February 25, 1948) or whether it should also cover the previous three years (May 1945–February 1948). Indeed, in this three-year period, the then-Czechoslovak president Beneš had implemented a nationalization scheme for heavy industry, banks, and transport. In the end it was decided to limit restitution to the years of the Communist regime, in light of the fact that the nationalization in the previous three years had been carried out by a legitimate government, on the basis of presidential decrees and in compliance with the Constitution. Moreover, if it had been decided otherwise, this would have meant addressing the question of compensation for the three million Sudeten Germans expelled from Czechoslovakia after the war. Indeed, these people would undoubtedly have requested compensation for the confiscations carried out in that period, and in all probability the question of the responsibility for the war would have re-emerged.

Another issue that was widely debated concerned *the entitlement to apply for the restitution of property*. It was decided to exclude institutions and political parties, and to grant this right only to physical persons. This category included the original owners, and their heirs and relatives, whereas immigrants were excluded, unless they had decided to settle permanently in the country, opting for the Czechoslovak nationality.

With regard to the *form of restitution*, after lengthy debate it was decided to proceed (wherever possible) with restitution of the original property (i.e., restitution in kind), rather than financial compensation, or the allocation of vouchers or coupons to exchange for shares in the companies that were due to be privatized.

These restitution policies represented a very effective instrument for the transfer of assets from the state to private citizens. Indeed, as noted, in 1989 the private sector was practically nonexistent, whereas "by 1991, owing largely to reprivatization, it accounted for 8.3% of GDP."[135]

The Constitutional Court of the Czech Republic handed down numerous rulings on the constitutional legitimacy of the laws concerning the restitution of property, showing (also in this field) *a certain degree of deference vis-à-vis the policies adopted by the legislator*. Indeed, the Court upheld a series of measures that had been impugned, such as those concerning the criterion of nationality,[136] the restriction of certain indemnification entitlements to legal persons,[137] the temporal restriction of restitution claims to the beginning of the Communist regime (thus considering as

[134] See Vojtech Cepl, "A Note on the Restitution of Property in Post-Communist Czechoslovakia" (1991) 7 *Journal of Communist Studies* 3, 368–375.

[135] Kraus 1995, note 129, at 587.

[136] Pl. ÚS 33/96.

[137] Pl. ÚS 46/95.

legitimate the exclusion of the three-year period 1945–1948),[138] the preferential treatment granted to individual farmers in the case of the transfer of agricultural land,[139] as well as the distinction between different categories of heirs of the original beneficiaries.[140] The Court also ruled on the form of restitution, always upholding the policies enacted by the legislator: "preference must in principle be given to turning over the original plot, or plots, of land," provided that those called on to return the property complied with this obligation and that the law did not prohibit it.[141] There were, however, certain exceptions, such as when the Court struck down the provision that citizens were not entitled to compensation in cases in which they did not have permanent residence in the Czech Republic.[142]

In the view of the Court, restitution represented a fundamental element of the political, economic, and social transformation.[143] According to the constitutional judges the nationalization and confiscation policies implemented by the Communist regime were completely incompatible with the principles and values laid down in the new Constitution. For this reason, restitution was deemed to be the "elimination of the illegality of property transfers," reflecting the "duty to restitute the original legal state of affairs."[144] The Court also stressed how these measures should be implemented: an approach that is "too restrictive or formalistic" should not be adopted, but rather the laws should be applied in a "very sensitive manner," always taking account of the "circumstances of the particular case," and above all in light of the "purpose and significance" of the law. According to the Court, "the *ratio legis* of the restitution acts is to redress, at least to a certain degree, the consequences of the infringement of the fundamental rights" that took place under the previous authoritarian regime.[145]

Whereas in Czechoslovakia, and subsequently the Czech Republic, an ambitious plan for the restitution of property was undertaken (as noted previously), in other post-Communist countries different strategies were adopted. In Hungary, for example, compensation vouchers were allocated, whereas Germany opted for a combination of restitution and compensation. In Romania the restitution of property was carried out in an uneven manner due to conflicting rulings by the courts and the public authorities, whereas in other countries it was decided not to adopt a policy of property restitution at all.[146] This lack of uniformity at the legislative level,

[138] Pl. ÚS 45/97.
[139] Pl. ÚS 15/99.
[140] Pl. ÚS 47/95.
[141] I. ÚS 754/01.
[142] Pl. ÚS 3/94.
[143] See Procházka 2002, note 40, at 150.
[144] Pl. ÚS 16/93.
[145] I. ÚS 38/02.
[146] For a comparative perspective see Andrzej K. Kozminski, "Restitution of Private Property: Re-Privatization in Central and Eastern Europe" (1997) 30 *Communist and Post-Communist Studies* 1, 95 ff.

followed by divergent court rulings,[147] was not due solely to the particular circumstances in the various countries, but also to the fact that there was no general consensus about the desirability of restitution. It was not clear, for example, whether restitution promoted or hindered economic growth, and whether it produced positive effects in terms of the rule of law.[148]

In general, the position of the European Court of Human Rights was to give priority to the present-day owners rather than to the claims of the previous owners.[149] Indeed, in the view of the Court, the restitution laws pursued a legitimate aim and served as a means to safeguard the socio-economic development of the country, but it was necessary "to ensure that the attenuation of those old injuries d[id] not create disproportionate new wrongs."[150] The Court also pointed out that "the legislation should make it possible to take into account the particular circumstances of each case, so that persons who acquired their possessions in good faith are not made to bear the burden of responsibility which is rightfully that of the State which once confiscated those possessions."[151]

5 THE COURT AND THE PROTECTION OF FUNDAMENTAL RIGHTS

Although the Czechoslovak Constitutions of 1948 and 1960 listed a number of rights and freedoms and the Communist regime formally ratified a series of international human rights treaties, in actual fact the provisions of these legal documents were rarely implemented.[152] The Velvet Revolution marked a real turning point in the protection of fundamental rights. Indeed, in the three-year period 1989–1992 (as in the case of Spain between 1975 and 1978,[153] but unlike what happened in Italy in the period 1943–1948),[154] numerous laws aimed at safeguarding fundamental rights and freedoms were approved, thus marking a break, for the first time, with the previous authoritarian legislation. Examples abound of these laws. Mention should be made of Law no. 83/1990 on freedom of association and the right to set up trade unions

147 Also in this field the Czech and Hungarian Courts adopted different approaches, though the common trait was that they both largely confirmed the choices of the legislator (see Procházka 2002, note 40, at 150).

148 See Tom Allen and Benedict Douglas, "Closing the Door on Restitution: The European Court of Human Rights" in Buyse and Hamilton (eds.) 2011, note 122, at 210–212.

149 See Antoine Buyse and Michael Hamilton, "Conclusions" in Buyse and Hamilton (eds.) 2011, note 122, at 291.

150 *Pincová and Pinc* v. *the Czech Republic*, November 5, 2002 (Appl. No. 36548/97).

151 *Pincová and Pinc* v. *the Czech Republic*, November 5, 2002 (Appl. No. 36548/97). Other cases involving the Czech Republic include *Malhous* v. *the Czech Republic*, December 13, 2000 (Appl. No. 33071/96); *Polacek* v. *the Czech Republic*, July 10, 2002 (Appl. No. 38645/97); *Myšáková* v. *the Czech Republic*, March 28, 2006 (Appl. No. 30021/03).

152 See Tereza Svobodova, "Les garanties des libertés fondamentales dans la République tchèque" (2003) 53 *Revue internationale de droit comparé* 3, 652 ff.

153 See Chapter 3, Section 3.C.

154 See Chapter 2, Section 3.

(bringing to an end the single trade union organization), Law no. 120/1990 (regulating the relations between the trade union organizations and the employers), and Law no. 84/1990 on freedom of assembly. Moreover, important measures were also taken in relation to the education system, such as Law no. 171/1990 and Law no. 172/1990, codifying academic rights and freedoms and introducing the principle of self-government of high schools. Constitutional Law no. 161/1990 laid down that the right to education could also be guaranteed in private schools: as a result, primary and middle schools run by the Church were established. Law no. 73/1990 introduced the right for citizens to perform civil service instead of military service. Parliament also approved Law no. 308/1991 on freedom of religion and the status of the Churches and religious societies, Constitutional Law no. 327/1991 on referenda, Law no. 490/1991 on procedures for holding a referendum, Law no. 424/1991 on the association in political parties, along with amendments to the Civil Code, the Code of Civil Procedure, and the Code of Criminal Procedure.[155]

However, the key achievement in terms of the protection of fundamental rights was the adoption of the Charter of Fundamental Rights and Basic Freedoms (Constitutional Law no. 23/1991), which, in addition to being considered a "milestone" in the new democratic order, represented "a return to the democratic traditions"[156] of the first Czechoslovak Republic. One of the distinguishing features of this Charter is that neither the Constitution of the Czech and Slovak Federal Republic nor the Constitution of the Czech Republic incorporated the Charter. Indeed, Article 3 of the Czech Constitution stipulates that "The Charter of Fundamental Rights and Basic Freedoms forms part of the constitutional order of the Czech Republic."[157] This *sui generis* collocation initially made the status of the Charter within the Czech constitutional order uncertain. It is significant that in commenting on the provisions laid down in the Charter, some scholars seemed unsure as to whether they were part of the Constitution, and whether they could be enforced before the Constitutional Court.[158] These doubts were soon dissipated because both the Federal and the Czech Constitutional Court upheld from the very beginning the *enforceability* of the provisions of the Charter, adopting its provisions as a parameter for constitutional review (*bloc de constitutionnalité*).[159]

In its role as the guardian of fundamental rights, the Czech Constitutional Court – along with the Slovak Court – has been described as a "champion in the application

[155] See Svoboda 1994, note 12, at 55 ff.

[156] Kresák 1992, note 64, at 440.

[157] The Constitution of the Slovak Republic, on the contrary, expressly includes a set of provisions (based on this Charter) guaranteeing fundamental rights and freedoms.

[158] See Cass R. Sunstein, "A Constitutional Anomaly in the Czech Republic?" (1995) 4 *East European Constitutional Review* 2, 50–51.

[159] In addition, Article 148(2) of the Law on the Constitutional Court stipulates that in ascertaining whether a violation of fundamental rights has taken place, the Court is required to rely on the Charter of Fundamental Rights and Basic Freedoms, as well as the international human rights treaties.

of the ECHR"[160] because both the European Convention on Human Rights and the case law of the Strasbourg Court (ECtHR) had a profound impact on its rulings. The Czech Court not only carefully avoided any potential conflict between the Constitution and the Charter of Fundamental Rights and Basic Freedoms, on the one hand, and the ECHR, on the other, but in certain cases it even "quashed the decisions of the ordinary courts with the use of highly contestable conclusions based on a very expansive reading of the ECHR and ECtHR's case law."[161]

The constant references to the Convention and other international human rights treaties clearly demonstrate the intention of the Court to strengthen its position and authority within the country, as well as the attempt to legitimize its own actions and rulings as far as possible, also with reference to external sources. This seems to be confirmed in the landmark judgment Pl. ÚS 36/01, in which the Court clarified the status of international human rights treaties following the 2001 constitutional reform (Constitutional Law no. 395/2001). Before this reform, Article 10 of the Constitution provided that "ratified and promulgated international treaties on human rights . . ., by which the Czech Republic is bound, are immediately binding and prevail over statute laws." This provision was required to be read alongside Article 87(1)(a) of the Constitution, which laid down that the Constitutional Court could strike down laws in contrast not just with the Constitution, *but also with international human rights treaties*, thus stipulating that these treaties were part of the parameter for constitutional review.

With the 2001 constitutional reform, the new Article 10 of the Constitution provided that "promulgated treaties, to the ratification of which Parliament has given its consent and by which the Czech Republic is bound, form part of the legal order; if a treaty provides something other than that which a statute provides, the treaty shall apply." The reform thus merely granted international treaties (all of them, not just those on human rights) precedence over ordinary legislation (a sort of "application priority"),[162] eliminating the hierarchical superiority (previously recognized) of treaties over domestic laws. In addition, it should be noted that the previously mentioned reference to international treaties envisaged in Article 87(1)(a) of the Constitution was eliminated. It is evident, then, that the aim of these amendments was *to prevent these treaties from continuing to be part of the parameter for constitutional review*.[163]

[160] Michal Bobek and David Kosař, "Report on the Czech Republic and Slovakia" in Giuseppe Martinico and Oreste Pollicino (eds.), *The National Judicial Treatment of the ECHR and EU Laws: A Comparative Constitutional Perspective* (Europa Law Publishing 2010), 138.

[161] Ibid., at 139.

[162] Ibid., at 135.

[163] Ibid.

In judgment Pl. ÚS 36/01 the Czech Court held that

> the inadmissibility of changing the substantive requirements of a democratic state based on the rule of law also contains an instruction to the Constitutional Court, that no amendment to the Constitution can be interpreted in such a way that it would result in limiting an already achieved procedural level of protection for fundamental rights and freedoms.

The Court ruled that the ordinary courts continued to be under an obligation to suspend the case and refer the question of constitutionality to the Court not only in the case of a contrast between domestic legislation and the Constitution but also in the case of conflict between such legislation and an international treaty. Therefore, in the view of the Constitutional Court, international human rights treaties, and especially the European Convention on Human Rights, *had retained their constitutional status*.[164]

Two main reasons explain this decision. First of all, the Court was, de facto, "forced" to grant constitutional status to international human rights treaties because otherwise, pursuant to the new Article 87 of the Constitution, it would have lost the power to verify the compatibility of domestic legislation with the treaties. The second reason concerns the lack of trust of the Court in the ordinary courts, who were deemed to be incapable of applying the ECHR in a satisfactory manner.[165]

Whereas in relation to transitional justice the approach of the Czech Constitutional Court was characterized by considerable self-restraint, in the field of human rights the Court was far more activist.[166] In addition to the rulings mentioned already, it struck down, for example, various provisions limiting the rights of defendants,[167] immigrants,[168] detainees,[169] and minorities (in particular, the Roma)[170] along with Article 102 of the Criminal Code (as amended by Law 290/1993), which envisaged prison sentences for those defaming Parliament, the government, and the Constitutional Court.[171] In the view of the Court, these provisions could not survive in a democratic system.

164 Ibid. See also Oreste Pollicino, *Allargamento dell'Europa ad Est e rapporto tra Corti costituzionali e Corti europee. Verso una teoria generale dell'impatto interordinamentale del diritto sovranazionale?* (Giuffrè 2010), 217.

165 Bobek and Kosař 2010, note 159, at 136.

166 See Procházka 2002, note 40, at 156.

167 Pl. ÚS 4/94.

168 Pl. ÚS 25/97, 27/97, and 29/98.

169 Pl. ÚS 5/94 and 2/97.

170 II. ÚS 2943/08, concerning a case of discrimination against Roma. See Sadurski 2014, note 107, at 234–235.

171 Pl. ÚS 43/93. Sadurski 2014, note 107, at 165, points out that "high penalties for defamation of high officials were not only the legacy of Communist era, where political criticism was identified with anti-state subversion, but also, more generally, of the long tradition going back to the feudal *crimen laese maiestatis*: a pattern of increasing the severity of punishment as a function of the relative height of position of the person defamed."

Moreover, the protection of fundamental rights was also strengthened by the intervention of the European Court of Human Rights, which handed down – *inter alia* – an important ruling on the rights of the Roma, one of the minorities most subject to discrimination in the country.[172]

A *The Right to Vote and the Electoral System*

In the first years of its activity, the Constitutional Court often dealt with issues concerning the right to vote, in an attempt to ensure the full application of Article 21 of the Charter of Fundamental Rights and Basic Freedoms. Among the most significant rulings, mention should be made of those concerning the electoral system and its corrective measures.[173] Unlike the Slovaks,[174] the Czech constitutional framers had decided to make provision for their electoral system in the Constitution, with a proportional representation system in the Chamber of Deputies and a majority voting system in the Senate (Article 18 of the Constitution).

In Judgment Pl. ÚS 25/96, in response to an appeal by one of the minor parties (DU), the Court ruled on the legitimacy of the 5 percent electoral threshold laid down by Law no. 247/1995.[175] The constitutional judges, adopting a line of reasoning similar to the one applied by the German *Bundesverfassungsgericht* in a well-known judgment delivered in 1957,[176] upheld this threshold, stating that the aim of the elections was not only to express the political preferences of the electorate and translate them into seats but also to allow the elected representatives to take decisions. In this regard, the risk of utilizing a pure proportional system was that of giving rise "to a political representation fragmented into a large number of small groups promoting diverse interests, which would make the formation of a majority much more difficult if not ... impossible." As a result, to ensure the smooth functioning of the parliamentary system, the introduction of corrective measures

[172] *D.H. and Others* v. *Czech Republic*, November 13, 2007 (Appl. no. 57325/00).

[173] It should be noted that the Constitutional Court is vested with important powers in the field of electoral justice. Indeed, it rules on decisions concerning the certification of the election of deputies and senators, and intervenes in cases concerning their loss of eligibility or the incompatibility in holding certain positions (Article 87 (e) and (f) of the Constitution). See e.g., the cases *Lastovecka* (I. ÚS 526/98) and *Nadvornik* (Pl. ÚS 73/04), discussed by Milan Podhrázký, "A Comparative Analysis of the Bodies in Charge of Electoral Control, Especially the Judicial Ones: The Czech Case" in M. Paloma Biglino Campos and Luis Esteban Delgado del Rincón (eds.), *La resolución de los conflictos electorales: un análisis comparado* (Centro de estudios políticos y constitucionales 2010), 89 ff.

[174] On the problems arising from the lack of constitutional provision for the electoral system in Slovakia, see M. Steven Fish, "A Vladimir Meciar Retrospective: The End of Meciarism" (1999) 8 *East European Constitutional Review* 1/2, 52–53.

[175] On this judgment see Richard H. Pildes, "The Inherent Authoritarianism in Democratic Regimes" in András Sajó (ed.), *Out of and into Authoritarian Law* (Kluwer Law International 2003), 138–140.

[176] 6 BVerfGE 84 *(Bavarian Party Case)*, 1957.

(such as the 5 percent threshold) was found to be reasonable. However, the Court specified that this threshold could not be increased without limits: for example, a 10 percent threshold would have been "an intrusion [into] the proportional system," with the potential "to threaten its democratic substance." The aim was therefore to strike a balance between the principle of proportional representation and that of parliamentary cohesion.[177]

In another particularly important ruling the Constitutional Court "defended" the process of democratization taking place in the country. As noted in the preceding text,[178] following the 1998 elections, an agreement between the Social Democratic Party (ČSSD) and the Civic Democratic Party (ODS) was concluded ("Opposition Agreement"), by which the ODS undertook to provide "external" support in Parliament for the minority government of the Social Democrats, that otherwise would have not been able to govern. In exchange, the ODS was to be consulted on major decisions. The situation was such that in actual fact an effective opposition was lacking. Indeed, the Civic Democratic Party had undertaken not to support a vote of no confidence, and the other parties (including the Communists) were too weak to cause any difficulties for the new executive. It is well known, however, that the lack of an effective opposition is always a danger to democratic systems, and in fact a serious threat to the Czech democracy (that was still in the making) soon arose. In the year 2000 the two main parties decided to amend the electoral law in such a way as to replace, de facto, the proportional system (that, as already noted, was provided by the Constitution for the election of the Chamber of Deputies) with a majority voting system (which was provided only for the Senate). This would have given to the two parties such an advantage that they would have been able to obtain an overwhelming majority, whereas the minor parties would have run the risk of not obtaining any seats in Parliament at all.

Law no. 204/2000 was thus approved, but it was immediately referred to the Constitutional Court by President Havel and a group of senators. The Court found itself in an extremely difficult position because the "political implications of its decision were to be enormous in any case. The guardian of the Constitution was expected to act as a strong political agent that could determine the political system and culture of the country for decades."[179] In Judgment Pl. ÚS 42/2000, the Court struck down most of the Law, ruling that increasing the number of constituencies to such a significant extent (from 8 to 35), setting the lowest number of mandates in a constituency to four, and amending the d'Hondt formula (increasing the coefficient from 1.0 to 1.4), would have meant setting aside the proportional system.

The Law also required each party to attach to the candidate list confirmation of payment of a deposit of 40,000 koruna. The Court established that requiring such a

[177] See Sadurski 2014, note 107, at 213–214.
[178] See Section 2 of this chapter.
[179] Přibáň 2002, note 78, at 390.

payment constituted a violation of the Constitution and the Charter of Fundamental Rights and Basic Freedoms because it was the duty of the state to enable political parties to take part in elections. The requirement to pay a deposit would have resulted in "*a priori* discrimination" because laying down economic and financial conditions would make it "impossible . . . for some parties to take part in elections." In the view of the constitutional judges, also the reduction in state financial support of political parties (from 90 to 30 koruna per vote) was in contrast with the constitutional principle safeguarding the free and voluntary formation of political parties and free competition among them.

The only provision that was upheld was the one requiring coalitions to reach a certain threshold to obtain seats in Parliament: 10 percent for a coalition consisting of two parties, 15 percent for one consisting of three parties, and so on.[180]

It does not seem to be far-fetched to draw a parallel (while taking account of the specific circumstances in each case)[181] between the "fraud law" (*legge truffa*) approved by the Italian Parliament in 1953 and Law no. 204/2000 adopted in the Czech Republic. Both laws were approved during the *substantive* transition to democracy and both were intended to introduce corrective measures to the proportional system, in order to favor the party (or the parties) in power at the time (and that were expected to win a majority once again in the forthcoming elections), to the detriment of the minor political parties. Also the reasons explaining the dangers arising from the changes to the electoral system were similar. In Italy and the Czech Republic, characterized by societies that were politically and ideologically divided, the system of proportional representation played an important function. Indeed, it was designed to avoid an excessive concentration of power for the benefit of the majority party or parties, with a view to enabling the survival of political and ideological forces that were quite distant from each other, as well as promoting mediation and compromise. These aspects are of the utmost importance especially in young democracies, as in the case both of Italy and the Czech Republic.

However, the reasons why the changes to the electoral systems failed are different. In the case of Italy, a pure proportional system was reinstated immediately because in the elections held on June 7, 1953, due to a shortfall of just 55,000 votes, the majority bonus was not awarded, thus preventing the Christian Democrats from obtaining 65 percent of the seats in Parliament.[182] The Constitutional Court had not

180 A short time after this ruling, the Court handed down another judgment along similar lines (Pl. ÚS 53/2000) striking down various provisions of the law on party funding, aimed at reducing state contributions to the smaller parties while increasing them to the larger and stronger parties.

181 It should be noted in particular that in the Czech Republic proportional representation was expressly provided in the Constitution for the election of the Chamber of Deputies. In Italy, although the 1948 Constitution did not make express provision for it, most legal scholars and political leaders of the period believed that this system was laid down implicitly by the Constitution.

182 See Chapter 2, Section 3.

yet been established and, even if it had, it would have been unlikely to claim jurisdiction to rule on the constitutional legitimacy of the electoral law.[183] In the Czech Republic, on the contrary, the intervention of the Constitutional Court was decisive. It should be stressed that its rulings were finely balanced. On the one hand, in striking down most of Law no. 204/2000, the Court "defended" the decision of the constitutional drafters to adopt a system of proportional representation for the Chamber of Deputies. On the other hand, it ruled that the 5 percent electoral threshold introduced by the legislator was in line with the Constitution, thus striking a balance between representation and governability.

6 THE GUARDIAN OF THE VELVET REVOLUTION

The Constitutional Court of the Czech Republic played a key role in the substantive transition to democracy, contributing to marking a clean break – in terms of principles and values – with the Communist regime. This is evident if one considers the decisions in the field of transitional justice, when in most cases the Court confirmed the legitimacy of measures directed against the previous regime. This high degree of *deference* toward the legislator may be partly explained by the fact that, especially at the beginning, the government's policies enjoyed the support of most of the experts, the media, and the public. As a result, "the *Zeitgeist* of the early years of the Czech Republic" was not particularly "permissive to interference by constitutional review."[184] In addition, the first constitutional judges (appointed by Havel) had been educated abroad and/or were fierce opponents of the Communist regime (including the first president of the Court, Zdeněk Kessler): for a Court that was "anticommunist in its political make-up"[185] it came naturally to confirm "decommunization measures."[186]

In the area of the protection of fundamental rights, the Court was much more *activist*. There was no contradiction with the self-restraint just mentioned in relation to transitional justice. Indeed, in striking down laws in contrast with the Constitution and the Charter of Fundamental Rights and Basic Freedoms, the

[183] As stressed by Andrea Pin and Erik Longo, "Judicial Review, Election Law, and Proportionality" (2016) 6 *Notre Dame Journal of International and Comparative Law* 1, 102–103, "the overwhelming Italian legal doctrine thought that there was no way that the Parliament's election law could be scrutinized by the [Constitutional Court], since the [Court] is the only organ in charge of the judicial review of legislation. Given the characteristics of Italian judicial review, it was hard to think of a situation in which individuals concretely challenge elections to the point of initiating a trial that will finally call on the [Court] to intervene. But the [Court] wanted to bring election law within its field of scrutiny precisely in order to avoid the denial of justice." The Court verified for the first time the constitutional legitimacy of the electoral law only in 2014 with Judgment 1/2014.

[184] Procházka 2002, note 40, at 145.

[185] Sadurski 2014, note 107, at 22.

[186] This was not the case, however, for all the opponents of the regime: Havel, e.g., as noted already, strenuously contested the lustration laws.

Constitutional Court simply confirmed its intention to mark a rupture with the previous Communist regime. In this field the Court was profoundly influenced by the ECHR and the case law of the Strasbourg Court, and it also made extensive use of foreign and comparative law.

Unlike other constitutional courts in the region (including above all the Hungarian Court), the Czech Court adopted neither a positivist nor a formalist approach, but rather promoted a *material conception of a state based on the rule of law*,[187] with the aim of defending the principles and values of the new legal order, as they emerged from the Velvet Revolution. This approach explains why the constitutional judges justified their decisions not only with legal reasoning strictly speaking, but also with *historical and political arguments*,[188] carrying out a detailed analysis of the ideology, the institutions, the laws, and practices of the Communist regime. Possibly partly influenced by the European Court of Human Rights (which made extensive use of historical narrative),[189] the Czech Court adopted this type of argumentation not only to reinforce its rulings or to make them more convincing but also to "explain" the meaning of the decision in the specific case. Especially in the field of transitional justice, the historical argument, combined with the constant exaltation of the new principles and values laid down in the Constitution and the Charter of Fundamental Rights and Basic Freedoms, often gave rise to rulings that appeared to be a "*manifesto*." Indeed, by means of these decisions, the constitutional judges clarified the inspiring principles and the ideals (arguably, the "program") of the new democratic state, in opposition to the Communist regime.

This line of reasoning was completely different from the one adopted by the Italian and Spanish Constitutional Courts, but also by the respective ordinary courts. Indeed, in these two countries the decisions dealing with the authoritarian past were usually based on purely legal reasoning. As a result, they were extremely technical, leaving little scope for historical and political considerations, and more in general for nonlegal reasoning. The example *par excellence* of this technical approach is to be found in the judgment of the Italian Court of Cassation of February 7, 1948 relating to transitional justice. In this case, in order to uphold the (retroactive) norms concerning the prosecution of Fascist crimes, the Court introduced for the first time the distinction between "programmatic constitutional provisions" and "preceptive constitutional provisions," and declared the programmatic nature of Article 25 of the Constitution.[190] Historical references to the previous Fascist regime, on the contrary, were entirely lacking.

[187] See Annabelle Hubeny-Belsky, *Le changement de régime politique en République tchèque (1989–2000): la place du droit constitutionnel* (Presses Universitaires de la Faculté de Droit de Clermont-Ferrand 2003), 452.

[188] See Di Gregorio 2003, note 18, at 281.

[189] See Andrea Buratti, "L'uso della storia nella giurisprudenza della Corte Europea dei Diritti dell'Uomo" (2012) 2 *Rivista dell'Associazione italiana dei costituzionalisti*, 1 ff.

[190] See Chapter 2, Section 4.

It is extremely difficult to evaluate the "historical" approach adopted by the Czech Constitutional Court. On the one hand, the use of historical argument is undoubtedly problematic (as history is almost always subject to divergent interpretations, and it is difficult to establish an objective reconstruction of events), whereas, on the other hand, the general clauses in the Constitution make it difficult to set aside a careful historical and contextual analysis, particularly when dealing with a country in transition, as in the case of the Czech Republic.[191]

Although it had to face the hostility of Parliament, President Klaus, the ordinary judiciary, and certain legal scholars, the Constitutional Court of the Czech Republic – like many other courts in post-Communist Europe – benefited not only from the experience of the courts of the previous generations but also from access to the European supranational organizations. Compared to the previous generations, a distinguishing feature of this third generation of constitutional courts is the interplay between the democratic transition, constitutional justice, and accession to the Council of Europe and the European Union. With regard to membership of the Council of Europe, as mentioned previously, an extraordinarily important role was played by the European Convention on Human Rights and the case law of the Strasbourg Court, to which the Czech Constitutional Court continually referred in order to strengthen its position and legitimacy within the country. Moreover, the process of accession to the EU guided and speeded up the transition, and as a result it provided assistance, albeit indirectly, to the activity of the Court. It is evident, then, that this European supranational dimension played a prominent role. Indeed, acting as the *guardian of the Velvet Revolution* – which was the intention of the Czech Constitutional Court – meant safeguarding the principles and values underlying the *European constitutional heritage*, such as pluralism, human rights, and the separation of powers.

[191] On the problematic use of history by the courts see Renáta Uitz, *Constitutions, Courts and History: Historical Narratives in Constitutional Adjudication* (Central European University Press 2005).

5

Comparing Three Generations

... it seems as though no country in Europe,
emerging from some form of undemocratic regime or serious domestic strife,
could find a better answer to the exigency of reacting against,
and possibly preventing the return of, past evils,
than to introduce constitutional justice
into its new system of government.

Mauro Cappelletti[1]

1 SHARED ACTIONS: THE UPHOLDING OF THE NORMATIVE VALUE OF THE CONSTITUTION AND THE PROTECTION OF FUNDAMENTAL RIGHTS

The action of the Constitutional Courts of Italy, Spain, and the Czech Republic in the democratic transition processes differed from one country to another in certain respects, whereas in other areas analogies are to be found. One common feature in the activity of all these constitutional courts – and more in general of all three generations of courts – is that *they upheld the normative value of the Constitution.*

It is important to consider that for a long time the European conception of the Constitution was radically different from the American one.[2] In the US "model," the Constitution was considered from the very beginning to be a legal norm, that could not be overridden by the state powers, especially the legislature. This conception found its greatest expression in the landmark case *Marbury* v. *Madison* (1803), in

[1] Mauro Cappelletti, "Repudiating Montesquieu? The Expansion and Legitimacy of 'Constitutional Justice'" (1985) 35 *Catholic University Law Review* 1, 7.

[2] On the distinction between the European "model" and the American "model" see Roberto L. Blanco Valdés, *Il valore della Costituzione. Separazione dei poteri, supremazia della legge e controllo di costituzionalità alle origini dello Stato liberale* (Cedam 1997).

which the US Supreme Court asserted for the first time the power of judicial review of legislation. According to Chief Justice John Marshall:

> Between these alternatives, there is no middle ground. The Constitution is either a superior, paramount law, unchangeable by ordinary means, or it is on a level with ordinary legislative acts, and like other acts, is alterable when the legislature shall please to alter it. If the former part of the alternative be true, then a legislative act contrary to the Constitution is not law; if the latter part be true, then written constitutions are absurd attempts, on the part of the people, to limit a power in its own nature illimitable.

The normativity and supremacy of the Constitution were thus indissolubly linked to judicial review. Marshall's opinion in *Marbury* was undoubtedly a bold one, but it must be recalled that he was not the first to mention the notion of judicial review. Even at the Philadelphia Convention numerous delegates, including Madison, had explicitly affirmed the power of the courts to rule on the constitutionality of state and federal laws.[3] Moreover, the fact that the Constitution was superior to ordinary legislation had been stated unequivocally by Alexander Hamilton in *The Federalist*:

> There is no position which depends on clearer principles, than that every act of a delegated authority, contrary to the tenor of the commission under which it is exercised, is void. No legislative act, therefore, contrary to the Constitution, can be valid. To deny this, would be to affirm, that the deputy is greater than his principal; that the servant is above his master; that the representatives of the people are superior to the people themselves; that men acting by virtue of powers, may do not only what their powers do not authorize, but what they forbid.[4]

According to Hamilton, the power of judges to exercise judicial review derived precisely from the superiority of the Constitution:

> Limitations [to the legislative power] can be preserved in practice no other way than through the medium of courts of justice, whose duty it must be to declare all acts contrary to the manifest tenor of the Constitution void. Without this, all the reservations of particular rights or privileges would amount to nothing.[5]

On the contrary, according to the European "model," which traces its origins back to the French Constitutions of the revolutionary period (1791, 1793, and 1795), the principle of the supremacy of statutory law, as the expression of the general will, implied the negation of the normative character of the Constitution, which was

3 See Saikrishna B. Prakash and John C. Yoo, "The Origins of Judicial Review" (2003) 70 *The University of Chicago Law Review*, 951–952.

4 Alexander Hamilton, *The Federalist*, no. 78, www.constitution.org/fed/federa78.htm (accessed July 30, 2019).

5 Ibid.

considered to be a "symbolic text,"[6] or in the best case scenario, a document of a political nature, aimed at regulating the organization of the public powers, in particular those of the head of state and Parliament. According to the classical Jacobin conception, the Assembly, as the sole representative of the people, could do and undo as it saw fit, without some superior norm being able to oppose its omnipotence. Even the Declaration of the Rights of Man and of the Citizen of 1789, although of extraordinary importance in that it laid down a new conception of the law and the idea of liberty, was characterized by a lack of effective normative value. This value was fully established only with the historic judgment of the *Conseil constitutionnel* of July 16, 1971 (*liberté d'association*), which held that the preamble to the 1958 French Constitution (that made reference also to the 1789 Declaration) was part of the parameter for constitutional review (*bloc de constitutionnalité*).[7]

Therefore, as pointed out by Eduardo García de Enterría, "before the last World War, the Constitution [was] not, anywhere in Europe, a norm that was actionable before the courts."[8] It is true that in the period between the two world wars constitutional courts had been set up in Czechoslovakia, Austria, and Spain, but these experiences – with the partial exception of the Austrian case – were not particularly successful.[9] It was only after World War II that in Europe the idea of the normativity of the Constitution and its superiority over ordinary legislation became established. This change in the way the Constitution was conceived was by no means easy. In Italy and Spain, for example, several constitutional provisions – especially those guaranteeing fundamental rights and freedoms – were considered by some legal scholars and judges to be mere programmatic provisions, and as such not immediately enforceable.

As happened in the United States at the beginning of the nineteenth century, it is mainly thanks to the action of the constitutional judges that in Europe the Constitution was recognized as a *legal norm*, and in particular as the *supreme norm*. Indeed, in each of the three generations of courts, these bodies considered the text of the Constitution to be *legally binding in its entirety*:[10] therefore, the normative

6 Louis Favoreu, "American and European Models of Constitutional Justice" in David S. Clark (ed.), *Comparative and Private International Law: Essays in Honor of John Henry Merryman on His Seventieth Birthday* (Duncker & Humblot 1990), 119.

7 See Eduardo García de Enterría, *La Constitución como norma y el Tribunal constitucional* (Aranzadi 2006), 282 ff.; on the ruling of the *Conseil Constitutionnel* and the value of the preamble to the 1958 Constitution, see Justin O. Frosini, *Constitutional Preambles: At a Crossroads between Politics and Law* (Maggioli 2012), 64 ff.; Wim Voermans, Maarten Stremler, and Paul Cliteur, *Constitutional Preambles: A Comparative Analysis* (Edward Elgar 2017), 105 ff.

8 García de Enterría 2006, note 7, at 288.

9 See Chapter 1, Section 4.

10 In addition to the analysis carried out in the previous chapters on Italy, Spain, and the Czech Republic, it is also important to consider the role played by the German Constitutional Court: according to Peter Häberle, "Il caso tedesco" in Associazione Italiana dei Costituzionalisti (ed.), *La nascita delle Costituzioni europee del secondo dopoguerra* (Cedam 2000), 158, "the

force of the Constitution, to use the expression of Alec Stone Sweet, became "a brute fact of the legislator's world."[11] The difference, compared to the United States, consisted in the model of constitutional review: "centralized" in Europe, "decentralized" in the United States.

The fact that constitutional review would give rise to a Constitution conceived as a legally binding norm had been underlined as early as the 1920s by Hans Kelsen:

> As long as a constitution lacks the guarantee ... of the annullability of unconstitutional acts it also lacks the character of full legal bindingness in the technical sense. A constitution according to which unconstitutional acts, and in particular unconstitutional statutes, must remain valid because they cannot be annulled on the ground of their unconstitutionality amounts to little more, from a legal-technical point of view, than a non-binding wish.[12]

Another aspect – a consequence of the first one – that is common to the action of the three generations of constitutional courts concerned *the safeguarding of fundamental rights and freedoms*. This protection was of crucial importance in light of the fact that all these countries had just emerged from long periods of authoritarian rule, characterized by severe constraints on individual freedoms. Certain autocratic regimes rejected the very idea of a constitution: Nazi Germany did not have a constitution, just as, in practical terms, there was no constitution in Fascist Italy, where the Albertine Statute, albeit formally in force, was in actual fact "an empty shell."[13] Under the Franco regime, Spain had adopted a series of Fundamental Laws, but at least those relating to citizens' rights (such as the *Fuero de los Españoles*) were simply not enforced. The case of Socialist States was different. Indeed, these countries adopted constitutions containing bills of rights, and special attention was devoted to social rights. However, these constitutions almost always

constitutional development of the Basic Law is ... unthinkable without the contribution of the Federal Constitutional Court. The 'normative force of the Constitution' (K. Hesse) has developed also thanks to Karlsruhe."

[11] Alec Stone Sweet, *Governing with Judges: Constitutional Politics in Europe* (Oxford University Press 2000), 196.

[12] Hans Kelsen, "Wesen und Entwicklung der Staatsgerichtsbarkeit" (1929) 5 *Veröffentlichtung der Vereinigung der Deutschen Staatrechtslehrer 2*/"La garantie jurisdictionnelle de la Constitution – La justice constitutionnelle" (1929) 5 *Revue de Droit Public et de la Science Politique en France et à l'étranger*. The English translation can be found in "Kelsen on the Nature and Development of Constitutional Adjudication" in Lars Vinx (ed.), *The Guardian of the Constitution: Hans Kelsen and Carl Schmitt on the Limits of Constitutional Law* (Cambridge University Press 2015), 69. See also Charles Eisenmann, *La justice constitutionnelle et la Haute Cour constitutionnelle d'Autriche* (Economica, Presses universitaires d'Aix-Marseille 1986) (reproduction of the 1928 edition), 22, who argued that constitutional review "turns constitutional rules into legally binding norms ...; without it the Constitution is simply a political program, ... morally obligatory, a collection of good advice for the use of the legislator, who is legally free to take account of it or not, considering that these [legislative] acts, even in violation of its precepts, will always be valid."

[13] Valerio Onida, *La Costituzione* (Il Mulino 2004), 9.

consisted of mere proclamations, without any kind of safeguards. For example, in many cases they left to ordinary legislation the concrete regulation of fundamental rights, with the result that this legislation often resulted in the full-scale "hollowing out" of those very same rights. This "technique of referral," combined with the absence of a constitutional court, facilitated the systematic violation of rights on the part of state bodies.[14]

In ensuring the normative value of the Constitution, constitutional courts guaranteed, first of all, the enforcement of fundamental rights. This was one of the fields in which the countermajoritarian role of constitutional judges emerged most forcefully, as they were called on to defend the respective countries from attacks coming from the ruling government.[15] The protection of rights by the courts was favored by a number of factors. In the first place, mention should be made of the *formulation of constitutional provisions*. For example, several norms relating to fundamental rights laid down in the Weimar Constitution were reproduced verbatim in the Bonn Constitution, with the difference, however, that "the Weimar Constitution recognized basic rights as 'goals,' but they were not directly enforceable."[16] Similarly, in Czechoslovakia, the provisions of the Constitution of 1960/1968 relating to rights and freedoms were formulated differently compared to those of the Charter of Fundamental Rights and Basic Freedoms adopted by the Federal Parliament in 1991. Indeed, the provisions of the Constitution of 1960/1968 mainly had a "programmatic nature," whereas the provisions of the Charter "were drafted in such a way as to be directly applied by the Constitutional Court."[17]

A further element that facilitated the role of the constitutional courts concerned the approval, already during the *formal* transition, of laws aimed at protecting fundamental rights. Whereas in Italy between 1943 and 1948 (but also in later years) most of the Fascist legislation was not replaced with laws more in line with democratic principles and values, in Spain (1975–1978) and Czechoslovakia (1989–1993), on the contrary, numerous laws aimed at ensuring the protection of rights were enacted, thus marking a discontinuity, for the first time, with the previous authoritarian legislation. The Spanish and Czech Constitutional Courts

[14] See Tereza Svobodova, "Les garanties des libertés fondamentales dans la République tchèque" (2003) 53 *Revue internationale de droit comparé* 3, 653.

[15] Giorgio Bongiovanni and Gustavo Gozzi, "Democrazia" in Augusto Barbera (ed.), *Le basi filosofiche del costituzionalismo* (Laterza 2005), 245, underline the fact that contemporary democracies are characterized "by the growing conflict between the *principle of the majority*, which is expressed by the production of legislation, and the *protection of rights and freedoms*, that finds in the jurisdiction of the Constitutional Courts and the Supreme Court the principle bulwark against the possible 'tyranny of the majority.'"

[16] Donald P. Kommers, *The Constitutional Jurisprudence of the Federal Republic of Germany* (Duke University Press 1989), 38. Moreover, Article 1(3) of the 1949 Constitution provides that fundamental rights are "directly applicable."

[17] Peter Kresák, "Le riforme costituzionali nella Repubblica federale cecoslovacca" (1992) 3 *Quaderni costituzionali*, 442.

were thus operating in a context that was undoubtedly much more favorable than that of the Italian constitutional judges.

As argued in greater detail in the following text, in many cases the constitutional courts managed to provide, at least initially, a considerable degree of protection of fundamental rights also thanks to the fact that several countries (but not all: suffice it to consider the case of Italy) had adopted procedural gateways to the constitutional court that were extremely diversified, and had vested a number of different actors with the power to apply to the court.

More in general, the role of the constitutional courts in relation to the protection of fundamental rights and freedoms was favored by the growing "internationalization" of constitutional law, and in particular by the increasing attention to human rights in the period after World War II:[18] the Universal Declaration of Human Rights (1948), the International Covenant on Civil and Political Rights (1966), and the International Covenant on Economic, Social and Cultural Rights (also 1966) are just a few examples of this trend. In addition to these international declarations and conventions, it is important to recall the various instruments for the protection of fundamental rights adopted at the regional level.[19] In the case of Europe, the reference is obviously to the European Convention on Human Rights, which (as highlighted in the text that follows), thanks in particular to the case law of the Strasbourg Court, provided enormous support to the second and, above all, the third generation of constitutional courts.

Finally, it should be noted that in their action to protect fundamental rights, constitutional courts were forced – from the very beginning of their activity – to address the issue of the *limits to rights*. It is well known that such limits are of two types: in addition to the *explicit* limits, expressly laid down in the constitutional provisions, there are also *implicit* limits, according to the principle that the rights of an individual find their limit in the rights of others. With the rise of constitutional courts after World War II, the balancing of rights and collective goods in conflict with each other became the task not just of the legislator at the drafting stage, but also of the constitutional judges in the constitutional review phase. In the case law of the Italian Constitutional Court, the roots of the balancing test are to be found in the "doctrine of natural limits" of fundamental rights,[20] that made its first appearance in the first ruling of the Court, namely Judgment 1/1956: "the concept of limit is implicit in the concept of law and ... within the legal order the various juridical

[18] See Wen-Chen Chang and Jiunn-Rong Yeh, "Internationalization of Constitutional Law" in Michel Rosenfeld and András Sajó (eds.), *The Oxford Handbook of Comparative Constitutional Law* (Oxford University Press 2012), 1165 ff.; Luca Mezzetti (ed.), *International Constitutional Law* (Giappichelli 2014).

[19] In addition to the European Convention on Human Rights, reference should be made to the American Convention on Human Rights (1969) and the African Convention on Human and Peoples' Rights (1981).

[20] See Roberto Bin, *Diritti e argomenti. Il bilanciamento degli interessi nella giurisprudenza costituzionale* (Giuffrè 1992), 56 ff.

spheres must mutually limit each other, in order for them to exist alongside each other in an orderly civil coexistence." Later, in Judgment 9/1965 the Court specified that no limit can be imposed upon fundamental rights by ordinary legislation unless the basis for such a limit is explicitly or implicitly contained in the Constitution.

Albeit with a few exceptions, in the case law of all three generations of constitutional courts balancing appears to be characterized by certain common traits. First of all, it must be referred to conflicts between rights or values with *the same constitutional status*.[21] Second, in carrying out the balancing test, the *essential content* of the right must be preserved, as emphasized, for example, by the Spanish Constitutional Court in one of its very first judgments (11/1981).[22] Third, the balancing test needs to be carried out in accordance with the criteria of *proportionality* and *reasonableness*.[23] The criterion of reasonableness is to be found in the case law of the Italian Constitutional Court starting in the early 1960s. In particular, Judgment 15/1960 expressly recognized the fact that "the principle of equality is violated also when the law, without a reasonable motive, provides for different treatment of citizens who find themselves in equal situations." Thus, by relying on Article 3 of the Constitution (principle of equality), the Court declared a prohibition on irrational laws, susceptible to giving rise to arbitrary discriminations between individuals who find themselves in the same situation, or arbitrary assimilations between individuals in different situations.[24]

In Germany the link between the principle of proportionality and the balancing of rights was laid down by the *Bundesverfassungsgericht* during the 1950s,[25] as for example in the *Lüth* case of January 15, 1958,[26] and the *Apothekenurteil* case of June 11, 1958.[27] In particular, in *Lüth* the Court held that "the right to express an opinion must yield if its exercise infringes interests of another which have a superior claim to protection. Whether such an interest exists depends on all the circumstances [of the specific case]." In this ruling the constitutional judges also expressly declared for the first time the status of the Basic Law as a "hierarchy of objective values."

The proportionality test of German origin, further finessed with a distinction between proportionality in the broad sense and proportionality strictly speaking,[28] has enjoyed an extraordinary success over the years, spreading to most of the

21 See, e.g., Judgment 91/1964 of the Italian Constitutional Court.

22 See Chapter 3, Section 3.C.

23 For a comparative perspective see Sara Pennicino, *Contributo allo studio della ragionevolezza nel diritto comparato* (Maggioli 2012).

24 See Enzo Cheli, *Il giudice delle leggi* (Il Mulino 1996), 87 ff.; Andrea Morrone, *Il custode della ragionevolezza* (Giuffrè 2001), 39 ff.

25 See Gertrude Lübbe-Wolff, "The Principle of Proportionality in the Case-Law of the German Federal Constitutional Court" (2014) 34 *Human Rights Law Journal* 1–6, 12 ff.

26 BVerfGE 7, 198.

27 BVerfGE 7, 377.

28 See Jörg Luther, "Ragionevolezza e *Verhältnismäßigkeit* nella giurisprudenza costituzionale tedesca" (1993) 1–2 *Diritto e società*, 307 ff.

European countries (including post-Communist Europe),[29] as well as Canada, South Africa, Israel, Australia, and New Zealand. Moreover, proportionality can also be found in the case law of the judicial authorities of supranational and international organizations, such as the European Union, the European Convention on Human Rights, and the World Trade Organization, to the point that it is currently considered to be one of the distinguishing features of "global constitutionalism."[30]

2 SPECIFIC ISSUES EXAMINED BY THE CONSTITUTIONAL COURTS

The intervention of the constitutional courts aimed at upholding the normative force of the Constitution and safeguarding the protection of fundamental rights was not the only way these bodies favored the substantive transition to democracy. Indeed, alongside these actions that were common to all three generations, each court was then called on to deal with *specific issues* arising from the individual processes of democratization.

In Italy, for example, the priority was *to break the legal continuity* that had characterized the country until 1956, when the Constitutional Court finally started to operate. Numerous laws enacted under the Fascist regime and clearly in contrast with the 1948 Constitution had remained in force, and therefore it was essential to eliminate, at least in part, this legislation. This "dismantling" was carried out by the Constitutional Court in the first 15 years of its activity. In this way the constitutional judges broke the legal continuity and ensured a more effective enforcement of the new Constitution.[31]

The issue of preconstitutional legislation was also addressed by the Spanish *Tribunal constitucional* and the German *Bundesverfassungsgericht*. Apart from the fact that each Court dealt with the relationship between "old legislation" and "new Constitution" in a different way, it must be emphasized that only in Italy (due to the transfer *en bloc* of the Fascist legislation to the new democratic regime) this question was decisive for the successful outcome of the transition. In Germany and Spain the problem was still significant, but much more limited.[32]

In the Spanish case the most sensitive issue in the democratization process concerned the *territorial organization of the State*. Indeed, the resolution of the question concerning the Autonomous Communities (in particular Catalonia and the Basque country) was crucial for an effective transition from the Francoist regime

[29] See Wojciech Sadurski, *Rights Before Courts: A Study of Constitutional Courts in Postcommunist States of Central and Eastern Europe* (Springer 2014), 387 ff.

[30] See Aharon Barak, *Proportionality: Constitutional Rights and Their Limitations* (Cambridge University Press 2012); Alec Stone Sweet and Jud Mathews, "Proportionality Balancing and Global Constitutionalism" (2008) 47 *Columbia Journal of Transnational Law*, 68 ff.

[31] See Chapter 2, Section 5.

[32] On the Spanish case in particular see Chapter 3, Section 3.B.

to a democratic state. Although the provisions of the Constitution governing this issue were lacking in clarity, the Constitutional Court managed to achieve a rational functioning of the State of Autonomies, playing a fundamental role in the interpretation of the constitutional provisions and in resolving the "conflicts of attribution" between the state and the Autonomous Communities, and among the Autonomous Communities.[33]

The German Constitutional Court also played a prominent role with regard to the territorial organization of the state.[34] It should be recalled that in Germany the federal system is one of the pillars of the constitutional order, to the point that the 1949 Basic Law prohibits any constitutional amendment "affecting the division of the Federation into Länder, their participation on principle in the legislative process" (Article 79(3)).[35] In particular, the *Bundesverfassungsgericht* established the doctrine of federal comity (*Bundestreue*), according to which the Federation and the member states are required to exercise their powers taking account not only of their own interests but also of those of the other *Länder* and the Federal Republic as a whole. In other words, they are required to be "loyal" in their mutual relations.[36] The Constitutional Court also handed down a number of rulings on "executive federalism" (that implies federal predominance in legislation, while the administration and implementation of federal law is the main responsibility of the *Länder*),[37] and on "cooperative federalism," especially with regard to fiscal matters, to "ensure uniformity of living standards throughout the federal territory" (as specified by Article 106(3) of the Basic Law).[38] Moreover, it was in a landmark judgment delivered in 1951 (*Southwest State*) on the territorial reorganization of the southwestern states that the Constitutional Court established certain fundamental principles of the new constitutional order. First of all, it held that once a law has been struck down as unconstitutional, Parliament cannot enact another one with the same content. Furthermore, it established that "an individual constitutional provision cannot be considered as an isolated clause and interpreted alone," but needs to be read in the context of the Constitution as a whole. The Court also specified that

33 See Chapter 3, Section 3.D.

34 See Kommers 1989, note 16, at 69 ff.; Jutta Kramer, "Judicial Federalism in Germany" in Hans-Peter Schneider, Jutta Kramer, and Beniamino Caravita di Toritto (eds.), *Judge Made Federalism? The Role of Courts in Federal Systems* (Nomos 2009), 89 ff.

35 It should be noted that the federal form of the state was one of the principles "imposed" on Germany by the Allied Forces. See Carl J. Friedrich, "Rebuilding the German Constitution" (1949) 43 *The American Political Science Review* 3, 461 ff.; Werner Heun, *The Constitution of Germany: A Contextual Analysis* (Hart 2011), 10–11; Luca Mezzetti, "Transizioni costituzionali e procedimenti esterni di formazione delle Costituzioni. L'esperienza tedesca fra corsi e ricorsi storici" in Silvio Gambino (ed.), *Costituzionalismo europeo e transizioni democratiche* (Giuffrè 2003), 415 ff.

36 I BVerfGE 299, 1952 *(Housing Funding Case)*; 12 BVerfGE 205, 1961 *(First Television Case)*.

37 8 BVerfGE 122, 1958.

38 I BVerfGE 117, 1952 *(Finance Equalization Case I)*; 4 BVerfGE 115, 1954 *(North Rhine – Westphalia Salaries Case)*.

even constitutional amendments can be found to be in contrast with the fundamental principles and values provided by the Constitution, thus paving the way for the doctrine of the "unconstitutional constitutional amendment."[39]

In comparison with Spain and Germany, in Italy the issue of the territorial organization of the state was not a crucial component of the transition process. The Constitutional Court did play an important role in the construction and regulation of the regional system, but until the 1970s its rulings only concerned the five "special" regions, namely Sicily, Sardinia, Trentino Alto Adige, Valle D'Aosta, and Friuli Venezia Giulia. This was due to the fact that "ordinary" regions were only established following the elections of the regional councils on June 7, 1970: thus, until that time the ordinary regions had existed only as a geographical subdivision.

The case of the Czech and Slovak Federal Republic was highly specific. Indeed, the decision to set up a Constitutional Court was linked to the federal structure of the state, but due to the dissolution of the Federation at the end of 1992, the Court was fully operational for less than a year.[40]

A sphere of intervention that was common to all the constitutional courts in post-Communist Europe was that of *transitional justice*. Indeed, all of them were called on to verify the constitutional legitimacy of lustration laws, laws on the restitution of property, and laws on the "reopening" of the statute of limitations.[41] The complexity of these issues is shown by the fact that the courts often reached divergent (if not opposite) conclusions, even in analogous cases: suffice it to mention the material conception of the state based on the rule of law adopted by the Czech Court, compared to the decidedly more formalistic approach of the Hungarian Constitutional Court.[42]

Many third-generation courts also dealt with the resolution of disputes among the branches of government, becoming embroiled in *political conflicts*.[43] Mention should be made, for example, of the interventions of the constitutional judges in the harsh clashes between the prime minister and the president that occurred in Poland, Hungary, and Slovakia, or in the conflicts between Parliament and the

39 I BVerfGE 14, 1951 *(Southwest State Case)*.

40 See Chapter 4, Sections 1 and 3.

41 For a comparative perspective see Angela Di Gregorio, *Epurazioni e protezione della democrazia. Esperienze e modelli di "giustizia postautoritaria"* (Franco Angeli 2012).

42 See Chapter 4, Sections 4.A, 4.B, and 6. It should be noted that also in Latin America both the Constitutional Courts and the Supreme Courts, as well as the Inter-American Court of Human Rights, have often ruled on issues concerning transitional justice, especially in relation to the review of the amnesty laws approved after the collapse of the military dictatorships. See Giuseppe de Vergottini, *Oltre il dialogo tra le corti. Giudici, diritto straniero, comparazione* (Il Mulino 2010), 87 ff.; Jessica Almqvist and Carlos Espósito (eds.), *The Role of Courts in Transitional Justice: Voices from Latin America and Spain* (Routledge 2012).

43 However (as noted in Chapter 4, Section 3), the Czech Constitutional Court was less involved than many other post-Communist courts in resolving political disputes.

president in Russia.[44] Through these decisions, the courts exerted a powerful influence on the dynamics of the system of government. As argued by Sergio Bartole, "when the Courts are dealing with issues connected to the form of government, they are in danger of being perceived as players in the constitutional conflicts that have also a political dimension."[45] This risk, according to Bartole, was particularly significant because the "diffidence about policy-makers" derived precisely from the "diffidence about communist regimes."[46]

Another sensitive matter concerned the constitutionality of political parties, an issue that was specifically addressed by the German Constitutional Court. Indeed, the Basic Law grants the *Bundesverfassungsgericht* the power to declare the unconstitutionality of parties "that, by reason of their aims or the behaviour of their adherents, seek to undermine or abolish the free democratic basic order or to endanger the existence of the Federal Republic of Germany" (Article 21(2)). It is above all by virtue of this provision (aimed at avoiding the repetition of what was considered to be one of the decisive errors committed by the Weimar Republic, that is to tolerate "antisystem" parties) that Germany became a "militant democracy," to use the well-known expression coined by Karl Loewenstein in 1937.[47] This constitutional provision did not remain a dead letter. In the first years of its activity the Court declared the unconstitutionality of a political party in two cases: in 1952 it ruled against a party of Nazi inspiration (the Socialist Reich Party),[48] and in 1956 it dissolved the Communist Party of Germany.[49] According to the Court, political parties could be eliminated "from the political scene if, but only if, they seek to topple supreme fundamental values of the free democratic order which are embodied in the Basic Law," and if they have made this intention clear in their political action, according to a predefined plan.[50] It is evident that in these decisions the *Bundesverfassungsgericht* had been profoundly influenced by the fact that the

44 For a comparative view see Wojciech Sadurski (ed.), *Constitutional Justice, East and West: Democratic Legitimacy and Constitutional Courts in Post-Communist Europe in a Comparative Perspective* (Kluwer Law International 2002), 89 ff.

45 Sergio Bartole, "Conclusions: Legitimacy of Constitutional Courts: between Policy Making and Legal Science" in Sadurski (ed.) 2002, note 44, at 424.

46 Ibid.

47 Karl Loewenstein, "Militant Democracy and Fundamental Rights" (1937) *The American Political Science Review*, 31. The literature on this topic is extensive. See Ruti G. Teitel, "Militating Democracy: Comparative Constitutional Perspectives" (2007) 29 *Michigan Journal of International Law* 1, 49 ff.; Samuel Issacharoff, *Fragile Democracies: Contested Power in the Era of Constitutional Courts* (Cambridge University Press 2015); Stefano Ceccanti, *Le democrazie protette e semi-protette da eccezione e regola. Prima e dopo le Twin Towers* (Giappichelli 2004); Stefano Ceccanti and Diletta Tega, "La protezione della democrazia dai partiti antisistema: quando un'esigenza può diventare un'ossessione" in Alfonso Di Giovine (ed.), *Democrazie protette e protezione della democrazia* (Giappichelli 2005); Ida Nicotra, *Democrazia "convenzionale" e partiti antisistema* (Giappichelli 2007).

48 2 BVerfGE I, 1952 *(Socialist Reich Party Case)*.

49 5 BVerfGE 85, 1956 *(Communist Party Case)*.

50 2 BVerfGE I, 1952 *(Socialist Reich Party Case)*.

country had just emerged from an authoritarian regime and therefore the need to preserve the democratic character of the new system was all the greater.[51]

Finally, it is also important to point out that the second- and third-generation courts often made reference in their decisions to foreign and comparative law, relying in particular on the experiences of other European courts (such as the Italian and German ones) that had had to address similar challenges in the democratic transition processes.[52] Especially for the courts of post-Communist Europe, the reference to the case law of such authoritative courts contributed to strengthening their legitimacy within the respective countries. Having said that, one should not overlook the fact that in certain cases the constitutional courts in new democracies made use of foreign and comparative law "for strategic purposes," with a view "to shield controversial and contestable decisions through reference to the constitutional jurisprudence of an established and respected constitutional democracy."[53]

3 THE SUCCESS OF THE CENTRALIZED SYSTEM

As noted,[54] in order to leave behind the previous authoritarian regime, most of the European constitutional drafters decided to adopt a centralized system of constitutional review, whereas only a few countries established a decentralized or partially decentralized system. With regard to the question as to whether this choice produced the desired results, the assessment must be largely positive.[55] A number of reasons explain why the constitutional courts, regardless of the generation to which they belonged, were so effective in their action. The first reason undoubtedly concerns the *nature* of these bodies. With reference to the Italian Constitutional Court, Enzo Cheli has underlined that it is

> a body with a very agile structure, and with a degree of stability that is superior to that of all the other constitutional bodies. Second, ... in spite of the fact that the

[51] On these judgments see also Justin Collings, *Democracy's Guardians: A History of the German Federal Constitutional Court, 1951–2001* (Oxford University Press 2015), 38 ff.; Paul Franz, "Unconstitutional and Outlawed Political Parties: A German-American Comparison" (1982) 5 *Boston College International and Comparative Law Review* 1, 51 ff.

[52] In particular, on the influence of the case law of the German *Bundesverfassungsgericht* on the Hungarian Constitutional Court, see Catherine Dupré, *Importing the Law in Post-Communist Transitions: The Hungarian Constitutional Court and the Right to Human Dignity* (Hart 2003). On the use of foreign and comparative law by the courts, see de Vergottini 2010, note 42; Tania Groppi and Marie-Claire Ponthoreau (eds.), *The Use of Foreign Precedents by Constitutional Judges* (Hart 2013).

[53] Norman Dorsen, Michel Rosenfeld, András Sajó, and Susanne Baer (eds.), *Comparative Constitutionalism: Cases and Materials* (West Thomson 2010), 33.

[54] See Chapter 1, Section 5.

[55] See Victor Ferreres Comella, *Constitutional Courts and Democratic Values: A European Perspective* (Yale University Press 2009); Francesco Biagi, "Three Generations of European Constitutional Courts in Transition to Democracy" (2014) 2 *Diritto pubblico comparato ed europeo*, 1003–1004.

> rationale for appointing its members is not only technical but also political, it tends to display a considerable cultural homogeneity, due to the background and experience of its members.[56]

Another reason concerns the *role and function* of the constitutional courts. Unlike the ordinary courts, these bodies are designed to perform a highly specific task, that is to defend the Constitution and to guarantee its supremacy over ordinary legislation. In addition, they "can provide a focal point for a new rhetoric of state legitimacy, one based on respect for democratic values and rights, and on the rejection of former rhetoric (of fascism, military or one-party rule, legislative sovereignty, the cult of personality, and so on)."[57]

Constitutional courts also played a fundamental role in *establishing and consolidating a constitutional culture* in the individual countries. The case law of these bodies facilitated the spread of a series of constitutional principles and values of crucial importance at a political and social level, such as the normativity of the Constitution and its supremacy over ordinary legislation,[58] as well as the inviolability of human rights. However, this educational role may also have a downside. Indeed, the risk of the "monopoly" on constitutional adjudication enjoyed by constitutional courts, which is a consequence of the centralized system of constitutional review, is to contribute "to a perception that other institutions – including 'regular' courts – do not really have a responsibility for constitutional maintenance because it is the exclusive domain of constitutional courts."[59]

In most cases the constitutional judges proved to be capable of meeting the expectations also with regard to the *timing* of their action. In commenting on the experience of the Spanish Constitutional Court, Pedro Cruz Villalón has argued that

> only a constitutional body conceived with this specific mission could have accomplished in such a short space of time the action carried out in our country by the Constitutional Court in favour of the effectiveness of the supremacy of the Constitution. By means of a "decentralized" system of constitutional review . . . this would not have been easily possible.[60]

[56] Cheli 1996, note 24, at 33.

[57] Alec Stone Sweet, "Constitutional Courts" in Rosenfeld and Sajó (eds.) 2012, note 18, at 827.

[58] This point is underlined by Alessandro Pizzorusso, "Italian and American Models of the Judiciary and of Judicial Review of Legislation: A Comparison of Recent Tendencies" (1990) 38 *The American Journal of Comparative Law*, 385 ff.

[59] Wojciech Sadurski, "Constitutional Courts and Constitutional Culture in Central and Eastern European Countries" in Alberto Febbrajo and Wojciech Sadurski (eds.), *Central and Eastern Europe after Transition: Towards a New Socio-Legal Semantics* (Ashgate 2010), 118. The author refers to constitutional courts in post-Communist Europe, but his observation appears to be applicable also to the other generations of courts.

[60] Pedro Cruz Villalón, "Dos años de jurisprudencia constitucional española" (1983) 17 *Revista de derecho político*, 41.

Indeed, in a decentralized system several courts may deliver judgments regarding a law's validity, and these judgments may conflict with each other. Only "after cases have worked their way through the judicial system to the country's highest courts will there be a degree of certainty, when appellate courts or the supreme court make a determination."[61] It should be recognized, however, that constitutional courts have not always managed to perform their role in an effective and timely manner. In the field of public order, for example, the Italian constitutional judges often adopted an excessively cautious approach, upholding the Fascist legislation even when it was manifestly in contrast with the Constitution.[62]

The analysis of the three generations of courts has also shown that a centralized system of constitutional review is preferable when the country, after a long period of autocratic rule, has not carried out an effective purge of the judiciary, as was the case in Italy (where from 1948 to 1956 a decentralized system was adopted) and in Spain. This *limited purge* helps to explain why the judiciary (and in particular the apex courts) of these two countries were so reluctant to recognize the full normative force of their respective constitutions, especially with regard to fundamental rights. The constitutional courts, on the contrary, declared from the very beginning the normativity of the entire Constitution, thus marking a clean break with the past.[63]

Another risk arising from the adoption of a decentralized model of constitutional review may occur when the judiciary tends to take an *excessively deferential stance toward the legislature and the executive*. In Greece, for example, due to such an approach, for a long time the judges were reluctant to strike down laws as unconstitutional, even when the compatibility of these laws with the Constitution was more than questionable. As a result, the 1975 Constitution was only partially implemented, at least until the mid-1980s. In actual fact, "in most cases, the courts made no use of the new Constitution's potential to conscientiously and comprehensively protect fundamental rights."[64] The risk of an excessively deferential approach vis-à-vis the legislator is obviously present also in a centralized system. However, unlike ordinary judges, constitutional courts are by their very nature countermajoritarian institutions, thus making an excessively "conciliatory" attitude toward the choices adopted by the majority less likely. It is significant that in Hungary, following the illiberal turn in recent years, the powers of the Constitutional Court (that had been accused of excessive activism in the past) have been severely constrained.[65]

61 Sujit Choudhry and Katherine Glenn Bass, *Constitutional Review in New Democracies* (The Center for Constitutional Transitions at NYU 2013).

62 See Chapter 2, Section 5.D.

63 See Chapters 2 and 3.

64 Julia Iliopoulos-Strangas and Stylianos-Ioannis G. Koutnatzis, "Greece" in Allan R. Brewer-Carías (ed.), *Constitutional Courts as Positive Legislators: A Comparative Law Study* (Cambridge University Press 2011), 558.

65 See Chapter 1, Section 5.A.

4 FACTORS INFLUENCING THE ACTION OF THE CONSTITUTIONAL COURTS

From the analysis of the three generations, it is evident that the action of the constitutional courts was either facilitated or hindered by a series of specific factors. In certain cases, these factors influenced all three generations, whereas in other cases they had an impact only on some generations or just one of them. The factors (that will now be examined) that appear to have most affected the activity of the constitutional judges are the following: (1) the time needed for the constitutional courts to be set up; (2) the appointment procedure and the status of constitutional judges; (3) the procedural gateways to the courts and the actors entitled to appeal; (4) the historical, political, and institutional context; and (5) the "Europe factor," namely the accession of the country to supranational European organizations and the influence of the European Convention on Human Rights and the case law of the Strasbourg Court on the decisions of the constitutional courts.

A *The Time Needed for the Constitutional Courts to Be Set Up*

The first factor influencing the action of the constitutional courts concerned the time needed for these bodies to be established. Various courts in Central and Eastern Europe were set up very rapidly, reflecting the fact that the establishment of these institutions, as symbols of the new democratic regime, was never seriously questioned.[66] The Hungarian Court, for example, was set up just two months after the approval of the constitutional amendments in October 1989, and the Romanian and the Czech Courts just six and seven months after the entry into force of their respective Constitutions (December 1991 in Romania, January 1993 in the Czech Republic).

In Germany and Spain, the interval was longer, but not excessive. In fact, the *Bundesverfassungsgericht* started to operate two and a half years after the entry into force of the 1949 Basic Law, whereas the *Tribunal constitucional* was established 19 months after the promulgation of the 1978 Constitution.

In Italy, on the contrary, the *Corte costituzionale* was set up only eight years after the adoption of the 1948 Constitution. This delay constitutes one of the reasons why the constitutional judges encountered numerous difficulties in the early stages of their activity. Certain criteria of interpretation that emerged during this lapse of time were by no means favorable to constitutional review: suffice it to mention, for example, the interpretation of several provisions of the Constitution as

[66] In the Czech Republic (as discussed in Chapter 4, Section 3) the introduction of a system of constitutional review was debated, but was not one of the main concerns of the constitutional drafters.

"programmatic provisions," with the result that only a limited number of preconstitutional laws were deemed to be in conflict with the new Constitution.[67]

As a result, it seems possible to apply also to constitutional courts the observation by Claudio Pavone that institutions that are set up in a timely manner have a greater "innovative force"[68] compared to those whose establishment has been postponed. The courts belonging to the first group (the majority) were able to uphold from the very beginning their "idea of the Constitution," which is particularly important in the case of a regime change. The Italian Court, on the contrary – resorting to a sports metaphor – had to face the difficulties of the player who is sent onto the field for the losing side when the match is already underway, in an attempt to turn the match round.

B *The Appointment Procedure and the Status of Constitutional Judges*

The procedure for appointing constitutional judges has often been extremely complex and sensitive, *regardless of the selection process adopted*. In Italy, for example, where a "mixed" model was adopted,[69] the considerable delay in the establishment of the Court was linked, *inter alia*, to the significant difficulties in reaching an agreement between the political parties. Also in Germany, that had opted, on the contrary, for an entirely "parliamentary" system,[70] the appointment of the first constitutional judges turned out to be quite difficult. Indeed, due to the two-thirds majority required in both houses of Parliament, the appointments were dependent on an agreement between the SPD and the CDU/CSU.[71]

The "US" model adopted by the Czech Republic did not fare any better.[72] It is true that during the Havel presidency the appointment system "functioned smoothly,"[73] but when Klaus became head of state, a conflict arose between him and the Senate over the appointment of the constitutional judges. The consequence

[67] See Chapter 2, Section 4.

[68] Claudio Pavone, *Alle origini della Repubblica. Scritti su Fascismo, antifascismo e continuità dello Stato* (Bollati Boringhieri 1995), 117.

[69] The 15 members of the Court are appointed as follows: one-third by the president of the republic, one-third by Parliament in joint sessions, and one-third by the superior courts. Spain also adopts a "mixed" system: initially the process of appointing the constitutional judges did not give rise to any problems, but over the years it became a matter of contention between the political parties. See Francisco Rubio Llorente, *La forma del poder (Estudios sobre la Constitución)* (Centro de estudios constitucionales 1993), 443 ff.

[70] The members of the Constitutional Court are appointed half each by the *Bundestag* and the *Bundesrat*.

[71] See Georg Vanberg, *The Politics of Constitutional Review in Germany* (Cambridge University Press 2005), 63.

[72] The 15 members of the Court are nominated by the president of the republic and confirmed by the Senate.

[73] Zdeněk Kühn and Jan Kysela, "Nomination of Constitutional Justices in Post-Communist Countries: Trial, Error, Conflict in the Czech Republic" (2006) 2 *European Constitutional Law Review* 2, 191.

of this contrast was that, between 2003 and 2004, the Court was forced to suspend its activity because the number of judges fell below 12, which was the quorum required for handing down rulings.[74]

The *involvement of different political and institutional actors* in the process of appointing the members of the constitutional courts appears to be of the utmost importance, above all in countries where democracy is still fragile and there is a greater risk of a return to authoritarian rule. Indeed, this type of selection process "fosters a broad sense of political investment in the court" because "all actors have an incentive to continue supporting the court even when they are on the losing side of its decisions."[75] In choosing the appointment procedure, another challenge for the constitutional drafters is to ensure that the court is independent and autonomous (in the sense that it is isolated from political interference), but at the same time is also in tune with the democratic society in which it operates. In fact, a court "whose decisions do not in any way reflect society's values and concerns is unlikely to retain the public's support, and will either come to be disregarded as an unjust body or dismantled by the elected branches."[76]

In addition to the fundamental role played by the provisions on the status of the judges – provisions aimed at ensuring their competence, professionalism, and independence – another extremely important element concerns the prestige and authority of those selected to perform this function. Suffice it to consider, for example, the first presidents of the Italian and Spanish Constitutional Courts, whose *auctoritas* was beyond reproach: in Italy it was Enrico De Nicola, previously head of state, whereas in Spain it was the *maestro* Manuel García-Pelayo.

Judges who are competent, independent, and well known for their prestige and authority are therefore crucial not only to ensuring the effective functioning of the constitutional court, but also to endowing it with greater legitimacy. This appears to be necessary especially when the court is an authentic innovation in the country (as was the case in Italy and many other countries), or when the country has been

[74] Mention should also be made of the developments in Italy in the 1960s. In response to the continuing inertia on the part of Parliament in electing the constitutional judges it was required to appoint, and fearful that it would have to suspend its deliberations due to the number of judges falling below the quorum of 11 members, the Court made an attempt to safeguard its proper functioning by adopting an internal regulation that, in the absence of any specific provision in the Constitution, allowed the extension of the term of office of constitutional judges (*prorogatio*). Parliament responded to this decision with Constitutional Law no. 2/1967, which reduced the term of office from 12 years to 9, ruled out the reappointment of the constitutional judges, and introduced clause 4 of Article 135 of the Constitution, explicitly prohibiting the extension of the term of office. See Antonio Ruggeri and Antonino Spadaro, *Lineamenti di giustizia costituzionale* (Giappichelli 2001), 64–65.

[75] Sujit Choudhry and Katherine Glenn Bass, *Constitutional Courts after the Arab Spring: Appointment Mechanisms and Relative Judicial Independence* (The Center for Constitutional Transitions at NYU 2014), 9.

[76] Ibid., at 28.

deprived of such a body for a long time (as in the case of Spain,[77] and to some extent also the Czech Republic).[78]

C The Procedural Gateways to the Courts and the Actors Entitled to Appeal

Germany, Spain, Portugal, and the post-Communist countries are characterized by a large number of procedural gateways to the constitutional courts, and by a large number of actors entitled to appeal to the courts.[79] Consider, for example, the claims lodged by constitutional bodies (such as the president of the republic, the prime minister, and the presidents of the Houses of Parliament),[80] substate entities (such as the members states and the regions in the case of decentralized countries), parliamentary minorities, the ombudsman (such as the *Defensor del Pueblo* in Spain), or specific actors (such as trade unions, national authorities of employers' organizations and occupational organizations, churches and religious organizations in Poland). Other procedural gateways include the questions of constitutionality referred to the constitutional court by ordinary courts ("concrete" review), and the individual constitutional complaints (such as the *recurso de amparo constitucional* in Spain, the *Verfassungsbeschwerde* in Germany, and the *actio popularis* in Hungary).[81]

In Italy, on the contrary, the main means of access to the Constitutional Court consisted of the "incidental" method of constitutional review (*ricorso in via incidentale*), which vested the ordinary courts with the power to challenge the constitutionality of laws before the *Corte costituzionale*. The "direct" method of constitutional review did not play a significant role because (as already mentioned) the ordinary regions were established only in 1970, and as a result for the first 15 years of its existence the Court was able to adjudicate only on the constitutional legitimacy of

[77] The *Tribunal de garantías constitucionales*, established by the Constitution of the Second Republic of 1931, had ceased to function in 1937 (see Chapter 1, Section 4).

[78] With the exception of the Constitutional Court of the Czech and Slovak Federal Republic that was established in 1992 and sat for only 11 months, the other *real* experience of constitutional justice in the region was the Constitutional Court envisaged by the Constitution of 1920, which suspended its deliberations in the early 1930s (see Chapter 1, Section 4).

[79] On the procedural gateways to European constitutional courts see Maartje De Visser, *Constitutional Review in Europe: A Comparative Analysis* (Hart 2014), 93 ff.

[80] These claims may be lodged subsequent to the approval of legislation, but also prior to its approval (*ex post* and *ex ante* constitutional review), as in the case of Portugal and Romania.

[81] The *actio popularis* consists of the right of every citizen to petition the Court *in abstract terms*, regardless of the existence of a specific juridical interest in the case in question. The *actio popularis* was abolished in Hungary with the 2012 Constitution. See Fruzsina Gárdos-Orosz, "The Hungarian Constitutional Court in Transition – From Actio Popularis to Constitutional Complaint" (2012) 53 *Acta Juridica Hungarica*, 302 ff.

the laws approved by the special regions (and the autonomous provinces of Trento and Bolzano), and only these regions were entitled to impugn state legislation.[82]

Because for an extended period the "incidental" method of constitutional review represented the only effective procedural gateway to the Italian Constitutional Court, *the success of the action of the Court depended in large part on the role of the ordinary courts*. Whereas the judges in the apex courts adopted a decidedly conservative stance, the judges in the lower courts formed an "alliance" with the Constitutional Court for the implementation of the Constitution. In light of the previously mentioned "stranglehold" on access (that prevented, e.g., parliamentary minorities, and citizens from appealing to the Court), it is evident that if the judges in the lower courts had not been "sensitive" to the values and principles laid down in the new Constitution, the elimination of Fascist legislation would have run into even greater difficulties.[83]

It should be noted that also the Constitutional Court itself attempted to find remedies, at least in part, to the limitations on access to constitutional justice. In fact, in the first phase of its case law, the constitutional judges did not hesitate to adjudicate on the matter even when the referrals from the ordinary courts did not fully respect all the procedural rules. Moreover, always with a view to widening access to the Court, constitutional judges interpreted the concepts of "judicial proceeding" and "jurisdictional authority" in a broad sense, legitimizing various categories of actors as judges *a quibus*, i.e. judges entitled to refer questions of constitutionality to the Court.[84]

The widening of access to the constitutional courts and the increase in the number of actors entitled to appeal give rise to significant advantages in the short term, when the country is still in the midst of the democratization process. Indeed, in this way the possibilities for the court to rule on issues that are relevant for the transition (fundamental rights, transitional justice, electoral laws, and so on) are much higher. In the long term, however, certain procedural gateways may hinder the activity of the courts. Suffice it to consider the case of Spain, where as a result of the extremely high number of individual constitutional complaints (*recursos de amparo*), the Constitutional Court ran the risk of "paralysis" due to the heavy caseload.[85]

82 See Roberto Romboli, "I rapporti tra giudici comuni e Corte costituzionale nel controllo sulle leggi in via incidentale in Italia: l'esperienza di 50 anni di giurisprudenza costituzionale" in Luca Mezzetti and Eduardo Ferrer Mac-Gregor (eds.), *Diritto processuale costituzionale* (Cedam 2010), 414. On the difference between the "incidental" method of constitutional review and the "direct" method see Chapter 2, Section 1.

83 In the view of John Ferejohn and Pasquale Pasquino, "Constitutional Adjudication, Italian Style" in Tom Ginsburg (ed.), *Comparative Constitutional Design* (Cambridge University Press 2012), 307, without the collaboration of the ordinary judges, the Constitutional Court would have been a "*vox clamans in deserto*."

84 See Chapter 2, Section 5.

85 See Chapter 3, Section 3.C.

D *The Historical, Political, and Institutional Context*

The historical, political, and institutional context clearly had a profound impact on the action of the constitutional courts. In the case of Italy, the opposition on the part of certain political forces (notably those belonging to the old liberal school of thought and the Communists) to the setting up of a constitutional court, the subsequent "obstructionism by the majority," as well as the predominantly conservative stance of the government and the judges in the superior courts, are some of the main factors explaining the difficulties in the establishment and operation of the Constitutional Court. In addition, it is important to bear in mind that the wounds of World War II had not yet healed, and that there were profound ideological differences between the political forces, reflecting at domestic level the features that characterized the Cold War. As argued by Enzo Cheli, the Constitutional Court came into existence

> within a political and social fabric that . . . appeared to be particularly uneven and fragmentary, a fabric where it was very difficult to identify fundamental shared values. The Constitution proclaimed these values, but within the framework of the various lexical expressions, bitter conflicts emerged between the different political groupings in relation to these values.[86]

In such a difficult context, especially for a body that represented an authentic novelty within the country, the Court found in the president of the republic and the judges of the lower courts its most important allies because they favored, respectively, its establishment and operation.

Although in Germany there was a much more favorable stance toward the *Bundesverfassungsgericht*, as shown by the fact that its establishment was "one of the least contentious issues,"[87] even in this country, due to the complex historical and political context, the task of the constitutional judges was by no means easy.[88] Suffice it to mention the conflict that arose shortly after the Court was set up between the Adenauer administration and the *Bundesverfassungsgericht*. This confrontation concerned a particularly sensitive issue from a political standpoint, namely the constitutionality of two very important treaties: the Convention on Relations between the Three Powers and the Federal Republic of Germany (that formally ended the occupation of West Germany) and the Treaty Establishing the European Defence Community (that was intended to set up a pan-European defence system, including German forces). For Adenauer, the ratification of these treaties was crucial for ensuring the integration of Germany into the Western bloc, as it represented "the only viable way to return Germany to full sovereignty, to

86 Cheli 1996, note 24, at 32.
87 Vanberg 2005, note 71, at 62.
88 See Collings 2015, note 51, at 1 ff.

secure its freedom from Soviet aggression, and to pave the way for eventual German 'reunification in liberty.'"[89] Adenauer and his government were accused of threatening the integrity and independence of the Court to obtain a favorable ruling, but the *Bundesverfassungsgericht* stood firm in its position.[90]

In the case of post-Communist Europe, the situation was ambivalent. On the one hand, the constitutional courts enjoyed widespread support among the population, in addition to the fact that they were operating in a world where international human rights instruments were increasingly gaining ground. On the other hand, these courts often had to face the hostility of some legal scholars, the apex courts and certain constitutional bodies, such as Parliament and the president of the republic. This particular situation (as already noted) was defined as the "paradox of the acceptance and rejection" of constitutional courts.[91] In the case of the Czech Republic, for example, the Supreme Court in certain circumstances did not consider the rulings of the Constitutional Court as binding, and in some cases Parliament ignored the judgments of the Constitutional Court (with the support of certain scholars, who relied on the principle of parliamentary sovereignty).[92]

The case of Romania is emblematic of the diffidence toward constitutional courts. Indeed, the constitutional drafters agreed to set up a Constitutional Court on condition that it was not a "strong" institution, and in fact in its original configuration this body was deprived of a series of powers that were granted to the other constitutional courts of Central and Eastern Europe.[93] The 1991 Constitution, for example, allowed Parliament to overrule by a two-thirds majority a ruling of the Court striking down a law as unconstitutional. Moreover, the law on the organization and functioning of the Court (no. 47/1992) envisaged the right to appeal against a ruling of the Court within a 10-day deadline: this provision was often used by the public prosecutor to oppose the jurisdiction of the Court to rule on the constitutionality of preconstitutional legislation. In addition, the Constitution did not grant the Court the power to resolve the conflicts between public institutions. Although these constraints were eliminated in later years,[94] they are indicative of the fears that the political forces in the Constituent Assembly had of this new body. Moreover, it is

89 Vanberg 2005, note 71, at 67.

90 Ibid., at 67 ff.

91 According to the expression used by Pavel Holländer, "The Role of the Czech Constitutional Court: Application of the Constitution in Case Decisions of Ordinary Courts" (1997) 4 *Parker School Journal of East European Law*, 445 (see Chapter 4, Section 3)

92 See Chapter 4, Section 3.

93 See Sadurski 2010, note 59, at 112.

94 The 2003 constitutional reform abolished the power of Parliament to override a ruling of unconstitutionality, and vested the Court with the power to rule on conflicts between public authorities. Moreover, in 1997, the possibility to appeal against a ruling of the Court within a 10-day time limit was eliminated.

significant that in Romania in 2007 voices called for the abolition of the Constitutional Court and for the transfer of its functions to the Senate.[95]

It is also important to recall the case of Poland, where until the adoption of the 1997 Constitution Parliament had the power to override by a two-thirds majority any judgment on the unconstitutionality of a law.[96] This prerogative had been granted as long ago as 1985 – when the Court started to operate – but it was not abolished even after the collapse of the Communist regime, and in fact between 1990 and 1997 "eight judgments were subjected to the parliamentary override that accounted for about 10% of the total number of judgments on unconstitutionality of statutes."[97]

In many respects, Spain constituted an exception to the scenario outlined in the preceding text, as the *Tribunal constitucional* encountered a hostile reception only in isolated cases. Indeed, with the exception of mild objections raised by the Communist Party, the establishment of the Court was never questioned, and once it started to operate, it enjoyed widespread support. In addition, at least until the mid-1980s, there was a lack of conflict between the Constitutional Court and the ordinary courts. As a result, the political and institutional context in which the constitutional judges began their deliberations, though by no means easy due to the issues that remained to be resolved (especially the question of the territorial organization of the state), was on the whole favorable to the action of the Court.

In conclusion, the constitutional courts, albeit with a few exceptions, were "feared," or at least *not easily accepted by the other constitutional bodies and political actors*. This was probably due to the suspicion that, in light of the importance of their role, they would take control (even if only partially) of the democratization process, to the detriment particularly of the political forces, which after a long period of democratic paralysis were reluctant to accept any limits on their activities.

E *The "Europe Factor"*

In the analysis of the role of the three generations of constitutional courts, it is important not to disregard the "Europe factor," in the sense of the accession of the countries to supranational European organizations (the Council of Europe and the European Union) and the influence of the European Convention on Human Rights (ECHR) and the case law of the European Court of Human Rights (ECtHR) on the decisions of the constitutional courts. This factor had a profound impact on

95 See Sadurski 2010, note 59, at 112 ff.

96 Though the Court had envisaged a transitory regime of two years, meaning that the power of Parliament would be eliminated only as from October 17, 1999.

97 Lech Garlicki, "Constitutional Court of Poland: 1982–2009" in Pasquale Pasquino and Francesca Billi (eds.), *The Political Origins of Constitutional Courts: Italy, Germany, France, Poland, Canada, United Kingdom* (Fondazione Adriano Olivetti 2009), 27. See also Lech Garlicki, "The Experience of the Polish Constitutional Court" in Sadurski (ed.) 2002, note 44, at 279–281.

the second and above all the third generation of courts, whereas for the German *Bundesverfassungsgericht* and the Italian *Corte costituzionale* the situation was different. The European Economic Community, established in 1957, was taking its first steps, and the instruments of the Council of Europe aimed at the protection of fundamental rights, such as the ECHR, the jurisdiction of the European Commission for Human Rights (abolished in 1998) and the ECtHR, were still not particularly effective.[98] As a result, from a practical point of view, the German and Italian Constitutional Courts could rely on these bodies only to a very limited extent. One need only consider that the Strasbourg Court had been set up in 1959 but by the end of 1973 it had taken a total of just 10 decisions on the merits.

On the contrary, the accession to the Council of Europe and the European Union had a favorable impact on the second and third generation of courts, as the reforms required to join these organizations had the effect of speeding up the process of democratization and acted to a certain extent as a "safety valve"[99] against new forms of authoritarianism. The conditions required to become a member of the Council of Europe became more and more stringent over the years. Indeed, from 1990 onward, the standard practice required that countries applying to join the Council of Europe ratified the ECHR,[100] and with the Vienna Declaration of 1993 also the respect for the rights of national minorities became a requirement. Moreover, an important element that counted in favor of a state in relation to its ability to safeguard the underlying principles of the Council of Europe (i.e., the rule of law and respect for fundamental rights) was the setting up of a system of constitutional justice. However, it should be pointed out that in the case of the accession of Central and Eastern European countries, the Council applied the conditions for membership in a less rigorous manner than in the case of previous enlargements. Indeed, for these countries the accession to the Council, rather than certifying the achievement of certain democratic standards, served as an incentive for the state to complete the necessary reforms.

In order to promote the democratization processes in post-Communist Europe, in 1990 it was decided to establish the European Commission for Democracy through

98 Not all the member states (notably the United Kingdom) took a favorable view of these instruments. A compromise was reached by which a Court was established with powers to determine violations of the Convention by the member states, whereas the states were granted the right (but not the obligation) to accept the individual right to petition the Commission, and it was established that the jurisdiction of the Court to rule on such petitions was optional, subject to specific acceptance by the states. See Oreste Pollicino, *Allargamento dell'Europa ad Est e rapporto tra Corti costituzionali e Corti europee. Verso una teoria generale dell'impatto interordinamentale del diritto sovranazionale?* (Giuffrè 2010), 28 ff.

99 Antoine Buyse and Michael Hamilton, "Conclusions" in Antoine Buyse and Michael Hamilton (eds.), *Transitional Jurisprudence and the European Convention on Human Rights: Justice, Politics and Rights* (Cambridge University Press 2011), 287.

100 The requirement to ratify the European Convention on Human Rights was formalized by the Vienna Declaration of 1993. Ratification was previously considered to be purely a political decision.

Law (better known as the Venice Commission), an advisory body of the Council of Europe on constitutional matters. This body was originally conceived for the purpose of supporting constitution-building processes in contexts of democratic transition. The Venice Commission played a key role in the adoption of constitutions in compliance with the standards of the European cultural heritage, and its activity has developed progressively to the point that it has become an internationally recognized independent body. In addition to its work in the area of elections, referendums, and political parties, the Commission has focused specifically on constitutional justice, that is considered to be a crucial component of a state based on the rule of law.

The Parliamentary Assembly of the Council of Europe, in an important resolution of 1996, also offered a series of guidelines and recommendations to the countries of Central and Eastern Europe to "dismantle the heritage of former communist totalitarian systems."[101] In the view of the Assembly, the principles to guide the transition processes were demilitarization, decentralization, demonopolization, and debureaucratization.[102]

With regard to accession to the European Union, the criteria drawn up by the Copenhagen Council of 1993, aimed at assessing the applications of Central and Eastern European countries, required not only respect for pluralist democracy and human rights (criteria that had already been laid down by the Copenhagen Council of 1978), but also for the principle of legality and the protection of minority rights. It should be pointed out that unlike the case of previous enlargements (in which the degree of effective enforcement of the constitutions was not closely monitored), in the case of the post-Communist European countries the Commission carefully examined that what was formally stated in the Constitution was really enforced.

The constitutional courts of the second and (above all) the third generation found *a crucial ally in the European Court of Human Rights*. The early 1970s constituted a watershed in the life of the ECtHR. Indeed, whereas (as noted previously) until then it had not managed to effectively perform its task as the guardian of fundamental rights, from then on, also thanks to the higher level of trust in the Strasbourg institutions and above all the "metabolization" by the member states of the "new" mechanism of individual petitioning, the Court, together with the European Commission of Human Rights, found itself facing the opposite challenge, that is managing to deal with the ever-increasing number of petitions.[103] The constitutional courts of the second generation, but even more the constitutional courts of Central

[101] Parliamentary Assembly of the Council of Europe (PACE) Resolution 1096 on "Measures to dismantle the heritage of former communist totalitarian systems," adopted by the Assembly on June 27, 1996.

[102] Ibid., para. no. 5.

[103] See Pollicino 2010, note 98, at 73. It should be noted that the *optional* recognition of the right of the individuals to apply directly to the Court was eliminated only with the entry into force of Protocol no. 11 in 1998, when the right of individual petition became mandatory.

and Eastern Europe, made constant reference to the ECHR and the case law of the Strasbourg Court. In the case of the post-Communist courts, the reference to the case law of such a prestigious jurisdictional body reinforced the legitimacy and reputation of the courts within the country (as well as at the international level), thus providing a shield against the powerful attacks (mentioned already) on the part of certain legal scholars, parts of the judiciary, and other constitutional bodies.[104]

Whereas for the constitutional courts of the first generation the *parameter* for constitutional review (*bloc de constitutionnalité*) was almost exclusively *internal*, represented by the domestic Constitution, in the case of the courts of the second and third generation this parameter became increasingly *supranational and international*. The Spanish Constitutional Court, for example, while not holding that the international human rights treaties constituted an autonomous parameter for the constitutional review of domestic legislation, recognized that to a certain extent the ECHR and the case law of the Court of Strasburg integrated the content of the fundamental rights laid down by the Constitution.[105] For its part, the Czech Court assigned constitutional status to the ECHR and the other human rights treaties, although Parliament had approved a constitutional law aimed at preventing international treaties from continuing to be a parameter for constitutional review.[106]

As evidence of the increasing importance of the international dimension in the action of the constitutional courts, it is emblematic that the closest allies of the Italian Court in the struggle to implement the Constitution were the *domestic* judges (in the lower courts), whereas for the constitutional judges in post-Communist Europe a fundamental "guarantee of the correct path and irreversibility of the democratic transition"[107] was the alliance with a *supranational* jurisdictional body, i.e. the European Court of Human Rights.

As a result, what emerged from the analysis of the three generations is that the more Europe became "a Europe of rights,"[108] the more the constitutional courts were able to increase their legitimacy and strengthen their actions, thus favoring the processes of democratic transition. It is unlikely that these bodies would have been able to contribute in such a significant manner to the construction and the safeguarding of the principles and values underlying the European constitutional heritage if they had not been placed in the supranational framework of the European Union and the Council of Europe.[109]

[104] See Wojciech Sadurski, "Partnering with Strasbourg: Constitutionalization of the European Court of Human Rights, the Accession of Central and East European States to the Council of Europe, and the Idea of Pilot Judgments" (2009) 9 *Human Rights Law Review*, 437 ff.

[105] See Chapter 3, Section 3.C.

[106] See Chapter 4, Section 5.

[107] Sadurski 2009, note 104, at 437.

[108] Helen Keller and Alec Stone Sweet (eds.), *A Europe of Rights: The Impact of the ECHR on National Legal Systems* (Oxford University Press 2008).

[109] On this point see Bartole 2002, note 45, at 421–425. However, the interactions between national courts and European supranational courts are often problematic: see Gertrude Lübbe-Wolff,

5 THE COUNTERMAJORITARIAN DIFFICULTY AND TRANSITION PROCESSES

The "countermajoritarian difficulty"[110] of constitutional review comes to the fore also in countries in transition toward democracy. The (apparent) paradox of this "mighty problem"[111] is evident: How is it possible, just when the representative institutions (Parliament above all) reacquire their full democratic powers, to grant unelected judges the power to strike down legislative acts adopted by the majority of elected representatives? Further complicating the issue, it should be noted that constitutional courts often rule on political conflicts, exert with their rulings a strong influence on extremely complex social and economic decisions, and in some cases even have the power to verify the constitutionality of political parties. In other words, these courts have a major impact on the trajectory of democratization processes, thus making their legitimacy even more problematic.

This argument, however, can be turned on its head. In fact, it may be objected that it is when a country is in transition, and therefore the democratic system is more vulnerable, that there is the most need for a body responsible for protecting fundamental rights and the rule of law: a constitutional court would thus constitute the principal mechanism for ensuring a transition from the previous "regime of horror"[112] to democracy. Due to the exceptional nature of the transition process, the courts would therefore enjoy greater legitimacy than they would in consolidated democracies.[113] It is significant that on the basis of this distinction between new democracies, on the one hand, and consolidated democracies, on the other, Aharon Barak argues in favor of the need for different approaches by Supreme Courts and Constitutional Courts: in his opinion, judicial minimalism appears to be appropriate in consolidated democracies, such as the United States, where "the main principles of the constitutional framework have already been established, and the judicial corrective – which assumes the existence of democracy – is limited in its role." In contrast, in new democracies, "minimalism is likely to be unsuitable."[114]

"Who Has the Last Word? National and Transnational Courts – Conflict and Cooperation" (2011) 30 *Yearbook of European Law* 1, 86 ff.

110 Alexander Bickel, *The Least Dangerous Branch: The Supreme Court at the Bar of American Politics* (Yale University Press 1986).

111 Mauro Cappelletti, "The 'Mighty Problem' of Judicial Review and the Contribution of Comparative Analysis" (1980) 53 *Southern California Law Review* 2, 409 ff.

112 Kim Lane Scheppele, "Constitutional Interpretation after Regimes of Horror" in Susanne Karstedt (ed.), *Legal Institutions and Collective Memories* (Hart 2009), 233 ff.

113 See Ruti G. Teitel, "Transitional Jurisprudence: The Role of Law in Political Transformation" (2009) 106 *The Yale Law Journal*, 2030–2034.

114 Aharon Barak, "A Judge on Judging: The Role of a Supreme Court in a Democracy" (2002) 116 *Harvard Law Review*, 63.

In actual fact, the analysis of the three generations has shown that the constitutional courts do not *in themselves* enjoy any more or any less legitimacy during transition processes, but this legitimacy depends to a large extent on the *type of action* carried out in such periods. Although certain factors certainly played an incisive role (suffice it to mention the appointment processes of constitutional judges, the "Europe factor," as well as the "dialogue" with Constitutional Courts and Supreme Courts of other countries), it is above all *thanks to the actions carried out during the transition processes* that the constitutional courts often managed to achieve full legitimation in their respective constitutional systems and within the dynamics of their respective forms of government. In Italy, for example, the legitimacy of the Court depended to a large extent on the action taken to strike down the authoritarian legislation, which promoted the standing of the Court as the first constitutional body to unequivocally uphold the normative force and supremacy of the entire Constitution: "thanks to [the Court] – observed Carlo Mezzanotte – the constitutional design was not purely an ideological projection of reality, but oriented towards its realization."[115]

In Spain, the Constitutional Court probably achieved the highest level of credibility and legitimacy by means of its interpretation of the provisions of the "territorial Constitution" and by means of the resolution of the conflicts over the distribution of powers between the central government and the Autonomous Communities, in other words, in dealing with the matter – the territorial organization of the country – on which the outcome of the process of transition largely depended. The possibility to appeal to the Constitutional Court represented a peaceful means of dispute resolution, without which it is likely that many political conflicts would have degenerated. It is significant that many years later the Court had to face a major crisis of legitimation arising precisely from its role as the guardian of territorial autonomy, a role in which it had in historical terms always been strong.[116] Therefore, the Spanish case provides confirmation of the argument put forward by Wojciech Sadurski, that the legitimacy of the constitutional courts "is more of a *process* than an end-state; it is constantly negotiated, fought-for and at best imperfectly attained, in rivalry with other political actors and in an uneasy relationship to the public opinion."[117] The legitimacy of constitutional courts thus appears to be analogous to democracy: neither of them is fully established once and for all.

[115] Carlo Mezzanotte, *Corte costituzionale e legittimazione politica* (Editoriale Scientifica 2014) (first published by Tipografia Veneziana in 1984), 117–118.

[116] The reference here is particularly to the ruling on the constitutional legitimacy of the Statute of Catalonia of 2006 (Judgment 31/2010), as discussed in Francesco Biagi, "*Estatut de Catalunya* e la crisi di legittimazione del *Tribunal constitucional*" (2011) 1 *Quaderni costituzionali*, 63 ff.

[117] Wojciech Sadurski, "Constitutional Courts in Transition Processes: Legitimacy and Democratization" (2011) *Sydney Law School Legal Studies Research Paper* 11/53, 18–19.

6 CONSTITUTIONAL COURTS AS GUARANTORS OF THE SUCCESS OF THE TRANSITIONS TO DEMOCRACY?

Regardless of the generation to which they belong, the chief merit of the constitutional courts has been *to reduce the high degree of uncertainty which*, as highlighted at the beginning of this book,[118] *characterizes the outcome of every transition process*. In fact, whereas the political forces managed to achieve extraordinary results in the course of the *formal* transition, culminating in the adoption of new democratic constitutions, they also displayed numerous limits and weaknesses in the second phase of this process, the *substantive* transition, when they were supposed to implement the constitutional provisions. This is the phase in which the constitutional courts emerged as key players: in striking down laws as unconstitutional or upholding certain decisions of the legislator, in clarifying the meaning of constitutional provisions or resolving conflicts in the distribution of powers, these bodies had a powerful impact on the process of democratization, *significantly increasing the chances of a positive outcome of such a process*. Although their action was not immune to criticism, with the result that it would not be appropriate to make an unconditionally positive appraisal of their activity, it is beyond doubt that the constitutional courts favored enormously the transition processes taking place in Europe in the twentieth century, heading off the risk of ending up in a situation of constitutions without constitutionalism.

However, the European experience *does not in any way lend support to the view that the presence of a constitutional court is in itself a guarantee of the success of democratic transitions*.[119] In the European countries facing these processes, the activity of the constitutional judges was very much favored by the fact that democracy was the ideology shared by the leading political and social forces. The same cannot be said, for example, of the North African or Middle Eastern countries currently experiencing transition processes, even though they have decided to set up constitutional courts for the first time in their history (as in the case of Jordan and Palestine) or to strengthen the powers of the existing ones (as in the case of Morocco, Tunisia, and Algeria). The Arab world continues to be strongly influenced by nondemocratic ideologies – such as authoritarian monarchy, authoritarian presidentialism, and authoritarian military, as well as Islamist fundamentalism – with the result that the *Zeitgeist* of the region is still largely unfavorable to fully embracing the democratic ideal.[120] This situation thus makes the role of these constitutional courts extremely complex. However, it should be noted that despite

[118] See Chapter 1, Section 1.

[119] The role of courts as democracy-builders is questioned by Tom G. Daly, *The Alchemists: Questioning Our Faith in Courts as Democracy-Builders* (Cambridge University Press 2017).

[120] See Francesco Biagi, "The Separation of Powers and Forms of Government in the MENA Region Following the 'Arab Spring': A Break with the Past?" (2018) 2 *Diritto pubblico comparato ed europeo*, 409–410.

the different contexts and historical periods, *the Arab constitutional courts can gain interesting insights from their European "counterparts."* Indeed, while it is undeniable that "each transition has its own story,"[121] it is also the case that the challenges to be faced by constitutional courts in transition processes are often analogous. One need only consider the ruling of 2012 in which the Egyptian Supreme Constitutional Court struck down the "political isolation law," a measure similar to the lustration laws adopted in Central and Eastern Europe following the collapse of the Communist regime.[122] Thus, past and present in this domain appear to be more than ever inextricably linked.

[121] Nino Olivetti Rason, "Alcune considerazioni conclusive" in Gambino (ed.) 2003, note 35, at 492.

[122] Judgment of June 14, 2012. See Ciro Sbailò, "Elezioni presidenziali in Egitto: quando le Corti vogliono guidare le transizioni" (2012) 3 *Quaderni costituzionali*, 646–647. More generally on the role played by the Egyptian Supreme Constitutional Court in the transition process, see Nathan J. Brown, "Egypt: A Constitutional Court in an Unconstitutional Setting" in Justin O. Frosini and Francesco Biagi (eds.), *Political and Constitutional Transitions in North Africa: Actors and Factors* (Routledge 2015), 33 ff.; Nathan J. Brown and Julian G. Waller, "Constitutional Courts and Political Uncertainty: Constitutional Ruptures and the Rule of Judges" (2016) 14 *International Journal of Constitutional Law* 4, 839 ff.

Bibliography

Ackerman, Bruce, *The Future of Liberal Revolution* (Yale University Press 1992).

"The Rise of World Constitutionalism" (1997) 83 *Virginia Law Review* 4.

Adam, Antal, "Il sistema di governo parlamentare in Ungheria" in Silvio Gambino (ed.), *Costituzionalismo europeo e transizioni democratiche* (Giuffrè 2003).

Adams, John Clarke, and Barile, Paolo, "The Implementation of the Italian Constitution" (1953) 47 *The American Political Science Review* 1.

"The Italian Constitutional Court in Its First Two Years of Activity" (1958) 7 *Buffalo Law Review*.

Aja, Eliseo, "Spain: Nation, Nationalities, and Regions" in John Loughlin (ed.), *Subnational Democracy in the European Union: Challenges and Opportunities* (Oxford University Press 2001).

Aja, Eliseo, and Pérez Tremps, Pablo, "Tribunal constitucional y organización territorial del Estado autonómico" in Eduardo Espín Templado and Francisco Javier Díaz Revorio (eds.), *La justicia constitucional en el Estado democrático* (Tirant lo Blanch 2000).

Ajani, Gianmaria, *Diritto dell'Europa orientale* (Utet 1996).

Albon, Mary, "Project on Justice in Times of Transition: Report of the Project's Inaugural Meeting" in Neil J. Kritz (ed.), *Transitional Justice: How Emerging Democracies Reckon with Former Regimes. Volume I: General Considerations* (United States Institute of Peace Press 1995).

Allen, Tom, and Douglas, Benedict, "Closing the Door on Restitution: The European Court of Human Rights" in Antoine Buyse and Michael Hamilton (eds.), *Transitional Jurisprudence and the European Convention on Human Rights: Justice, Politics and Rights* (Cambridge University Press 2011).

Almqvist, Jessica, and Espósito, Carlos (eds.), *The Role of Courts in Transitional Justice: Voices from Latin America and Spain* (Routledge 2012).

Aragón Reyes, Manuel, "La sentencia del Tribunal constitucional sobre leyes relativas al regimen local, anteriores a la Constitución" (1981) 1 *Revista española de derecho constitucional*.

"25 años de justicia constitucional en España" in Manuel Carrasco Durán, Francisco Javier Pérez Royo, Joaquín Urías Martínez, and Manuel José Terol Becerra (eds.), *Derecho constitucional para el siglo XXI, Actas del VIII Congreso Iberoamericano de Derecho constitucional* (Thomson-Aranzadi 2006, vol. II).

Araújo, António, "A construção da justiça constitucional portuguesa: o nascimento do Tribunal Constitucional" (1995) 30 *Análise Social* 134.

Arzoz, Xabier, "Constitutional Court of Spain" in Rainer Grote, Frauke Lachenmann, and Rüdiger Wolfrum (eds.), *The Max Planck Encyclopedia of Comparative Constitutional Law* (Oxford University Press 2018).

Ascarelli, Tullio, "Interpretazione del diritto e studio del diritto comparato" in *Saggi di diritto commerciale* (Giuffrè 1955).

Azzariti, Gaetano, "La retroattività di leggi penali anteriori alla nuova Costituzione" (1948) II *Foro italiano*.

Problemi attuali di diritto costituzionale (Giuffrè 1951).

"La mancata attuazione della Costituzione e l'opera della magistratura" (1956) IV *Foro italiano*.

Baldassarre, Antonio, "Structure and Organization of the Constitutional Court of Italy" (1996) 40 *Saint Louis University Law Journal*.

Baldassarre, Antonio, and Mezzanotte, Carlo, *Gli uomini del Quirinale. Da De Nicola a Pertini* (Laterza 1985).

Balladore Pallieri, Giorgio, "La Costituzione italiana nel decorso quinquennio" (1954) *Il Foro Padano*.

Barak, Aharon, "A Judge on Judging: The Role of a Supreme Court in a Democracy" (2002) 116 *Harvard Law Review*.

Proportionality: Constitutional Rights and Their Limitations (Cambridge University Press 2012).

Barbera, Augusto, "Le basi filosofiche del costituzionalismo" in Augusto Barbera (ed.), *Le basi filosofiche del costituzionalismo* (Laterza 2005).

"Dalla Costituzione di Mortati alla Costituzione della Repubblica" in Costantino Mortati, *Una e indivisibile* (Giuffrè 2007).

"I principi della Costituzione repubblicana: dal 'compromesso' al radicamento progressivo" (2009) 2 *Rassegna parlamentare*.

Barile, Paolo, "La pubblica sicurezza" in Paolo Barile, *Scritti di diritto costituzionale* (Cedam 1967).

"La salutare scomparsa del potere prefettizio di scioglimento delle associazioni" (1967) *Giurisprudenza costituzionale*.

"Il caso italiano" in Associazione Italiana dei Costituzionalisti (ed.), *La nascita delle Costituzioni europee del secondo dopoguerra* (Cedam 2000).

Barile, Paolo, and Predieri, Alberto, "Efficacia abrogante delle norme della Costituzione italiana" in Piero Calamandrei and Alessandro Levi (eds.), *Commentario sistematico alla Costituzione italiana* (Barbera 1950).

Barrera, Carlos, *Historia del proceso democrático en España. Tardofranquismo, transición y democracia* (Fragua 2002).

Barros, Robert, *Constitutionalism and Dictatorship: Pinochet, the Junta, and the 1980 Constitution* (Cambridge University Press 2002).

Barsotti, Vittoria, Carozza, Paolo G., Cartabia, Marta, and Simoncini, Andrea, *Italian Constitutional Justice in Global Context* (Oxford University Press 2016).

Bartole, Sergio, *Riforme costituzionali nell'Europa centro-orientale. Da satelliti comunisti a democrazie sovrane* (Il Mulino 1993).

"Introduzione: The Crisis of the Czechoslovak Federalism and the Prospects for Federalism in Europe" in Viktor Knapp and Sergio Bartole (eds.), *La dissoluzione della Federazione cecoslovacca* (La Rosa 1994).

"Le nuove democrazie dell'Europa centro-orientale alle loro prime prove" in Sergio Bartole and Pietro Grilli di Cortona (eds.), *Transizione e consolidamento democratico nell'Europa centroorientale. Élites, istituzioni partiti* (Giappichelli 1998).
"Conclusions: Legitimacy of Constitutional Courts: Between Policy Making and Legal Science" in Wojciech Sadurski (ed.), *Constitutional Justice, East and West: Democratic Legitimacy and Constitutional Courts in Post-Communist Europe in a Comparative Perspective* (Kluwer Law International 2002).
Interpretazioni e trasformazioni della Costituzione repubblicana (Il Mulino 2004).
Basso, Lelio, *Il principe senza scettro* (Feltrinelli 1958).
Bassols Coma, Martín, *La jurisprudencia del Tribunal de garantías constitucionales de la II República española* (Centro de estudios constitucionales 1981).
Battaglia, Achille, *I giudici e la politica* (Laterza 1982).
Battaglini, Mario, *Contributi alla storia del controllo di costituzionalità delle leggi* (Giuffrè 1957).
Battaglini, Mario, and Mininni, Mattia, *Codice della Corte costituzionale* (Cedam 1960).
Baylos, Antonio Pedro, "Diez años de jurisprudencia constitucional: el derecho de huelga" in Manuel Ramón Alarcón Caracuel (ed.), *Constitución y derecho del trabajo: 1981–1991 (Análisis de diez años de jurisprudencia constitucional)* (Marcial Pons 1992).
Becerra, Ricardo, Salazar, Pedro, and Woldenberg, José, *La mecánica del cambio político en México. Elecciones, partidos y reformas* (Cal y Arena 2000).
Biagi, Francesco, "*Estatut de Catalunya* e la crisi di legittimazione del *Tribunal constitucional*" (2011) 1 *Quaderni costituzionali*.
"Three Generations of European Constitutional Courts in Transition to Democracy" (2014) 2 *Diritto pubblico comparato ed europeo*.
"The Pilot of *Limited* Change: Mohammed VI and the Transition in Morocco" in Justin O. Frosini and Francesco Biagi (eds.), *Political and Constitutional Transitions in North Africa: Actors and Factors* (Routledge 2015).
"The 2011 Constitution-Making Process in Morocco: A Limited and Controlled Public Participation" in Tania Abbiate, Markus Böckenförde, and Veronica Federico (eds.), *Public Participation in African Constitutionalism* (Routledge 2018).
"The Separation of Powers and Forms of Government in the MENA Region Following the 'Arab Spring': A Break with the Past?" (2018) 2 *Diritto pubblico comparato ed europeo*.
Bickel, Alexander, *The Least Dangerous Branch: The Supreme Court at the Bar of American Politics* (Yale University Press 1986).
Bignami, Marco, *Costituzione flessibile, Costituzione rigida e controllo di costituzionalità in Italia (1848–1956)* (Giuffrè 1997).
Bin, Roberto, *Diritti e argomenti. Il bilanciamento degli interessi nella giurisprudenza costituzionale* (Giuffrè 1992).
Bin, Roberto, and Pitruzzella, Giovanni, *Diritto costituzionale* (Giappichelli 2014).
Bisogni, Giovanni, "Le leggi istitutive della Corte costituzionale" in Ugo De Siervo, Sandro Guerrieri, and Antonio Varsori (eds.), *La prima legislatura repubblicana. Continuità e discontinuità nell'azione delle istituzioni* (Carocci 2004).
Blanco Valdés, Roberto L., *Il valore della Costituzione. Separazione dei poteri, supremazia della legge e controllo di costituzionalità alle origini dello Stato liberale* (Cedam 1997).
"La politica e il diritto: vent'anni di giustizia costituzionale e di democrazia in Spagna (appunti per un bilancio)" in Lucio Pegoraro, Angelo Rinella, and Roberto Scarciglia (eds.), *I vent'anni della Costituzione spagnola nella giurisprudenza del Tribunale costituzionale* (Cedam 2000).

Blanco Valdés, Roberto L., and Sanjurjo Rivo, Vicente A., "Per comprendere la transizione politica spagnola (un contributo)" in Silvio Gambino (ed.), *Costituzionalismo europeo e transizioni democratiche* (Giuffrè 2003).
Bobek, Michal, "The Fortress of Judicial Independence and the Mental Transitions of the Central European Judiciaries" (2008) 14 *European Public Law* 1.
"Quantity or Quality? Reassessing the Role of Supreme Jurisdiction in Central Europe" (2009) 57 *The American Journal of Comparative Law* 1.
Bobek, Michal, and Kosař, David, "Report on the Czech Republic and Slovakia" in Giuseppe Martinico and Oreste Pollicino (eds.), *The National Judicial Treatment of the ECHR and EU Laws: A Comparative Constitutional Perspective* (Europa Law Publishing 2010).
Bognetti, Giovanni, *Introduzione al diritto costituzionale comparato* (Giappichelli 1994).
Lo spirito del costituzionalismo americano. Breve profilo del diritto costituzionale degli Stati Uniti. La Costituzione liberale (Giappichelli 1998).
The American Constitution and Italian Constitutionalism: An Essay in Comparative Constitutional History (CLUEB 2008).
Bongiovanni, Giorgio, and Gozzi, Gustavo, "Democrazia" in Augusto Barbera (ed.), *Le basi filosofiche del costituzionalismo* (Laterza 2005).
Boni, Massimiliano, "Gaetano Azzariti: dal Tribunale della razza alla Corte costituzionale" (2014) 4 *Contemporanea*.
Borón, Atilio A., "Latin America: Constitutionalism and the Political Traditions of Liberalism and Socialism" in Douglas Greenberg, Stanley N. Katz, Melanie Beth Oliviero, and Steven C. Wheatley (eds.), *Constitutionalism and Democracy: Transitions in the Contemporary World* (Oxford University Press 1993).
Bradley, John F. N., *Czechoslovakia's Velvet Revolution: A Political Analysis* (Columbia University Press 1992).
Brewer-Carías, Allan R., *Judicial Review in Comparative Law* (Cambridge University Press 1989).
Brown, Nathan J., "Egypt: A Constitutional Court in an Unconstitutional Setting" in Justin O. Frosini and Francesco Biagi (eds.), *Political and Constitutional Transitions in North Africa: Actors and Factors* (Routledge 2015).
Brown, Nathan J., and Waller, Julian G., "Constitutional Courts and Political Uncertainty: Constitutional Ruptures and the Rule of Judges" (2016) 14 *International Journal of Constitutional Law* 4.
Brunelli, Giuditta, *Donne e politica* (Il Mulino 2006).
"Lili, ebrea e donna, discriminata due volte" (2007) 2 *Quaderni costituzionali*.
Brzezinski, Mark, *The Struggle for Constitutionalism in Poland* (Macmillan 2000).
Bunce, Valerie, "Should Transitologists Be Grounded?" (1995) 54 *Slavic Review* 1.
Bunce, Valerie, and Wolchik, Sharon L., "Mixed Regimes in Postcommunist Eurasia: Tipping Democratic and Tipping Authoritarian" (2008) *Società per lo studio della diffusione della democrazia Working Paper* 1.
Buratti, Andrea, "L'uso della storia nella giurisprudenza della Corte Europea dei Diritti dell'Uomo" (2012) 2 *Rivista dell'Associazione italiana dei costituzionalisti*.
Buyse, Antoine, and Hamilton, Michael, "Conclusions" in Antoine Buyse and Michael Hamilton (eds.), *Transitional Jurisprudence and the European Convention on Human Rights: Justice, Politics and Rights* (Cambridge University Press 2011).
Buyse, Antoine, and Hamilton, Michael (eds.), *Transitional Jurisprudence and the European Convention on Human Rights: Justice, Politics and Rights* (Cambridge University Press 2011).
Calamandrei, Piero, "La Corte costituzionale e il processo civile" in *Studi in onore di Enrico Redenti nel XL anno del suo insegnamento* (Giuffrè 1951).

"L'ostruzionismo di maggioranza" (1953) *Il Ponte*.
"La Costituzione e le leggi per attuarla" in *Dieci anni dopo. 1945–1955* (Laterza 1955).
"Viva vox Constitutionis" (1955) *Il Ponte*.
"La prima sentenza della Corte Costituzionale" (1956) II *Rivista di diritto processuale*.
Campanelli, Giuseppe, *Incontri e scontri tra Corte suprema e Corte costituzionale in Italia e in Spagna* (Giappichelli 2005).
Candela Soriano, Mercedes, "The Reception Process in Spain and Italy" in Helen Keller and Alec Stone Sweet (eds.), *A Europe of Rights: The Impact of the ECHR on National Legal Systems* (Oxford University Press 2008).
Canosa, Romano, and Federico, Pietro, *La magistratura in Italia dal 1945 ad oggi* (Il Mulino 1974).
Cappelletti, Mauro, "The 'Mighty Problem' of Judicial Review and the Contribution of Comparative Analysis" (1980) 53 *Southern California Law Review* 2.
"Repudiating Montesquieu? The Expansion and Legitimacy of 'Constitutional Justice'" (1985) 35 *Catholic University Law Review* 1.
"Dimensioni della giustizia nelle società contemporanee" in *Studi di diritto giudiziario comparato* (Il Mulino 1994).
Cappelletti, Mauro, and Cohen, William, *Comparative Constitutional Law: Cases and Materials* (Bobbs-Merrill Company Publishers 1979).
Cappuccio, Laura, "Le condizioni costituzionali di adesione all'Unione europea" (2005) *Forum di Quaderni costituzionali*, www.forumcostituzionale.it
Carcassonne, Guy, "Les 'nationalités' dans la Constitution" (1978) 8 *Pouvoirs*.
Carothers, Thomas, "The End of the Transition Paradigm" (2002) 13 *Journal of Democracy* 1.
Carré de Malberg, Raymond, *La loi, expression de la volonté générale* (Sirey 1931).
Carrozza, Paolo, "Alcuni problemi della giustizia costituzionale in Spagna" in Alessandro Pizzorusso and Vincenzo Varano (eds.), *L'influenza dei valori costituzionali sui sistemi giuridici contemporanei* (Giuffrè 1985, vol. II).
Casanas Adam, Elisenda, "The Constitutional Court of Spain: From System Balancer to Polarizing Centralist" in Nicholas Aroney and John Kincaid (eds.), *Courts in Federal Countries: Federalists or Unitarists?* (University of Toronto Press 2017).
Cascajo Castro, José Luis, and Gimeno Sendra, Vicente, *El recurso de amparo* (Tecnos 1988).
Cassese, Sabino, "La giustizia costituzionale: bilancio di un'esperienza; ovvero il dilemma del porcospino, Prolusione dell'anno accademico 2014–15, Accademia delle Scienze di Torino, 10 novembre 2014" in Sabino Cassese, *Dentro la Corte. Diario di un giudice costituzionale* (Il Mulino 2015).
Castellà Andreu, Josep M.ª, "Tribunal constitucional y proceso secesionista catalán: respuestas jurídico-constitucionales a un conflicto político-constitucional" (2016) 37 *Teoría y realidad constitucional*.
Ceccanti, Stefano, *Le democrazie protette e semi-protette da eccezione e regola. Prima e dopo le Twin Towers* (Giappichelli 2004).
Ceccanti, Stefano, and Tega, Diletta, "La protezione della democrazia dai partiti antisistema: quando un'esigenza può diventare un'ossessione" in Alfonso Di Giovine (ed.), *Democrazie protette e protezione della democrazia* (Giappichelli 2005).
Cepl, Vojtech, "A Note on the Restitution of Property in PostCommunist Czechoslovakia" (1991) 7 *Journal of Communist Studies* 3.
"Ritual Sacrifices" (1992) 1 *East European Constitutional Review* 1.
Cepl, Vojtech, and Franklin, David, "Senate, Anyone?" (1993) 2 *East European Constitutional Review* 2.
Cercas, Javier, *Anatomía de un instante* (Literatura Mondadori 2009).

Chang, Wen-Chen, and Yeh, Jiunn-Rong, "Internationalization of Constitutional Law" in Michel Rosenfeld and András Sajó (eds.), *The Oxford Handbook of Comparative Constitutional Law* (Oxford University Press 2012).

Cheli, Enzo, *Il giudice delle leggi* (Il Mulino 1996).

Choudhry, Sujit, and Glenn Bass, Katherine, *Constitutional Review in New Democracies* (The Center for Constitutional Transitions at NYU 2013).

Constitutional Courts after the Arab Spring: Appointment Mechanisms and Relative Judicial Independence (The Center for Constitutional Transitions at NYU 2014).

Clementi, Marco, "Un aspetto della transizione in Cecoslovacchia e nella Repubblica Ceca: la legge di lustrazione" in Silvio Gambino (ed.), *Costituzionalismo europeo e transizioni democratiche* (Giuffrè 2003).

Collings, Justin, *Democracy's Guardians: A History of the German Federal Constitutional Court, 1951–2001* (Oxford University Press 2015).

Córdova Vianello, Lorenzo, "La reforma electoral y el cambio político en México" in Daniel Zovatto and J. Jesús Orozco Henríquez (eds.), *Reforma política y electoral en América Latina 1978–2007* (Editorial UNAM 2008).

Costanzo, Pasquale, "VII disposizione transitoria e finale" in Giuseppe Branca (ed.), *Commentario alla Costituzione* (Zanichelli-Il Foro italiano 1981).

Crisafulli, Vezio, *La Costituzione e le sue disposizioni di principio* (Giuffrè 1952).

Crisafulli, Vezio et al., "Dibattito sulla competenza della Corte costituzionale in ordine alle norme anteriori alla Costituzione" (1956) *Giurisprudenza costituzionale*.

Crowder, Richard W., "Restitution in the Czech Republic: Problems and Prague-nosis" (1994) 5 *Indiana International and Comparative Law Review*.

Cruz Villalón, Pedro, "Dos años de jurisprudencia constitucional española" (1983) 17 *Revista de derecho político*.

"¿Reserva de Constitución? Comentario al fundamento jurídico cuarto de la sentencia del Tribunal Constitucional 76/1983, de 5 de agosto, sobre la Loapa" (1983) 9 *Revista española de derecho constitucional*.

La formación del sistema europeo de control de constitucionalidad (1918–1939) (Centro de estudios constitucionales 1987).

"La jurisprudencia del Tribunal constitucional sobre autonomías territoriales" in Sebastián Martín-Retortillo (ed.), *Estudios sobre la Constitución española. Homenaje al Profesor Eduardo García de Enterría* (Civitas 1991).

"El recurso de amparo constitucional" in Pedro Cruz Villalón, Luis López Guerra, Javier Jiménez Campo, and Pablo Pérez Tremps (eds.), *Los procesos constitucionales* (Centro de estudios constitucionales 1992).

"Constitución y cultura constitucional" in Pedro Cruz Villalón, Julio D. González Campos, and Miguel Rodríguez-Piñero y Bravo-Ferrer, *Tres lecciones sobre la Constitución* (Mergablum Edición 1999).

La curiosidad del jurista persa, y otros estudios sobre la Constitución (Centro de estudios políticos y constitucionales 1999).

"El estado del Tribunal constitucional" (2009) 191 *Claves de razón práctica*.

Cruz Villalón, Pedro, and Pardo Falcón, Javier, "Los derechos fundamentales en la Constitución española de 1978" (2000) 97 *Boletín mexicano de derecho comparado*.

"Czech Republic" (1998) 7 *East European Constitutional Review* 4.

Daly, Tom G., *The Alchemists: Questioning Our Faith in Courts as Democracy-Builders* (Cambridge University Press 2017).

de Almeida Ribeiro, Gonçalo, "Judicial Review of Legislation in Portugal: A Brief Genealogy" in Francesco Biagi, Justin O. Frosini, and Jason Mazzone (eds.), *Constitutional History: Comparative Perspectives* (Brill forthcoming).

De Blas, Andrés, "El problema nacional-regional español en la transición" in José Félix Tezanos, Ramón Cortarelo, and Andrés de Blas (eds.), *La transición democrática española* (Editorial sistema 1989).

de Carreras, Francesc, "The Inevitable Jurisprudential Construction of the Autonomous State" in Alberto López-Basaguren and Leire Escajedo San Epifanio (eds.), *The Ways of Federalism in Western Countries and the Horizons of Territorial Autonomy in Spain* (Springer 2013).

"Prólogo. El federalismo en España" in Javier Tajadura Tejada and Josu de Miguel Bárcena (eds.), *Federalismos del siglo XXI* (Centro de estudios políticos y constitucionales 2014).

de Esteban, Jorge, "El proceso constituyente español, 1977–1978" in José Félix Tezanos, Ramón Cortarelo, and Andrés de Blas (eds.), *La transición democrática española* (Editorial sistema 1989).

Tratado de Derecho constitucional (Universidad Complutense Madrid 1998).

De Fina, S., "Testo unico di pubblica sicurezza e Costituzione" (1959) *Giurisprudenza costituzionale*.

De La Oliva Santos, Andrés, "Tribunal constitucional y jurisdicción ordinaria: causas, ámbitos y alivios de una tensión" in Andrés De La Oliva Santos and Ignacio Díez Picazo Giménez (eds.), *Tribunal constitucional, jurisdicción ordinaria y derechos fundamentales* (McGraw-Hill 1996).

Della Cananea, Giacinto, "Mortati and the Science of Public Law: A Comment on La Torre" in Christian Joerges and Navraj Singh Ghaleigh (eds.), *Darker Legacies of Law in Europe* (Hart 2003).

de Lojendio Irure, I. M.ª, "Prólogo" in Pedro Cruz Villalón, *La formación del sistema europeo de control de constitucionalidad (1918–1939)* (Centro de estudios constitucionales 1987).

de Miguel Bárcena, Josu, "El proceso soberanista ante el Tribunal constitucional" (2018) 113 *Revista española de derecho constitucional*.

De Siervo, Ugo, "Attuazione della Costituzione e legislazione antifascista" (1975) *Giurisprudenza costituzionale*.

"L'istituzione della Corte costituzionale in Italia: dall'Assemblea costituente ai primi anni di attività della Corte" in Paolo Carnevale and Carlo Colapietro (eds.), *La giustizia costituzionale tra memoria e prospettive. A cinquant'anni dalla pubblicazione della prima sentenza della Corte costituzionale* (Giappichelli 2008).

De Vega, Pedro, "Prólogo" in Javier Ruipérez, *La reforma del Estatuto de Autonomía para Galicia* (Servicio de publicacións da Universidade da Coruña 1995).

"Prólogo" in Santiago A. Roura, *Federalismo y justicia constitucional en la Constitución Española de 1978* (Biblioteca nueva 2003).

de Vergottini, Giuseppe, *Le origini della seconda Repubblica portoghese* (Giuffrè 1977).

"Principio di legalità e revisione della Costituzione portoghese del 1982" in Alessandro Pizzorusso and Vincenzo Varano (eds.), *L'influenza dei valori costituzionali sui sistemi giuridici contemporanei* (Giuffrè 1985).

Le transizioni costituzionali (Il Mulino 1998).

"Costituzionalismo europeo e transizioni democratiche" in Marina Calamo Specchia, Maddalena Carli, Giampiero Di Plinio, and Roberto Toniatti (eds.), *I Balcani occidentali. Le Costituzioni della transizione* (Giappichelli 2008).

Oltre il dialogo tra le corti. Giudici, diritto straniero, comparazione (Il Mulino 2010).

Diritto costituzionale comparato (Cedam 2013).
De Visser, Maartje, *Constitutional Review in Europe: A Comparative Analysis* (Hart 2014).
Diamond, Larry, *Developing Democracy: Towards Consolidation* (The Johns Hopkins University Press 1999).
Di Gregorio, Angela, "La transizione in Cecoslovacchia. Principali profili di diritto costituzionale" in Silvio Gambino (ed.), *Costituzionalismo europeo e transizioni democratiche* (Giuffrè 2003).
Repubblica Ceca (Il Mulino 2008).
Epurazioni e protezione della democrazia. Esperienze e modelli di 'giustizia postautoritaria' (Franco Angeli 2012).
"Lo scioglimento della Cecoslovacchia: aspetti politico-costituzionali" in Angela Di Gregorio and Alessandro Vitale (eds.), *Il ventennale dello scioglimento pacifico della Federazione ceco-slovacca. Profili storico-politici, costituzionali, internazionali* (Maggioli 2013).
"Ricorso incidentale e ruolo dei cittadini nella tutela dei diritti e libertà fondamentali dinanzi alla Corte costituzionale ceca" (2014) 1 *Diritto pubblico comparato ed europeo*.
Dogliani, Mario, *Interpretazioni della Costituzione* (Franco Angeli 1982).
D'Orlando, Elena, *La funzione arbitrale della Corte costituzionale tra Stato centrale e governi periferici* (Libreria Bonomo Editrice 2005).
Dornbach, Alajos, "Retroactivity Law Overturned in Hungary" (1992) 1 *East European Constitutional Review* 1.
Dorsen, Norman, Rosenfeld, Michel, Sajó, András, and Baer, Susanne (eds.), *Comparative Constitutionalism: Cases and Materials* (West Thomson 2010).
Dupré, Catherine, *Importing the Law in Post-Communist Transitions: The Hungarian Constitutional Court and the Right to Human Dignity* (Hart 2003).
Eisenmann, Charles, *La justice constitutionnelle et la Haute Cour constitutionnelle d'Autriche* (Economica, Presses universitaires d'Aix-Marseille 1986) (reproduction of the 1928 edition).
"Ekman Report" in Council of Europe, *Documents. Working Papers*, vol. VII, Strasbourg 1991.
Elia, Leopoldo, "De Gasperi e Dossetti" (1974) 521, 2084 *Nuova Antologia*, 109.
Ellis, Mark S., "Purging the Past: The Current State of Lustration Laws in the Former Communist Bloc" (1996) 59 *Law and Contemporary Problems* 4.
Elster, Jon, *Closing the Books: Transitional Justice in Historical Perspective* (Cambridge University Press 2004).
Esposito, Carlo, "Leggi vecchie e Costituzione nuova" (1948) III *Giurisprudenza italiana*.
Eula, Ernesto, "Magistratura e Costituzione" (1956) IV *Foro padano*.
European Commission for Democracy through Law, *Constitution Making as an Instrument of Democratic Transition* (Council of Europe Press 1993).
Meeting with the Presidents of Constitutional Courts and Other Equivalent Bodies (Council of Europe Press 1993).
The Role of the Constitutional Court in the Consolidation of the Rule of Law (Council of Europe Press 1994).
Evans, Malcolm, "The Italian Constitutional Court" (1968) 17 *International and Comparative Law Quarterly*.
Falzone, Vittorio, *La Costituzione ed i culti non cattolici* (Giuffrè 1953).
Farrelly, David G., and Chan, Stanley H., "Italy's Constitutional Court: Procedural Aspects" (1957) 6 *The American Journal of Comparative Law*.
Favara, E., "Ancora sul controllo giurisdizionale di costituzionalità dei provvedimenti legislativi" (1950) IV *Foro padano*.
Favoreu, Louis, *Les Cours Constitutionnelles* (Presses Universitaires de France 1986).

"American and European Models of Constitutional Justice" in David S. Clark (ed.), *Comparative and Private International Law: Essays in Honor of John Henry Merryman on His Seventieth Birthday* (Duncker & Humblot 1990).
Ferejohn, John, and Pasquino, Pasquale, "Constitutional Adjudication, Italian Style" in Tom Ginsburg (ed.), *Comparative Constitutional Design* (Cambridge University Press 2012).
Fernández Farreres, Germán, *El recurso de amparo según la jurisprudencia constitucional. Comentarios al Título III de la LOTC* (Marcial Pons 1994).
Ferreres Comella, Victor, "The Spanish Constitutional Court: Time for Reforms" (2008) 3 *Journal of Comparative Law* 2.
Constitutional Courts and Democratic Values: A European Perspective (Yale University Press 2009).
The Constitution of Spain: A Contextual Analysis (Hart 2013).
"The Spanish Constitutional Court Confronts Catalonia's 'Right to Decide' (Comment on the Judgment 42/2014)" (2014) 10 *European Constitutional Law Review* 3.
Fiorillo, Mario, *La nascita della Repubblica italiana e i problemi giuridici della continuità* (Giuffrè 2000).
Fish, M. Steven, "A Vladimir Meciar Retrospective: The End of Meciarism" (1999) 8 *East European Constitutional Review* 1/2.
Flauss, Jean-François, "Les conditions d'admission des pays d'Europe centrale et orientale au sein du Conseil de l'Europe" (1994) 5 *European Journal of International Law* 1.
"Forum. Statuto catalano e giurisprudenza costituzionale" (2011) *Diritto pubblico comparato ed europeo*.
Franz, Paul, "Unconstitutional and Outlawed Political Parties: A German-American Comparison" (1982) 5 *Boston College International and Comparative Law Review* 1.
Friedrich, Carl J., "Rebuilding the German Constitution" (1949) 43 *The American Political Science Review* 3.
Fromont, Michel, *La justice constitutionnelle dans le monde* (Dalloz 1996).
Frosini, Justin O., "Constitutional Justice" in Giuseppe Franco Ferrari (ed.), *Introduction to Italian Public Law* (Giuffrè 2008).
Constitutional Preambles: At a Crossroads between Politics and Law (Maggioli 2012).
"Constitutional Court of Italy" in Rainer Grote, Frauke Lachenmann, and Rüdiger Wolfrum (eds.), *The Max Planck Encyclopedia of Comparative Constitutional Law* (Oxford University Press 2017).
Frosini, Justin O., and Biagi, Francesco (eds.), *Political and Constitutional Transitions in North Africa: Actors and Factors* (Routledge 2015).
Frosini, Justin O., and Pegoraro, Lucio, "Constitutional Courts in Latin America: A Testing Ground for New Parameters of Classification?" (2008) 3 *Journal of Comparative Law* 2.
Ganino, Mario, "Democrazia e diritti umani nelle costituzioni dei Paesi dell'Europa orientale" in Mario Ganino and Gabriella Venturini (eds.), *L'Europa di domani: verso l'allargamento dell'Unione* (Giuffrè 2002).
García de Enterría, Eduardo, "La posición juridica del Tribunal constitucional en el sistema español: posibilidades y perspectivas" (1981) 1 *Revista española de derecho constitucional* 1.
La Constitución como norma y el Tribunal constitucional (Aranzadi 2006).
García de Enterría, Eduardo, and Fernandez, Tomás-Ramón, *Curso de derecho administrativo* (Civitas 1980).
García-Escudero Márquez, Piedad, and Pendás García, Benigno, "Régimen jurídico del derecho de reunión (análisis de la Ley orgánica 9/1983, de 15 de julio)" (1986) 22 *Revista de derecho político*.

García-Pelayo, Manuel, "El 'status' del Tribunal constitucional" (1981) 1 *Revista española de derecho constitucional* 1.

Gárdos-Orosz, Fruzsina, "The Hungarian Constitutional Court in Transition – From Actio Popularis to Constitutional Complaint" (2012) 53 *Acta Juridica Hungarica*.

Garlicki, Lech, "The Experience of the Polish Constitutional Court" in Wojciech Sadurski (ed.), *Constitutional Justice, East and West: Democratic Legitimacy and Constitutional Courts in Post-Communist Europe in a Comparative Perspective* (Kluwer Law International 2002).

"Constitutional Courts versus Supreme Courts" (2007) 5 *International Journal of Constitutional Law* 1.

"Constitutional Court of Poland: 1982–2009" in Pasquale Pasquino and Francesca Billi (eds.), *The Political Origins of Constitutional Courts: Italy, Germany, France, Poland, Canada, United Kingdom* (Fondazione Adriano Olivetti 2009).

Garrido Falla, Fernando, "Artículo 1" in Fernando Garrido Falla (ed.), *Comentarios a la Constitución* (Civitas 2001).

"Artículo 53" in Fernando Garrido Falla (ed.), *Comentarios a la Constitución* (Civitas 2001).

Garton Ash, Timothy, *The Magic Lantern: The Revolution of '89 Witnessed in Warsaw. Budapest, Berlin and Prague* (Random House 1990).

Ghisalberti, Carlo, *Storia costituzionale d'Italia 1848–1994* (Laterza 2002).

Giannini, Massimo Severo, "Sull'intervento nel processo dinanzi alla Corte costituzionale (giudizi di legittimità costituzionale)" (1956) *Giurisprudenza costituzionale*.

Gil Gil, Alicia, "Spain as an Example of Total Oblivion with Partial Rehabilitation" in Jessica Almqvist and Carlos Espósito (eds.), *The Role of Courts in Transitional Justice: Voices from Latin America and Spain* (Routledge 2012).

Gillis, Mark, "Lustration and Decommunisation" in Jiří Přibáň and James Young (eds.), *The Rule of Law in Central Europe: The Reconstruction of Legality, Constitutionalism and Civil Society in the Post-Communist Countries* (Ashgate 1999).

Ginsburg, Tom, *Judicial Review in New Democracies: Constitutional Courts in Asian Cases* (Cambridge University Press 2003).

Ginsburg, Tom, and Moustafa, Tamir (eds.), *Rule by Law: The Politics of Courts in Authoritarian Regimes* (Cambridge University Press 2008).

Gonzáles Enríquez, Carmen, *Crisis y cambio en Europa del Este: la transición húngara a la democracia* (Centro de investigaciones sociológicas 1993).

González-Trevijano Sánchez, Pedro J., *El Tribunal constitucional* (Aranzadi 2000).

Groppi, Tania, *Il sistema di distribuzione delle competenze tra lo Stato e le Comunità Autonome* (Giappichelli 1992).

"The Italian Constitutional Court: Towards a 'Multilevel System' of Constitutional Review?" (2008) 3 *Journal of Comparative Law* 2.

Groppi, Tania, and Ponthoreau, Marie-Claire (eds.), *The Use of Foreign Precedents by Constitutional Judges* (Hart 2013).

Guarino, Giuseppe, "Stato e regioni speciali nella giurisprudenza della Corte costituzionale" in Ettore Rotelli (ed.), *Dal regionalismo alla regione* (Il Mulino 1973).

Guarnieri, Carlo, *Magistratura e politica in Italia* (Il Mulino 1992).

Guazzarotti, Andrea, *Giudici e minoranze religiose* (Giuffrè 2001).

L'autoapplicabilità delle norme. Un percorso costituzionale (Jovene 2011).

"Art. 11. Libertà di riunione e di associazione" in Sergio Bartole, Pasquale De Sena, and Vladimiro Zagrebelsky (eds.), *Commentario breve alla Convenzione Europea dei Diritti dell'Uomo* (Cedam 2012).

Guillén López, Enrique, "Judicial Review in Spain: The Constitutional Court" (2008) 41 *Loyola of Los Angeles Law Review*.

Gunther, Richard, Puhle, Hans-Jürgen, and Diamandouros, P. Nikiforos, "Introduction" in Richard Gunther, P. Nikiforos Diamandouros, and Hans-Jürgen Puhle (eds.), *The Politics of Democratic Consolidation: Southern Europe in Comparative Perspective* (The Johns Hopkins University Press 1995).

Gutteridge, Harold C., *Comparative Law: An Introduction to the Comparative Method of Legal Study and Research* (Cambridge University Press 1946).

Häberle, Peter, "Il caso tedesco" in Associazione Italiana dei Costituzionalisti (ed.), *La nascita delle Costituzioni europee del secondo dopoguerra* (Cedam 2000).

Hamilton, Alexander, *The Federalist*, no. 78, www.constitution.org/fed/federa78.htm.

Harding, Andrew, Leyland, Peter, and Groppi, Tania, "Constitutional Courts: Forms, Functions and Practice in Comparative Perspective" (2008) 3 *Journal of Comparative Law* 2.

Hayner, Priscilla B., *Unspeakable Truths: Transitional Justice and the Challenge of Truth Commissions* (Routledge 2011).

Hendrych, Dušan, "Constitutionalism in the Czech Republic" in Jiří Přibáň and James Young (eds.), *The Rule of Law in Central Europe: The Reconstruction of Legality, Constitutionalism and Civil Society in the Post-Communist Countries* (Ashgate 1999).

Hermet, Guy, "Environnement international et dimension historique de la transition politique en Espagne" (1984) 8 *Pouvoirs*.

Hernández Gil, Antonio, *El cambio político español y la Constitución* (Planeta 1982).

Herrero de Miñon, Miguel, "Les sources étrangères de la Constitution" (1984) 8 *Pouvoirs*.

Heun, Werner, *The Constitution of Germany: A Contextual Analysis* (Hart 2011).

Hirschl, Ran, "From Comparative Constitutional Law to Comparative Constitutional Studies" (2013) 11 *International Journal of Constitutional Law* 1.

Holländer, Pavel, "The Role of the Czech Constitutional Court: Application of the Constitution in Case Decisions of Ordinary Courts" (1997) 4 *Parker School Journal of East European Law*.

Holmes, Stephen, "Constitutions and Constitutionalism" in Michel Rosenfeld and András Sajó (eds.), *The Oxford Handbook of Comparative Constitutional Law* (Oxford University Press 2012).

Hubeny-Belsky, Annabelle, *Le changement de régime politique en République tchèque (1989–2000): la place du droit constitutionnel* (Presses Universitaires de la Faculté de Droit de Clermont-Ferrand 2003).

Huntington, Samuel P., *The Third Wave: Democratization in the Late Twentieth Century* (University of Oklahoma Press 1991).

Huyse, Luc, "Justice after Transition: On the Choices Successor Elites Make in Dealing with the Past" in Neil J. Kritz (ed.), *Transitional Justice: How Emerging Democracies Reckon with Former Regimes. Volume I. General Considerations* (US Institute of Peace Press 1995).

Iliopoulos-Strangas, Julia, and Koutnatzis, Stylianos-Ioannis G., "Greece" in Allan R. Brewer-Carías (ed.), *Constitutional Courts as Positive Legislators: A Comparative Law Study* (Cambridge University Press 2011).

Imholz, Kathleen, "A Landmark Constitutional Court Decision in Albania" in Neil J. Kritz (ed.), *Transitional Justice: How Emerging Democracies Reckon with Former Regimes. Volume II. Country Studies* (US Institute of Peace Press 1995).

"States of Emergency as Pretexts for Gagging the Press: Word Play at Albania's Constitutional Court" (1997) 6 *East European Constitutional Review* 4.

Issacharoff, Samuel, "Constitutional Courts and Democratic Hedging," *Public Law and Legal Theory Research Paper Series* (New York University School of Law 2010).

Fragile Democracies: Contested Power in the Era of Constitutional Courts (Cambridge University Press 2015).

Jakab, András, and Sonnevend, Pál, "Continuity with Deficiencies: The New Basic Law of Hungary" (2013) 9 *European Constitutional Law Review* 1.

Jemolo, Arturo Carlo, "Le libertà garantite dagli artt. 8, 19, 21 della Costituzione" (1952) *Diritto ecclesiastico*.

Tra diritto e storia (1960–1980) (Giuffrè 1982).

Jiménez Campo, Javier, "Comentario al artículo 53. Protección de los derechos fundamentales" in Óscar Alzaga Villaamil (ed.), *Comentarios a la Constitución española de 1978*, vol. IV (Cortes Generales, Editoriales de derecho reunidas 1996).

Jover, Pedro, "Tribunal de Garantias Constitucionales" in Gregorio Peces-Barba et al., *La izquierda y la Constitución* (Taula de Canvi 1978).

Kawagishi, Norikazu, "The Birth of Judicial Review in Japan" (2007) 5 *International Journal of Constitutional Law* 2.

Keller, Helen, and Stone Sweet, Alec (eds.), *A Europe of Rights: The Impact of the ECHR on National Legal Systems* (Oxford University Press 2008).

Kelsen, Hans, "Wesen und Entwicklung der Staatsgerichtsbarkeit" (1929) 5 *Veröffentlichtung der Vereinigung der Deutschen Staatrechtslehrer* 2/"La garantie jurisdictionnelle de la Constitution – La justice constitutionnelle" (1929) 5 *Revue de Droit Public et de la Science Politique en France et à l'étranger* (English translation: "Kelsen on the Nature and Development of Constitutional Adjudication" in Lars Vinx (ed.), *The Guardian of the Constitution: Hans Kelsen and Carl Schmitt on the Limits of Constitutional Law* [Cambridge University Press 2015]).

"Judicial Review of Legislation. A Comparative Study of the Austrian and the American Constitution" (1942) 4 *The Journal of Politics* 2.

Klíma, Karel, *Constitutional Law of the Czech Republic* (Aleš Čeněk 2008).

Klug, Heinz, "South Africa's Constitutional Court: Enabling Democracy and Promoting Law in the Transition from Apartheid" (2008) 3 *Journal of Comparative Law* 2.

Knapp, Viktor, "The Czechoslovak State from Its Origin to Its Extinction" in Viktor Knapp and Sergio Bartole (eds.), *La dissoluzione della Federazione cecoslovacca* (La Rosa 1994).

Kommers, Donald P., *The Constitutional Jurisprudence of the Federal Republic of Germany* (Duke University Press 1989).

Kosař, David, "Lustration and Lapse of Time: 'Dealing with the Past' in the Czech Republic" (2008) 4 *European Constitutional Law Review* 3.

Perils of Judicial Self-Government in Transitional Societies (Cambridge University Press 2016).

Kosař, David, and Vyhnánek, Ladislav, "The Constitutional Court of Czechia" in Armin von Bogdandy et al. (eds.), *Constitutional Judicial Review* (Oxford University Press forthcoming).

Kovács, Kriszta, and Attila Tóth, Gábor, "Hungary's Constitutional Transformation" (2011) 7 *European Constitutional Law Review* 2.

Kozminski, Andrzej K., "Restitution of Private Property: Re-Privatization in Central and Eastern Europe" (1997) 30 *Communist and Post-Communist Studies* 1.

Kramer, Jutta, "Judicial Federalism in Germany" in Hans-Peter Schneider, Jutta Kramer, and Beniamino Caravita di Toritto (eds.), *Judge Made Federalism? The Role of Courts in Federal Systems* (Nomos 2009).

Kraus, Michael, "Settling Accounts: Postcommunist Czechoslovakia" in Neil J. Kritz (ed.), *Transitional Justice: How Emerging Democracies Reckon with Former Regimes. Volume II. Country Studies* (US Institute of Peace Press 1995).

Kresák, Peter, "Le riforme costituzionali nella Repubblica federale cecoslovacca" (1992) 3 *Quaderni costituzionali*.

Kühn, Zdeněk, "Making Constitutionalism Horizontal: Three Different Central European Strategies" in András Sajó and Renáta Uitz (eds.), *The Constitution in Private Relations: Expanding Constitutionalism* (Eleven International Publishing 2005).

"The Democratization and Modernization of Post-Communist Judiciaries" in Alberto Febbrajo and Wojciech Sadurski (eds.), *Central and Eastern Europe after Transition: Towards a New Socio-Legal Semantics* (Ashgate 2010).

"Judicial Independence in Central-Eastern Europe: The Experience of the 1990s and 2000s" (2011) 1 *The Lawyer Quarterly*.

"Ultra Vires Review and the Demise of Constitutional Pluralism: The Czecho-Slovak Pension Saga, and the Dangers of State Courts' Defiance of EU Law" (2016) 23 *Maastricht Journal of European and Comparative Law*.

Kühn, Zdeněk, and Kysela, Jan, "Nomination of Constitutional Justices in Post-Communist Countries: Trial, Error, Conflict in the Czech Republic" (2006) 2 *European Constitutional Law Review* 2.

Kysela, Jan, "Bicameralism in the Czech Republic: Reasons, Functions, Perspectives" in Jörg Luther, Paolo Passaglia, and Rolando Tarchi (eds.), *A World of Second Chambers* (Giuffrè 2006).

Lach, Kasia, and Sadurski, Wojciech, "Constitutional Courts of Central and Eastern Europe: Between Adolescence and Maturity" (2008) 3 *Journal of Comparative Law* 2.

Lamarque, Elisabetta, *Corte costituzionale e giudici nell'Italia repubblicana* (Laterza 2012).

Lambert, Edouard, *Le gouvernement des juges et la lutte contre la législation sociale aux États-Unis* (Marcel Giard & Cie 1921).

La Torre, Massimo, "The German Impact on Fascist Public Law Doctrine – Costantino Mortati's 'Material Constitution'" in Christian Joerges and Navraj Singh Ghaleigh (eds.), *Darker Legacies of Law in Europe* (Hart 2003).

Lembcke, Oliver W., and Boulanger, Christian, "Between Revolution and Constitution: The Roles of the Hungarian Constitutional Court" in Gábor Attila Tóth (ed.), *Constitution for a Disunited Nation: On Hungary's 2011 Fundamental Law* (Central European University Press 2012).

Lener, Salvatore, "Leggi vecchie e Costituzione nuova" (1953) III *La civiltà cattolica*.

Liebman, Enrico Tullio, "Invalidità e abrogazione delle leggi anteriori alla Costituzione" (1956) *Rivista di diritto processuale*.

Linz, Juan J., "La transición a la democracia en España en perspectiva comparada" in Ramón Cotarelo (ed.), *Transición politica y consolidación democrática. España (1975–1986)* (Centro de investigaciones sociológicas 1992).

Linz, Juan J., and Stepan, Alfred, *Problems of Democratic Transition and Consolidation: Southern Europe, South America, and Post-Communist Europe* (The Johns Hopkins University Press 1996).

lo Calzo, Antonello, "Protosistemi di giustizia costituzionale: il Corpo degli Efori nella Costituzione della Repubblica napoletana del 1799" (2013) 14 *Historia constitucional*.

Loewenstein, Karl, "Militant Democracy and Fundamental Rights" (1937) *The American Political Science Review*.

Lollini, Andrea, *Constitutionalism and Transitional Justice in South Africa* (Berghahn Books 2011).

Lollini, Andrea, and Palermo, Francesco, "Comparative Law and the 'Proceduralization' of Constitution-Building Processes" in Julia Raue and Patrick Sutter (eds.), *Facets and Practices of State-Building* (Martinus Nijhoff 2009).

Lombardi, Clark B., "Egypt's Supreme Constitutional Court: Managing Constitutional Conflict in an Authoritarian, Aspirationally 'Islamic' State" (2008) 3 *Journal of Comparative Law* 2.

Long, Gianni, *Alle origini del pluralismo confessionale. Il dibattito sulla libertà religiosa nell'età della Costituente* (Il Mulino 1990).

Le confessioni religiose "diverse dalla cattolica." Ordinamenti interni e rapporti con lo Stato (Il Mulino 1991).

López Guerra, Luis, "La segunda fase de la construcción del Estado de las Autonomías" (1993) *Revista vasca de administración pública*.

"The Role and Competences of the Constitutional Court" in European Commission for Democracy through Law, *The Role of the Constitutional Court in the Consolidation of the Rule of Law* (Council of Europe Press 1994).

Las sentencias básicas del Tribunal constitucional (Centro de estudios políticos y constitucionales 1998).

"The Application of the Spanish Model in the Constitutional Transitions in Eastern and Central Europe" (1998) 19 *Cardozo Law Review*.

Lorca Corrons, Alejandro, "The Spanish Experience Following Accession," paper presented at the University Association for Contemporary European Studies (1988), cited by Geoffrey Pridham, "The International Context of Democratic Consolidation: Southern Europe in Comparative Perspective" in Richard Gunther, P. Nikiforos Diamandouros, and Hans-Jürgen Puhle (eds.), *The Politics of Democratic Consolidation: Southern Europe in Comparative Perspective* (The Johns Hopkins University Press 1995).

Lübbe-Wolff, Gertrude, "Who Has the Last Word? National and Transnational Courts – Conflict and Cooperation" (2011) 30 *Yearbook of European Law* 1.

"The Principle of Proportionality in the Case-Law of the German Federal Constitutional Court" (2014) 34 *Human Rights Law Journal* 1–6.

Ludwikowski, Rett R., *Constitution-Making in the Region of Former Soviet Dominance* (Duke University Press 1996).

Luther, Jörg, *Idee e storie di giustizia costituzionale nell'Ottocento* (Giappichelli 1990).

"Ragionevolezza e *Verhältnismäßigkeit* nella giurisprudenza costituzionale tedesca" (1993) 1–2 *Diritto e società*.

Malfatti, Elena, Panizza, Saulle, and Romboli, Roberto, *Giustizia costituzionale* (Giappichelli 2007).

Mancini, Susanna, "Il fallimento di un *mariage de raison*: la dissoluzione della Repubblica federativa ceca e slovacca" (1993) 4 *Nomos. Le attualità del diritto*.

"Secession and Self-Determination" in Michel Rosenfeld and András Sajó (eds.), *The Oxford Handbook of Comparative Constitutional Law* (Oxford University Press 2012).

Un affare di donne. L'aborto tra eguale libertà e controllo sociale (Cedam 2012).

Mańko, Rafał, "'War of Courts' as a Clash of Legal Cultures: Rethinking the Conflict between the Polish Constitutional and Supreme Court over 'Interpretive Judgements'" in Antonia Geisler, Michael Hein and Siri Hummel (eds.), *Law, Politics, and the Constitution: New Perspectives from Legal and Political Theory* (Peter Lang 2014).

Marada, Radim, "The 1998 Czech Elections" (1998) 7 *East European Constitutional Review* 4.

Maravall, José M., *La política de la transición* (Taurus 1985).

Maravall, José M., and Santamaria, Julián, "Political Change in Spain and the Prospects for Democracy" in Guillermo O'Donnell, Philippe C. Schmitter, and Laurence Whitehead (eds.), *Transitions from Authoritarian Rule. Southern Europe* (The Johns Hopkins University Press 1986).

"Transición política y consolidación de la democracia en España" in José Félix Tezanos, Ramón Cortarelo, and Andrés de Blas (eds.), *La transición democrática española* (Editorial sistema 1989).

Martín-Retortillo Baquer, Lorenzo, "Eficacia y garantía de los derechos fundamentales" in Sebastián Martín-Retortillo (ed.), *Estudios sobre la Constitución española. Homenaje al Profesor Eduardo García de Enterría*, vol. II (Civitas 1991).

Martínez-Herrera, Enric, and Miley, Thomas Jeffrey, "The Constitution and the Politics of National Identity in Spain" (2010) 16 *Nations and Nationalism*.

Massias, Jean-Pierre, *Justice constitutionnelle et transition démocratique en Europe de l'Est* (Les Presses Universitaires de la Faculté de Droit de Clermont-Ferrand 1998).

Mathernova, Katarina, "Czecho?Slovakia: Constitutional Disappointments" in A. E. Dick Howard (ed.), *Constitution-Making in Eastern Europe* (Woodrow Wilson Center Press 1993).

Merli, Gianfranco, and Sparisci, Emo (eds.), *Giovanni Gronchi. Discorsi parlamentari* (Senato della Repubblica 1986).

Merlini, Stefano, "La Corte costituzionale e le leggi di pubblica sicurezza" (1972) *Quale giustizia*.

Merryman, John Henry, and Vigoriti, Vincenzo, "When Courts Collide: Constitution and Cassation in Italy" (1967) 15 *The American Journal of Comparative Law*.

Mezzanotte, Carlo, *Il giudizio sulle leggi. Le ideologie del costituente* (Editoriale Scientifica 2014) (first published by Giuffrè 1979).

Corte costituzionale e legittimazione politica (Editoriale Scientifica 2014) (first published by Tipografia Veneziana in 1984).

Mezzetti, Luca, *Le democrazie incerte. Transizioni costituzionali e consolidamento della democrazia in Europa orientale, Africa, America Latina, Asia* (Giappichelli 2000).

Teoria e prassi delle transizioni costituzionali e del consolidamento democratico (Cedam 2003).

"Transizioni costituzionali e procedimenti esterni di formazione delle Costituzioni. L'esperienza tedesca fra corsi e ricorsi storici" in Silvio Gambino (ed.), *Costituzionalismo europeo e transizioni democratiche* (Giuffrè 2003).

Mezzetti, Luca (ed.), *International Constitutional Law* (Giappichelli 2014).

Monereo Pérez, José Luis, *Derecho de huelga y conflictos colectivos* (Editorial Comares 2002).

Morlino, Leonardo, "The Two 'Rules of Law' between Transition to and Quality of Democracy" in Leonardo Morlino and Gianluigi Palombella (eds.), *Rule of Law and Democracy: Inquiries into Internal and External Issues* (Brill 2010).

Morodo, Raúl, "Socialistes et communistes dans la transition" (1984) 8 *Pouvoirs*.

La transición política (Tecnos 1985).

Morrone, Andrea, *Il custode della ragionevolezza* (Giuffrè 2001).

Mortati, Costantino, *La Costituzione in senso materiale* (Giuffré 1940).

"Corte costituzionale e Alta Corte per la regione siciliana" (1956) *Giurisprudenza costituzionale*.

"Appunti per uno studio sui rimedi giurisdizionali contro comportamenti omissivi del legislatore" (1970) V *Foro italiano*.

Morvai, Krisztina, "Retroactive Justice Based on International Law: A Recent Decision by the Hungarian Constitutional Court" (1993–1994) *East European Constitutional Review* 2, 4/3, 1.

Moustafa, Tamir, *The Struggle for Constitutional Power: Law, Politics and Economic Development in Egypt* (Cambridge University Press 2007).

Muller, Ingo, *Hitler's Justice: The Courts of the Third Reich* (Harvard University Press 1991).
Muñoz Machado, Santiago, *Derecho público de las Comunidades Autónomas* (Civitas 2007).
Muro, Diego, and Quiroga, Alejandro, "Building the Spanish Nation: The Centre-Periphery Dialectic" (2004) 4 *Studies in Ethnicity and Nationalism* 2.
Nardini, William J., "Passive Activism and the Limits of Judicial Self-Restraint: Lessons for America from the Italian Constitutional Court" (1999) 30 *Seton Hall Law Review*.
Neff, Michael L., "Eastern Europe's Policy of Restitution of Property in the 1990's" (1992) 10 *Dickinson Journal of International Law* 2.
Neumayer, Karl H., "Law in the Books, Law in Action et les méthodes du droit comparé" in Mario Rotondi (ed.), *Buts et méthodes du droit comparé* (Cedam 1973).
Nicotra, Ida, *Democrazia "convenzionale" e partiti antisistema* (Giappichelli 2007).
O'Donnell, Guillermo, and Schmitter, Philippe C., "Tentative Conclusions about Uncertain Democracies" in Guillermo O'Donnell, Philippe C. Schmitter, and Laurence Whitehead (eds.), *Transitions from Authoritarian Rule* (The Johns Hopkins University Press 1986).
Okoth-Ogendo, H. W. O., "Constitutions without Constitutionalism: Reflections on an African Political Paradox" in Douglas Greenberg, Stanley N. Katz, Melanie Beth Oliviero, and Steven C. Wheatley (eds.), *Constitutionalism and Democracy: Transitions in the Contemporary World* (Oxford University Press 1993).
Olivetti Rason, Nino, "Alcune considerazioni conclusive" in Silvio Gambino (ed.), *Costituzionalismo europeo e transizioni democratiche* (Giuffrè 2003).
Onida, Valerio, "Luci e ombre nella giurisprudenza costituzionale in tema di sciopero" (1969) *Giurisprudenza costituzionale*.
"L'attuazione della Costituzione tra magistratura e Corte costituzionale" in *Aspetti e tendenze del Diritto costituzionale. Scritti in onore di Costantino Mortati* (Giuffrè 1977).
La Costituzione (Il Mulino 2004).
Pace, Alessandro, "Spunti per una delimitazione 'costituzionale' dello sciopero" (1964) *Giurisprudenza costituzionale*.
Paladin, Livio, "Costituzione, preleggi e codice civile" (1993) 1 *Rivista di diritto civile*.
Per una storia costituzionale dell'Italia repubblicana (Il Mulino 2004).
Palomeque López, Manuel Carlos, "El derecho constitucional de huelga y su regulación en España" in *Derecho del trabajo y razón crítica* (Varona 2004).
Panunzio, Sergio, "Lo sciopero politico fra Costituzione e Corte costituzionale" in *Aspetti e tendenze del Diritto costituzionale. Scritti in onore di Costantino Mortati* (Giuffrè 1977).
Parejo Alfonso, Luciano, "El contenido esencial de los derechos fundamentales en la jurisprudencia constitucional; a propósito de la sentencia del Tribunal constitucional de 8 abril de 1981" (1981) 1 *Revista española de derecho constitucional* 3.
"La Constitución y las leyes preconstitucionales. El problema de la derogación y la llamada incostitucionalidad sobrevenida" (1981) 94 *Revista de administración pública*.
Pasquino, Gianfranco, "The Demise of the First Fascist Regime and Italy's Transition to Democracy: 1943–1948" in Guillermo O'Donnell, Philippe C. Schmitter, and Laurence Whitehead (eds.), *Transition from Authoritarian Rule: Southern Europe* (The Johns Hopkins University Press 1986).
Pasquino, Pasquale, "The Debates of the Italian Constituent Assembly Concerning the Introduction of a Constitutional Court (1947–1948)" in Pasquale Pasquino and Francesca Billi (eds.), *The Political Origins of Constitutional Courts: Italy, Germany, France, Poland, Canada, United Kingdom* (Fondazione Adriano Olivetti 2009).
Pavone, Claudio, *Alle origini della Repubblica. Scritti su fascismo, antifascismo e continuità dello Stato* (Bollati Boringhieri 1995).

"Peaceful Transitions to Constitutional Democracy: Transcript of the Proceedings" (1998) 19 *Cardozo Law Review*.

Peces-Barba, Gregorio, et al., *La izquierda y la Constitución* (Taula de Canvi 1978).

Pehe, Jiri, "Parliament Passes Controversial Law on Vetting Officials" in Neil J. Kritz (ed.), *Transitional Justice: How Emerging Democracies Reckon with Former Regimes. Volume II. Country Studies* (US Institute of Peace Press 1995).

Peñaranda Ramos, José Luis, "Disposición derogatoria. Constitución y ordenamiento pre-constitucional" in Óscar Alzaga Villaamil (ed.), *Comentarios a la Constitución española de 1978* (Cortes Generales, Editoriales de derecho reunidas 1996).

Pennicino, Sara, *Contributo allo studio della ragionevolezza nel diritto comparato* (Maggioli 2012).

Perone, Gian Carlo, "La giurisprudenza costituzionale in materia di sciopero e serrata" in Renato Scognamiglio (ed.), *Il lavoro nella giurisprudenza costituzionale* (Franco Angeli 1978).

Peyrot, Giorgio, "Provvedimenti ostativi dell'autorità di polizia e garanzie costituzionali per il libero esercizio dei culti ammessi" (1951) *Diritto ecclesiastico*.

Piana, Daniela, "Bureaucratic and Managerial Cultures in Central Eastern European Courts" in Alberto Febbrajo and Wojciech Sadurski (eds.), *Central and Eastern Europe after Transition: Towards a New Socio-Legal Semantics* (Ashgate 2010).

Pierandrei, Franco, "Ancora sul conflitto fra il Governo-legislatore provvisorio e il potere giudiziario" (1947) I *Giurisprudenza italiana*.

Pildes, Richard H., "The Inherent Authoritarianism in Democratic Regimes" in András Sajó (ed.), *Out of and into Authoritarian Law* (Kluwer Law International 2003).

Pin, Andrea, and Longo, Erik, "Judicial Review, Election Law, and Proportionality" (2016) 6 *Notre Dame Journal of International and Comparative Law* 1.

Pinelli, Cesare, "Cinquant'anni dopo: Gronchi, Tambroni e la forma di governo" (2010) 4 *Quaderni costituzionali*.

Pištan, Čarna, "I sistemi di giustizia costituzionale nei paesi dell'Europa centro-orientale e dell'area post-sovietica" in Luca Mezzetti (ed.), *Sistemi e modelli di giustizia costituzionale*, vol. II (Cedam 2011).

Tra democrazia e autoritarismo. Esperienze di giustizia costituzionale nell'Europa centro-orientale e nell'area post-sovietica (Bononia University Press 2015).

Pizzorusso, Alessandro, "Obiettivo sulle ordinanze di rimessione alla Corte costituzionale" (1970) 1 *Quale giustizia*.

"Meriti e limiti del processo costituzionale" (1972) *Politica del diritto*.

"Garanzie costituzionali. Art. 134" in Giuseppe Branca (ed.), *Commentario della Costituzione* (Zanichelli-Il Foro italiano 1981).

"Le stagioni della Costituzione," preface to the final volume of Giuseppe Branca (ed.), *Commentario alla Costituzione* (Zanichelli-Il Foro italiano 1981).

"Italian and American Models of the Judiciary and of Judicial Review of Legislation: A Comparison of Recent Tendencies" (1990) 38 *The American Journal of Comparative Law*.

Pizzorusso, Alessandro, Vigoriti, Vincenzo, and Certoma, G. L., "The Constitutional Review of Legislation in Italy" (1983) 56 *Temple Law Quarterly*.

Podhrázký, Milan, "A Comparative Analysis of the Bodies in Charge of Electoral Control, Especially the Judicial Ones: The Czech Case" in M. Paloma Biglino Campos and Luis Esteban Delgado del Rincón (eds.), *La resolución de los conflictos electorales: un análisis comparado* (Centro de estudios políticos y constitucionales 2010).

Pogány, István, "Minority Rights and the Roma of Central and Eastern Europe" (2006) 6 *Human Rights Law Review* 1.

Poggeschi, Giovanni, *Le nazioni linguistiche della Spagna autonómica* (Cedam 2002).
Pollicino, Oreste, "Corti europee e allargamento dell'Europa: evoluzioni giurisprudenziali e riflessi ordinamentali" (2009) 1 *Il Diritto dell'Unione europea*.
Allargamento dell'Europa ad Est e rapporto tra Corti costituzionali e Corti europee. Verso una teoria generale dell'impatto interordinamentale del diritto sovranazionale? (Giuffrè 2010).
Pombeni, Paolo, *La Costituente. Un problema storico-politico* (Il Mulino 1995).
Powell, Charles T., *El piloto del cambio. El Rey, la monarquía y la transición a la democracia* (Planeta 1991).
Prakash, Saikrishna B., and Yoo, John C., "The Origins of Judicial Review" (2003) 70 *The University of Chicago Law Review*.
Přibáň, Jiří, "Judicial Power vs. Democratic Representation: The Culture of Constitutionalism and Human Rights in the Czech Legal System" in Wojciech Sadurski (ed.), *Constitutional Justice, East and West: Democratic Legitimacy and Constitutional Courts in Post-Communist Europe in a Comparative Perspective* (Kluwer Law International 2002).
Pridham, Geoffrey, "The International Context of Democratic Consolidation: Southern Europe in Comparative Perspective" in Richard Gunther, P. Nikiforos Diamandouros, and Hans-Jürgen Puhle (eds.), *The Politics of Democratic Consolidation: Southern Europe in Comparative Perspective* (The Johns Hopkins University Press 1995).
Prieto Sanchís, Luis, "Dos años de jurisprudencia del Tribunal Supremo sobre cuestiones constitucionales" (1981) 1 *Revista española de derecho constitucional* 1, 2, 3.
Estudios sobre derechos fundamentales (Editorial Debate 1990).
Prochàzka, Radoslav, *Mission Accomplished: On Founding Constitutional Adjudication in Central Europe* (Central European University Press 2002).
Pulido Quecedo, Manuel, *El Estatuto de Autonomía de Cataluña. Anotado con la jurisprudencia sistematizada de la STC 31/2010, de 28 de junio* (Aranzadi 2010)
"Rassegna di giurisprudenza sulla Costituzione e sugli Statuti regionali" (1956) *Giurisprudenza costituzionale*.
Reinares, Fernando, "Democratización y terrorismo en el caso español" in José Félix Tezanos, Ramón Cortarelo, and Andrés de Blas (eds.), *La transición democrática española* (Editorial sistema 1989).
Requejo Pagés, Juan Luis (ed.), *Comentarios a la Ley Orgánica del Tribunal Constitucional* (Tribunal Constitucional, Boletín Oficial del Estado 2001).
Robertson, David, "A Problem of Their Own, Solutions of Their Own: CEE Jurisdictions and the Problems of Lustration and Retroactivity" in Wojciech Sadurski, Adam Czarnota, and Martin Krygier (eds.), *Spreading Democracy and the Rule of Law? The Impact of EU Enlargement on the Rule of Law, Democracy and Constitutionalism in Post-Communist Legal Orders* (Springer 2006).
Rodotà, Stefano, "La svolta 'politica' della Corte costituzionale" (1970) 1 *Politica del diritto*.
Rolla, Giancarlo, *Indirizzo politico e Tribunale costituzionale in Spagna* (Jovene 1986).
Romagnoli, Umberto, "Art. 40" in Giuseppe Branca (ed.), *Commentario alla Costituzione* (Zanichelli-Il Foro italiano 1981).
Romboli, Roberto, *Il giudizio costituzionale incidentale come processo senza parti* (Giuffrè 1985).
"I rapporti tra giudici comuni e Corte costituzionale nel controllo sulle leggi in via incidentale in Italia: l'esperienza di 50 anni di giurisprudenza costituzionale" in Luca Mezzetti and Eduardo Ferrer Mac-Gregor (eds.), *Diritto processuale costituzionale* (Cedam 2010).

Rosenfeld, Michel, "Constitution Making, Identity Building and Peaceful Transition to Democracy: Theoretical Reflections Inspired by the Spanish Example" (1998) 19 *Cardozo Law Review*.

"Editorial. Constitutionalism, Moderation and Compromise: Confronting Threats within and beyond the Constitution" (2011) 9 *International Journal of Constitutional Law* 3–4.

Rubio Llorente, Francisco, "Del Tribunal de garantías constitucionales al Tribunal constitucional" (1982–1983) 16 *Revista de derecho político*.

"El bloque de costitucionalidad" (1989) 27 *Revista española de derecho constitucional*.

La forma del poder (Estudios sobre la Constitución) (Centro de estudios constitucionales 1993).

Rubio Llorente, Francisco, and Aragón Reyes, Manuel, "La jurisdicción constitucional" in Alberto Predieri and Eduardo García de Enterría (eds.), *La Constitución española de 1978* (Civitas 1980).

Rubio-Marín, Ruth, "Women and the Cost of Transition to Democratic Constitutionalism in Spain" (2003) 18 *International Sociology*.

Ruggeri, Antonio, and Spadaro, Antonino, *Lineamenti di giustizia costituzionale* (Giappichelli 2001).

Ruiz Lapeña, Rosa María, *El Tribunal de garantías constitucionales en la II República española* (Bosch 1982).

Sadurski, Wojciech, "Constitutional Justice, East and West: Introduction" in Wojciech Sadurski (ed.), *Constitutional Justice, East and West: Democratic Legitimacy and Constitutional Courts in Post-Communist Europe in a Comparative Perspective* (Kluwer Law International 2002).

"Judicial Review in Central and Eastern Europe: Rationales or Rationalizations?" (2009) 42 *Israel Law Review* 3.

"Partnering with Strasbourg: Constitutionalization of the European Court of Human Rights, the Accession of Central and East European States to the Council of Europe, and the Idea of Pilot Judgments" (2009) 9 *Human Rights Law Review*.

"Constitutional Courts and Constitutional Culture in Central and Eastern European Countries" in Alberto Febbrajo and Wojciech Sadurski (eds.), *Central and Eastern Europe after Transition: Towards a New Socio-Legal Semantics* (Ashgate 2010).

"Constitutional Courts in Transition Processes: Legitimacy and Democratization" (2011) *Sydney Law School Legal Studies Research Paper* 11/53.

Rights before Courts: A Study of Constitutional Courts in Postcommunist States of Central and Eastern Europe (Springer 2014).

"How Democracy Dies (in Poland): A Case Study of Anti-Constitutional Populist Backsliding" (2018) *Sydney Law School Research Paper* 18/01.

Poland's Constitutional Breakdown (Oxford University Press 2019).

Sadurski, Wojciech (ed.), *Constitutional Justice, East and West: Democratic Legitimacy and Constitutional Courts in Post-Communist Europe in a Comparative Perspective* (Kluwer Law International 2002).

Salvemini, Gaetano, "Fu l'Italia prefascista una democrazia?" (1952) *Il Ponte*.

Šamalík, František, "Political Parties and the Split of Czechoslovakia" in Viktor Knapp and Sergio Bartole (eds.), *La dissoluzione della Federazione cecoslovacca* (La Rosa 1994).

Sánchez Navarro, Ángel J., *La transición española en sus documentos* (Centro de estudios políticos y constitucionales 1998).

Sandulli, Aldo, *Rapporti tra giustizia comune e giustizia costituzionale in Italia* (Cedam 1968).

Santoni, Francesco, *Lo sciopero* (Jovene 1991).

Sartori, Giovanni, *Elementi di teoria politica* (Il Mulino 1995).

Sbailò, Ciro, "Elezioni presidenziali in Egitto: quando le Corti vogliono guidare le transizioni" (2012) 3 *Quaderni costituzionali*.

Scheppele, Kim Lane, "Constitutional Interpretation after Regimes of Horror" in Susanne Karstedt (ed.), *Legal Institutions and Collective Memories* (Hart 2009).

"The Unconstitutional Constitution" (January 2, 2012) *The New York Times*, https://krugman.blogs.nytimes.com/2012/01/02/the-unconstitutional-constitution/.

Schmitter, Philippe C., "Transitology: The Science or Art of Democratization?" in Joseph S. Tulchin and Bernice Romero (eds.), *The Consolidation of Democracy in Latin America* (Lynne Rienner 1995).

Schwartz, Herman, "The New East European Constitutional Courts" in A. E. Dick Howard (ed.), *Constitution-Making in Eastern Europe* (Woodrow Wilson Center Press 1993).

"The Czech Constitutional Court Decision on the Illegitimacy of the Communist Regime" (1994) 1 *Parker School Journal of Eastern European Law*.

The Struggle for Constitutional Justice in Post-Communist Europe (University of Chicago Press 2000).

Segretariato della Presidenza della Repubblica. Servizio archivio storico, documentazione e biblioteca, *Discorsi e messaggi del Presidente della Repubblica Giovanni Gronchi* (2005).

Serna de la Garza, José Maria, "Amparo" in Rainer Grote, Frauke Lachenmann, and Rüdiger Wolfrum (eds.), *The Max Planck Encyclopedia of Comparative Constitutional Law* (Oxford University Press 2016).

Serra Cristóbal, Rosario, *La guerra de las Cortes* (Tecnos 1999).

Šiklová, Jirina, "Lustration or the Czech Way of Screening" (1996) 5 *East European Constitutional Review* 1.

Šiklová, Jirina, and Miklusakova, Marta, "Law as an Instrument of Discrimination: Denying Citizenship to the Czech Roma" (1998) 7 *East European Constitutional Review* 2.

Silvestri, Gaetano, "Alle origini del modello italiano di giurisdizione costituzionale" in *Genesi ed evoluzione dei sistemi di giustizia costituzionale in Italia, Francia e Spagna*, Quaderni del dottorato di ricerca in Diritto ed Economia dell'Università Federico II di Napoli, no. 5 (2012), www.federalismi.it

Simoncini, Andrea, "L'avvio della Corte costituzionale e gli strumenti per la definizione del suo ruolo: un problema storico aperto" (2004) *Giurisprudenza costituzionale*.

Slosarcik, Ivo, "Rapports: Czech Republic. The Reform of the Constitutional Systems of Czechoslovakia and the Czech Republic in 1990–2000" (2001) 7 *European Public Law* 4.

Solé Tura, Jordi, and Aja, Eliseo, "Une élaboration consensuelle" (1984) 8 *Pouvoirs*.

Solozábal Echavarría, Juan José, "La configuración constitucional del derecho de reunión" (2001) 5 *Parlamento y Constitución*.

Sólyom, László, "The Role of Constitutional Courts in the Transition to Democracy: With Special Reference to Hungary" (2003) 18 *International Sociology*.

Spadaro, Antonino, "La transizione costituzionale. Ambiguità e polivalenza di un'importante nozione di teoria generale" in Antonino Spadaro (ed.), *Le "trasformazioni" costituzionali nell'età della transizione* (Giappichelli 2000).

Stasio, Donatella, "Consulta garante della democrazia" (April 21, 2006) *Il Sole-24 Ore*.

Stone Sweet, Alec, *Governing with Judges: Constitutional Politics in Europe* (Oxford University Press 2000).

"Why Europe Rejected American Judicial Review: And Why It May Not Matter" (2003) 101 *Michigan Law Review* 8.

"Constitutional Courts" in Michel Rosenfeld and András Sajó (eds.), *The Oxford Handbook of Comparative Constitutional Law* (Oxford University Press 2012).

Stone Sweet, Alec, and Mathews, Jud, "Proportionality Balancing and Global Constitutionalism" (2008) 47 *Columbia Journal of Transnational Law*.

Sunstein, Cass R., "A Constitutional Anomaly in the Czech Republic?" (1995) 4 *East European Constitutional Review* 2.

Svoboda, Karel, "Legal and Political Events between 1989 and 1992" in Viktor Knapp and Sergio Bartole (eds.), *La dissoluzione della Federazione cecoslovacca* (La Rosa 1994).

Svobodova, Tereza, "Les garanties des libertés fondamentales dans la République tchèque" (2003) 53 *Revue internationale de droit comparé* 3.

Tajadura Tejada, Javier, "La legitimidad de la Monarquía parlamentaria" in Carolina León Bastos and Víctor Alejandro Wong Meraz (eds.), *Homenaje al Doctor Jorge Carpizo en Madrid* (Porrúa 2010).

Tarchi, Rolando, "VI disp. trans. e fin." in Giuseppe Branca (ed.), *Commentario alla Costituzione* (Zanichelli-Il Foro italiano 1981).

Teitel, Ruti G., *Transitional Justice* (Oxford University Press 2000).

"Transitional Justice Genealogy" (2003) 16 *Harvard Human Rights Journal*.

"Militating Democracy: Comparative Constitutional Perspectives" (2007) 29 *Michigan Journal of International Law* 1.

"Transitional Jurisprudence: The Role of Law in Political Transformation" (2009) 106 *The Yale Law Journal*.

Toharia, José J., "Judicial Independence in an Authoritarian Regime: The Case of Contemporary Spain" (1975) 9 *Law and Society Review* 3.

Tomás y Valiente, Francisco, *Escritos sobre y desde el Tribunal constitucional* (Centro de estudios políticos y constitucionales 1993).

"La primera fase de construcción del Estado de las Autonomías (1978–1983)" (1993) 36 *Revista vasca de administración pública*.

Tomoszek, Maxim, "The Czech Republic" in Dawn Oliver and Carlo Fusaro (eds.), *How Constitutions Change: A Comparative Study* (Hart 2011).

Torres del Moral, Antonio, *Principios de Derecho constitucional español* (Atomo ediciones 1984).

"El Tribunal constitucional español en negativo: lagunas y rectificaciones; cuestiones disputadas, inéditas, irresueltas, menores y de lege ferenda" in Víctor Bazán (ed.), *Derecho procesal constitucional americano y europeo*, vol. I (Abeledo Perrot 2010).

Torres Pérez, Aida, "Report on Spain" in Giuseppe Martinico and Oreste Pollicino (eds.), *The National Judicial Treatment of the ECHR and EU Laws: A Comparative Constitutional Perspective* (Europa Law Publishing 2010).

Toscano, Mario, "L'abrogazione delle leggi razziali: l'Egeli e le restituzioni" in *Commissione per la ricostruzione delle vicende che hanno caratterizzato in Italia le attività di acquisizione dei beni dei cittadini ebrei da parte di organismi pubblici e privati, Rapporto generale* (Presidenza del Consiglio dei Ministri, Dipartimento per l'informazione e l'editoria 2001).

Tosi, Silvano, *Il Governo davanti alla Corte nei giudizi incidentali di legittimità costituzionale* (Giuffrè 1963).

Tóth, Gábor Attila (ed.), *Constitution for a Disunited Nation: On Hungary's 2011 Fundamental Law* (Central European University Press 2012).

Tranfaglia, Nicola, "Per una storia politica della Corte costituzionale" in *Dallo Stato liberale allo Stato fascista* (Feltrinelli 1973).

Treves, Giuseppino, "Judicial Review of Legislation in Italy" (1958) 7 *Journal of Public Law*.

Tribunal constitucional. Trabajos parlamentarios (Cortes Generales 1980).

Trochev, Alexei, *Judging Russia: The Role of the Constitutional Court in Russian Politics 1990–2006* (Cambridge University Press 2008).

Trujillo, Gumersindo, "Juicio de legitimidad e interpretación constitucional: cuestiones problematicas en el horizonte constitucional español" (1979) 7 *Revista de estudios políticos*.

Tushnet, Mark, "Authoritarian Constitutionalism" (2015) 100 *Cornell Law Review* 2.

Uitz, Renáta, *Constitutions, Courts and History: Historical Narratives in Constitutional Adjudication* (Central European University Press 2005).

Vanberg, Georg, *The Politics of Constitutional Review in Germany* (Cambridge University Press 2005).

Vandelli, Luciano, *L'ordinamento regionale spagnolo* (Giuffrè 1980).

Varela, Santiago, and Satrústegui, Miguel, "Constitución nueva y leyes viejas" (1979) 4 *Revista del departamento de derecho político*.

Vepřek, Jaromír, "The Economic Dimension of the Split of Czechoslovakia" in Viktor Knapp and Sergio Bartole (eds.), *La dissoluzione della Federazione cecoslovacca* (La Rosa 1994).

Verdú, Pablo Lucas, *La octava Ley fundamental: crítica jurídicopolítica de la reforma Suárez* (Tecnos 1976).

Vida Soria, José, and Gallego Morales, Ángel, "Art. 28.2" in Óscar Alzaga Villaamil (ed.), *Comentarios a la Constitución española de 1978*, vol. III (Cortes Generales, Editoriales de derecho reunidas 1996).

Vigoriti, Vincenzo, "Italy: The Constitutional Court" (1972) 20 *The American Journal of Comparative Law*.

Virga, Pietro, "Origine, contenuto e valore delle dichiarazioni costituzionali" (1948) *Rassegna di diritto pubblico*.

Voermans, Wim, Stremler, Maarten, and Cliteur, Paul, *Constitutional Preambles. A Comparative Analysis* (Edward Elgar 2017).

Volcansek, Mary L., *Constitutional Politics in Italy: The Constitutional Court* (Macmillan Press 2000).

"Bargaining Constitutional Design in Italy: Judicial Review as Political Insurance" (2010) 33 *West European Politics* 2.

Volpe, Giuseppe, *L'ingiustizia delle leggi. Studi sui modelli di giustizia costituzionale* (Giuffrè 1977).

Walker, Neil, "Central Europe's Second Constitutional Transition: The EU Accession Phase" in Adam Czarnota, Martin Krygier, and Wojciech Sadurski (eds.), *Rethinking the Rule of Law after Communism* (Central European University Press 2005).

Wheaton, Bernard, and Kavan, Zdeněk, *The Velvet Revolution: Czechoslovakia, 1988–1991* (Westview Press 1992).

Woelk, Jens, *La transizione costituzionale della Bosnia ed Erzegovina* (Cedam 2008).

Wolchik, Sharon L., "The Politics of Ethnicity in Post-Communist Czechoslovakia" (1994) 8 *East European Politics and Societies* 1.

Woller, Hans, *I conti con il Fascismo. L'epurazione in Italia 1943–1948* (Il Mulino 1997).

Zagrebelsky, Gustavo, *La giustizia costituzionale* (Il Mulino 1988).

Index